First World War
and Army of Occupation
War Diary
France, Belgium and Germany

34 DIVISION
102 Infantry Brigade
Northumberland Fusiliers
23rd Battalion (Tyneside Scottish)
19 December 1915 - 20 March 1919

WO95/2463/2

The Naval & Military Press Ltd
www.nmarchive.com
Published in association with The National Archives

Published by

The Naval & Military Press Ltd

Unit 10 Ridgewood Industrial Park,

Uckfield, East Sussex,

TN22 5QE England

Tel: +44 (0) 1825 749494

www.naval-military-press.com

www.nmarchive.com

This diary has been reprinted in facsimile from the original. Any imperfections are inevitably reproduced and the quality may fall short of modern type and cartographic standards.

© **Crown Copyright**
Images reproduced by permission of The National Archives, London, England, 2015.

Contents

Document type	Place/Title	Date From	Date To
Heading	WO95/2463 34 Division 102 Infantry Brigade 23 Battalion Northumberland Fusiliers Jan 1916-Mar 1919		
Heading	34th Division 102nd Infy Bde 23rd Bn North'd Fus. Jan 1916-1919 Mar		
Heading	23rd Northumberland Fus. Vol I Dec 19-31 Jan.		
War Diary	Longbridge	19/12/1915	31/12/1915
War Diary	Deverill	19/12/1915	31/12/1915
War Diary	Sandhill Camp 2015	19/12/1915	08/01/1916
War Diary	Sandhill Camp, 15	09/01/1916	09/01/1916
War Diary	Folkstone	09/01/1916	09/01/1916
War Diary	Boulogne	09/01/1916	10/01/1916
War Diary	Wardrecques	10/01/1916	23/01/1916
War Diary	Steenbecque	23/01/1916	31/01/1916
Heading	War Diary for February 1916 of 23rd Northumberland Fusiliers (4th Tyneside Scottish)		
War Diary	Estaires	01/02/1916	02/02/1916
War Diary	Sailly	02/02/1916	03/02/1916
War Diary	Fleurbaix	03/02/1916	04/02/1916
War Diary	In the Trenches	04/02/1916	08/02/1916
War Diary	Estaires	09/02/1916	09/02/1916
War Diary	Steenbecque	09/02/1916	13/02/1916
War Diary	Estaires	13/02/1916	14/02/1916
War Diary	Near Fleurbaix (H.26.d.4.7)	15/02/1916	16/02/1916
War Diary	Nr Fleurbaix	17/02/1916	17/02/1916
War Diary	In trenches	17/02/1916	18/02/1916
War Diary	In the Trenches	19/02/1916	21/02/1916
War Diary	Bac St Maur	21/02/1916	25/02/1916
War Diary	L'Hallobeau	25/02/1916	29/02/1916
Operation(al) Order(s)	102nd (Tyneside Scottish) Brigade. Operation Order No. 7.	13/02/1916	13/02/1916
Operation(al) Order(s)	102nd (Tyneside Scottish) Brigade. Operation Order No. 8.	16/02/1916	16/02/1916
Miscellaneous	Operation Orders. By. Lieut. Col. W. Lyle. Cmdg. 23rd Battn. Northumberland Fusiliers.	17/02/1916	17/02/1916
Map	Trench Map Scale 1:10,000.		
Operation(al) Order(s)	102nd (Tyneside Scottish) Brigade. Operation Order No. 9.	20/02/1916	20/02/1916
Miscellaneous	March Table. 102nd (Tyneside Scottish) Bde.		
Operation(al) Order(s)	102nd (Tyneside Scottish) Brigade. Operation Order No: 10.	24/02/1916	24/02/1916
Miscellaneous	102nd (Tyneside Scottish) Brigade. March Table.		
War Diary	L'Hallobeau	01/03/1916	04/03/1916
War Diary	In Trenches	05/03/1916	08/03/1916
War Diary	Rue Marle	09/03/1916	14/03/1916
War Diary	In the Trenches	15/03/1916	20/03/1916
War Diary	Rue Marle	21/03/1916	25/03/1916
War Diary	Trenches	26/03/1916	30/03/1916
War Diary	Rue Marle	30/03/1916	31/03/1916
Operation(al) Order(s)	102nd (Tyneside Scottish) Brigade. Operation Order No. 11. Appendix "A".	02/03/1916	02/03/1916

Type	Description	Date From	Date To
Miscellaneous	102nd (Tyneside Scottish) Brigade. March Table.		
Miscellaneous	Battalion Orders by Lieut. Col. W. Lyle, Cmdg., 23rd. Battalion Northumberland Fusiliers. 4th. Battalion Tyneside Scottish.	19/03/1916	19/03/1916
Miscellaneous	March Table	04/03/1916	04/03/1916
Miscellaneous	Operation Orders. by Lieut. Col. Lyle, Cmdg. 23rd. Battalion Northumberland and Fusiliers.		
Map			
War Diary	Rue Marle	01/04/1916	06/04/1916
War Diary	L'Hallobeau	07/04/1916	07/04/1916
War Diary	Vieux Berquin	08/04/1916	08/04/1916
War Diary	Morbecque	09/04/1916	09/04/1916
War Diary	Renescure	09/04/1916	10/04/1916
War Diary	Tatinghem	11/04/1916	11/04/1916
War Diary	Bayenghem	12/04/1916	30/04/1916
Operation(al) Order(s)	The 102nd (Tyneside Scottish) Brigade. Operation Order No. 17.	05/04/1916	05/04/1916
Miscellaneous	Table "A".		
Miscellaneous	Table "B".		
Miscellaneous	Battalion Orders by Lieut. Col. W. Lyle, Cmdg., 23rd. Battalion Northumberland Fusiliers. (4th. Battalion Tyneside Scottish).	06/04/1916	06/04/1916
Miscellaneous	34th Divn: No 806/Q.	02/04/1916	02/04/1916
War Diary	Bayenghem	01/05/1916	06/05/1916
War Diary	St Gratien	06/05/1916	10/05/1916
War Diary	Behencourt	11/05/1916	31/05/1916
Operation(al) Order(s)	The 102nd (Tyneside Scottish) Brigade. Operation Order No. 26.	09/05/1916	09/05/1916
Miscellaneous	Fatigues.		
Operation(al) Order(s)	The 102nd (Tyneside Scottish) Brigade. Operation Order No. 23.	03/05/1916	03/05/1916
Miscellaneous	Issued with Operation Order No. 23.	03/05/1916	03/05/1916
Miscellaneous	Provisional Billetting Arrangements.	04/05/1916	04/05/1916
Miscellaneous	Reference 1:40,000. Albert-Combined Sheet.	29/05/1916	29/05/1916
Miscellaneous	Table "A".		
War Diary	Behencourt	01/06/1916	04/06/1916
War Diary	Albert	04/06/1916	06/06/1916
War Diary	La Boisselle Trenches.	07/06/1916	11/06/1916
War Diary	Albert	12/06/1916	23/06/1916
War Diary	Trenches	24/06/1916	30/06/1916
Operation(al) Order(s)	The 102nd (Tyneside Scottish) Brigade. Operation Order No. 26.	01/06/1916	01/06/1916
Miscellaneous	Table "A" Issued with Operation Order No. 26.	01/06/1916	01/06/1916
Miscellaneous	Working Parties to be Relieved by 103rd Inf. Brigade.		
Operation(al) Order(s)	The 102nd (Tyneside Scottish) Brigade. Operation Order No. 27.	06/06/1916	06/06/1916
Miscellaneous	Barrier at 4 pm Signrs Sgt. Major Sgt. Ledley.		
Miscellaneous	Battalion Orders by Lieut. Col., W. Lyle, Cmdg., 23rd. Battalion Northumberland Fusiliers 4th. Battalion Tyneside Scottish).	06/06/1916	06/06/1916
Miscellaneous	Operation Order by Lt. Col. W. Lyle Cmdg. 23rd Btn. Northd. Fusiliers.	10/06/1916	10/06/1916
Miscellaneous	Operation Order by Lieut. Col., W. Lyle., Cmdg., 23rd. Battalion Northumberland Fusiliers. (4th. Battalion Tyneside Scottish).	21/06/1916	21/06/1916
Miscellaneous	Appendix "D" Signalling and Communication.		

Miscellaneous	Operation Orders by Lieut. Col. W. Lyle, Cmdg., 23rd. Battalion Northumberland Fusiliers.	23/06/1916	23/06/1916
Operation(al) Order(s)	102nd. (Tyneside Scottish) Brigade. Operation Order No. 34.	23/06/1916	23/06/1916
Map	Appendix A		
Miscellaneous	Ref. Albert.-1:40,000 (Combined) Table 'A'.		
Miscellaneous	Appendix "C".		
Heading	102nd Bde. 34th Div. War Diary Brigade was temporarily transferred to 37th Division 6th July-Rejoined 34th Division 22nd August. 23rd Battalion Northumberland Fusiliers July 1916.		
War Diary	Trenches	01/07/1916	04/07/1916
War Diary	Millencourt.	05/07/1916	06/07/1916
War Diary	La Cauchie	07/07/1916	11/07/1916
War Diary	Warlincourt	12/07/1916	14/07/1916
War Diary	Beaufort	15/07/1916	15/07/1916
War Diary	Villers Brulin	16/07/1916	16/07/1916
War Diary	Divion	17/07/1916	26/07/1916
War Diary	Mesnil Bouche	27/07/1916	27/07/1916
War Diary	Trenches	28/07/1916	31/07/1916
War Diary	Trenches	02/07/1916	04/07/1916
War Diary	Millencourt	05/07/1916	06/07/1916
War Diary	La Cauchie	07/07/1916	11/07/1916
War Diary	Warlincourt	12/07/1916	14/07/1916
War Diary	Beaufort	15/07/1916	15/07/1916
War Diary	Villers Brulin	16/07/1916	16/07/1916
War Diary	Divion	17/07/1916	17/07/1916
Heading	102nd Brigade 37th Division till 21.8.16. 34th Division from 22.8.16. 1/23rd Battalion Northumberland Fusiliers. August 1916.		
War Diary	Trenches	01/08/1916	02/08/1916
War Diary	Reserve Trenches Dalys	02/08/1916	06/08/1916
War Diary	Reserve Trenches	07/08/1916	07/08/1916
War Diary	Villers Au Bois.	08/08/1916	14/08/1916
War Diary	Estree Cauchie	15/08/1916	15/08/1916
War Diary	Frevillers.	16/08/1916	22/08/1916
War Diary	Erquinghem	22/08/1916	23/08/1916
War Diary	Rue Marle	24/08/1916	31/08/1916
War Diary	Trenches	01/09/1916	04/09/1916
War Diary	Rue Marle Area.	07/09/1916	11/09/1916
War Diary	Trenches	12/09/1916	30/09/1916
War Diary	Trenches B2 Sector Armentieres	01/10/1916	03/10/1916
War Diary	Rue Marle Area	04/10/1916	08/10/1916
War Diary	Trenches	09/10/1916	12/10/1916
War Diary	Trenches B2 Sub Sector	12/10/1916	14/10/1916
War Diary	Subsidiary Line	15/10/1916	21/10/1916
War Diary	B2 Sector Front System	22/10/1916	22/10/1916
War Diary	B2. Sector	23/10/1916	27/10/1916
War Diary	Rue Marle	27/10/1916	31/10/1916
War Diary	Trenches B.2 S-Sector. Armentieres	01/11/1916	04/11/1916
War Diary	Trenches	04/11/1916	06/11/1916
War Diary	Reserve Trenches of B.2. Subsector Armentieres	07/11/1916	10/11/1916
War Diary	B.2 Sub Sector of Trenches	11/11/1916	11/11/1916
War Diary	Trenches	12/11/1916	16/11/1916
War Diary	Rue Marle	16/11/1916	21/11/1916
War Diary	Trenches B.2 Sector Armentieres	22/11/1916	24/11/1916

War Diary	Trenches	25/11/1916	30/11/1916
Operation(al) Order(s)	Operation Order No. 72 by Brigadier-General T.P.B. Terman, C.M.G. D.S.O. commanding 102nd. (Tyneside Scottish) Brigade.	10/11/1916	10/11/1916
Miscellaneous	Table "A". To accompany Operation Order No. 72. Left Group Divisional Artillery Programme.		
Miscellaneous	Report on a Raid on the Enemy's Trenches at Point I.22.a.7.5. on the night of 12/13th November 1916.	12/11/1916	12/11/1916
Heading	23rd (S) Bn Northd Fusiliers (4th Tyneside Scottish) War Diary-December 1916. Vol 12.		
War Diary	Trenches B.2. S-Sector Armentieres	01/12/1916	05/12/1916
War Diary	Trenches	05/12/1916	11/12/1916
War Diary	Fort Rompu	11/12/1916	22/12/1916
War Diary	B 2 Sub-Sector Trenches, Armentieres	23/12/1916	26/12/1916
War Diary	Spring Port C Battn.	27/12/1916	30/12/1916
War Diary	B2 Subsector Trenches	31/12/1916	31/12/1916
War Diary	B 2 Sub-Sector of Trenches Armentieres	01/01/1917	03/01/1917
War Diary	Rue Marle	04/01/1917	08/01/1917
War Diary	B2. Sub-Sector Trenches	08/01/1916	20/01/1916
War Diary	Erquinghem	21/01/1916	26/01/1916
War Diary	Mont Des Cats.	26/01/1917	27/01/1917
War Diary	Godewaers-Velde	28/01/1917	31/01/1917
Heading	War Diary of 23rd (S) Bn. Northumberland Fusiliers (4th Tyneside Scottish) Month-February, 1917 Vol 14.		
War Diary	Godewaers-Velde	01/02/1917	10/02/1917
War Diary	Armentiers Trenches S.E. B.2. Sub-Sector.	11/02/1917	11/02/1917
War Diary	Armentieres	11/02/1917	11/02/1917
War Diary	Godewaers Velde.	13/02/1917	20/02/1917
War Diary	Villers Brulin.	22/02/1917	23/02/1917
War Diary	Arras	24/02/1917	24/02/1917
War Diary	Norrent Fontes.	25/02/1917	25/02/1917
War Diary	Arras	25/02/1917	02/03/1917
War Diary	Roclincourt. Trenches.	02/03/1917	07/03/1917
War Diary	Ecoivres	08/03/1917	09/03/1917
War Diary	Houvelin	09/03/1917	09/03/1917
War Diary	Houvelin & Rocourt	10/03/1916	20/03/1916
War Diary	Ecoivres	21/03/1916	24/03/1916
War Diary	Arras	24/03/1916	28/03/1916
War Diary	Arras	29/03/1916	29/03/1916
War Diary	Roclincourt Trenches	29/03/1917	31/03/1917
Miscellaneous	34th Div. No. SQ.34/25/2.	30/03/1917	30/03/1917
Miscellaneous	Administrative Instructions No. 1. Part Five.		
Miscellaneous	Administrative Instructions No. 2. Part Ten.		
Miscellaneous	Administrative Instructions No. 2. Part Thirteen.		
Operation(al) Order(s)	Divisional Routine Order No. 167-"March Discipline".		
Miscellaneous	Ammunition. Appendix "T"		
Operation(al) Order(s)	Operation Order No. 41 by Lieut. Col. C.P. Porch, D.S.O., Cmdg. 23rd Northumberland Fusiliers, (4th Battn. Tyneside Scottish)	31/03/1917	31/03/1917
Heading	War Diary. April 1917. 23rd N.F. (4th Tyneside Scottish) Northumberland Fus. 102 Inf Bde. Vol 16.		
War Diary	Trenches Roclincourt	01/04/1917	02/04/1917
War Diary	Arras.	03/04/1917	04/04/1917
War Diary	X Huts Ecoivres	04/04/1917	07/04/1917
War Diary	Louez	07/04/1917	08/04/1917
War Diary	Roclincourt.	08/04/1917	14/04/1917

Type	Description	Start	End
War Diary	Orlencourt.	15/04/1917	28/04/1917
War Diary	Trenches in front of Chemical Works I.13.d.	29/04/1917	30/04/1917
Miscellaneous	23rd Bn. Northumberland Fusiliers. Instructions No. 1.		
Miscellaneous	Action of Stores Mortars.		
Miscellaneous	Contact Patrol Aeroplane.		
Miscellaneous	Strong Points. Appendix I.	06/05/1917	06/05/1917
Miscellaneous	Appendix II. To accompany "Instructions No. 1" Contents of Dumps.		
Miscellaneous	23rd Bn. Northumberland Fusiliers. Instructions No. 2.		
Miscellaneous	Amendment No. 2 to 102nd (Tyneside Scottish) Bde. Instructions No. 3.	07/04/1917	07/04/1917
Miscellaneous	23rd Bn. Northumberland Fusiliers. Instructions No. 3.		
Miscellaneous	23rd Bn. Northumberland Fusiliers. Instructions No. 4.		
War Diary	Trenches Opposite Chemical Works I.13.d.	01/05/1917	09/05/1917
War Diary	Autheux	10/05/1917	29/05/1917
War Diary	St Nicholas Near Arras	30/05/1917	04/06/1917
War Diary	Trenches in Front of Greenland Hill.	05/06/1917	05/06/1917
War Diary	Trenches	05/06/1917	11/06/1917
War Diary	Sunken Road H.7.a.	11/06/1917	13/06/1917
War Diary	Trenches	14/06/1917	17/06/1917
War Diary	Sunken Rd H.7.a.	18/06/1917	27/06/1917
War Diary	Moncheaux	28/06/1917	07/07/1917
War Diary	Trenches Hargicourt	08/07/1917	25/07/1917
War Diary	Hancourt (Q.8.d)	26/07/1917	31/07/1917
Heading	23rd Bn Northumberland and Fusiliers Brigade Operation Orders. During August and September 1917.		
War Diary	Hancourt (Q.8.d)	01/08/1917	02/08/1917
War Diary	Trenches	02/08/1917	04/08/1917
War Diary	Trenches A.2. Sub Sector	05/08/1917	10/08/1917
War Diary	Hancourt	11/08/1917	15/08/1917
War Diary	Trenches Left Sub Sector B. Sector.	15/08/1917	15/08/1917
War Diary	Hargicourt	16/08/1917	19/08/1917
War Diary	Hervilly	20/08/1917	22/08/1917
War Diary	Intermediate Line "B" Sector Bde Div.	23/08/1917	24/08/1917
War Diary	Left Sub-Sector Of B Sector of Trenches Hargicourt	24/08/1917	25/08/1917
War Diary	Left Sub-Sector of "B" Section Hargicourt.	26/08/1917	26/08/1917
War Diary	B Section of Trenches Hargicourt.	26/08/1917	29/08/1917
War Diary	Sunken Road L.22.c-L.28.a.	29/08/1917	31/08/1917
Miscellaneous	General Instructions No. 1 for Operation Against Cologne Ridge.	22/08/1917	22/08/1917
Operation(al) Order(s)	Operation Order No. 64 (Part II) by Lt. Col. C.P Porch D.S.O. Commdg. 23rd Northumberland Fusiliers (4th Tyneside Scottish)	22/08/1917	22/08/1917
Operation(al) Order(s)	Operation Order No. 65 by D.S.O., Cmdg. 23rd Northld. Fusiliers	24/08/1917	24/08/1917
Miscellaneous	T.S. 66/199	24/08/1917	24/08/1917
Miscellaneous	H.C. B & D Companies	24/08/1917	24/08/1917
Miscellaneous	T.S. 66/198.	24/08/1917	24/08/1917
Miscellaneous	Amendment No. 1 to General Instructions No. 1 For Operation Against Cologne Ridge.	24/08/1917	24/08/1917
Miscellaneous	Amendment No. 2 to General Instructions No. 1 For Operations Against Cologne Ridge.	24/08/1917	24/08/1917
Operation(al) Order(s)	Operation Order No. 66 by Lt. Col. C.P. Porch, D.S.O. Cmdg. 23rd Northumberland Fusiliers	29/08/1917	29/08/1917
Map	GN/M/II		
Map	Ref GN/M/1.		

Type	Description	From	To
Map	Ref GN/M		
War Diary	Sunken Road L.22.c. L.28.a.	01/09/1917	02/09/1917
War Diary	Bouvincourt	03/09/1917	07/09/1917
War Diary	Trenches G.13.B.	08/09/1917	11/09/1917
War Diary	Bernes.	12/09/1917	17/09/1917
War Diary	Trenches F.24.D F.29.B F.30.C.	18/09/1917	25/09/1917
War Diary	Trenches Hargicourt	26/09/1917	26/09/1917
War Diary	Doingt	27/09/1917	28/09/1917
War Diary	Boisleux Au Mont	29/09/1917	29/09/1917
War Diary	Bailleul M	30/09/1917	30/09/1917
Operation(al) Order(s)	Operation Order No. 67 by Lieut. Col. C.P. Porch, D.S.O., Cmdg. 23rd Northld. Fus.	02/09/1917	02/09/1917
Operation(al) Order(s)	Addendum to O.O. 67 by Lt. Col. C.P. Porch D.S.O. Cmdg. 23rd Northld. Fusiliers.	02/09/1917	02/09/1917
Operation(al) Order(s)	Operation Order No. 68 by Lt. Colonel C.P. Porch D.S.O. Commanding 23rd Northumberland Fusiliers (4th Tyneside Scottish)	06/09/1917	06/09/1917
Operation(al) Order(s)	Operation Order No. 69 by Lt. Colonel C.P. Porch D.S.O. Comdg. 23rd Northumberland Fusiliers (4th Tyneside Scottish)	07/09/1917	07/09/1917
Miscellaneous	23rd Northumberland Fusiliers (4th Tyneside Scottish)	13/09/1917	13/09/1917
Operation(al) Order(s)	Operation Order No. 70 by Major J.I. Gracie, Commanding, 23rd Northld. Fusiliers (4th Tyneside Scottish)	16/09/1917	16/09/1917
Miscellaneous	Amendment to 23rd N.F. O.O. No. 70.		
Operation(al) Order(s)	23rd N.F., (4th T.S.). Operation Order No. 71.	22/09/1917	22/09/1917
Operation(al) Order(s)	23rd N.F., (4th T.S.). Operation Order No. 72.	25/09/1917	25/09/1917
Operation(al) Order(s)	23rd N.F., (4th T.S.). Operation Order No. 73.	26/09/1917	26/09/1917
Miscellaneous	23rd (S) Bn. Northumberland Fusiliers.	27/09/1917	27/09/1917
Operation(al) Order(s)	23rd N.F., (4th T.S.). Operation Order No. 74.	24/09/1917	24/09/1917
Miscellaneous	Operation Orders by Lieut. Col., C.P. Porch, Cmdg., 23rd. Battn. Northd. Fusiliers. (4th Battalion Tyneside Scottish)	25/09/1916	25/09/1916
Miscellaneous	No. 2 Scheme.		
Operation(al) Order(s)	Addendum No. 2 to 102nd Infantry Brigade Operation Order No. 155.	27/09/1917	27/09/1917
Miscellaneous	Q.102/33.	28/09/1917	28/09/1917
Miscellaneous	Reference Map Sheet 62c. Lens. 11. 102nd Brigade Group, 1st Line Transport Orders for Route March on 29th and 30th Sept. 1917.	29/09/1917	29/09/1917
Miscellaneous	March Table 1.	29/09/1917	29/09/1917
War Diary	Bailleulmont	01/10/1917	07/10/1917
War Diary	Proven	07/10/1917	12/10/1917
War Diary	Elverdinghe	13/10/1917	13/10/1917
War Diary	Wolfe Camp B.22.d.8.6.	14/10/1917	16/10/1917
War Diary	Kortebeek Farm Area.	16/10/1917	23/10/1917
War Diary	Ferdan House Area.	24/10/1917	25/10/1917
War Diary	Proven	25/10/1917	31/10/1917
War Diary	Trenches Cojeul Sec to Rt 51.B. S.W.	01/11/1917	08/11/1917
War Diary	Cojeul Sector Trenches.	09/11/1917	12/11/1917
War Diary	York Lines (Huts)	13/11/1917	15/11/1917
War Diary	York Lines	15/11/1917	16/11/1917
War Diary	Coseul Sub Sector of Trenches	17/11/1917	21/11/1917
War Diary	N.16.c Billets	22/11/1917	23/11/1917
War Diary	N.16.c	23/11/1917	26/11/1917
War Diary	Cojeul Sub Sector of Trenches.	27/11/1917	30/11/1917

War Diary	York Lines	01/12/1917	04/12/1917
War Diary	Cojeul Subsector 57.B.S.W.2.	05/12/1917	06/12/1917
War Diary	Trenches Cojeul Subsector	06/12/1917	08/12/1917
War Diary	Support N.16.c.	09/12/1917	13/12/1917
War Diary	North bl'd Lines	14/12/1917	20/12/1917
War Diary	Fortaine Subsector	21/12/1917	24/12/1917
War Diary	Hindenberg Tunnel	25/12/1917	28/12/1917
War Diary	Fontaine Subsector	29/12/1917	06/01/1918
War Diary	Front Line	06/01/1918	06/01/1918
War Diary	Cherisy. Special Sheet. U.1.a.40.75 to O.31.B.70.20.	06/01/1918	09/01/1918
War Diary	Front Line Trench. Ref Special Sheet Cherisy. U.1.a.40.75 to O.31.B.70.20. Right Sector of 102nd Bgde Sector.	10/01/1918	10/01/1918
War Diary	Reserve Line Sheet No. 260 U.T.S.N. 35 (c) 5.0.	10/01/1918	10/01/1918
War Diary	Shaft Avenue Sheet 260 U.T.S. N.35.C.5.0	11/01/1918	13/01/1918
War Diary	Front Line Centre Subsector Ref. Heinel Trench Map Sheet No. 260 U.T.S. V.1.B.50.95 O.31.b.65.5.	14/01/1918	17/01/1918
War Diary	Support Line The Nest Ref. Heninel Trench Map U.T.S. No. 360 N.30.a.40.30	17/01/1918	20/01/1918
War Diary	Front Line Ref. Heninel Trench Map U.T.S. No. 360 U.I.B.50-95 O.21.B.65-85	20/01/1918	20/01/1918
War Diary	Front Line	21/01/1918	23/01/1918
War Diary	Shaft. Avenue Ref. Heninel Trench Map. U.T.S. No. 260 N.35.C.50.10.	23/01/1918	25/01/1918
War Diary	York Lines France Sheet 51.B.S.W. M.22.B.	25/01/1918	25/01/1918
War Diary	York Lines Trench Map Sheet 51.B.S.W. Rd. 5.a.	25/01/1918	28/01/1918
War Diary	York Lines M.22.b. Ref. Sheet 51.b S.W.	29/01/1918	31/01/1918
War Diary	York Lines Ref. Trench Map Sheet. 51.B.S.W. M.22.b.	01/02/1918	08/02/1918
War Diary	York Lines until 9.30 am Blairville remainder of day.	09/02/1918	09/02/1918
War Diary	Blairville until 9 am. Barly remainder of day.	10/02/1918	10/02/1918
War Diary	Barly to 10.15 am Penin remainder of day	11/02/1918	11/02/1918
War Diary	Penin Ref. Map France 51.c. Edition 2.	12/02/1918	25/02/1918
War Diary	Penin Ref Map Lens. Sheet 11. Ed: 2.	26/02/1918	27/02/1918
War Diary	Pommier	27/02/1918	28/02/1918
War Diary	Hamelincourt	28/02/1918	28/02/1918
Heading	34th Division. 102nd Infantry Brigade. War Diary 23rd Battalion The Northumberland Fusiliers March 1918.		
War Diary		01/03/1918	31/03/1918
Miscellaneous	Casualties		
War Diary		20/03/1918	22/03/1918
Miscellaneous	34th Divn. No. A/222.	29/03/1918	29/03/1918
War Diary	The Officer Commanding 23rd Bn. Northumberland Fusrs.	31/03/1918	31/03/1918
Heading	34th Division. 102nd Infantry Brigade War Diary 23rd Battalion Northumberland Fusiliers April 1918		
War Diary	Ref Map Sheet 36 N.W. 1/10000 Bde in Divl. Res.	01/04/1918	04/04/1918
Miscellaneous	Part II.		
War Diary		05/04/1918	08/04/1918
War Diary	Ref. Map. Houplines 1/10000	09/04/1918	12/04/1918
War Diary	Ref Map Sheet 28 S.W.	13/04/1918	25/04/1918
War Diary	Ref Map Sheet 28 N.W.	25/04/1918	30/04/1918
Miscellaneous	102nd Infantry Brigade.	17/04/1918	17/04/1918
Miscellaneous	102nd Inf. Bde.	18/04/1918	18/04/1918
Miscellaneous	First Army G.S. 1152. Second Army No. G.56 XV Corps 128/13G.	18/04/1918	18/04/1918
Miscellaneous	34th Div. No. A/222.	22/04/1918	22/04/1918

Miscellaneous	Special order of the Day by Major General C.L. Nicholson. CB, CMG. Commanding 34th Division.	22/04/1918	22/04/1918
Miscellaneous	Special order of the Day by Major General C.L. Nicholson. CB, CMG. Commanding 34th Division.	28/04/1918	28/04/1918
Heading	102nd Brigade. 34th Division. War Diary 23rd Northumberland Fusiliers. May 1918		
War Diary	Sheet 28 N.W.	01/05/1918	04/05/1918
War Diary	Sheet 28.	05/05/1918	09/05/1918
War Diary	K.12.b.6.4.	10/05/1918	11/05/1918
War Diary	Sheet Hazebrouck 5.A. Calais. 13.	12/05/1918	31/05/1918
Heading	102nd Brigade. 34th Division Battalion transferred to 39th Division 17.6.18. War Diary 23rd Northumberland Fusiliers June 1918.		
War Diary	Ref Map Calais 13 Hennessy	01/06/1918	03/06/1918
War Diary	Boursin	04/06/1918	30/06/1918
Operation(al) Order(s)	102nd. (Tyneside Scottish) Brigade Operation Order No. 32.	18/06/1918	18/06/1918
Operation(al) Order(s)	102nd (Tyneside Scottish) Bde. Operation Order No. 32. Dated 18/6/16.	18/06/1916	18/06/1916
Miscellaneous	Amendment. Operation Order No. 32 of 18/6/16.	18/06/1916	18/06/1916
Operation(al) Order(s)	Operation Order 32. dated 18/6/16. Appendix B.	18/06/1916	18/06/1916
Operation(al) Order(s)	Operation Order 32. Dated 18/6/16. Appendix C.	18/06/1916	18/06/1916
Operation(al) Order(s)	Operation Order No. 32. Dated 18/6/16. Appendix C.	18/06/1916	18/06/1916
Miscellaneous Diagram etc	Table "A".		
Heading	66th Division Training Cadres 34 Div 23rd Bn Northum'D Fus Aug-Dec 1918 July 1918 to 1919 Mar. 34 Div. 102 Bde Served with 197 Bde L of C from Sept 1918		
War Diary	Boursin	01/07/1918	16/07/1918
War Diary	Lens 11. Bouningues	17/07/1918	19/07/1918
War Diary	Hautcloque	20/07/1918	28/07/1918
War Diary	Magnicourt en Comte	29/07/1918	31/07/1918
Heading	War Diary of 23rd Battn Northumd Fus From Aug 1st 1918 To Aug 31st 1918 Vol No. 32.		
War Diary	Rf. Map Lens II Magnicourt En Courte	01/08/1918	03/08/1918
War Diary	Licques	04/08/1918	15/08/1918
War Diary	Abancourt	16/08/1918	22/08/1918
War Diary	Handricourt	23/08/1918	31/08/1918
Heading	War Diary Of 23rd. Northumberland Fusiliers. From 1st. Septr. 1918 to 30th. September 1918. (Volume 9)		
War Diary	Haudricourt	01/09/1918	30/09/1918
Heading	War Diary of 23rd. Bn. Northumberland Fusiliers. From 1st October, 1918. To. 31st October, 1918. (Volume 10).		
War Diary	No. 1 L of C. Aera Reception Camp.	01/10/1918	31/10/1918
War Diary		15/10/1918	28/10/1918
Heading	War Diary of 23rd North'd Fusiliers From 1st November, 1918 To 30th November, 1918 (Volume 11)		
War Diary	No. 1 L of C. area Reception Camp.	01/11/1918	30/11/1918
War Diary		01/11/1918	08/11/1918
War Diary		06/11/1918	30/11/1918
Heading	War Diary of 23rd Northumberland Fusiliers From 1st December 1918 To 31st December 1918 (Volume 12).		
War Diary	No. 1 L of C area Reception Camp	01/12/1918	15/12/1918
War Diary	No. 1 Rest Camp Sec. B Haore	20/12/1918	31/12/1918

War Diary	War Diary 23rd Northumberland Fusiliers From 1st January 1919 To 31st January 1919 (Volume 13)			
War Diary Heading	Havre		01/01/1919	31/01/1919
			24/01/1919	24/01/1919
	War Diary 23rd. Northumberland Fusiliers From 1st. February 1919 To: 28th. February 1919 (Volume 14)			
War Diary	Havre		01/02/1919	31/03/1919
War Diary Map			13/03/1919	20/03/1919

(2)

WO 95/24963

3rd Division
13 Infantry Brigade
2 Inniskillen Northern Ireland
Tulley

Tom Larkin - about 1910

34TH DIVISION
102ND INFY BDE

23RD BN NORTH'D FUS.

JAN 1916 - ~~JUN 1916.~~

1919 MAR

34TH DIVISION
102ND INFY BDE

1-23   1st

102/34

23rd W/Minnesota: Fros:
Vol I

Dec 15-31
TAV

34

23rd Northumberland Fusiliers
(4th Tyneside Scottish)

Army Form C. 2118.

WAR DIARY
or
INTELLIGENCE SUMMARY.
(Erase heading not required.)

Instructions regarding War Diaries and Intelligence Summaries are contained in F.S. Regs., Part II. and the Staff Manual respectively. Title pages will be prepared in manuscript.

Place	Date	Hour	Summary of Events and Information	Remarks and references to Appendices
Haybridge Deverill Sandhill Camp 2015	Dec. 19th to 31st		Continual alarms as to departure of Btn. for Egypt (finally cancelled) and then for France. Finally, a notification that we are off to France — no date given.	
"	Jan 1st–4th		Still in doubt as to our departure. Mobilization has begun again!	
"	Jan 5th		Word received that this is the 3rd day before departure, so work on mobilizing has commenced in earnest.	
"	Jan 6th to 7th		Mobilization proceeding, and time tables received. The transport embarks on Saturday 8th from Southampton, and the rest of the Btn. from Folkestone on the 9th	
"	Jan 8th		Transport, machine guns, cooks, grooms & horses etc. parade 12 midnight and march to WARMINSTER STN. under Major BURGE; Lt HUNTER (transport Officer) & Lt NELSON ( ) also go, and 106 O.R. Train ( ) then again until France in...	

Army Form C. 2118.

WAR DIARY
or
INTELLIGENCE SUMMARY.
(Erase heading not required.)

Instructions regarding War Diaries and Intelligence Summaries are contained in F. S. Regs., Part II. and the Staff Manual respectively. Title pages will be prepared in manuscript.

Place	Date	Hour	Summary of Events and Information	Remarks and references to Appendices
Sandhill Camp, 15	Jan 9th 1916	—	Mobilization was completed as far as possible yesterday, and we are in possession of practically all essential requirements. Reveille sounded at 2.30 A.M.,	
		2.30 A.M.	and hot tea was served at 3 A.M.. The first party, consisting of A & B Coys. and Hd. Qrs., paraded at 3.45 A.M.; was inspected by the Commanding Officer and marched off at 4.15 A.M.. The second party (C & D Coys.) under Major MACKINTOSH marched from Camp at 4.45 A.M..	
		7 A.M.	The first party entrained at WARMINSTER and left punctually at 7 A.M., being closely followed by the second party at 7.40 A.M.. The train journey was uneventful, FOLKESTONE being reached a few minutes ahead of	
Folkestone	"		time, at 1 P.M.. The second train quickly followed, and the whole Btn. was embarked on a small paddle steamer, and we sailed at	
		2.30 P.M.	We had a calm crossing, and were escorted over by a destroyer — a small air-ship also came some of the way with us.	
Boulogne	"	4 P.M.	BOULOGNE was reached at 4 P.M., and the Btn. marched with bands playing up a very steep hill to ST MARTIN'S CAMP, arriving at 6 P.M..	

Army Form C. 2118.

WAR DIARY
or
INTELLIGENCE SUMMARY.
(Erase heading not required.)

Instructions regarding War Diaries and Intelligence Summaries are contained in F. S. Regs., Part II. and the Staff Manual respectively. Title pages will be prepared in manuscript.

Place	Date	Hour	Summary of Events and Information	Remarks and references to Appendices
BOULOGNE	9/1/16	7 P.M.	Rations were issued, and our deficiencies in ground sheets & clasp knives were made up. A good move without any difficulties. The men were very tired.	
"	10/1/16	8 A.M.	Reveille 5.30 A.M., and Btn. marched at 8 A.M.. The men over-slept and unfortunately the camp was left dirty. Entrained at PONT DE BRIQUES, where Maj. BURGE. We saw a Tauke being shelled by an anti-aircraft guns over ST OMER, and detrained at BLENDECQUES (near ARQUES) at 1.30 P.M.. The transport took some time unloading, and a forced wait ensued as no guide was available to show us our billets. In the end the Staff Capt. arrived, and took the Interpreter	Map of HAZEBROUCK Sheet 5A (1:100000)
WARDRECQUES			& Capt K. ANDERSON (the adjutant) ahead in his motor to arrange billets. We are in a small village called WARDRECQUES, and the men are crowded, but we have to take close billets, that of the officers are in a monastery; men in	
		4 P.M.	The Btn. arrived at 4.15 P.M, very tired; G Coy. is in another village some way off. Transport did not fully arrive till 10.30 P.M..	

Army Form C. 2118.

WAR DIARY
or
INTELLIGENCE SUMMARY.
(Erase heading not required.)

Place	Date	Hour	Summary of Events and Information	Remarks and references to Appendices
WARDRECQUES	9/11/16	—	been had a good sleep, and the day was spent in cleaning up & settling down; straw for sleeping on was obtained, rations & stores issued, and as many light transport animals as possible put under cover. The rain luckily holding off. Our strength on landing in FRANCE is:— Officers 30 Lt-Col W. Lyle Major A. Burge Major S.H. Mackintosh Capt J.G. Todd Capt H.J. Whitehead Capt J.B. Gulvey Capt C.R. Longhurst Capt T.B. Goule Capt T.A. Anderson Capt H.A. Balles Lt. H.D. Whittaker Lt. R. Phillips Lt. Sharkey R. Pallister Lt. Officer Lt. Terry (Acting Q-Mr) Lt. Dunn Lt. S. Macdonald Lt. Leach 2/Lt. Young 2/Lt. Tyler 2/Lt. Campbell 2/Lt. Wilson 2/Lt. Williams 2/Lt. Hall 2/Lt. R. Macdonald 2/Lt. Hunter 2/Lt. Hamilton 2/Lt. Chapman Capt & Adjt K. Anderson attached Lt Muirhead M.O. Rev. W. Gould Jean Millet Interpreter O.R. 984 (excluding 9 attached men & A.S.C. drivers & 5 water duty men)	HAZEBROUCK & many sheet 5A (1/100000)

Army Form C. 2118.

WAR DIARY
or
INTELLIGENCE SUMMARY
(Erase heading not required.)

Place	Date	Hour	Summary of Events and Information	Remarks and references to Appendices
WARDRECQUES	12/1/16	—	Quiet day in billets. Company route marches in morning. Rain still held off. C.O. inspected A & B Coys. in afternoon. Casualties: 1 Sick	HAZEBROUCK Sheet 5A (1:100,000)
"	13/1/16	—	Concentration march in the morning. Practise in billets after lunch. Inspection of gas helmets, iron rations etc. The Hd-Qrs Party (signallers, orderlies etc.) organised and put on a proper basis. A practice Alarm at 9 P.M. — not a great success. Casualties: nil	
"	14/1/16	—	Practised the Alarm, paying attention to the points which were wrong last night — stacking of blankets, officers' kits, filled water bottles etc... Casualties: nil	
"	15/1/16	—	Concentration march for companies. The DUKE OF NORTHUMBERLAND came round billets in morning, but C.O. was out. Practised rapid loading with ball cartr. after lunch. Men were paid out in evening. G.O.'s. are to visit Brigade Hd-Qrs every evening at 6 P.M. Casualties: 2 Sick	

Army Form C. 2118.

WAR DIARY
or
INTELLIGENCE SUMMARY.
(Erase heading not required.)

Instructions regarding War Diaries and Intelligence Summaries are contained in F.S. Regs., Part II. and the Staff Manual respectively. Title pages will be prepared in manuscript.

Place	Date	Hour	Summary of Events and Information	Remarks and references to Appendices
WARDRECQUES	16/1/16		Presbyterian Service in School at 9 A.M. Roman Catholics use village Church. Quiet day; the men washed their clothes and played football in the afternoon. Casualties: 1 sick	HAZEBROUCK Sheet 5A (1:100,000) 10
"	17/1/16		Bn. route march in morning. Coys. practised rapid loading with ball cartridge in afternoon. Fine. Casualties: 1 sick	
"	18/1/16		Practised dressing on markers for Ceremonial parade in morning. Raised Govt- hosted on Cpl. ROCHESTER, B Coy. all afternoon. Casualties: 1 sick	
"	19/1/16		Fine & sunny day. Bn. parade in morning, and parade under coy. arrangements after lunch. Five marksmen practised with the new "hyperscope" rifle on the miniature range constructed by C Coy. Casualties: nil	

Army Form C. 2118.

WAR DIARY
or
INTELLIGENCE SUMMARY.
(Erase heading not required.)

Place	Date	Hour	Summary of Events and Information	Remarks and references to Appendices
WARDRECQUES	20/1/16	—	Battalion paraded at 11 A.M. (coys. sized) and marched to take up our position along the AIRE – ST. OMER road, just near BELLE CROIX, for inspection by GEN. JOFFRE. The whole division was drawn up along the road, two-deep, facing West. The inspecting Officer arrived late, and it was very cold waiting – a strong wind & showers of rain. GEN. JOFFRE passed down the line slowly in a motor car at 2.10 P.M.; the coy. commanders gave the order to present arms. Btns. marched back to billets independently. Dinners on return at 2.45 p.m. Casualties: nil	HAZEBROUCK Sheet 3A (1:100,000)
	21/1/16		Hutments at the Tile Factory allotted to the Btn. for the day; coys. in order B, D, A sent 20 men at a time at ½ hr. intervals. C Coy. have made an open air bath of their own, and did not go. Parades near billets in morning, and short coy. route marches in afternoon. Twenty officers (including G.O. & Medical Officer) & 10 N.C.O.s went to a gas lecture at CHAU LE NIEPPE at 2 P.M. MJR. BURGE and CAPT. GUBBY attended a one days course at the machine gun school at WISQUES. Casualties: nil	

Army Form C. 2118.

WAR DIARY
or
~~INTELLIGENCE SUMMARY.~~
(Erase heading not required.)

Instructions regarding War Diaries and Intelligence Summaries are contained in F. S. Regs., Part II. and the Staff Manual respectively. Title pages will be prepared in manuscript.

Place	Date	Hour	Summary of Events and Information	Remarks and references to Appendices
WARDRECQUES	22/1/16		Concentration march for Companies in morning. Musketry & handling of arms after lunch. Quiet day. Casualties: 1 sick	HAZEBROUCK Sheet 5A (1:100,000)
WARDRECQUES	23/1/16	4.30 A.M.	Orders were received at 12.30 A.M. for the Brigade to move into a new Billetting area, the starting point to be BLARINGHEM STN. at 9 A.M., 23rd N.F. to lead. Reveille was sounded at 4.30 A.M. Rations, gas helmet satchels were issued to Coys., and Blankets stacked ready for loading. The Battalion marched off at 7.30 A.M., all complete (except for Blankets, which were taken by motor lorry independently). The Brigade marched via LES CISEAUX and STEENBECQUE. The Brigade is billetted round the latter place. We ourselves are in a very muddy camp about 3/4 mile out of the village just off the	
STEENBECQUE	"	1 P.M.	HAZEBROUCK main road (No 4 Camp). This camp was left by it's late occupants in a most disgustingly filthy condition, apart from the mud. The men are in Bell tents (10 per tent). Fatigue parties were at once put on to clean up - a weak job. Fine, cold day. Casualties: nil	

Army Form C. 2118.

WAR DIARY
or
INTELLIGENCE SUMMARY.
(Erase heading not required.)

Place	Date	Hour	Summary of Events and Information	Remarks and references to Appendices
STEENBECQUE	24/1/16	10 A.M.	Bttn. was suddenly ordered to parade for inspection by our Corps Commander (LT-GEN. PULTENEY, Comdg. 3rd Corps.). Marched from camp at 9.10 A.M. and formed up in a field near in mass with the rest of the Brigade by 10 A.M.. Inspecting Officer did not arrive until 11 a.m.. He inspected each Bttn., and then closed them in and gave a short speech of welcome. After dinners, practically the whole Bttn. was on fatigue cleaning up camp, and also drawing it under superintendence of an R.E. Officer. Dull, but no rain. Casualties: nil	Ref: HAZEBROUCK Sheet 5 A (1:100000)
"	25/1/16		Concentration march in morning. Brigade Hd-Qrs with the 21st & 22nd M.F. marched up to SAILLY to undergo their instructional tour in the trenches, and we are left under direct orders of the Division. Large fatigue party on cleaning up. Fine & frosty. Casualties: nil	

Army Form C. 2118.

WAR DIARY
or
INTELLIGENCE SUMMARY.
(Erase heading not required.)

Place	Date	Hour	Summary of Events and Information	Remarks and references to Appendices
STEENBECQUE	26/1/16		Concentration march in morning. Div. Commander visited our camp, and inspected the drainage together with the C.R.E. Football match between B & G Coys. in afternoon. Fatigue parties at work again. Casualties: nil	HAZEBROUCK Sheet 5A (1:100,000)
	27/1/16		Lt OLIVER, 2Lt HAMILTON and 11 O.R. were taken to SAILLY in a motor lorry for a course of instruction in trench mortar (Stokes gun). Coy. route marches in morning. Platoon football competition starts. Fatigues as usual. Casualties: 1 sick	
	28/1/16		Btn. route march in morning, with advance guard out. Gen. PULTENEY visited Camp while Btn. was out. Work continued on draining & clearing camp. Football in afternoon. At 11 pm Secret orders were received giving route etc. in case we were ordered up to 3rd Corps to repel a German attack; we will be at 2 hrs. notice to move. Coys. warned to see that stores, gas helmets etc. were ready at hand for issue in case of need. Casualties: nil	

Army Form C. 2118.

WAR DIARY
or
INTELLIGENCE SUMMARY
(Erase heading not required.)

Instructions regarding War Diaries and Intelligence Summaries are contained in F. S. Regs., Part II. and the Staff Manual respectively. Title pages will be prepared in manuscript.

Place	Date	Hour	Summary of Events and Information	Remarks and references to Appendices
STEENBECQUE	29/1/16		Baths available in a cottage near STEENBECQUE STN. from 7am – 6pm, twelve men at a time, each batch being allowed ½ hr.. Each coy. gets 72 men. Parades under coy. arrangements. Football in afternoon. Fatigue work continued. Lt PHILLIPS, P/t MEADOWS and 2 N.C.O.'s went to ST-VENANT for a short course of instruction in trench mortars. Casualties: nil	HAZEBROUCK Sheet 5A (1:100,000)
"	30/1/16		Church Parades in morning. Rehearsal in afternoon of bombing attack on a small section of trench dug in field just north of Camp. This attack was ordered to take place tonight; we had [crossed out] it at 8 p.m. and about 20 live bombs were thrown. Casualties: nil	
"	31/1/16		1 sgt., 2 cpls, & 12 men marched at 8 am to MORBECQUE, where they were picked up in motor buses & taken on to 23rd Div. Bombing School for a 10 days course. Lt WHITTAKER & 20 men started at 9 am and went ahead to ESTAIRES to arrange billets for us to-morrow. Short coy. route marches in morning. Roaming up camp in afternoon. Casualties: 1 sick.	

War Diary
for
February 1916
of
23rd Northumberland Fusiliers
(4th Tyneside Scottish)

K. Anderson
Capt & Adjt
23rd Northd Fus!

29/2/16

WAR DIARY
or
~~INTELLIGENCE SUMMARY~~

Army Form C. 2118.

23rd Northumberland Fusiliers
(4th Tyneside Scottish)

16

Place	Date	Hour	Summary of Events and Information	Remarks and references to Appendices
Lillers	1st Feb 1916	6 a.m. 7.45 a.m. 9 a.m.	Reveille 6 a.m.; breakfasts 7.45 a.m. Btn. marched off at 9 a.m. to ESTAIRES via STEENBECQUE STN., road junction at J.3.d.3/9; PRÉ À VIN; K.15.c.4/2;	Sheet 36A (1:40000)
ESTAIRES			NEUF BERQUIN; arriving ESTAIRES at 3 p.m. Went into billets for the night. Casualties: NIL	
"	2nd Feb	10 A.M.	The 1st Btn returned from the trenches to our billets at 7 a.m., but we did not move off till 10 a.m. The Btn. was split into 2 parts for attachment and instruction. Hd-Qrs & A and B marched via ESTAIRES and cross-roads at G.16.a.3/1 and were billetted with the 8/York & Lancaster Regt. C and D Coys under Major Burge marched via ESTAIRES and were billetted in SAILLY with 8/K.O.Y.L.I.. Very crowded, but it is only for one night. Our coys are split up and lived with the coys of the Btns. we are attached to. Casualties: NIL	Sheet 36 (1:40,000)
SAILLY				
"	3rd Feb		Machine guns under Lt NELSON went into the trenches at 8 a.m. under arrangements made by 70th Bde. M.G.Officer. The rest of the Btn. marched off at 5.30 p.m. with the Btns. they are attached to, moving at intervals of 10 mins. between coys. as far as G.17.d.7/10, and thence onwards to FLEURBAIX by platoons at 2 min. intervals (via G.30.a.8/8, H.19.a.5/0, H.26.d.1/2). Casualties: NIL	

Army Form C. 2118.

WAR DIARY
or
INTELLIGENCE SUMMARY.
(Erase heading not required.)

Place	Date	Hour	Summary of Events and Information	Remarks and references to Appendices
FLEURBAIX	3rd Feb	8 pm	Coys were billetted with the 8/Y.L.R. and 8/K.O.Y.L.I in FLEURBAIX. After arrival in billets #3 officers and 14 N.C.O.'s per Coy. proceeded to the trenches and were attached as follows for 24 hrs. instruction (A & B Coy. to the 9/Y.L.R. and C.O. and Adjt. to 9/Y.L.R. with headquarters at FORAY HOUSE – H.35 c 6/1; C & D Coys. to 11th Notts & Derby with headquarters at WYE FARM – H.36 A 2/2).	Sheet 36 A (1/40000)
"	4th Feb		The other officers & men remained in FLEURBAIX. The remaining officers and N.C.O.'s per Coy. went into the trenches at 6 pm, and those who were in last came out and rejoined their Coy.	Casualties: NIL Casualties: 1 sick.
In the Trenches	5th Feb		The whole of the coys. came in to the trenches, leaving FLEURBAIX at 6 pm, and were split among the 9/Y.L.R. (A & B Coys) and 11th N & D (C & D Coys). Two Sections being attached to each platoon of these regiments. The men seemed to be very interested and were put on sentry etc. with men of the two Bns., we are attached to. Fairly quiet day, but a certain amount of hostile shelling. Sgt BELL was wounded in the leg while on patrol (slight).	Casualties: { 1 wd. { 3 sick.

17

Army Form C. 2118.

WAR DIARY
or
INTELLIGENCE SUMMARY.
(Erase heading not required.)

Instructions regarding War Diaries and Intelligence Summaries are contained in F. S. Regs., Part II. and the Staff Manual respectively. Title pages will be prepared in manuscript.

Place	Date	Hour	Summary of Events and Information	Remarks and references to Appendices
In the Trenches	Feb. 6th		Very fine day. Front line shelled in morning. Men took their share of working parties and fatigues, as well as sentry go. Two men wounded (one seriously) (Ptes 584 THOMPSON and 89 YOUNG) Casualties — 2 wounded (initials of party)	Sheet 36A (1:40000)
"	Feb. 7th		The 9/Y.L.R. were relieved in evening by the 8/Y.L.R., and the 11th N.&D. by the 8/K.O.Y.L.I.. Coys are now collected together and hold a portion of the line by themselves. Pte HARRISON of C Coy was accidentally shot by a man of the 11th N.&D. and died of wounds; Pte YOUNG, wounded yesterday, also died. Dull day. Certain amount of shelling. Casualties - 2 killed, 2 wounded	
"	Feb. 8th		Billetting party under Lt WHITTAKER left for ESTAIRES at 7am — so into the billets we occupied on the 21st Feb. The Coys left the trenches (A&B at 5.45pm.; C&D at 6pm) and marched to billets via FLEURBAIX, CROIX DE ROME, FORT ROMPU and SAILLY — marching by platoons as far as CROIX DE ROME, where Coys were assembled. Transport collected Officers mess kits, dixies, etc... and firing trench stores & tools. Did not reach billets till 12.30 am. Casualties : NIL	died of wounds, 4 sick.

Army Form C. 2113.

WAR DIARY
or
INTELLIGENCE SUMMARY.
(Erase heading not required.)

Instructions regarding War Diaries and Intelligence Summaries are contained in F. S. Regs., Part II. and the Staff Manual respectively. Title pages will be prepared in manuscript.

Place	Date	Hour	Summary of Events and Information	Remarks and references to Appendices
ESTAIRES	9th		Arrived in billets at 12.20 a.m.. Transport got in earlier and had dumped Blankets and got left tea ready. Men dead tired. Ordered to march at 9 a.m., but we postponed this till 10.15 a.m. The 3rd Btn passed us at 9 a.m.. Men's feet were very bad, and 18 had to go in an ambulance. Marched back to STEENBECQUE (same billets as before), arriving 4 p.m.; we had an hour's halt for dinner. Passed 3rd Btn who had lost their way. Blankets, which had been left behind under a guard, to be picked up by motor lorries, did not arrive — in spite of repeated messages. Very cold night with frost, and owing to this men were most uncomfortable. Casualties: NIL	Blanket Sheet 36A (1:40,000)
STEENBECQUE	10th		Fine & cold. Spent day cleaning up and checking stores. New Boots issued. 30 men & 2 Officers per coy had to attend an anti-gas demonstration in No. 2 Camp at 11 a.m.. Blankets did not arrive till 7 p.m., but then we also got a second blanket — making 2 per man. Casualties: 3 sick.	NIL
"	11th		Continued cleaning up & resting. Saluting drill & handling of arms in afternoon. Very wet and rained almost all day. We were ordered to parade for inspection by Lord KITCHENER at 10 a.m., but luckily for our comfort this was postponed.	Casualties: NIL

Army Form C. 2118.

WAR DIARY
or
INTELLIGENCE SUMMARY
(Erase heading not required.)

Instructions regarding War Diaries and Intelligence Summaries are contained in F. S. Regs. Part II. and the Staff Manual respectively. Title pages will be prepared in manuscript.

20

Place	Date	Hour	Summary of Events and Information	Remarks and references to Appendices
STEENBECQUE	Feb 12th		Fine again. Quiet day in Camp, packing up as far as possible ready for the move to-morrow. Lt WHITTAKER and billetting party started off at 2 pm for ESTAIRES. Casualties: 1 sick.	Sheet 36 A (1:40000)
"	Feb 13th		The Btn paraded ready to move off at 8.50 am, and marched in rear of the brigade to ESTAIRES, via PRÉ À VIN and LE PARC. The Officers' kits and Q-Mrs Stores were left behind and followed in a lorry. We were billetted along roads running through L 23 b, L17 d, and L 24 a & c. After arrival in billets (4 pm) all G.O's and Adjts were called for to meet G.O.C. 25th Bde at Bde Hd-Qrs, and discuss the trenches we are going to take over. The men were very tired, and a good many cases of sore feet occurred. Casualties: NIL	
ESTAIRES	Feb 14th		A quiet morning spent in preparing for the move this afternoon. The Q-M Stores & Transport moved off ahead to their new lines in G 20 d. An advanced party of 1 M.G.O, 4 men & the 2-in-Command of each coy. left at 10 am to take over billets from the 2nd LINCOLNS. The Btn. marched off at	Sheet 36

Army Form C. 2118.

WAR DIARY
or
INTELLIGENCE SUMMARY.
(Erase heading not required.)

Place	Date	Hour	Summary of Events and Information	Remarks and references to Appendices
ESTAIRES	Feb 14th	4 pm	4 pm via LE NOUVEAU MONDE, SAILLY Cross-roads, ROUGE DE BOUT. After crossing the railway at G.29.b.2.5, Companies moved at 10 mins. intervals. The Btn. is in left reserve to the Brigade, and is billetted round LA CROIX LESCORNEX and CROIX BLANCHE, with Btn Hd-Qrs at JERRY VILLA (M.26 d.4.7). D Coy. is at CROIX BLANCHE in close support to the 22nd Batt'd Bre: (3rd Tyneside Scottish) who are holding the trenches on our front. The Btn. is in readiness to move up at ½ hr's notice if required, but D Coy and 1 platoon per Coy. are always ready to move in 5 minutes. Btn. all correctly in billets by 8 pm. (Appendix A attached).	Sheet 36 (1:40000) Appendix A
near FLEURBAIX (H.26 d 4-7)	Feb 15th		Officers reconnoitred the way to the trenches, and to the Alarm Arsenal. Very windy morning & rainy night — no Shelling. Some firing by our artillery between 9 – 9.30 pm., otherwise quiet. Working parties of 100 men from C Coy required by R.E. Casualties: 3 sick.	Casualties: 2 sick.
"	Feb 16th		V. windy & rainy. Quiet day. 120 men of A Coy on working parties. Casualties; NIL	

Army Form C. 2118.

WAR DIARY
or
INTELLIGENCE SUMMARY.
(Erase heading not required.)

Place	Date	Hour	Summary of Events and Information	Remarks and references to Appendices
Ln FLEURBAIX	Feb 17th		Coy. Commanders, and 2n Gun Officer, Signalling Officer and Adjt, visited the trenches we are taking over from the 22nd M.F. (3rd Tyneside Scottish) in the morning. All the mens' blankets and officers' kits etc were stacked by Coys., and one man left in charge, until the kits are picked up by the transport and taken back to the Transport Lines. The Btn. marched off at 6 p.m. by platoons, passing CROIX BLANCHE at 2 mins. intervals. Btn. H.Q is at EATON HALL (M 3 & 4/4). Relief completed at 9 p.m. Four men wounded by shrapnel in morning. Fairly quiet night. Casualties: { 2 sick. { 4 wd. Appendix "B" attached.	Sheet 36. (1:40000) Appendix B
In trenches	Feb 18th		The trenches are more "breastworks", and require a very great deal of work, as in many places the parapet is too low and the parados non-existent, while the communication trenches are all flooded and only one (CELLAR FARM AVENUE) is in use for the whole Btn. There is no proper support line owing to the wet state of the ground. Each company has 3 platoons in the front line and one in a "post" in rear (see attached plan – Appendix "C"). A wet & rainy day, and both sides were fairly quiet. Our trench mortars fired at about 11 p.m., and enemy retaliated vigorously but with little effect. The men worked hard at filling sandbags and erecting parados; this is the first time the Btn. has been up in the trenches as a single unit, and they seemed been, but not "quite "at home" yet. Casualties: 2 wd.	Appendix "C"

Army Form C. 2118.

WAR DIARY
or
INTELLIGENCE SUMMARY.
(Erase heading not required.)

Instructions regarding War Diaries and Intelligence Summaries are contained in F. S. Regs., Part II. and the Staff Manual respectively. Title pages will be prepared in manuscript.

Place	Date	Hour	Summary of Events and Information	Remarks and references to Appendices
In the Trenches	Feb. 19th		Very dull morning & drizzling rain, but cleared up later. Hostile artillery very active 3-4 pm on our front line, and swished in G Gap parapet in one place, but no casualties from this fire. We used the periscope rifles a lot. Work continued on improving the trench. A carrying party of 75 from 2nd Btn. reported in evening. Brilliant moonlight night. Casualties: 1 died of wounds, 1 killed	Sheet 36 (1:40000)
"	Feb. 20th		Very fine & frosty morning, and no artillery fire. German aeroplanes extremely active in afternoon, while 14 of us went over their lines. From 3.30-5.30 pm hostile guns were very active and heavily shelled CELLAR FARM AV:, V.C. AVENUE, also CROIX BLANCHE and RUE PETILLON. Officers of 2/LINCOLNS went round the line — they relieve us to-morrow. Work carried on as usual, and 50 men from 3rd Btn. came down. A machine gun & trench mortar "strafe" took place at 1 A.M., and the enemy retaliated vigorously, causing our guns to reply. Otherwise the night was quiet. Information received that the Germans launched a gas attack at GIVENCHY (7 miles South), but no details. Casualties: 1 Sick, 2 wd, 1 killed	

23

Army Form C. 2118.

WAR DIARY
or
~~INTELLIGENCE SUMMARY.~~
(Erase heading not required.)

Instructions regarding War Diaries and Intelligence Summaries are contained in F. S. Regs., Part II. and the Staff Manual respectively. Title pages will be prepared in manuscript.

24

Place	Date	Hour	Summary of Events and Information	Remarks and references to Appendices
In the Trenches	Feb 21st		Considerable reciprocal shelling in the morning. Advance parties (1 Officer & 1 man per coy, 1 N.C.O. for machine guns & 1 for Hd-Qrs) left at 7 am to take over billets from the 2nd Rifle Brigade at BAC ST MAUR. Adv. parties from 2nd Lincolns arrived at 1 pm to take over all stores, Bombs, S.A.A. etc. The relieving Btn. arrived at 7.10 pm, and relief was completed at 10 pm. Coys. marched independently to billets, by platoons, and were all in by 11.30 pm — very quiet night. Casualties: 2 wd. sick	Sheet 36 (1:40,000) Appendix "A"
BAC ST MAUR	22nd		Quiet day. Spent in cleaning up and making good deficiencies; new boots and mackintosh capes were issued. Very cold, and snowed all morning. Casualties: NIL	
"	23rd		The baths at SAILLY were allotted to the Btn., and every man had a bath and clean under-clothes given him in exchange for his dirty ones. Billetting parties left at 2 pm to take over our billets at FORT ROMPU, where we move to-morrow. V. cold & frosty. The working parties (225/men) got under the R.E. at 7.15 pm. Sudden alarm received at 3 pm that we are to move to-night back to JERRY VILLA, but this was cancelled. Billetting parties were recalled, as we are not to move to-morrow either. Began to snow in afternoon. Casualties: 4 sick.	

Army Form C. 2118.

WAR DIARY
or
INTELLIGENCE SUMMARY.
(Erase heading not required.)

Instructions regarding War Diaries and Intelligence Summaries are contained in F. S. Regs., Part II. and the Staff Manual respectively. Title pages will be prepared in manuscript.

Place	Date	Hour	Summary of Events and Information	Remarks and references to Appendices
BAC ST MAUR	Feb. 24th		Bitterly cold. Some long range shells fell near BAC ST MAUR about 2-3 pm. One man was injured by the after explosion of a blind shell. Orders received that we are to march to-morrow to new billets at L'HALLOBEAU (H.I.C.78). Casualties: NIL	Sheet 36 (1:40000) Appendix E
"	25th		Coys. to move at 10 mins. interval with transport in rear. Billeting party started at 6.30 am; Btn. was originally ordered to move at 11.30 am, but this was postponed by one hour. New billets reached at 2.30 pm; the new billets are very dirty. Began to snow again in evening - very cold.	
L'HALLOBEAU			We are now back again in the 34th Division, and our Brigade is in Divisional Reserve - the other two brigades being in the line. Casualties: 1 wd. 1 sick.	
L'HALLOBEAU	26th		Cold & Snowy. Quiet day. Gas alarm received at 11.45 pm, but it turned out to be false. Casualties: NIL.	

Army Form C. 2118.

WAR DIARY
or
INTELLIGENCE SUMMARY.
(Erase heading not required.)

26

Place	Date	Hour	Summary of Events and Information	Remarks and references to Appendices
L'HALLOBEAU	Feb 27th	9.30 a.m.	110 men required for fatigues at Div. Coal depot and G.R.E's yard at 9.30 a.m.. C.O., Capt TOD & Capt WHITEHEAD went to visit the trenches. We are to occupy. Church parades for all denominations in morning. Slightly warmer. Casualties: NIL	Sheet 36 (1:40000)
"	28th		Majr MACKINTOSH and Capt CUBEY went up to the trenches, and Capt TOD is attached to the artillery for the day, in order to see how work is carried out in an observation post. Quiet day. C.O. inspected "A" Coy. Casualties: 4 sick	
"	29th		8 Officers & 160 men required for fatigues on the various defensive posts in the left sector; paraded 7 a.m., Back again 3.30 p.m.. Capt WHITEHEAD attached to the artillery for the day. Three German aeroplanes over in the morning. Fine & warm. Inspection of "B" Coy.. New P.H. gas helmets issued. Casualties: 1 Officer sick 5 sick	

S E C R E T.

Reference Sheet 36.   1/40,000.

102nd (TYNESIDE SCOTTISH) BRIGADE.

OPERATION ORDER NO. 7.

13th FEB 1916.

1.. The Brigade will take over the trenches, posts and billets, in the Right Brigade Area from the 25th Brigade on the evening of FEB:14th, 1916.

2.. Battalions will march in accordance with the attached March Table.

3.. Trenches and works will be taken over as under :-

   21st(S)Bn.Northd. Fusiliers (2nd Tyneside Scottish) to hold trenches from right of N.8.3 to Left of N.9.4.   Battalion Headquarters, Rifle Villa, N.2.b.6.0

   22nd(S)Bn.Northd. Fusiliers (3rd Tyneside Scottish) to hold trench from right of N.10.1 to left of N.10.5.
   Battalion Headquarters, Eaton Hall, N.3.b.5.5.

   20th(S)Bn.Northd. Fusiliers (1st Tyneside Scottish) will be in Right Reserve.   Battalion Headquarters, Rouge de Bout. G.36.d.6.7

   23rd(S)Bn.Northd. Fusiliers (4th Tyneside Scottish) will be in left reserve.   Battalion Headquarters, Jerry Villa. N.28.d.4.7

4.. GUIDES supplied by Royal Berkshire Regiment for Lewis Machine Guns of 22nd (S) Bn Northd Fusiliers (3rd Tyneside Scottish) will be met at Cross Roads, LA CROIX LES CORNEX at 4 p.m., and guides for Platoons at Cross Roads, LA CROIX LES CORNEX at 5-30 p.m.

   GUIDES for Lewis Machine Guns of 21st (S) Bn Northd Fusiliers (2nd Tyneside Scottish) supplied by 1st Royal Irish Rifles will be met at Road Junction G.36.d.6.7 at 4 p.m., and guides for Platoons at the same place at 5-30 p.m.

5.. Company Commanders of 22nd (S) Bn Northd Fusiliers (3rd Tyneside Scottish) will be met at EATON HALL at 2 p.m. by an Officer, 15th Field Company, R. E.

   Company Commanders of 21st (S) Bn Northd Fusiliers (2nd Tyneside Scottish) will be met at RIFLE VILLA at 2 p.m. by an Officer, 1st Home Counties Field Company, R.E.

   These R.E. Officers will show Company Commanders the general system of the work to be carried on in the front line of trenches and posts.

6.. Advanced Parties of :-
   22nd (S) Bn Northd Fusiliers) will be at EATON HALL at 3 p.m.
   (3rd Tyneside Scottish).....) N.3.b.5.5
   21st (S) Bn Northd Fusiliers) will be at RIFLE VILLA at 3 p.m.
   (2nd Tyneside Scottish).....) N.2.b.6.0
   23rd (S) Bn Northd Fusiliers) will be at JERRY VILLA at 1 p.m.)to take
   (4th Tyneside Scottish).....) N.28.d.4.7   )over
   20th (S) Bn Northd Fusiliers) will be at ROUGE DE BOUT at 1 p.m.)billets
   (1st Tyneside Scottish).....) G.36.d.6.7   )and

2.

7.. 25th Infantry Brigade Machine Gun Companies will be attached to the Brigade. Their Vickers Guns will remain in the present positions.

8.. The 36th Trench Mortar Battery and A/25 Light Trench Mortar Battery will be attached to the Brigade.
A/102 Light Trench Mortar Battery will be billetted at G.36.a.6.9

9.. Transport of Battalions will move to the following localities under Battalion arrangements :-

20th (S) Bn. Northd. Fusiliers (1st Tyneside Scottish).. G.16.c.2.9
21st (S) Bn. Northd. Fusiliers (2nd Tyneside Scottish).. G.14.d.2.2
22nd (S) Bn. Northd. Fusiliers (3rd Tyneside Scottish).. G.14.d.9.5
23rd (S) Bn. Northd. Fusiliers (4th Tyneside Scottish).. G.21.a central

Officers Commanding Units will send a representative of the Transport to reconnoitre these localities.

10.. All Trench Stores are to be carefully checked before taking over, and a receipt given for them.
Vermoral Sprayers and solution to be taken over correctly.

11.. Battalions will report immediately reliefs have been completed.

Reports to Brigade Headquarters H.20.d.6.6.

Major.
BRIGADE MAJOR.
102nd (TYNESIDE SCOTTISH) BRIGADE.

Copies issued to :-

    34th Division.
    8th Division.
    25th Brigade.
    20th (S) Bn Northd Fusiliers (1st Tyneside Scottish)
    21st   "   "   "   (2nd   "   "   )
    22nd   "   "   "   (3rd   "   "   )
    23rd   "   "   "   (4th   "   "   )

SECRET.

Reference Sheet 57.
1/40,000.

"B"

102nd (TYNESIDE SCOTTISH) BRIGADE.

OPERATION ORDER NO. 8

16th FEBRUARY, 1916.

1. The two Battalions of the 102nd (Tyneside Scottish) Brigade now in Brigade Reserve will relieve the two Battalions at present in the trenches on the evening of 17th FEBRUARY, 1916.

    20th(S)Bn.Northd.Fus:) will relieve the (21st(S)Bn.Northd.Fus.
    (1st TYNESIDE SCOTTISH).)   (2nd TYNESIDE SCOTTISH).

    23rd(S)Bn.Northd.Fus:) will relieve the (22nd(S)Bn.Northd.Fus.
    (4th TYNESIDE SCOTTISH))   (3rd TYNESIDE SCOTTISH).

2. Details of relief will be arranged mutually between Commanding Officers concerned.

3. Battalion Transport will remain in the present lines now occupied by it.

4. Battalions in reserve will send representatives in daylight to take over ammunition bombs, stores, gum boots, etc., from Battalions in front line of trenches.
   Battalions in trenches will send parties to take over the billets now occupied by the reserve Battalions.

5. Brigade Machine Gun Sections of the 20th and 23rd (S) Bns. Northd. Fusiliers (1st and 4th Tyneside Scottish) will take over the Lewis Gun positions from the 21st and 22nd (S) Bns. Northd. Fusiliers (2nd and 3rd Tyneside Scottish) during daylight.

6. No movement other than Machine Gun Sections, Billeting and taking over representatives to take place before 5-45p.m.

7. The Trench Mortar Batteries will remain in their present positions.

8. Care must be taken that the Communication Trenches are kept clear of all carrying parties until the relief has been completed.

9. Reports to Brigade Headquarters when relief has been effected.

                                                        Major.
                                                BRIGADE MAJOR.
                                    102nd (TYNESIDE SCOTTISH) BRIGADE.

Copies to : 8th Division
            34th Division.
            23rd Brigade & 25th Brigade.
            70th Brigade.
            All Units, 102nd (Tyneside Scottish) Brigade.
            Brigade Transport Officer.
            25th Brigade Machine Gun Company.
            36/Medium Trench Mortar Battery.
            25/Light Trench Mortar Battery.
            A/102 Trench Mortar Battery.

SECRET.   "B"

OPERATION ORDERS.

By. Lieut. Col. W. Lyle. Cmdg. 23rd Battn. Northumberland Fusiliers
17th Feberuary, 1916.

1. The Battalion will relieve the 22nd Battalion Northumberland Fusiliers in the trenches this evening.

2. Guides at the rate of one per Platoon and one for Head Quarter Party will be at CROIX BLANCHE at 6pm - Machine Gun Guides will be at CROIX LESCORNET at 3.30pm.

3. Companies will move up by Platoons at 4 minutes interval;
   "A" Company No. 1. Platoon to pass CROIX BLANCHE at 6pm.
   Headquarter Party   "   "   "   "   " 6.16pm
   "B" Company No. 5 Platoon " "   "   "   " 6.20pm
   "D" Company No. 13   " "   "   "   " 6.36pm
   "C" Company No. 9   " "   "   "   " 6.52pm

4. Company Signallers will march at the head of the leading platoon of their Companies. The Signallers will take over the instruments already in the trenches, and will leave their own instruments ready for use where they are now.
Lieutenant R. MACDONALD and 1 N.C.O. will meet the 3rd Battalion Signalling Officer at EATON HALL at 2pm.

5. Companies will take in their Verey Pistols and 1½" illuminating pistols.

6. All the Blankets and Officers' Kits must be stacked in one place at Company Head Quarters, together with any other articles not required in the trenches, under the charge of two men per Company. The Transport Officer will collect these to-morrow morning, and take them back to the Transport Lines. The men in charge will them rejoin their Companies.

7. A limbered wagon is at Battalion Head Quarters; any stores to be taken to the trenches, and which cannot be carried, must be loaded on on this limber by 4pm.

8. Companies will take dixies into the trenches for cooking purposes; as far as possible the "cooker-cart" dixies should not be taken.

9. The transport Officer will arrange to withdraw to the Transport Lines all "cookers"; he will bring the limbered wagon from Head Quarters and the 2 water carts to EATON HALL, with the rations to-night.

10. The Water Carts will remain at EATON HALL, and will be filled every night. Companies must take up with them every receptacle they can find, for carrying water. Water bottles must be filled before marching in.

11. No fatigue or ration parties will move until the relief is complete.

12. The Battalion dump and water supply will be at Battalion Head Quarters (XXXX EATON HALL).
No water parties are to move during daylight.
13. Report by wire as soon as relief is completed.

K. A. N.   ANDERSON

CAPTAIN AND ADJUTANT.

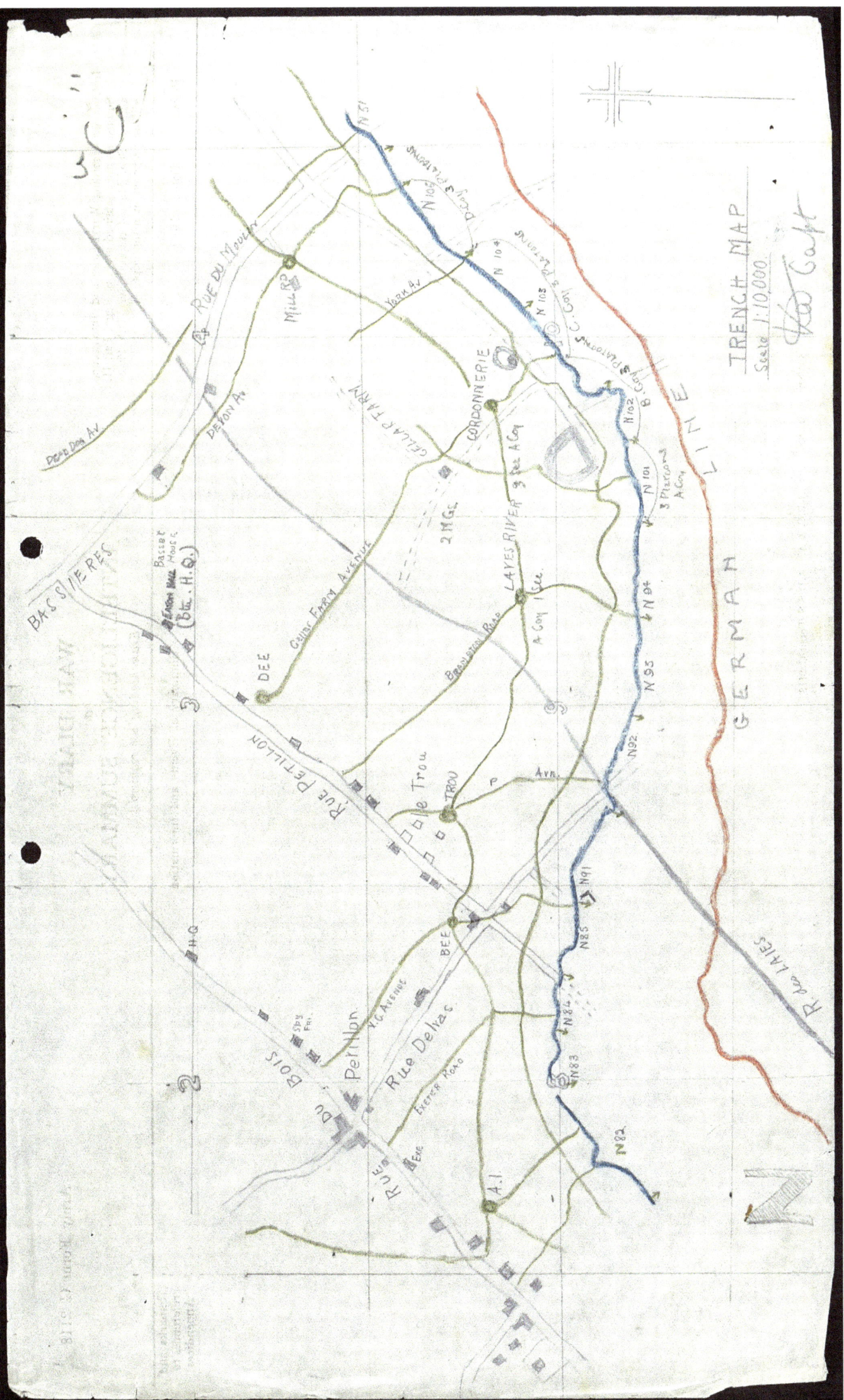

Reference Sheet 36. 1/40,000.

102nd (TYNESIDE SCOTTISH) BRIGADE.

OPERATION ORDER NO. 9

1.. The 102nd (Tyneside Scottish) Brigade will be relieved by the 25th Brigade in the centre area of the 8th Divisional Line of TRENCHES on the evening of FEBRUARY 21st, 1916, and will after being relieved go into Divisional Reserve Billets.

2.. Battalions will march in accordance with attached March Table.

3.. Trenches and Advanced Posts will be handed over as under :-

    (a) To - 2/RIFLE BRIGADE trenches N8/3 to N9/4 (both inclusive) BEE and TROU posts.

    (b) To - 2/LINCOLNS REGT: trenches N10/1 to N10/5 (both inclusive) LAIES RIVER CONDONNERIE and DEE POSTS)

Billets and Supporting Posts will be handed over as under :-

    (c) To - 1/ROYAL IRISH RIFLES - CHARRED POST and WINDY POST and billets ROUGE DE BOUT.

    (d) To - 2/ROYAL BERKS REGT:, WINTERS NIGHT POST, JUNCTION POST, CROIX BLANCHE POST, and billets about LA CROIX LES COMETS

Details of relief to be arranged mutually between Commanding Officers concerned.

4.. The 25th Brigade Machine Gun Company will cease to be attached to the Brigade.
The 36/Medium Trench Mortar Battery and A/25 Light Trench Mortar Battery will also cease to be attached to the Brigade.

5.. A/102 Trench Mortar Battery will withdraw from trenches at dusk and proceed to billets at G.9.C (with 21st (S) Bn Northd Fusiliers (2nd Tyneside Scottish)
The necessary transport for the Officers baggage etc., to be supplied by 21st (S) Bn Northd Fusiliers (2nd Tyneside Scottish).

6.. Advanced Billetting parties will take over billets in daylight.

7.. Battalion representatives will hand over in daylight - ammunition bombs, gum boots, vermorel sprayers, stores, etc., and obtain receipt for same.

8.. Transport will remain in its present lines.

9.. Battalions will report immediately moves have been completed. Reports to present Brigade Headquarters (Mares Nest) H.20.d.3.6.. When reliefs have been completed - Brigade report centre will be at SAILLY BRIDGE HOUSE, G.13.d.1.5.

20th FEBRUARY, 1916.
Issued at 5 p.m.
Copies issued to -
All Units, 102nd (Tyneside Scottish) Bde.
Brigade Transport Officer.
A/102 Trench Mortar Battery.
8th Division.   34th Division.   ) For information.
70th Brigade.   23rd Brigade.   )
Centre Group Artillery Commander.   )
1st Home Counties R.E.   )

Major.
BRIGADE MAJOR.
102nd (TYNESIDE SCOTTISH) B

MARCH TABLE.

S.I.G. A.
Reference Sheet 53.   1/40,000   102nd (TYNESIDE SCOTTISH) BDE.

UNIT.	STARTING POINT.	TIME.	ROUTE.	TAKING OVER TRENCHES OR BILLETS TO:	TAKING OVER BILLETS FROM:	REMARKS.
21st (S) Bn. Northd. Fusiliers (2nd Tyneside Scottish).	G.36.a.5.8	5.50 p.m	G.29.d.3.8 G.30.a.2.0 G.17.d.1.7 SAILLY CROSS ROADS G.9.c.	1/ROYAL IRISH RIFLES.	1/ROYAL IRISH RIFLES. G.9.c.	Precedence of road to be given to relieving Battalions. ******** Advanced Company to remain at ??? until relieved, then it will proceed independently by Platoons to billets. 3 remaining Companies will move by Platoons at 2 minutes intervals.
22nd (S) Bn. Northd. Fusiliers (3rd Tyneside Scottish).	H.23.d.1.3	5:40 p.m	H.23.a.1.2 .22.a.0.0 H.19.a.4.0	2/ROYAL BERKS: 3/GL.STP.	ROYAL BERKS: 3/GL.STP. RUE DU QUESNOY	Advanced Company to remain at CROIX BLANCHE until relieved, when it will proceed to billets independently by Platoons. 3 remaining Companies will move by Platoons at 2 minutes intervals.
20th (S) Bn. Northd. Fusiliers (1st Tyneside Scottish).	) on relief, by most direct route) to billets.			2/RIFLE BRIGADE.	2/LH-COLNS. SAILLY.	
23rd (S) Bn. Northd. Fusiliers (4th Tyneside Scottish).	) on relief, by most direct route) to billets.			2/LH-COLNS.	RIFLE BRIGADE. BAC ST. MAUR.	

BRIGADE MAJOR.
102nd (TYNESIDE SCOTTISH) BDE.

SECRET. "E" COPY NO: 4

Reference Sheet 36. 1/40,000.

102nd (TYNESIDE SCOTTISH) BRIGADE

OPERATION ORDER NO: 10

1.. The 102nd (Tyneside Scottish) Brigade will relieve the 68th Infantry Brigade in the 34th Divisional Reserve Area on FEBRUARY 25th, 1916.

2.. No. 3 Company, A.S.C., 34th Divisional Train, will accompany the Brigade to the new area.

3.. Units will march in accordance with the attached March Table.

4.. Units will be billeted as follows :-

    BRIGADE HEAD QUARTERS .... ERQUINGHEM.

    20th (S) Bn. Northd. Fusiliers
    (1st TYNESIDE SCOTTISH).......... JESUS FARM (B.26.d.4.0)

    21st (S) Bn. Northd. Fusiliers
    (2nd TYNESIDE SCOTTISH).......... FORT ROMPU (H.8.c.8.5)

    22nd (S) Bn. Northd. Fusiliers
    (3rd TYNESIDE SCOTTISH).......... RUE DORMOIRE (H.8.b.9.3)

    23rd (S) Bn. Northd. Fusiliers
    (4th TYNESIDE SCOTTISH).......... L'HALLOBEAU (B.25.c.8.5)

    No. 3 Coy: A. S. C.,
    34th Divisional Train............ STEENWERCK

5.. Units will march by Companies at 10 minutes interval.

6.. All Units will send Advanced Billeting Parties to take over billets in their new areas to arrive by 7-30 a.m. on 25th inst.

7.. A/102 Light Trench Mortar Battery will march with the rear Company of the 21st (S) Bn. Northd. Fusiliers (2nd Tyneside Scottish). The necessary transport for the battery to be supplied by this Battalion.

8.. Brigade Report Centre will close at SAILLY at 10-30 a.m. on the 25th instant, and re-open at ERQUINGHEM (H.4.d.4.7) at 10-30 a.m. the same day.

24:2:1916.

Issued at 9 p.m.

Major.
BRIGADE MAJOR.
102nd (TYNESIDE SCOTTISH) BRIGADE.

Copies to :-
  All Units, 102nd (Tyneside Scottish) Brigade.
  A/102 Light Trench Mortar Battery.
  Brigade Transport Officer.
  No. 3 Company, A. S. C. (34th Div:Train).

  8th Division.   )
  34th Division.   ) For information.
  68th Brigade.   )

S E C R E T.   Reference Sheet 53.   1/40,000

102nd (TYNESIDE SCOTTISH) BRIGADE.

MARCH TABLE.

UNIT.	STARTING POINT.	TIME.	ROUTE.	REMARKS.
Headquarters, 102nd (Tyneside Scottish)Bde:		10:30 a.m	direct to ERQUINGHEM.	
20th (S) Bn. Northd.Fus: (1st TYNESIDE SCOTTISH).	G.22.b.2.9	10 a.m	BAC ST.MAUR ERQUINGHEM. B.27.d.5.8 JESUS FARM.	To march by Companies at 10 minutes intervals. Field Kitchens will march in rear of Companies. One Water Cart in rear of 1st and 3rd Companies. One Baggage wagon in rear of 2nd and 4th Companies. Officers Mess Cart and Maltese Cart to march in rear of Head Quarter Company. Remainder of transport in rear of Battalion.
* 23rd (S) Bn. Northd.Fus: (4th TYNESIDE SCOTTISH).	H.13.c.5.9	11:30 a.m	FORT ROMPU ERQUINGHEM B.27.d.3.8 H.1.b.4.3 L'HALLOBEAU.	* To follow 209th Field Coy. R.E.
21st (S) Bn. Northd.Fus: (2nd TYNESIDE SCOTTISH).	G.22.b.2.9	12 noon.	BAC ST.MAUR FORT ROMPU.	- do -
22nd (S) Bn. Northd.Fus: (3rd TYNESIDE SCOTTISH).	H.13.c.5.9	1 p.m.	FORT ROMPU H.8.b.9.2 RUE DORMOIRE.	- do -
No. 3 Coy. A. S. C. 34th Divisional Train.	Via LE VERRIER to STEEN BECK direct.			To take over billets from 191st Coy. A.S.C.

Army Form C. 2118.

Instructions regarding War Diaries and Intelligence
Summaries are contained in F. S. Regs., Part II.
and the Staff Manual respectively. Title pages
will be prepared in manuscript.

WAR DIARY
or
INTELLIGENCE SUMMARY.
(Erase heading not required.)

27

Place	Date	Hour	Summary of Events and Information	Remarks and references to Appendices
L'HALLOBEAU	March 1st		Quiet day. Huts were sprayed by medical authorities. 150 men for fatigue at 8 a.m. – 2 p.m. Casualties: 6 sick.	Sheet 36 (1/40,000)
"	March 2nd		Fine & warmer. 2 Officers and 400 O.R. for fatigues. Parades under Coy. arrangements. Casualties: 7 sick.	
"	March 3rd		The Signallers under 2/Lt R. MACDONALD left billets at 8 a.m., and the machine gunners at 10 a.m. They are to relieve the Signals & machine guns of the 25th Northd Fus: (2nd Tyneside Irish). Route marches by Coys. in morning. Orders re the relief to-morrow received from Brigade. 25 men per coy. for baths at ERQUINGHEM at 10 a.m. Casualties: 1 sick.	
"	March 4th		All blankets, Officers kits & surplus stores collected by Q-M during morning, and stacked in a shed in the Transport lines. Orders attached (Appendix "A"). Relief completed 10.45 p.m.; somewhat delayed by A Coy. being guided by wrong track. Enemy very quiet. Work begun on thickening parapet & the wire was examined. Casualties: 1 sick.	3 · 3 [illegible] A

2353 Wt W2544/1454 700,000 5/15 D. D. & L. A.D.S.S./Forms/C. 2118.

Army Form C. 2118.

WAR DIARY
~~INTELLIGENCE SUMMARY~~
(Erase heading not required.)

Instructions regarding War Diaries and Intelligence Summaries are contained in F. S. Regs., Part II. and the Staff Manual respectively. Title pages will be prepared in manuscript.

28

Place	Date	Hour	Summary of Events and Information	Remarks and references to Appendices
In Trenches	March 5th		We held the left half of the left sector of our Divnl. front. The 22nd Yorkk'd Fus: are on our right, and the 2nd Army on our left. 20th Yorkk'd Fus: are in reserve behind us. A very long line extending from I.16.1 — I.21.2, and the front line is in an advanced state of decay, particularly on our right flank (D Coy.). In other ways, the position is not a bad one as there are 3 distinct lines behind the front line, and 3 commun. trenches also. The wire is not too bad on the whole, but requires a lot of improvement in places, while the parapet is tumbling down & the dug-outs are flooded. Work was begun on revetting & thickening the parapet. Hostile artillery fairly active in morning, wounding 2 men — our guns replied. Two Officer's patrols went out, but met no enemy ones. Working party of 100 from the 20th N.F. Casualties:	Sheet 36 (1:40,000) Trench map 36 N.W.4 Edition 6 2 wounded
"	March 6th		Quiet morning. At 1.50 pm a small "scheme" took place. We opened rapid fire on hostile parapet; 2 pm our guns shelled hostile line opposite I.16.1 and down enemy commun. trench at same place. They retaliated & killed one man & wounded another. Work continued on wire & parapet. Quiet night. 3rd Bn. on our right raised gas alarm at 9 pm, which proved false. Very cold night. Casualties:	1 Sick 1 killed 1 wounded

WAR DIARY
or
INTELLIGENCE SUMMARY.
(Erase heading not required.)

Army Form C. 2118.

29

Place	Date	Hour	Summary of Events and Information	Remarks and references to Appendices
In Trenches near	7th		Quiet day owing to weather. Snow & sleet all day. Capt T.A. Anderson of B Coy. was placed under arrest for drunkenness at 7.30 a.m. Worked on parapet. Practically no hostile fire. Lt Williams & 6 O.R. went out on patrol.	
"	8th		Bitterly cold day. Carr. parties left to take over billets from 1st Btn in RUE MARLE, and parties from 1st Btn arrived to take over all trench stores etc. from us. Quiet day on the whole; our support line was shelled at intervals — no damage. Transport brought officer's kits & blankets & dumped them in billets before our arrival. Relief was delayed owing to a platoon of the 1st Btn losing Sheet 36 their way & refusing to follow the guide. Back in billets by 11.30 p.m. Casualties: 2 sick; 1 died of wounds. (1/40,000)	
RUE MARLE	9th		Day devoted to cleaning up. Billets are filthy & have never been cleaned for weeks; their condition reported to Brigade. The detailed report of Lt Williams' patrol, together with a recommendation for his work, forwarded to Brigade. V. cold. 190 men on fatigue. Casualties: 1 sick.	
"	10th		Nothing of interest occurred. Large working parties of over 250 men out. Draft of 29 O.R. inspected by G.O.C. & G.O.C. Brigade. Casualties: 1 sick. & posted to Coys.	

Army Form C. 2118.

WAR DIARY
or
INTELLIGENCE SUMMARY
(Erase heading not required.)

Instructions regarding War Diaries and Intelligence Summaries are contained in F.S. Regs., Part II. and the Staff Manual respectively. Title pages will be prepared in manuscript.

Place	Date	Hour	Summary of Events and Information	Remarks and references to Appendices
RUE MARLE	March 11th		Very quiet day; raw & cold. 250 men on fatigues. Casualties: 5 sick.	Sheet 36 (1:40000)
"	12th		We were to have returned to the trenches this evening, but relief is postponed till 14th owing to the Brigade having to do a total spell of 20 days instead of 16 days. 160 men on fatigue. Church parades in morning. Casualties: 4 sick.	
"	13th		Lovely warm day. Two officers (Lt J.N. COLLINGS and Lt COLLINGS) joined and posted to B & D Coys respectively. Lt DUNN, & 30 O.R. join Brigade Bombing School for a 4 days course of instruction. Casualties: NIL.	
"	14th		Very warm day. Lt WHITTAKER and Lt HAMILTON sent to hospital. As the Brigades on our right & left are both carrying out reliefs to-night, we do not start ours until 11 p.m.. We go into the same trenches as before, relieving the 20th M.F.; the only change is that C Coy holds the right of the line & D Coy is in reserve. Casualties: 3 sick.	

Army Form C. 2118.

WAR DIARY
or
INTELLIGENCE SUMMARY.
(Erase heading not required.)

30

Place	Date	Hour	Summary of Events and Information	Remarks and references to Appendices
In the Trenches	March 15th		Relief completed 1 am. A & B Coys held same portion as before, but C now holds the right of the line and D is in reserve. The reserve Coy has been moved up from the BOIS GRENIER line, & now has 2 platns in the S-S line on each side of WINE ST, and Coy Hd-Qrs in the S-S line. A quiet night. Patrols examined our wire and found it extremely weak all along. Trenches drying up. 2nd HAMILTON & 2nd WHITTAKER to hospital. Casualties: 2 Officers sick.	French map 36 N.W.4. Edition 6
"	16th		Very fine & dry. Much work done on repairing parapet & re-modelling parados, also drainage. 100 men from 20th M.F. as working parties in morning. The Brigadier visited the trenches in morning. Owing to there being no tramway, very large carrying parties are required every night for rations & R.E. Stores; this prevents work being done on the front line. Hostile artillery quiet. Several patrols out at night, but bright moon prevented them from closely approaching hostile lines. Casualties: Nil	
"	17th		V. fine & hot again. Work as before, and 100 men from 20th M.F. came down in morning as working party. Slight shelling of our S line in afternoon. Bright moonlight night. 1 platn moved to FME DE BIEZ. The railway was used for rations. Casualties: 1 sick	
"	18th		Our batteries in rear were v. heavily shelled all morning. Aeroplanes active on both sides. Patrols out as usual, and usual parties on on wire. Btn Hd-Qrs was re-roofed with steel girders & concrete. 1 Platoon moved from back from FME DE BIEZ. Rations for C & D Coys brought up city. Casualties; 3 sick	

WAR DIARY
or
INTELLIGENCE SUMMARY.
(Erase heading not required.)

Army Form C. 2118.

Place	Date	Hour	Summary of Events and Information	Remarks and references to Appendices
In the Trenches	March 19th		Quiet day except between 1 & 2 pm when the right of the S-S line on the rly was shelled. Rations & stores brought up by railway; this effects a great saving in carrying parties. Bright moon; patrols & wiring parties out as usual. 2nd Lt F.O. DUNN was unfortunately killed by a bomb accident at the Brigade Bombing School. Casualties: 2 wounded at duty. 1 Officer killed (accidentally)	Trench Map 36 N.W.4 Edition 6
"	20th		Quiet morning until 11 am when Hd-Qrs & WHITE AV: were shelled till 1 pm, some damage being done. Our guns retaliated. Aeroplanes v. active. The 6th. relieved us Evening & going into Brigade Reserve (disposition as shewn in Appendix "B"). The 20th M.F. was to relieve us [Appendix "B"]. Sketch of our trench position also attached. Relief completed 9.30 pm. B & C Coys complete in billets by 10.30 pm. At F.O. DUNN buried at ERQUINGHEM Church Cemetery (Row H, X°11); Officers from Each Coy in the Brigade attended. Court-Martial on Capt. T.A. ANDERSON took place at 111th S.[?] (sick). Hd-Qrs 10 am. Casualties: 7 wounded, 3 sick	
RUE MARLE	21st		Dull & misty. Quiet day with nothing in particular doing. Two platoon parades in morning of 20 min each. Casualties: NIL	
"	22nd		Drizzling. 195 men on fatigues at different hours. 100 men B Coy & 100 men C Coy had baths. Casualties: NIL	

WAR DIARY
or
INTELLIGENCE SUMMARY.
(Erase heading not required.)

Army Form C. 2118.

32

Place	Date	Hour	Summary of Events and Information	Remarks and references to Appendices
RUE MARLE	March 23rd		"Quiet day." The draft were put through a short course of musketry (15 rds per man) at a miniature range at L'ARMÉE. 250 men on fatigues. All arrangements are once again altered, and the brigade is not to be relieved on the 24th; we remain on, and return to the same line of trenches in relief of the 20th N.F. on Saturday, 25th. Casualties: 3 Sick 1 wd	Sheet 36 (1:40000)
"	24th		Snow again. Quiet day. 150 men on fatigue. Casualties: 1 sick	
"	25th		Fine & sunny. We relieve the 20th N.F. in the same trenches as before, starting at 7 p.m. Relief completed plan.. "A" Coy is in "reserve this time, and "D" Coy holds the left of the line — "B" and "C" returning to the same sectors. Casualties: nil	
Trenches	26th		Quiet day & rain at intervals. Usual work on wire etc.; Lt PATTERSON leaves for a short sniping course. Officers' patrols out. Casualties: nil	
"	27th		Hostile guns active against our rear positions, and a few shells near Btn Hd Qrs; very quiet night, but heavy rain, which interfered very much with work. Casualties: 2 wounded (1 remains at duty) 1 Sick	

Army Form C. 2118.

WAR DIARY
or
INTELLIGENCE SUMMARY.

(Erase heading not required.)

Instructions regarding War Diaries and Intelligence Summaries are contained in F.S. Regs., Part II. and the Staff Manual respectively. Title pages will be prepared in manuscript.

33

Place	Date	Hour	Summary of Events and Information	Remarks and references to Appendices
Trenches	March 28th		Nothing doing. 22nd N.F. carried out a small scheme on our right, for which we got the retaliation — 2 men wounded. Patrols & wiring parties out as usual. Casualties: 2 wd.	
"	29th		Slight shelling in afternoon; 3 casualties. Fine day. Casualties: 3 wd.	
"	30th		Very fine & sunny. Quiet day. We were relieved by the 20th N.F. as usual, commencing 7.30 p.m. Relief completed 9.30 p.m. We become "D" Bn. now, and have all 4 Coys in billets in RUE MARLE and on the ERQUINGHEM road. Casualties: [Sick 2, wd. 3]	
RUE MARLE	31st		Another v. fine day. 400 men to baths; 170 for the new Arrault Course, and 265 on fatigues. [illegible] Casualties: nil	

S E C R E T.   COPY NO: 6

Reference Sheet 36. N.W. 1/20,000.

102nd (TYNESIDE SCOTTISH) BRIGADE.

OPERATION ORDER NO. 11.

(Appendix "A")

2nd MARCH, 1916.

1.. The 102nd (Tyneside Scottish) Brigade will relieve the 103rd (Tyneside Irish) Brigade in the Left Section of the 34th Division on the night of MARCH 4/5th, 1916.

2.. Battalions will move in accordance with the attached March Tables.

3.. Trenches will be taken over as under :-

22nd (S) Bn. Northd. Fusiliers (3rd Tyneside Scottish) to hold trenches I.26.5 inclusive to Road Junction I.21.2 exclusive.
Headquarters - I.20.b.4.0
(1 Company in BOIS GRENIER Line.)

23rd (S) Bn. Northd. Fusiliers (4th Tyneside Scottish) to hold trenches I.21.2 inclusive to I.16.1 inclusive less 2 bays held by 2nd Army.
Headquarters I.15.c.7.5
(3 Platoons in BOIS GRENIER Line).

Brigade Reserve -

21st (S) Bn. Northd. Fusiliers (2nd Tyneside Scottish) will be in Brigade Reserve.
Headquarters, RUE MARLE, H.6.d.8.8

20th (S) Bn. Northd. Fusiliers (1st Tyneside Scottish) will be in Brigade Reserve.
Headquarters, RUE MARLE, H.6.d.8.4

4.. Details of relief will be arranged mutually by Commanding Officers concerned.

5.. Guides for 22nd (S) Bn. Northd. Fusiliers (3rd Tyneside Scottish) will be supplied by 24th (S) Bn. Northd. Fusiliers (1st Tyneside Irish), and will be at the South end of the RUE DES ACQUETS (H.18.c.3.5) at 7 p.m.
Guides for 23rd (S) Bn. Northd. Fusiliers (4th Tyneside Scottish) will be supplied by 25th (S) Bn. Northd. Fusiliers (2nd Tyneside Irish), and will be at SANDBAG CORNER (I.1.d.7.3) at 6:55 p.m.
Guides for the Company of 21st (S) Bn. Northd. Fusiliers (2nd Tyneside Scottish) proceeding to the BOIS GRENIER Line and FME DU BIEZ will be supplied by 26th (S) Bn. Northd. Fusiliers (3rd Tyneside Irish) and will be at RUE MARLE Road Junction H.6.d.7.7 at 7:35 p.m.

6.. Signallers of 22nd and 23rd (S) Bns. Northd. Fusiliers (3rd and 4th Tyneside Scottish) will report at 103rd (Tyneside Irish) Bde. Headquarters, RUE MARLE, at 10 a.m., and will relieve the signallers of 24th and 25th (S) Bns. Northd. Fusiliers (1st and 2nd Tyneside Irish) before noon on MARCH 3rd, 1916.
Machine Gunners of 22nd and 23rd (S) Bns. Northd. Fusiliers (3rd and 4th Tyneside Scottish) will report at 103rd (Tyneside Irish) Brigade Headquarters, RUE MARLE, at 12 noon, and will relieve the Machine Gunners of 24th and 25th (S) Bns. Northd. Fusiliers (1st and 2nd Tyneside Irish) before 3 p.m. on MARCH 3rd, 1916.

7.. The Battalion Bombing Officer and 8 Bombers of each Battalion in the trenches will take over Bombing Posts on the morning of 4th MARCH, 1916.
A Sniping Officer and 8 Snipers of each Battalion in the trenches will take over Snipers Posts by daylight on 4th MARCH, 1916.

8.. Advanced Parties from Battalions to hold the forward line will be sent to take over Trench Stores, maps, ammunition, bombs, log books, etc., on the morning of MARCH 4th 1916.

9.. Billeting Parties of the 20th and 21st (S) Bns. Northd. Fusiliers (1st and 2nd Tyneside Scottish) will take over billets etc. from Battalions now in 'D' and 'C' area on the morning of MARCH 4th, 1916.

10.. No movement of troops is to take place South of the BAC ST MAUR/LILLE Railway before 6-40 p.m.

11.. No transport is to move South of the BAC ST MAUR/LILLE Railway before 8-15 p.m.

12.. The A/102 Light Trench Mortar Battery will relieve the A/103 Light Trench Mortar Battery at 12 noon on the morning of MARCH 4th 1916.

13.. No. 3 Section Signal Company will remain in Divisional Reserve.

14.. Rations for consumption on 5th MARCH, 1916, will be carried on the men of the Battalions taking over front line of trenches.

15.. Gum boots and waders to be handed over to incoming units of 103rd (Tyneside Irish) Brigade, and receipts for them obtained.

16.. One Officer per Company will proceed to the trenches on the morning of MARCH 4th 1916, to take over work in progress.

17.. The 60th Medium Trench Mortar Battery will remain in its present position, and will be attached to the Brigade.

18.. One Section No. 6 Motor Machine Gun Battery will remain in the BOIS GRENIER Line, and will be attached to the Brigade.

19.. Transport will remain in its present lines.

20.. Battalions will report immediately by wire when moves have been completed.
Reports to Brigade Headquarters, RUE MARLE, (H.6.d.8.3).

21.. Please acknowledge.

Issued at 10 p.m.

Signature Major.
BRIGADE MAJOR.
102nd (TYNESIDE SCOTTISH) BRIGADE.

Copies Nos. 1 and 2 retained.
Copy No. 3 20th (S) Bn. Northd. Fusiliers (1st Tyneside Scottish)
         4 21st   "   "   "   "   (2nd   "   "   )
         5 22nd   "   "   "   "   (3rd   "   "   )
         6 23rd   "   "   "   "   (4th   "   "   )
         7 102nd Brigade Machine Gun Officer.
         8 102nd Brigade Transport Officer.
         9 A/102 Light Trench Mortar Battery.
        10 34th Division.
        11 63rd Brigade.
        12 101st Brigade.
        13 103rd Brigade.
        14 "B" Group Royal Artillery.
        15 60th Medium Trench Mortar Battery.
        16 No 6 Section Motor Machine Gun Battery.
        17 209th Field Company R.E.

SECRET. Reference Sheet 36. 1/20,000. To accompany Operation Order No. 11.

102nd (TYNESIDE SCOTTISH) BRIGADE.

MARCH TABLE.

UNIT.	STARTING POINT.	TIME.	ROUTE.	TAKING OVER TRENCHES OR BILLETS FROM	HANDING OVER BILLETS TO:	REMARKS.
22nd (S) Bn. Northd. Fusiliers (3rd TYNESIDE SCOTTISH)...	H.8.b.9.3	5-10 p.m	ERQUINGHEM SECHE RUE RUE DES ACQUETS GRIS POT LA VESSEE PARK ROW AVENUE.	24th (S) Bn. Northd. Fus. (1st Tyneside Irish).		By Companies at 10 minutes interval to the RUE DELETREE/RUE ALLEE Line, thence by Platoons at 2 minutes interval.
23rd (S) Bn. Northd. Fusiliers (4th TYNESIDE SCOTTISH)...	H.1.b.4.6	5-25 p.m	B.27.d.2.7 ERQUINGHEM. CHAPELLE D'ARMENTIERES. COWGATE - WINE & HAYSTACK AVENUES.	25th (S) Bn. Northd. Fus. (2nd Tyneside Irish).		- do -
21st (S) Bn. Northd. Fusiliers (2nd TYNESIDE SCOTTISH)...	FORT ROMPU.	6-30 p.m	ERQUINGHEM ARMENTIERRES STATION.	26th (S) Bn. Northd. Fus. (3rd Tyneside Irish).		By Companies at 5 minutes interval.
20th (S) Bn. Northd. Fusiliers (1st TYNESIDE SCOTTISH)...	B.26.c.2.6	7 p.m	B.27.d.2.7 ERQUINGHEM. ARMENTIERRES STATION.	27th (S) Bn. Northd. Fus. (4th Tyneside Irish).		- do -

Major.
BRIGADE MAJOR.
102nd (TYNESIDE SCOTTISH) BRIGADE.

Battalion Orders   by
Lieut. Col. W. Lyle, Cmdg., 23rd. Battalion Northumberland Fusiliers.
          4th. Battalion Tyneside Scottish.
                                            B.E.F. 19/3/16.

Orders for Monday March 20 th. 1916.

1.
   The Battalion will be relieved by the 20th. Battalion Northd. Fusiliers on the evening 20/21st. March, and will become "C" Battalion in Brigade Reserve.   Machine Gun Detachments, Signallers, Bombers and Snipers will be relieved in the afternoon.

2.
   When relieved the Battalion will be distributed as under, in billets and trenches at present held by the 20th. Northd. Fusiliers.
```
           HEADQUARTERS.........RUE MARLE.
           "A" COMPANY..........3 Platoons in LOOP LINE.
(to relieve "A" Coy.            1 Platoon in FME DE BIEZ
 20th. Northd. Fusrs.)
           "B" COMPANY..........3 Platoons in billets at RUE MARLE
(to relieve "C" Company         1 Platoon in PARADISE ALLEY.
 20th. Northd. Fusrs.)
           "C" COMPANY..........3 Platoons in billets at L'ARMEE
(to relieve "D" Company         1 Platoon in DOG LEG ROAD.
 20th. Northd. Fusrs.)
           "D" Company..........in BOIS GRENIER Line
(to relieve "B" Company 20th.
 Northd. Fusiliers )
```

3.
  "A" Company will relieve "A" Company 20th. Northd. Fus., starting at 5 p.m.-via COWGATE AVENUE; relieving by Platoons.

4.
   The usual Advance Parties will take over billets or trenches from the 20th. Northd. Fusiliers before 3 p.m., receipt being given for all stores taken over.
              Advance Parties from 20th. Northd. Fusrs. will take over during the morning, all trench stores &c and steel helmets. Duplicate lists of all stores &c. handed over to be at Battalion Head-quarters by 4 p.m.

5.
   All dixies, mess stores &c. to be taken out of the trenches by "B" and "C" Companies and Headquarters must be stacked at the dump by 6p.m. Other stores must be carried under Company arrangements.

6.
   Rations for "A" and "D" Companies and the platoons of "B" in the trenches will be at the dump at about 9.30 p.m.

7.
   The Companies in the trenches will send sick report and wounded to Medical Officer, 20th. Battn Northd. Fusrs.

8.
   Report when relieved and arrival in new billets.

                                            K.A.N.ANDERSON.

                                              CAPTAIN AND ADJUTANT.

MARCH TABLE.

Company.	Starting Point.	Time.	Route	Remarks.
"D" & Hd.Qrs. Party.	N.1.b.4/6	5.25 p.m.	B.27.d.2/7 ERQUINGHEM CHAPELLE D'ARMENTIERES COWGATE, WINE AND HAYSTACK AVENUES.	By Companies at 10 minutes interval to the RUE DELETREE/RUE ALLEE Line, thence by Platoons at 2 minutes interval.
"A"	do.	5.35 p.m.	do.	do.
"B"	do.	5.45 p.m.	do.	do.
"C"	do.	5.55 p.m.	do.	do.

Watches to be synchronized with Orderly Room Time at 12.0 noon on the 4th. March 1916.

OPERATION ORDERS.

By. Lieut. Col. Lyle, Comdg. 23rd. Battalion Northumberland Fusiliers.

1. The Battalion will relieve the 25th. (S) Battalion Northumberland Fusiliers in the trenches on the night of March 4/5th. 1916, holding trenches I.21.2 inclusive to I.16.1 inclusive less 2 bays held by 2nd. Army. 3 platoons of "C" Company will be in BOIS GRENIER Lines.

2. Companies will move in accordance with attached March Table.

3. Guides from the 25th. (S) Battalion Northd. Fusiliers (2nd. Tyneside Irish) will be at SANDBAG CORNER (I.1.d.7/3) at 6.30 p.m.

4. Advance Parties consisting of one Officer and 4 men per Company, the Regimental Sergt. Major for Headquarters, Lieut. Oliver and 2 bombers to take over bombing posts, Lieut. Patterson and 2 Snipers to take over Snipers posts, will parade outside Orderly Room ready to march at 3.0.p.m. and will report at the Headquarters 25th. Northumberland Fusiliers (I.15.c.7/5). All Trench Stores, maps, ammunition, bombs, gum boots leg books etc. must be taken over. All work in progress must be taken over.

5. All blankets and Officers kits must be stacked by Companies ready for loading by 2.0 p.m. The transport will pick these up, commencing with "C" Company and store them in the transport lines.

6. Rations for consumption on the 5th. March will be waiting for issue ready labelled in 8 bags per platoon at Railway Crossing at I.1.d.4/2. Companies will pick these up in passing and carry them into the trenches.

7. Officers Mess Stores, Orderly Room boxes, water buckets etc. will be loaded on a limbered wagon by 3 p.m., this wagon together with the Mess Cart will follow the Battalion to the trenches. Ground sheets will be stacked separately ready for loading by 3.0.p.m. and will be carried to the trenches by the transport.

8. No transport is to move South of the SAC ST MAUR/LILLE railway before 8.15 p.m.

9. The Quartermaster will hand over to the 25th. Northumberland Fusiliers all gum boots and waders (retaining sufficient for use of the transport personnel) and obtain receipts for them.

10. Companies to report by wire immediately the relief is completed.

K. Anderson
Capt & Adjt

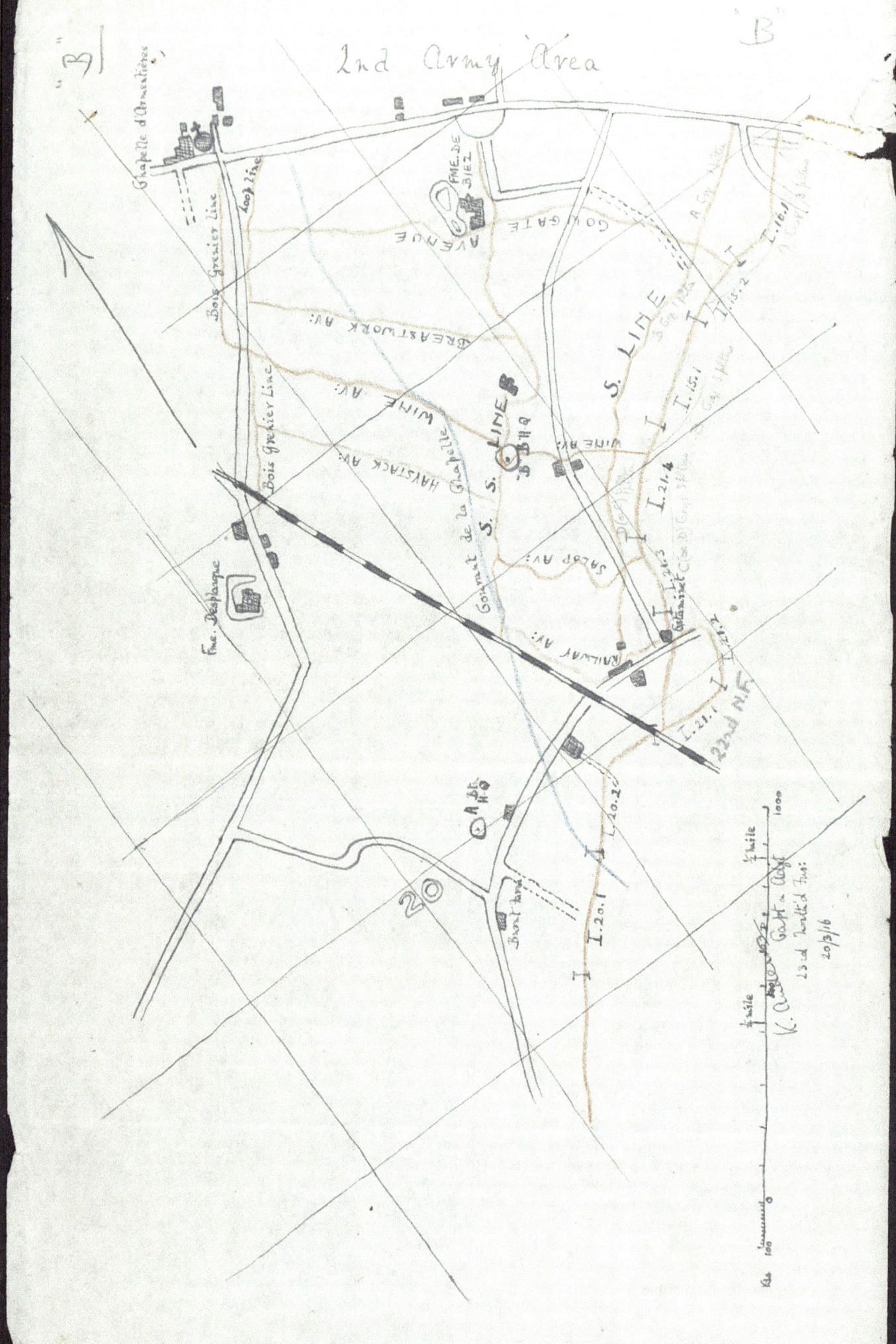

23 Northumberland
Army Form C. 2118.
vol 4
34

XXXIV

WAR DIARY
or
INTELLIGENCE SUMMARY.
(Erase heading not required.)

Instructions regarding War Diaries and Intelligence
Summaries are contained in F. S. Regs., Part II.
and the Staff Manual respectively. Title pages
will be prepared in manuscript.

Place	Date	Hour	Summary of Events and Information	Remarks and references to Appendices
RUE MARLE	April 1st		Lovely day. Two Australian G.O.'s came to lunch and we showed them round front trench area — they are to relieve us soon. 200 men at Baths, and 170 on fatigues. One man at Bow. Casualties:	36 M, N, H Sheet 6
"	2nd		Another glorious day. 160 men at Baths and Church Service in morning. Brigade Commander went round the W.E.B. Casualties: Nil	
"	3rd		V. fine. 150 men at Baths, 250 on fatigues, 150 on Assault Course, 50 men went to the Divisional Theatre at ERQUINGHEM. Board of Survey held on all fur coats, mittens and mufflers, which are to be returned to-night to Ordnance. Casualties:	
"	4th		Dull day. Lt WHITAKER & Cpl JONES left for THIENNES as a Salvaging party. 150 men at Baths, 115 on fatigue. Casualties:	
"	5th		V. fine again. 150 men at Baths. One blanket per man returned to O.C. Salvage Coy. Casualties: 1 Sick	

Army Form C. 2118.

WAR DIARY
or
INTELLIGENCE SUMMARY.
(Erase heading not required.)

Instructions regarding War Diaries and Intelligence Summaries are contained in F. S. Regs., Part II. and the Staff Manual respectively. Title pages will be prepared in manuscript.

Place	Date	Hour	Summary of Events and Information	Remarks and references to Appendices
RUE MARIE	April 6th		Fine day. 200 men at Baths & only 40 on fatigues. Casualties:	Map Sheet 36 N.W.4 Edition 6
L'HALLOBEAU	7th		40 men on fatigue. Relieved by 26th Australian Inf: Bn at 8.30 pm and marched by coys to some billets as we occupied before at L'HALLOBEAU; Bn complete in billets 12 midnight. Casualties:	Sheet 36 Appendix "A"
VIEUX BERQUIN	8th	8.30 am	The Brigade marched to billets in VIEUX BERQUIN area, the Bn leading. "A" Echelon Transport marched with the Bn, "B" Echelon in rear of Brigade. Bn was complete in billets (in VIEUX BERQUIN village) by 1 pm, and men had dinners out of the cookers. Blankets, officers valises & coy stores were brought on by a motor lorry which made two journeys. 9½ mile march. Casualties:	
MORBECQUE	9th	8.30 am	Bn again led the Brigade, but on arrival at MORBECQUE found we still had a long way to go — we were billetted in a camp just south of SERCUS, which we reached at 2 pm. The kits & blankets came on by lorry. 10 mile march. Casualties:	
RENESCURE	10th	9.30 am	Left camp at 9.30 am & marched at head of Brigade to billets near RENESCURE, just N. of WARDRECQUES STATION, arriving 12.30 pm. Kits by lorry as usual. 7 mile march. Casualties:	Sheet 5A

WAR DIARY
or
INTELLIGENCE SUMMARY
(Erase heading not required.)

Army Form C. 2118.

36

Place	Date	Hour	Summary of Events and Information	Remarks and references to Appendices
TATINGHEM	April 11th	8.30am	Marched in rear of Brigade to Gillets at TATINGHEM (X 7 central), arriving 12.30 p.m. Up till now the weather has been gloriously fine & sunny, but it rained heavily all the march, clearing up in the afternoon. Very good Billets. 10½ mile march. Casualties:	Sheet 27A S.E. 1st Edition
BAYENGHEM	12th	8.30am	March to our final destination at BAYENGHEM (K3) central) in pouring rain, arriving 1 p.m. very wet. A small village, but the Billets are not too bad. A, B & D Coys are in the village, C being 1½ mile away at WESTROVE; the men mostly in good barns with plenty of straw. Lorries lost their way & then got stuck in a ditch. Can't had to be sent to take over A & B Coys' kits, & the lorry did not return from the second journey with C & D Coys kits till 11 p.m. 8 mile march. Casualties:	Sheet 27A N.E. 1st Edition
"	13th		Fine day, devoted to drying clothes, cleaning up & kit inspection. All paulubents taken off the men & stacked at Coy Stores. G.O. visited Brigade Hd Qrs at PELINCOVE (D.29.d 7/7), which is 4½ miles away. Casualties: 2 sick.	
"	14th		Windy with occasional showers. Platoon training began - every man has a short run or Physical drill before breakfast, the rest of the time being devoted to Saluting, handling of arms, guard mounting & close order drill. Casualties: nil	

Army Form C. 2118.

WAR DIARY
or
INTELLIGENCE SUMMARY.
(Erase heading not required.)

Instructions regarding War Diaries and Intelligence Summaries are contained in F.S. Regs., Part II. and the Staff Manual respectively. Title pages will be prepared in manuscript.

37

Place	Date	Hour	Summary of Events and Information	Remarks and references to Appendices
BAYENGHEM	April 15th		Fine but windy. Platoon training & drilling continued. A Coy starts using the range in the Sandpit. Subaltern Officers have an hour's drill under the Sergt-Major. No work after lunch (Saturday). A field has been hired and prepared for football; first game this afternoon. Casualties: nil	Sheet 37A M.E. 1st Edition
"	16th		Sunday; usual services. V. fine & sunny. Brigade passed word that Div'l & Army Comdrs were coming to inspect us, but it proved a false alarm. Short parade in afternoon; holiday for remainder of day. Casualties: nil	
"	17th		Drizzling rain early, but cleared up. Same work & parades continued. A Coy continues using the range. Efforts are being made to start baths for the men in an old vat in a brewery; coal bought & the furnace put in working order, but a pump is required to free the vat. The bath was calculated to pass 5/six a day on hire for the furnace a vat, and being our own coal, but it is well worth it. The expenses will be paid out of Imprest Account and every man will now get washed. Casualties: 4 Sick.	

Army Form C. 2118.

WAR DIARY
~~INTELLIGENCE SUMMARY~~
(Erase heading not required.)

38

Place	Date	Hour	Summary of Events and Information	Remarks and references to Appendices
BAYENGHEM	April 18th		The Batt. is allotted to I.B. Coy a Machine Gun Section. Coy at the disposal of OC Coys for drill on a complete unit on the Training Area; C Coy started digging a trench for use later on. B Coy firing on the small range. Casualties: Sick	Sheet 37A N.E. & S.E.
"	19th		D Coy are allotted the range at MORDAUSQUES which allows 20 men to fire at a time. A Coy for the batt at the small range. If OLIVER and 8 men per Coy form a Bn Bombing Platoon and proceed to MORDAUSQUES for instruction under the Brigade Bombing Officer. C Coy continue work on the new trench, and B Coy for training in the Area. Major BURGE leaves for BOULOGNE on 48 hrs leave. Squalls & showers at intervals. Casualties: NIL	
"	20th		B Coy use the range at MORDAUSQUES. C Coy for the batt at the small range. A & D Coys on the training area for close & extended order drill; exercise if could be use in the assault. More showers & a high wind. Casualties: NIL	
"	21st		Small tactical scheme for A, B, & D Coys on the Area in morning. Afternoon under Coy arrangements. C Coy at the MORDAUSQUES range. The Batt is headed for washing clothes starting with D Coy at 4–5.30 pm. The C.O.H. is lent to 34th Div. Train at 34th Inf. Bde. Casualties: Sick	Sheet 37A N.E. A.S.C.

2353 Wt. W2544/1454 700,000 5/15 D. D. & L. A.D.S.S. Forms/C. 2118.

Army Form C. 2118.

WAR DIARY
or
INTELLIGENCE SUMMARY.
(Erase heading not required.)

Place	Date	Hour	Summary of Events and Information	Remarks and references to Appendices
BAVENGHEM	April 22nd		The Batt. is allotted to A Coy & G Coy for washing clothes. One officer & 50 O.R. per coy for bathing instruction in morning; and Btn Cookers in the afternoon, under 2/Lt GOLLINGS, N.E. & Lie. Bombs being thrown. Parades in morning under coy arrangements (inspections & lectures); S.E. Coy not very wet all afternoon, and no out-door work done. 2/Lt T. G. WHITTAKER joined from Home, & is posted to A Coy.. Casualties: NIL	Sheets 2/A & S.E.
"	23rd		Easter Sunday; usual Church services. Very fine & sunny again, after a week's unsettled weather. Semi-final of Platoon football competition. 2/Lt G.H. DAGGETT joined from Home, & is posted to A Coy.. Casualties: NIL	
"	24th		Batt. & small range to A Coy. Remaining Coys on Training Area. A Staff ride under the Brigadier of all C.O.s, 2nd-in-Commands and Adjutants, to go over the ground selected for the Divisional practice Trench Attack. By an extensive system of trenches & posts have been spit-locked out, and each Btn has to write detailed orders for the attack. In the afternoon no work was done, and a Sports meeting held on the football ground; it went off very successfully. Capt F.C.A. NICHOLLS joined from Home & is posted to D Coy.. Casualties: 2 sick	
"	25th		The Btn practiced the part allotted to it in the practice Trench Attack (we are in Bde reserve), taking dinners out in Cookers to the Training Area. Some 6th drill also carried out. Hot & sunny. Back in Billets 5 pm... Casualties: NIL	

39

WAR DIARY or INTELLIGENCE SUMMARY

Army Form C. 2118.

Place	Date	Hour	Summary of Events and Information	Remarks and references to Appendices
BAYENGHEM	April 26th		Out on the area all day practising the Trench Attack as a Brigade; drivers sent as Scout ut. Bad at 4 pm. Hot & Sunny. Baths allotted to B Coy on return from parade. Casualties NIL	Sheets 27A N.E. & S.E.
"	27th		The whole division practised the attack, starting at 11.45 am. Dinners sent out but we did not get them till 3 pm; Back in Billets 5 pm. Baths allotted to D Coy on return. Very hot. Casualties NIL	
"	28th		Another glorious day; inspections & cleaning up. Battn. range to 6 Coys. Hot-Grs & Machine Gunners. Small range to G Coy; Quarry range to Machine Gunners. Bombers out under 2 L/Galliers. D Coy at 10 Quarry held a all woollen test on F.S. kit which have to be returned to A.A.D.O.S. Leave ???? on Sunday. All rifles & the Battn inspected by the Armourer Sgt. Casualties NIL	
"	29th		V. fine & sunny. Quiet day with parades in morning under Coy arrangements. D Coy for Bath. Machine Gunners on the range. Football in afternoon (A Coy beat G Coy in final of inter-platoon cup; 1-0). Casualties NIL	

Army Form C. 2118.

WAR DIARY
~~INTELLIGENCE SUMMARY.~~
(Erase heading not required.)

Instructions regarding War Diaries and Intelligence Summaries are contained in F. S. Regs., Part II. and the Staff Manual respectively. Title pages will be prepared in manuscript.

41

Place	Date	Hour	Summary of Events and Information	Remarks and references to Appendices
BAYENGHEM	April 30th		Sunday. The Div: Trench Attack was repeated in morning, an early start being made; Btn left billets at 5.45 am... then had some actual entrenching work this time. Back in billets at 11 am.. Voluntary Church Services in Evening. Casualties: NIL.	Sheets 27A N.E. & S.E.

SECRET.
Reference Sheet 36. 1:40,000

COPY NO. 1

The 102nd (TYNESIDE SCOTTISH) BRIGADE.

OPERATION ORDER NO....17.

1.. The 102nd (Tyneside Scottish) Brigade will be relieved by the 7th Australian Infantry Brigade in the Left Sector of the Divisional Line on the night of 7/8th April, 1916.

The 208th Field Company R.E. will be relieved by the 7th Field Company R.E. on the night of 7/8th April, 1916.

2.. The relief will be carried out in accordance with the attached Tables "A" and "B".

3.. The "A" Battalion 21st N.F. (2nd Tyneside Scottish) will be relieved by the 28th Australian Infantry Battalion which will become "A" Battalion.

The "B" Battalion 20th N.F. (1st Tyneside Scottish) will be relieved by the 27th Australian Infantry Battalion which will become "B" Battalion.

The "C" Battalion 22nd N.F. (3rd Tyneside Scottish) will be relieved by the 25th Australian Infantry Battalion which will become "C" Battalion.

The "D" Battalion 23rd N.F. (4th Tyneside Scottish) will be relieved by the 26th Australian Infantry Battalion which will become "D" Battalion.

Further details of relief to be mutually arranged between Commanding Officers concerned.

4.. Each Commanding Officer of the Outgoing Battalions will remain in command of his Battalion Area until the relief of his Battalion is complete, and will be responsible for all details of traffic management, while it is taking place.

5.. Guides at the rate of 1 Officer per Company and 1 N.C.O. per Platoon from the 21st N.F. (2nd Tyneside Scottish) will meet the 28th Australian Infantry Battalion at Road Junction H.5.d.2.9 at 7:40 p.m.

Guides at the rate of 1 Officer per Company and 1 N.C.O. per Platoon from the 20th N.F. (1st Tyneside Scottish) will meet the 27th Australian Infantry Battalion at Road Junction B.30.c.3.1 at 7:20 p.m.

Guides at the rate of 1 Officer per Company and 1 N.C.O. per Platoon from the 22nd N.F. (3rd Tyneside Scottish) will meet the 25th Australian Infantry Battalion at Road Junction B.30.c.3.1 at 8 p.m.

Guides at the rate of 1 Officer per Company and 1 N.C.O. per Platoon from the 23rd N.F. (4th Tyneside Scottish) will meet the 26th Australian Infantry Battalion at H.5.b.9.8 at 8:30 p.m.

Guides from the 208th Field Company R.E. will meet the 7th Field Coy. R.E. at time and place to be arranged by O.C's concerned.

6.. Signallers, Snipers and Machine Gunners of the 21st N.F. (2nd Tyneside Scottish) 20th N.F. (1st Tyneside Scottish) and 22nd N.F. (3rd Tyneside Scottish) (in the FME DU BIEZ and BOIS GRENIER Line) will be relieved at 2 p.m. on 7th April, 1916, and remain in the trenches until there Battalions are relieved on the evening of 7th April, 1916.

/ 7.. Advance

7.. Advance parties of Battalions of the 7th Australian Infantry Brigade will take over trenches and billets and sign for all stores handed over on morning of 7th April, 1916. Periscope rifles, Steel Helmets, Box Respirators, Periscopes, Bomb buckets, on charge of Battalions will not be handed over.

8.. Guides from Battalions of 102nd (Tyneside Scottish) Brigade for advance parties, Signallers, Snipers and Machine Gunners, at the rate of 1 N.C.O. per Battalion will report at Brigade Headquarters, RUE MARLE at 11 a.m. on 7th inst., to conduct parties to Battalion Headquarters.

9.. There will be no movement of troops other than advance parties and Guides South of the BAC ST MAUR/LILLE Railway before 7:30 p.m. Up to the point at which they meet their guides Battalions of the 7th Australian Infantry Brigade will move in Companies at 5 minutes interval, after that by Platoons at 2 minutes interval. Battalions of the 102nd (Tyneside Scottish) Brigade after being relieved will move in Platoons at 2 minutes interval until North of the BAC ST MAUR/LILLE Railway, and thereafter in Companies at 5 minutes interval.

10.. No Transport of the 102nd (Tyneside Scottish) Brigade will move South of the BAC ST MAUR/LILLE Railway before 8.15 p.m., and no Transport of the 7th Australian Infantry Brigade will move South of the BAC ST MAUR/LILLE Railway before 9:30 p.m.

11.. No trench or billet is to be vacated by the 102nd (Tyneside Scottish) Brigade, and 208th Field Company R.E., until occupied by the 7th Australian Infantry Brigade and 7th Field Company R.E. respectively.

12.. Billetting Parties of the 102nd (Tyneside Scottish) Brigade will take over billets on the morning of 7th April, 1916, as detailed in Table "A".
Battalions will be billetted as follows :-

"A" BATTALION .... 21st (S) Bn. Northd. Fusiliers) FORT ROMPU
                   (2nd TYNESIDE SCOTTISH).......) H.7.d.9.4.

"B" BATTALION .... 20th (S) Bn. Northd. Fusiliers) JESUS FARM
                   (1st TYNESIDE SCOTTISH).......) B.28.d.4.0

"C" BATTALION .... 22nd (S) Bn. Northd. Fusiliers) RUE DORMOIRE
                   (3rd TYNESIDE SCOTTISH).......) H.8.b.9.3.

"D" BATTALION .... 23rd (S) Bn. Northd. Fusiliers) L'HALLOBEAU
                   (4th TYNESIDE SCOTTISH).......) (H.1.b.4.7)

13.. Attention is directed to the instructions that parties moving South of RUE MARLE during daylight must not number more than six and move in single file, keeping well to the side of the road with 200x interval between parties.

14.. Duplicate copies of all receipts given and received are to be forwarded to Brigade Headquarters.

15.. Battalions of the 102nd (Tyneside Scottish) Brigade in the Forward Area will retain their D3 Telephone Instruments.

/ 16.. The

16.. The Brigade Bombing Officer, 7th Australian Infantry Brigade, will take over the Bomb School and Brigade Reserve Bomb Stores at 10.a.m on the morning of April 7th, 1916, and will meet the Bombing Officer, 102nd (Tyneside Scottish) Brigade at Brigade Headquarters at 10 a.m. 7th inst.

17.. Instructions regarding Trench Mortar Batteries will be issued later.

18.. The Section of No. 4 Motor Machine Gun Battery will remain in the BOIS GRENIER Line, and be attached to 7th Australian Infantry Brigade (2nd Australian Division.).

19.. Brigade Guards will be relieved at 4 p.m. on April 7th, 1916.

20.. Until all reliefs are complete, the General Officer Commanding 102nd (Tyneside Scottish) Brigade remains in command of the Left Sector, and when all reliefs are complete Brigade Headquarters move to ERQUINGHEM H.4.d.4.7.

21.. The completion of reliefs will be reported to Brigade Headquarters H.6.d.7½.5 by wire.

22.. Acknowledge.

102 B.H.Q.
5:4:1916.

Issued at 7 p.m.

Major.
Acting BRIGADE MAJOR.
102nd (TYNESIDE SCOTTISH) BRIGADE.

```
Copies  1 -  3  retained.
             4  20th N.F. (1st Tyneside Scottish)
             5  21st   *  (2nd      *       *   )
             6  22nd   *  (3rd      *       *   )
             7  23rd   *  (4th      *       *   )
             8  Brigade Transport Officer.
             9  Brigade Machine Gun Officer.
            10  Brigade Bombing Officer.
            11  102/1 Trench Mortar Battery.
            12  X 34th    *       *      *  R.A.
            13  208th Field Company R.E.
            14  4/Motor Machine Gun Battery.
            15  War Diary.
            16  34th Division.           )
            17  2nd Australian Division  )
            18  51st Infantry Brigade.   )
            19  103rd Infantry Brigade.  ) For information.
            20  7th Australian Inf. Bde. )
            21  "B" Group R. F. A.       )
            22  O.C. No.3 Coy. A.S.C.     
                     34th Divisional Train)
            23  7th Aus. Field Coy. R.E. )
```

SECRET.
Reference Sheet 36 .. 1/40,000.

TABLE "A"   Issued with Operation Order No... 17

DATE.		UNIT.	HAND OVER TRENCHES OR BILLETS TO	TAKE OVER BILLETS FROM	ROUTE TO BILLETS.	REMARKS.
1916 APRIL 7th.	A	21st (S) Bn. N. F. (2nd TYNESIDE SCOTTISH).........	28th Australian Infantry Battn:	28th Australian Infantry Battn:	PARK ROW AVENUE. LA VESEE. GRIS POT. RUE DES ACQUETS. FORT ROMPU.	South of the BAC ST MAUR/LILLE Railway all movement will be by Platoons at 2 minutes interval, and thereafter in Companies at 5 mins: interval.
7th	B	20th (S) Bn. N. F. (1st TYNESIDE SCOTTISH).........	27th Australian Infantry Battn:	26th Australian Infantry Battn:	HAYSTACK, WINE & COWGATE AVENUES. I.8.a.9.3 RUE MARLE. B.30.c.3.1. ERQUINGHEM BRIDGE. JESUS FARM.	
7th	C	22nd (S) Bn. N. F. (3rd TYNESIDE SCOTTISH).........	25th Australian Infantry Battn:	27th Australian Infantry Battn:	B.30.c.3.1. ERQUINGHEM. RUE DORMOIRE.	
7th	D	23rd (S) Bn. N. F. (4th TYNESIDE SCOTTISH).........	26th Australian Infantry Battn:	25th Australian Infantry Battn:	B.30.c.3.1 ERQUINGHEM BRIDGE. L'HALLOBEAU.	
7th		208th Field Coy.R.E.	7th Field Coy. R.E.	7th Field Coy. R.E.	B.30.c.3.1 ERQUINGHEM.	

Admacantoch Major.
Acting BRIGADE MAJOR.
102nd (TYNESIDE SCOTTISH) BRIGADE.

SECRET.
Reference Sheet 36.. 1/40,000.   Issued with Operation Order No. 17

TABLE "B"

DATE		UNIT.	TAKE OVER TRENCHES OR BILLETS FROM.	ROUTE TO TRENCHES OR BILLETS.	HAND OVER BILLETS TO	MEET GUIDES AT	TIME.	REMARKS.
1916 APRIL 7th.	A	28th Australian Infantry Battn:	21st (S) Bn. N.F. (2nd TYNESIDE SCOTTISH)......	H.5.d.2.9 RUE DES ACQUETS. GRIS POT. LA VESEE.	21st N.F. (2nd TYNESIDE SCOTTISH).	H.5.d.2.9	7:40 p.m	Up to the point at which they meet their guides, Units will move in Companies at 5 minutes interval, add thereafter in Platoons at 2 mins: interval.
7th.	B	27th Australian Infantry Battn:	20th (S) Bn. N.F. (1st TYNESIDE SCOTTISH)......	B.30.c.3.1 RUE MARLE I.8.a.9.3 COWGATE, WINE, & HAYSTACK AVENUES.	22nd N.F. (3rd TYNESIDE SCOTTISH	B.30.c.3.1	7:20 p.m	
7th.	C	25th Australian Infantry Battn:	22nd (S) Bn. N.F. (3rd TYNESIDE SCOTTISH)......	B.30.c.3.1 RUE MARLE. Units in trenches. I.8.a.9.3. BOIS GRENIER Line. COWGATE AV:	23rd N.F. (4th TYNESIDE	P.30.c.3.1	8 p.m.	2 Companies and 2 Platoons in billets at RUE MARLE - L'ARMEE 1 Company and 2 Platoons in trenches at BOIS GRENIER Line RUE DU BIEZ- PARADISE ALLEY.
7th.	D	26th Australian Infantry Battr:	23rd (S) Bn. N.F. (4th TYNESIDE SCOTTISH)......	H.5.b.9.3	20th N.F. (1st TYNESIDE SCOTTISH)	H.5.b.9.5	8:30 p.m	
7th		7th Field Company R. E.	209th Field Company R. E.	B.30.c.3.1 RUE MARLE.	209th Field Coy. R. E.			To be arranged by O.O's concerned.

Acting BRIGADE MAJOR.
102nd (TYNESIDE SCOTTISH) BRIGADE.

Battalion Orders
by
Lieut. Col. W. Lyle, Cmdg., 23rd. Battalion Northumberland Fusiliers.
(4th. Battalion Tyneside Scottish)

RUE MARLE.   April 6th. 1916.

<u>Orders for Friday the 7th. April 1916.</u>

1.   The Battalion will be relieved on the night of 7/8th. April by the 26th. Australian Infanrty Battalion, which will become "D" Battalion.

2.   Guides at the rate of 1 Officer per Company, 1 N.C.O. per platoon and 1 N.C.O. for Headquarters will meet the 26th. Battalion Australian Infantry at M.5.b.9/8 at 8.30 p.m. and conduct them direct to their billets.
   "A" Company, 26th. Australian Infantry Battalion to relieve our "A" Coy
   "B"   do   do   do   do   do   "B" do.
   "C"   do   do   do   do   do   "C" do
   "D"   do   do   do   do   do   "D" do
               One N.C.O. from the Lewis Gun Detatchmant will report at Brigade Headquarters at 11.0 a.m. and will guide the Machine Gun Detatchment of the 26th. Australian Infantry Battalion to billets.

3.   As soon as they have been relieved Companies will move off in Platoons at 2 minutes interval until NORTH of BAC ST MAUR / LILLE RAILWAY, and thereafter in Companies at 5 minutes interval.
"C" and "D" Companies will report relief to Headquarters by telephone; "A" and "B" by orderly.

4.   All S.A.A. and Stores which are not Battalion property will be handed over and receipts obtained. Bomb buckets are not to be handed over. Duplicate lists to be sent to Headquarters by 12.0 noon.

5.   The usual Advance Parties will take over billets from the 26th. Australian Infantry Battalion at L'HALLOBEAU before 3 p.m., Companies to occupy exactly the same billets as before.

6.   All blankets, Officers Valises, bomb buckets, Mess Stores, Medical Stores etc. will be picked up by the transport before 2.0 p.m. and taken on to the new billets at L'HALLOBEAU. "A" and "B" Companies will carry thier blankets etc. up to the railway, where they will be loaded Cookers will be called for at 5.30 p.m. The Officers Mess Cart will be at Battalion Headquarters at 8.0 p.m. to pick up surplus Mess Stores for Headquarters, "A" and "B" Companies and will then call at "D" Companys Headquarters for "C" and "D" Companies Stores, These Stores must be kept as low as possible.

7.   Arrival in billets will be reported by wire or orderly to Battalion Headquarters.

                                        K.A.N. ANDERSON.

                                             CAPTAIN AND ADJUTANT.

SECRET

34th Divn: No 806/0.

1. In continuation of 34th Divisional Operation Order No. 9 dated 30/4/16, the Division will entrain at St OMER and WIZERNES on the 4th., 5th., and 6th. May for LONGEAU. ~~A time table will be issued later.~~
    Order of entrainment and roads to be used are shown on Table "A" attached.

2. ROUTES.
    Roads are available to the Entraining Station for Units as shown on Table "A".
    Routes from Detraining Station to the new billeting area will be allotted on arrival at the detraining station; arrangements are being made for guides to meet units and conduct them to their billets.

3. BILLETING PARTIES.
    (a) Billeting parties as under will be sent by motor lorry on the 3rd instant. Lorries will be at Headquarters 103rd Infantry Brigade at TATINGHEM at 9 a.m. where each billeting party should meet them. 1 bicycle will be taken by each billeting party; the officer from Bde Hdqrs will be in charge of all billeting parties, and on arrival in the new area will take steps to ascertain the routes to and from detraining station to billets; he will arrange for guides to meet units on arrival at the Detraining station. Detailed instructions will be handed to him at the embussing place by a Divisional Staff Officer.

Billeting parties.

Unit.	Offrs.	O.R.
24th Bn: Northl'd Fus.	1	6
25th " " "	1	6
26th " " "	1	6
27th " " "	1	6
103rd Infy Bde H.Q.) Signal Sec. &) M. G. Coy.)	1	2
Cyclist Coy		1
Train Hdqrs.		1
Headqr. Coy Train		1
No. 4. Coy Train		1
103rd Fd. Amb.	1	2
Totals	5	33

Sheet 2.

   (b) Billeting parties for the remainder of the Division in proportion, as detailed in para. 3(a), will proceed by the 1st train on the day previous to that on which their respective units entrain. Guides to be provided as in para. 3(a).

4. RATIONS.

   All units will entrain with rations for the day following the day of entrainment; all billeting parties vide para 3 will take three days rations with them. All units are to carry Iron Rations on the man.

5. BAGGAGE & SUPPLY WAGONS.

   Baggage and Supply wagons will entrain with Units and not with Train Companies.

6. MOTOR VEHICLES.

   Motor vehicles, except motor cars with Staff Officers, will proceed to following destinations, in convoys in chrage of an officer, via ST OMER - AIRE - LILLERS - ST POL - FREVENT - DOULLENS - TALMAS.

   SUPPLY COLUMN to BEHENCOURT; one section on the 4th., one section and Headquarters on the 5th., and one section on the 6th May, 1916.

   34th DIVNL. AMMN. SUB PARK to FRANVILLERS on 4th May.

   Motor Ambulances to the place where their Field Ambulance is billeted, moving on the same day on which it entrains.

   Hours of departure to be notified to Divisional Headquarters.

   The SANITARY SECTION lorry will proceed with the Motor Ambulances of the 102nd Field Ambulance.

7. SUPPLIES.

   (a) Supply Column will be loaded at Railhead on the morning of the 4th May, i.e., first day of entrainment, in such a manner as to ensure that the supplies for consumption on the 6th May, for those units which entrain on the 4th May, are loaded separately. These lorries should be despatched immediately after loading. Similarly the lorries which load on the 5th and 6th May, for units entraining on those days, should proceed immediately after loading with supplies for consumption on 7th and 8th.

   (b) Units which entrain between midnight 3rd/4th and midnight 4th/5th, will draw supplies for consumption on the 4th, at Refilling Point as usual; the supply wagons when unloaded, will return at 3 p.m. to the Refilling Point, and draw supplies for consumption on the 5th May. They will then return to their units and entrain "loaded" on the 4th. The same procedure will be carried out by units entraining be-
on 4th tween midnight 4th/5th and 5th/6th and midnight 5th/6th and
& 5th 6th/7th May.
May

8. STAFF OFFICERS AT ENTRAINING AND DETRAINING STATIONS.

   (a) Infantry Brigades and Headquarters Artillery will detail one Staff Officer to be at the entraining and detraining stations during the whole period during which their formation is entraining or detraining.

Sheet 2.

These officers will be responsible that all men of their formation are either entrained or clear of the detraining before they rejoin their brigade. In the case of the entraining officer, he will proceed as soon as he has reported to the R.T.O. that all the units of his formation are entrained with transport complete.

(b) A Staff Officer from Divisional Headquarters will be at the R.T.O.'s office at ST OMER and WIZERNES during the whole of the entrainment. Similarly another Staff Officer from Divisional Headquarters will be at the R.T.O.'s office LONGPRE during the whole period of detrainment.

ROAD CONTROL (c) Brigades, portions of which pass through ST MARTIN au LAERT on route to entrain, will detail an officer to control traffic at T roads at that place until all troops of their Brigade are clear.

9. HEAVY BAGGAGE.

Lorries will be provided to convey heavy baggage and blankets to the entraining station. Details etc will be issued later.

All packages are to be clearly labelled with two labels with the name of the units to which they belong.

It must be borne in mind that transport has only been demanded for the amount of baggage as estimated in replies to this office letter No. 718/Q dated 14/4/16.

10.
On arrival in new area units will billet as follows:-

103rd Infy Bde. in area ST GRATIEN (Bde Hdqrs) and RAINNEVILLE.

101st Bde in area LAHOUSSOYE (Bde Hdqrs), FRANVILLERS

102nd Infy Bde will replace the 103rd Infy Bde on the 8th and the latter will then move to BRESLE.

R. A. on arrival will billet and bivouac in and around BEHENCOURT and BEAUCOURT. The D.A.C. in the neighbourhood of LAHOUSSOYE.

Details as to Divisional Headquarters will be issued later.

11. RAILHEAD.

The Railhead at WATTEN will remain open up to and including the 5th May, and a new Railhead will be opened at MIRICOURT on this date.

12. GENERAL INSTRUCTIONS.

The Instructions (Notes on Entrainment) issued under this office number 806/Q dated 19/4/16 are to be strictly complied with.

1st May 1916.

Lieut-Colonel,
A.A. & Q.M.G., 34th Division

P.T.O

Copies 1 - 3 filed.
    4 A.D.C. for G.O.C.
    5 - 9 Second Army
   10 II Corps
   11 IIIrd Corps.
   12 101st Infy Bde.
   13 102nd Infy Bde.
   14 103rd Infy Bde.
   15 C.R.A.
   16 207 Fd Coy R.E.
   17 208 Coy R.E.
   18 209 Coy R.E.
   19 Div Mtd Troops.
   20 G. S.

21 A.D.M.S.
22 A.A. and Q.
23 B.O.
24 P.M.
25 D.A.D.O.S.
26 Signals
27 I.G.C.
28 A.D.V.S.
29 A.D.R.T. Northern
30 A.D.R.T. Southern
31/

Vol 5

SECRET
XXXIV

Army Form C. 2118.

23 Month Year 1917

WAR DIARY
or
INTELLIGENCE SUMMARY.
(Erase heading not required.)

Instructions regarding War Diaries and Intelligence Summaries are contained in F. S. Regs., Part II. and the Staff Manual respectively. Title pages will be prepared in manuscript.

Place	Date	Hour	Summary of Events and Information	Remarks and references to Appendices
BAYENGHEM	May 1st		Quiet day. Conference of all Officers at Bde H-Q in morning. B Coy for the Bath, and for bowling. Other Coys under Coy arrangements. Adjt went on leave. Casualties: 1 sick.	Sheets 27A N.E.& S.E.
	2nd		The Div trench attack was again repeated in the morning, our early start being made. Bn left billets at 6.0 a.m. Conference of officers after the attack was finished. Coys under Coy arrangements in the afternoon. Casualties NIL	5-23
	3rd	7.30 1.30	The Bn again took part in the Div trench attack - leaving billets at 7.30. - returning 1.30. Thunder storm in afternoon. Coys paraded under Coy arrangements in the afternoon. Casualties NIL	A99
	4th		Fine + sunny. C Coy for the Bath, other Coys under Coy arrangements. Extra Coy walking competition - 10 miles. - Battle order. Result 1st D Coy. 2nd C Coy. 3rd A Coy. - 4th B Coy. - D Coy did Test to make in 2 hrs. 11 minutes - Lieut Whitaker + Burning party left for St. GRATIEN. Casualties 2 sick	5-23

Army Form C. 2118.

WAR DIARY
or
INTELLIGENCE SUMMARY.
(Erase heading not required.)

Instructions regarding War Diaries and Intelligence Summaries are contained in F.S. Regs., Part II. and the Staff Manual respectively. Title pages will be prepared in manuscript.

Place	Date	Hour	Summary of Events and Information	Remarks and references to Appendices
BAYENGHEM.	May 5th		Quiet day, generally cleaning up trucks. Begin the move. Fine & sunny. The transport left at 11.15pm for St Omer station together with "C" Coy. who detailed working parties. Casualties & sick.	Sheet 27A NE + SE.
	6th		A.B. & D Coys paraded & ready to move off at 1.0 am - met cool. arrived at Omer Station 4.40. - entrained the train left up to time at 5.43. It was 2 hrs late in arriving at LONGEAU at 3.30. The Battalion detrained marched clear of the station & then halted - the dinners cooked & served out. He much to ST. GRATIEN. the distance about 12 miles the Bn arriving in billets between 9.30pm & 10.0 pm. - a very long day, everybody being very tired & dirty. Casualties NIL	Appendix "A" SHEET AMIENS 17.
ST GRATIEN.	May 7th		Sunday. a very quiet day in billets. Voluntary Church Service. the water supply very bad. A government supply tank is situated about 1 mile from the village. also deep well in the village was tested & found good for cooking purposes Casualties	

#353 Wt. W2544/1454 700,000 5/15 D. D. & L. A.D.S.S./Forms/C. 2118.

Army Form C. 2118.

WAR DIARY
or
INTELLIGENCE SUMMARY.
(Erase heading not required.)

45

Place	Date	Hour	Summary of Events and Information	Remarks and references to Appendices
ST. GRATIEN	May 8.		Coys paraded under Coy arrangements, handling of arms etc. all Coys paraded under an officer to the WD's cart to fill all their water bottles. The water cart (2) carts were arranged for carrying to the cook water from the well was observed for cooking purposes. Casualties nil.	Sheet AMIENS 17. Yes
	9.		Coys paraded under Coy arrangements. Church day - Coys went to church route march. - weather favoured.	Yes
				Casualties nil Yes.
	10.		Fine & sunny. Lieut Whitcher's stabling party left for BEHENCOURT. Coys generally cleaning up kits, the Wash left in the morning. + cleaning up Parties left about 3.0 pm to clean up the new billets where we are to go to next Coys to be in a on duty state. The Bn paraded at 7.0 pm & marched to BEHENCOURT - about 3 miles. - everything working like clock work.	Casualties 2 Sick yes

WAR DIARY
or
INTELLIGENCE SUMMARY.

(Erase heading not required.)

Army Form C. 2118.

Instructions regarding War Diaries and Intelligence Summaries are contained in F.S. Regs., Part II. and the Staff Manual respectively. Title pages will be prepared in manuscript.

Place	Date	Hour	Summary of Events and Information	Remarks and references to Appendices
BEHENCOURT.	May 11th		Leave party left at 6.0 am. under Capt Cuter. The 102/1 French Mis Bautz, & the Bde snipers rejoined the Bde. Conference of Company officers at Bde. at 10.0 am. D Coy went for a short route march in the evening. Short course in Lewis gun for Coy Comdrs starts at Brig H.Q. Capt & Adjt K. ANDERSON returns from leave. Casualties: nil	Sheet AMIENS 17
"	12th		Quiet day in billets. Bn. bombers paraded under Lt Gollings at 2 pm. A Coy went for short march in evening; D Coy gave a concert at 8 pm. Lewis guns are divided up among the companies (2 to A, 2 to B, 1 to C, 1 to D coys.), Lt NELSON remains in general supervision. A class started for instruction of 1 Officer, 1 N.C.O. & 7 men per Coy in the Lewis Gun. Casualties: nil	
"	13th		Rainy morning. Lt H.D. WHITTAKER and 3 O.R. proceed on leave. Parades in vicinity of billets; half holiday in afternoon. Casualties: nil	
			Church parade in morning. Head-Quarters party were billeted in the afternoon. Football in evening. Casualties: nil	
			Lt J.L. COLLINGS, 1 Sergt, 2 cpls & 8 ptes proceeded to Bde H.Q at FRANVILLERS for a week's course in the Stokes mortar. Lt OLIVER also goes for a short course. Steady rain, which hindered work. Casualties: 1 sick	

Wt. W2544/1454 700,000 5/15 D. D. & L. A.D.S.S./Forms/C. 2118.

WAR DIARY
or
INTELLIGENCE SUMMARY.

(Erase heading not required.)

Army Form C. 2118.

Place	Date	Hour	Summary of Events and Information	Remarks and references to Appendices
BEHENCOURT	May 16th		Very fine & warm. An alarm was raised that the Army Commander was coming round to inspect us, and all the Coys were sent out on to unculivated ground to trench attack practice etc.; but he never turned up. Short route marches in the evening. Capt WHITEHEAD went on leave. Casualties 1 sick	Received S/List 17
"	17th		The Bn. used the Baths at FRANVILLERS, and this prevented any concerted work during the day. Specialists paraded as usual. Very fine & warm. Casualties 1 sick	
"	18th		Very hot day. The men were given a bathe in the river in the afternoon. Parades on the Training Area in the morning. A practice alarm took place at night & was fairly satisfactory. Casualties 1 sick	
"	19th		The G.O.C., Lt. CAMPBELL & the REV. GAULD went on leave. V. hot again. Coys spent the morning on the area & had a quiet afternoon; short marches in the evening. Casualties 1 sick	
"	20th		The Reg-Sgt-Major & 9 O.R. on leave. A practice Brigade Trench Attack took place in the morning on ground the other side of FRANVILLERS; we worked from Billets at 6 am & were Back at 1 pm; extremely hot. Quiet afternoon & evening. Casualties 1 NCO	

Army Form C. 2118.

WAR DIARY
or
INTELLIGENCE SUMMARY.
(Erase heading not required.)

Instructions regarding War Diaries and Intelligence
Summaries are contained in F. S. Regs, Part II.
and the Staff Manual respectively. Title pages
will be prepared in manuscript.

46

Place	Date	Hour	Summary of Events and Information	Remarks and references to Appendices
BEHENCOURT	May 21st		Usual Church Services. Bowling hot again. Major BURGE went up to visit the trenches. Spots in the afternoon. Casualties: nil	Amiens Sheet 17
"	22nd		25 O.R. (6 per Coy) are to be taken daily for wiring under G.R.E. 3rd Corps, leaving here at 7.20 a.m, commencing from to-day. The Inter-Company bowling competition was held in the morning; each Coy entered 2 teams of 8 ptes & 1 cpl. — D Coy wins A second. An extremely hot & sultry day, with a thunderstorm in the evening. The range in the morning. Casualties: nil C & D Coy for baths at the village hall.	
"	23rd		Cooler but fine. A Conference for all G.O's and Adjutants at Brigade H.Q. No draft. D Coy & the Lewis Gunners use the range in the afternoon. A & B Coys use the baths in the morning. A daily party of 2 officers & 100 men to work under the G.R.E. taken away at 8am in motor lorries. Parade: unde Coy arrangements. Casualties: nil	
"	24th		Fine till lunch, but steady rain afterwards. A Coy provided the fatigue of 2 officers & 100 men, but they start at 6.30 a.m now. B Coy practiced digging a "strong-point". B Coy for baths in afternoon. C & D Coys had their billets sprayed & all clothes disinfected & ironed. All leave for officers stopped. Casualties: nil	

2353 Wt. W2544/1454 700,000 5/15 D. D. & L. A.D.S.S./Forms/C. 2118.

Army Form C. 2118.

WAR DIARY
or
INTELLIGENCE SUMMARY.
(Erase heading not required.)

47

Place	Date	Hour	Summary of Events and Information	Remarks and references to Appendices
BEHENCOURT	May 25th		Leave open again. Showery weather. 6 platoons practiced carrying drill at ST LAURENT'S F.M.E. B Coy provided fatigue party. Signallers & M.G. Coy out from 8-11 p.m. Sheet 17. A Coy on range in afternoon, & Lewis gunners.	Amiens Casualties: nil
	26th		Finer. 5 officers (4 coy comdrs & adjt) visited trenches at LA BOISELLE returning at 5 pm, being taken both ways in a motor lorry. C Coy for fatigue. Regt 5 pltns for carrying drill. Remaining pltns on area.	Casualties: 1 Sick
	27th		V. fine. 8 officers (including Q-Mr) to trenches for 24 hrs instruction, returning tomorrow. D Coy for fatigue. Football in afternoon. Capt LONGHURST & L.O. R.A. Coy.	Casualties: nil
	28th		Church Service in evening. Capt WHITEHEAD & 2Lt MACDONALD visit the trenches. An additional fatigue party of 2 officers & 100 men is required by C.R.E. daily, thus A & C each provide one party. Quiet day. No G.O. returns from Bans. G.O's & adjts inspected a flagged position. Raid out for another practice. Attack tomorrow. Capt GOULL left to attend a month's course at 4th Army School at FLIXECOURT, with Sgt MORGAN. A Div: water carrying tests took place, & all Watts, carts & cookers were out.	Casualties: 1 Sick

WAR DIARY
or
INTELLIGENCE SUMMARY.
(Erase heading not required.)

Army Form C. 2118.

48

Place	Date	Hour	Summary of Events and Information	Remarks and references to Appendices
BEHENCOURT	May 29th		B & D Coys on fatigue, & A Coy had 100 O.R. inoculated but right, so there was a very weak parade for the trench attack to-day, & the Btn was found into 2 Coys. A very early start – moving at 5.30 a.m.; the attack took place over ground between LA HOUSSOYE and FRANVILLERS. Back in billets by 10.30 a.m. Salts allotted to the Btn at the hill, starting with G Coy at 11 a.m. The water carrying unit was repeated. 9 O.R. on leave. 100 O.R. of A Coy inoculated. Casualties: 2 Sick.	Amiens Sheet 17
"	30th		Orders received to send 2 working parties (5 Officers & 200 O.R.) and 3 Officers & 200 O.R.) to relieve parties found by the 20th & 21st M.F. at DERNANCOURT. These parties were found by B & C Coys, made up to the requisite strength by A & D Coys. Parties marched under Capt T.O.S. by Platoons starting at 8 a.m.; a 9 mile march. In addition, orders received late at night for another 1 Officer & 50 O.R. to report to O.G. 2nd Labour Bn at DERNANCOURT; this party will leave at 5 a.m. to-morrow, & will be found by D Coy under Lt TYLER. Apart from these permanent parties, we now find daily parties as under: a) 2 Officers & 100 O.R. } go & return in lorries b) 1 Officer & 31 O.R. } c) 25 O.R. } daily C.O. & Adjt visited billets at DERNANCOURT. Casualties: 1 O.R. died in hospital.	Appendix "B"

Army Form C. 2118.

WAR DIARY
or
INTELLIGENCE SUMMARY.
(Erase heading not required.)

Instructions regarding War Diaries and Intelligence Summaries are contained in F. S. Regs., Part II. and the Staff Manual respectively. Title pages will be prepared in manuscript.

49

Place	Date	Hour	Summary of Events and Information	Remarks and references to Appendices
BEHENCOURT	May 31st		Owing to the numerous fatigues given to tending of the troops Billetted in DERNANCOURT, and So not many men are left with M.O. visited trenches. very little work is possible, but preference is We now have 9 Officers & 450 O.R. and find daily parties of 3 Officers & 156 O.R., G. O. a. Bn Hd Qrs." There is warnin Casualties: 1 O.R. Killed (Arthur Bradshaw 9063)	Amiens Sheet 17

SECRET.
Reference - AMIENS - 17
Scale 1/100,000.

COPY NO. 4

The 102nd (TYNESIDE SCOTTISH) BRIGADE.

OPERATION ORDER NO. 26.

9th MAY, 1916.

1.. Units of the 102nd (Tyneside Scottish) Brigade will be billeted for the night of 10/11th MAY, 1916, as follow :-

    Brigade Headquarters .... FRANVILLERS.
    20th N.F. (1st TYNESIDE SCOTTISH) .... LA HOUSSOYE.
    21st "   (2nd   "   "   ) .... FRANVILLERS.
    22nd "   (3rd   "   "   ) .... FRANVILLERS.
    23rd "   (4th   "   "   ) .... BEHENCOURT.

2.. Units moving into new Billeting Area will march as under :-

UNIT.	STARTING POINT & TIME.	ROUTE.
22nd N.F. (3rd TYNESIDE SCOTTISH)	Church at ST. GRATIEN... 6:50 p.m.	Via FRECHENCOURT. BEHENCOURT.
23rd N.F. (4th TYNESIDE SCOTTISH)	Church at ST. GRATIEN... 7 p.m.	Via FRECHENCOURT.

3.. Billeting parties from Battalions will proceed to FRANVILLERS and BEHENCOURT respectively on the morning of the 10th instant. These parties will report to the Town Major of their new Billeting Area, who will allocate billets to them.

4.. Acknowledge.

102 B.H.Q.
9:5:1916.

Major.
BRIGADE MAJOR.
102nd (TYNESIDE SCOTTISH) BRIGADE.

    Copies 1 - 3 retained.
           4 20th N.F. (1st Tyneside Scottish)
           5 21st "   (2nd   "   "   )
           6 22nd "   (3rd   "   "   )
           7 23rd "   (4th   "   "   )
           8 102 Machine Gun Coy.
           9 34th Division ....)
          10 101st Inf. Bde. ..) For information.
          11 103rd Inf. Bde. ..)
          12 War Diary.

REFERENCE 1:40000.
ALBERT (Combined Sheet.)

B

FATIGUES.

The following working parties not found by the 20th. Northumberland
Fusiliers will be found by the 23rd. Battalion Northumberland Fusiliers.

A)   5 Officers and 100 other ranks. (for work under orders of the C.R.A.
                                                        DERNANCOURT.)

B)   1 Officer and 31 other ranks   do.   do.

This latter party (B) is a daily party, and will be found tomorrow
by "D" Company. A bus will call at Headquarters for this party at
7.30a.m.
The 23rd. Battalion Northumberland Fusiliers will also relieve the
following parties of the 21st. Battalion Northumberland Fusiliers.

(C) 3 Officers and 100 other ranks (for work under the orders of the
                                           C.R.E., DERNANCOURT.)

(D) 2 Officers and 100 other ranks (for work under the orders of the
                                           C.R.E., ALBERT.)

This latter party (D) is a daily party, and will be found tomorrow
by "D" Company. Lorries will pick up this party at 7.15a.m.

Party "A"
   This will be provided by "B" Company under Capt. TODD, made
up to the requisite strength by "A" Company if necessary.

Party "C"
   This will be provided by "C" Company, under Lieut. SHAPLEY,
made up to the requisite strength by "D" Company, if necessary.
   Lewis Gun Detachments will proceed with their Companies, and
will be counted in the total strength.
   Capt. TODD will be in command of both parties on arrival in
DERNANCOURT.
   Parties will march by platoons at 5 minutes interval, the
first platoon starting at 8.0a.m. and follow the following route.
D.17.a.3/3.
       South to LA BUIRE.
       Thence along the road running N of Railway to DERNANCOURT.
       An Officer will march with each platoon

TRANSPORT.
       The Transport Officer will provide the following Transport
to march in rear of the last platoon of each party.

       1 Limber for 2 Lewis Guns and S.A.A.
       1 Limber for Officers Valises and Company Stores.
       1 Limber for mens' ground sheets.
       1 Cooker.
The limbers will return to BEHENCOURT after unloading at the
billets in DERNANCOURT.
       One Water Cart will also accompany the first party.
       Blankets are not to be taken, and must be handed to the
Quarter Master before departure.
       Billets are to be left clean and all latrines filled in.

                                   K.A.N. ANDERSON.

                                       CAPTAIN AND ADJUTANT.

SECRET.   Copy No. 6.

The 102nd (TYNESIDE SCOTTISH) BRIGADE.

OPERATION ORDER NO... 23.

3rd MAY, 1916.

1. The Brigade will entrain at ST.OMER on the 5th and 6th May, for LONGEAU.
   Order of entrainments and roads to be used, are shown on attached Table "A".

ROUTES —
2. Routes from the Detraining Station to the new Billetting Area will be allotted on arrival at Detraining Station.
   Arrangements are being made for guides to meet units and conduct them to their billets.

BILLETTING PARTIES.
3. Billetting parties - strength as under - will proceed to ST.OMER Station by the 9.45 a.m. train on the 5th inst.
   Billetting parties to be at ST.OMER Station at 1 a.m.

	OFF.	O.R.
Brigade Headquarters)		
Signal Section.)	1	7
102 Machine Gun Coy.)		
20th N.F. (1st Tyneside Scottish)	1	6
21st " (2nd " ")	1	6
22nd " (3rd " ")	1	6
23rd " (4th " ")	1	6
102 Field Ambulance	1	2
No. 3 Coy Train		1 1
204th Field Coy. R.E.		1

RATIONS
4. All units will entrain with the unexpended portion of the day's rations - and rations for the day following that of entrainment.
   The Billetting parties mentioned in para.3 will take 3 days rations with them.
   All Units including Billetting parties will carry Iron Rations on the men, extra to the rations referred to above.
   The 3 days rations for billetting parties will be conveyed in a G.S. limbered wagon to ST.OMER Station under Battalion arrangements.

BAGGAGE AND SUPPLY WAGONS.
5. Baggage and Supply wagons will entrain with units and not with Train Companies.

SUPPLIES
6. Units which entrain between midnight 4/5th and midnight 5/6th will draw supplies for consumption on the 5th at Refilling Point as usual - i.e. on the 4th.
   The Supply wagons when unloaded will return to the Refilling Point at 3 p.m. on the 4th inst., and draw supplies for consumption on the 5th. These wagons will then return to their units and entrain "loaded" on the 5th.

   Units which entrain between midnight 5/6th and midnight 6/7th will draw supplies for consumption on the 6th at Refilling Point as usual - i.e. on the 5th.
   The Supply wagons when unloaded will return to the Refilling Point at 3 p.m. on the 5th inst., and draw supplies for consumption on the 7th. These wagons will then return to their units and entrain "loaded" on the 6th.

/ 7.. STAFF

STAFF OFFICERS
AT ENTRAINING
& DETRAINING
STATIONS.   7.. There will be a Staff Officer at Entraining and
                          Detraining Stations for the whole period during which
                          units of the Brigade will be either entraining or
                          detraining.
                                The Brigade Major will be at the Entraining Station.
                                The Staff Captain will be at the Detraining Station.

ROAD
CONTROL...   8.. The O.C. 52nd Bn., (4th Canadian Scottish) will detail
                          an officer to be present to control traffic at the
                          Cross Roads at ST GEORGE AUBIGNY during the whole period that
                          various units of the Brigade are passing that point for
                          the Rail Station.
                          This Officer will rejoin his unit when the last section
                          of his battalion has passed that point.

LIGHT TRENCH
MORTAR BATTERIES   9.. The personnel of the 103/1 and 103/2 Trench Mortar
                          Batteries will for the purposes of this move be attached
                          to units to which they originally belonged, but will be
                          kept as far as possible as a distinct unit during the
                          move.

BILLETS.......   10.. On arrival in the new area - the Brigade will be
                          billetted in the area of ST MARTIN and RAINNEVILLE.
                          Brigade Headquarters will be at RAINNEVILLE.

RAILHEAD......   11.. The Railhead at MAILLY will remain open up to and
                          including 6th MAY, 1916, and a new Railhead will be
                          opened at LONGUEAU on that day.

GENERAL
INSTRUCTIONS.   12.. The instructions "Notes on Entrainment" issued to Units
                          of the Brigade - 24th Div No. 309/2 dated 12:4:1916, are
                          to be strictly complied with.

REPORT CENTRE...13.. Brigade Headquarters will close at MAILLY MAILLET at 12 noon
                          on 6th MAY, 1916, and reopen at ST. GRATIEN at the same
                          hour.

                                                                    Major.
103 B.G.C.   BRIGADE MAJOR.
6:5:1916.   103rd (CANADIAN COUNTIES) BRIGADE.
        Issued at   D.H.
        Copies 1 & 2 retained.
                3 50th Bn. (1st Canadian Scottish)
                4 51st "   (2nd   "   ")
                5 52nd "   (3rd   "   ")
                6 53rd "   (4th   "   ")
                7 511th Field Coy. C.E.
                8 103 Machine Gun Coy.
                9 No.3 Coy. A.S.C.
                10 War Diary.

S E C R E T.

Issued with Operation Order No. 53.

TRAIN NO.	CONVEYING.	LEAVES.	AT	ON	DUE AT LONGREAU.	ON	REMARKS.
23	20th N.F. (1st TYNESIDE SCOTTISH)	ST OMER.	5:53 p.m	5th	1.31 a.m.	6th.	Any road.
25	102nd Bde. Head Qrs. Signal Section...... Machine Gun Coy.....	ST OMER.	8:43 p.m	5th	4.31 a.m	6th	Any road.
27	21st N.F. (2nd TYNESIDE SCOTTISH)	ST OMER.	11:43 p.m.	5th	7.31 a.m.	6th	Any road.
29	22nd N.F. (3rd TYNESIDE SCOTTISH)	ST OMER.	2:43 a.m	6th	10.31 a.m.	6th	Via CALAIS---ST OMER road.
31	23rd N.F. (4th TYNESIDE SCOTTISH)	ST OMER.	5:43 a.m.	6th	1.31 p.m.	6th	Via CALAIS---ST OMER road.
33	102nd Field Ambulance No. 3 Coy. A.S.C. D.T. }	ST OMER.	8:33 a.m.	6th	4.31 p.m.	6th	Any road.
55	226th Field Coy. R.E.	ST OMER.	11.43 a.m.	6th	7.31 p.m.	6th	Any road - North of LUMBRES.

5:5:1916.

Major
BRIGADE MAJOR
102nd (TYNESIDE SCOTTISH) BRIGADE

Provisional Billeting Arrangements.   34. 806/5.

Unit.	Time of arrival London.	Date of arrival	Approximate time of arrival at billets.	Billet	Strength NCO/Men OR/Men
10th Bn. R.W.F. Signal Section. } 135 R.E. Coys... }		8th	10.30 a.m. 8th	OSWESTRY	
20th ... (1st Brigade Section)......	11:30 a.m	8th	7.00 a.m. 8th		
21st ... (2nd Bn. Pyrennées Section)......	7:30 a.m	8th	1.00 p.m. 8th		
22nd R.F. (3rd Bn. Pyrennées Section)......	10:30 a.m	8th	4.00 p.m. 8th		
23rd R.F. (4th Bn. Pyrennées Section)......	1:30 p.m	8th	7.00 p.m. 8th		
15th Suss. Regt.....	4:30 p.m	8th	10.00 p.m. 8th	LA PANNE	
13th Lond. Regt......	4:30 p.m	8th	11.00 p.m. 8th		
10th Bn. R. Coys.......	7:30 p.m	8th	2.00 a.m. 9th		

For information.

Reference 1:40,000
ALBERT - Combined Sheet.
Ref No... 102/
Ref No... 102/2028/

Headquarters,
   20th N.F. (1st Tyneside Scottish)
   21st " (2nd   "   ")
   23rd " (4th   "   ")

C.R.E., 34th Div., ... for information.

The following Working Parties now found by the 20th N.F. (1st Tyneside Scottish) will be found by the 23rd N.F. (4th Tyneside Scottish) :-

   5 Officers & 200 Other Ranks - for work under the orders
                                                  of the C.R.E., DERNANCOURT.

* 1 Officer & 31 men - for work under the orders
                                    of the C.R.E., DERNANCOURT.

* This latter party is a daily party; a bus will call at the Headquarters of the 23rd N.F. (4th Tyneside Scottish) at 7:30 a.m., daily, for the conveyance of this party.

The 23rd N.F. (4th Tyneside Scottish) will also relieve the following Working Parties of the 21st N.F. (2nd Tyneside Scottish) :-

   3 Officers & 200 Other Ranks - for work under the orders
                                                  of the C.R.E., DERNANCOURT.

ø 2 Officers & 100 Other Ranks - for work under the orders
                                    of the C.R.E., ALBERT.

ø This latter working party now found by the 21st N.F. (2nd Tyneside Scottish) is a daily working party. Arrangements will be made to collect this party at the Headquarters, 23rd N.F. (4th Tyneside Scottish) at 7:15 a.m. daily.

As regards the 5 Officers and 200 Other Ranks and 3 Officers and 200 Other Ranks for work under the C.R.E., DERNANCOURT, these will proceed to DERNANCOURT to-morrow morning (30:5:16) at 6 a.m., and report to the C.R.E.

Parties will march by Platoons at 5 minutes interval - and follow the following route from A.17.a.2.2 - then South to LA BUIRE - thence along the road running North of the Railway to DERNANCOURT.

In order, however, that a full days work may be got out of all available men relieving and about to be relieved - the parties of the 20th and 21st N.F. (1st and 2nd Tyneside Scottish) whom the 23rd N.F. (4th Tyneside Scottish) relieve will not return to their respective Battalions until to-morrow evening, starting back at 6 p.m.

                                                               Major.

102 B.H.Q.   BRIGADE MAJOR.
29:5:1916.   102nd (TYNESIDE SCOTTISH) BRIGADE.

TABLE "A".

Train No.	Conveying	Leaves	At	On	Due at LONGUEAU at	On	Remarks.
1.	24th N.F.	St. Omer	8.35	4th	15.31	4th	Any road
2.	25th N.F.	Wizernes	9.52	"	17.31	"	-do-
3.	23rd N.F.	O.	11.43	"	18.31	"	-do-
4.	103rd Bde H.Q.) Signal Sect.) N.G. Coy.)	W.	11.52	"	20.31	"	-do-
5.	D. H. Q.) R. A. Hdqrs.) H.A. & 1 Sec) Sig. Coy.)	O.	14.43	"	22.31	"	-do-
6.	27th N.F.	W.	14.52	"	23.31	"	Train to move by Setques & Tattinghem
7.	Div. Cyclist Coy Train Hdqrs & Hdqr Coy.	O.	17.55	"	1.31	5th	
8.	103rd Fd Amb. & No. 4 Coy Train)	W.	17.52	"	2.31	"	(N.O. 4 Coy train via St Martin au Laert, thence by Wostove Road as far as main St. Omer - Wizernes ...
9.	15th R. Scots.	O.	20.45	"	4.31	"	Any road.
10.	H.E. Hdqrs & 207 Coy R.E.	W.	20.52	"	5.31	"	-do-
11.	101st Bde H.Q.) Signal Sec.) ½ N.F. & Coy.)	O.	23.45	"	7.31	"	By main road from Houlle.
12.	A/152 Bde R.F.A.) ½ B.A.C. 152)	W.	23.52	5th	8.31	"	Any road.
13.	18th Royal Scots.	O.	2.45	"	10.31	"	" "
14.	B/152 Bde R.F.A.) ½ 152 B.A.C.)	W.	2.52	"	11.31	"	" "
15.	10th Lincolns.	O.	5.45	"	13.31	"	" "
16.	C/15. Bde R.F.A.) ½ 152 B.A.C.)	W.	5.52	"	14.31	"	" "
17.	11th Suffolks.	O.	8.35	"	15.31	"	To join ST OMER-CALAIS road W. of HOULLE.
18.	D/152 Bde R.F.A.) ½ 152 B.A.C.)	W.	8.52	"	17.31	"	Any road.

Page 2. - Contd.

Train No.	Convoying.	Loaves.	At.	On.	Due at LONGEAU at.	On.	Remarks.
19.	No. 3 Co. Div. Train.) 104th Fld Amb.	O.	11.43	5th.	19.31	5th.	Any road.
20.	A/130 Bde R.F.A. & ½ 130 B.A.C.	W.	11.52	"	20.51	"	"
21.	209th Fld Co. R.E.	O.	14.43	"	22.51	"	"
22.	B/130 Bde R.F.A.) ½ 130 B.A.C.	W.	14.52	"	23.51	"	"
23.	30th N.F.	O.	17.55	"	1.31	6th	
24.	C/1.0 Bde R.F.A. ½ 160 B.A.C.	W.	17.52	"	2.31	"	"
25.	102nd Bde H.Q., Signal Sect., L.C. Coy.	O.	20.43	"	4.31	"	"
26.	D/130 Bde R.F.A.) ½ 160 B.A.C.	W.	20.52	"	5.51	"	"
27.	21st N.F.	O.	23.43	"	7.51	"	"
28.	H.Qrs 153, 160,175 & 173 Bdes R.F.A.	W.	23.52	"	8.31	"	"
29.	22nd N.F.	O.	2.43	6th.	10.31	"	via CALAIS-ST OMER road.
30.	A/173 Bde R.F.A.) ½ 175 B.A.C.	W.	2.52	"	11.31	"	Any road.
31.	23rd N.F.	O.	5.43	"	13.51	"	"
32.	B/173 Bde R.F.A.) ½ 175 B.A.C.	W.	5.52	"	14.31	"	"
33.	No. 3 Co. Div. Train.) 102nd Fld Amb.	O.	8.33	"	13.31	"	"
34.	C/175 Bde R.F.A.) ½ 175 B.A.C.	W.	8.52	"	17.31	"	"
35.	203th Fld Co. R.E.	O.	11.43	"	19.51	"	Any roads N. of LEULINGEN.
36.	D/175 Bde R.F.A.) ½ 175 B.A.C.	W.	11.52	"	20.31	"	Any road.
37.	Div. Cavalry, Sanitary Sect. & A.V.Sect.	O.	14.43	"	22.51	"	"
38.	A/173 Bde R.F.A.) 1/3rd 175 B.A.C.	W.	14.52	"	23.51	"	"
39.	C/173 Bde R.F.A.) 1/3rd 173 B.A.C.	O.	17.55	"	1.51	7th	"

Table A. - Page 5 - Contd.

Train No.	Conveying.	Leaves.	At.	On.	Due at LONGEAU at	On.	Remarks.
40.	2/173 Bde A.F.A.) 1/3rd 173 B.A.C.)	V.	17.52	6th	2.51	7th	Any road.
41.	H.Q. D.A.C.,)	O.	21.65	"	5.31	"	"
42.	1/3rd No. 1 Section) 2/3rds No. 2 Section) D.A.C.	V.	21.52	"	3.51	"	"
43.	2/3rds No. 1 Section) D.A.C.	O.	1.25	7th	5.51	"	"
44.	2/3rds No. 3 Section) D.A.C.	V.	1.42	"	10.31	"	"
45.	1/3rd No. 2 Section) 1/3rd No. 3 Sect. D.A.C.)	O.	3.46	"	13.31	"	"

Army Form C. 2118.

WAR DIARY
or
INTELLIGENCE SUMMARY.
(Erase heading not required.)

Instructions regarding War Diaries and Intelligence Summaries are contained in F.S. Regs., Part II. and the Staff Manual respectively. Title pages will be prepared in manuscript.

Place	Date	Hour	Summary of Events and Information	Remarks and references to Appendices
BETTENCOURT	June 1st		A Coys practice Trench Attack was held, but we only had to provide 1 Officer & 50 O.R. (found from D Coy) to form part of a Skeleton Bde. In addition 3 Officers were attached for liaison work to various Bdes. This party moved off at 5.15 am, and were back by 10 am. Usual fatigues & practically none left in billets; those who remained were practised in bombing & handling of arms. D Coy on range 4-6 pm. Casualties: nil	Officers Sheet 17
"	2nd		Fine & quiet day. Bombing & handling of arms in morning. Over score have thrown 3 live bombs. The C.O. rode over to visit the Coys in DERNANCOURT. A Court of Enquiry was held at 4 pm at the 20th M.F. Hd-Qrs (Lt-Col SILLERY as President) to enquire into the conduct of Lts YOUNG and WILLIAMS in leaving their working parties at ALBERT and being found at lunch in the town, over 1½ miles away. A Coy used the range in the evening. Casualties: Scott P.	

WAR DIARY
or
INTELLIGENCE SUMMARY.
(Erase heading not required.)

Army Form C. 2118.

Place	Date	Hour	Summary of Events and Information	Remarks and references to Appendices
BEHENCOURT	June 3rd		The morning was spent in cleaning up billets & inspections, and the a[fternoon] in rest. The Btn. [?] (less 2 Coys) paraded at 9.30 p.m. and marched by Coys at 10 mins interval, via FRANVILLERS, to ALBERT, where we were to relieve the 20th N.F. Billetting party went ahead in the morning (& also the Q-M with rations). Major MACKINTOSH returned (from leave) had his an arrangements for the march of B & C Coys from DERNANCOURT to ALBERT. Showery day.	Orders Sheet 17 Appendix A. Casualties Nil.
"	4th		The Btn was not complete in billets in ALBERT in full & arms) till 5+ A & D Coys arrived at 1.0 a.m. and B & C Coys at 1.40 a.m. D Coy has 3 pltns in redoubts in close support to front line (2 pltns in TARA and 1 pltn in TARA redoubt). The delay was owing to the heavy shelling on line & gun pits heavily, this delayed the 20th F. and our the 3 platoons of D Coy, a cut all wires. Luckily, [?] all our wires used, & they made everyone [?] as we not cover the support march[?]	

Army Form C. 2118.

WAR DIARY
or
INTELLIGENCE SUMMARY.
(Erase heading not required.)

Instructions regarding War Diaries and Intelligence Summaries are contained in F.S. Regs., Part II. and the Staff Manual respectively. Title pages will be prepared in manuscript.

Place	Date	Hour	Summary of Events and Information	Remarks and references to Appendices
ALBERT	June 4th	1-4am	on to Bate. no casualties. The Btn is billeted in the eastern outskirts of ALBERT, and Btn Hd-Qrs is in RUE DE PERONNE at E.4.D 2/4). Btn Hd-Qrs is in RUE DE PERONNE at E.4.D 2/4. A, B & C Coys sent left --- 3 pltns of D Coy are in redoubts (2 pltns in USNA and 1 in TARA; Cott in Square W.24.D.) A quiet day; all the officers reconnoitred the route to the trenches & to the Assembly point in case of alarm. The heavy shelling in the early morning was due to the Boches having raided the Btn on the right of on Bde, but without much success; both the 20th & 21st M.F. Cost about 30 O.R. each owing to shell fire. Heavy shelling again at night & a Boche raid was undertaken against the 21st M.F. but only a few raiders penetrated the line. B Coy was sent up urgently at 9pm to support the 21st M.F.; they had an exciting journey up and had narrow escapes from shell fire. Their rations were sent up later, and the 21st M.F. provided hot tea. One man was wounded while on guard & two on the way up. Shelling died down at 2 am. Casualties;	52 ALBERT Sheet (1/40000)

Army Form C. 2118.

WAR DIARY
or
INTELLIGENCE SUMMARY.
(Erase heading not required.)

Instructions regarding War Diaries and Intelligence Summaries are contained in F.S. Regs., Part II. and the Staff Manual respectively. Title pages will be prepared in manuscript.

Place	Date	Hour	Summary of Events and Information	Remarks and references to Appendices
ALBERT	June 5th		A very quiet day. Btn Hd-Qrs moved to the Chateau des Rochers in RUE DE BRAY at 4 p.m. A Coy provided fatigue parties to carry up ammunition for trench mortars. The 103rd Bde are arranging to raid the Boche lines opposite LA BOISELLE to-night, and A Coy was sent up into the USNA-TARA line at 9 p.m. to Go in close support of the 20th N.F. in Cave of necessity. The raiding parties are to Cave from the Line held by the 20th N.F. All the men remaining in Billets (C Coy & 1 plt. D Coy) & Hd-Qrs were put in cellars & the Motto at Hd-Qrs by 11 p.m. when the Bombardment started, but the Boche did not retaliate at all. All was quiet by 1 a.m., and the men came up out of the cellars. A Coy remained in the trenches for the night. No details of the raid received yet. 6 men on Leave. Casualties: nil.	ALBERT Sheet 1:40000 and OVILLERS French Map
"	6th		Wet & rainy morning. A Coy returned at 10 a.m. The G.O. went to meet the Brigadier at BECOURT Chateau at 11 a.m. A quiet day, all the Shelling appears to be done here By night. Orders suddenly received that we are to relieve the 20th N.F. in the left sector trenches	

Army Form C. 2118.

54

WAR DIARY
or
INTELLIGENCE SUMMARY.
(Erase heading not required.)

Instructions regarding War Diaries and Intelligence Summaries are contained in F.S. Regs., Part II and the Staff Manual respectively. Title pages will be prepared in manuscript.

Place	Date	Hour	Summary of Events and Information	Remarks and references to Appendices
ALBERT	June 6th		to-night. Coys to go up by platoons at 10 mins. interval. D Coy carried out their relief during the afternoon, & B Coy having to cross over from BECOURT Chateau arrived last. Casualties: nil	OVILLERS Trench map "Appendix A"
LA BOISSELLE trenches			A very long relief, owing to the delay of B Coy, and not complete until 4 a.m. The trenches are very wet & muddy, but it was a quiet night. For disposition of Btn see attached sketch (B); A Coy has by far the worst sector opposite the craters — it was very confused & broken and gets nearly all the "minnies" and "sausages" (large & small minenwerfer shells) & the shelling. A Coy also has 2 platoons of D Coy & one of B Coy attached. Trench mortars & rifle grenades active on both sides all day, but a quiet night once more. 400 men from the 20th H.F. came up to dig. Casualties: nil	Appendix B
"	8th		Mutual activity all day, the Boche seeming to send over more than we do; A Coy had an unpleasant day. Lt TYTLER (D Coy) did very well & set a good example to his men under trying circumstances. More large parties on digging. Raining again, and the mud is much worse. Casualties: nil	

#353 Wt. W2544/T454 700,000 5/15 D.D. & L. A.D.S.S./Forms/C. 2118.

Army Form C. 2118.

WAR DIARY
or
INTELLIGENCE SUMMARY.
(Erase heading not required.)

Place	Date	Hour	Summary of Events and Information	Remarks and references to Appendices
LA BOISSELLE Trenches	June 9th		Our miners sprang a camouflet against the Boche system at 11.15 a.m., and blew in OVILLERS their gallery, but no artillery action followed. The Boche later in the day became very active with canisters. In the evening D Coy relieved their 2 pltns, but A remained on. Rain again with fine intervals, but the trenches get worse & worse. The labour of carrying is very great; no cooking is allowed in the trenches, and all the food has to be carried up 3 times a day in food containers from the Cook House up to the Coys; the 2 plutoons of D Coy in USNA [?] don't do this carrying.	Trench map
"	10th		Our artillery & trench mortars were more in evidence & gave the Boche a lively time; but he retaliated quite effectively. It was decided to relieve A Coy, as they had had a bad time, but as we are only to be in one more night, the C.O. decided against it. The trenches are filthy; a quiet night again and we had wiring parties out, and a party from the 10th N.F. did heavy bombardment on our left took place at 9.... Casualties: [?]	
"	11th		Boche much less active, and we gave him a good shelling. We did to be relieved to-night and [crossed out] the usual advanced parties went out in the morning. The 20th N.F. commenced coming in about 9.30 p.m., and the	

Army Form C. 2118.

56

WAR DIARY
or
INTELLIGENCE SUMMARY.
(Erase heading not required.)

Place	Date	Hour	Summary of Events and Information	Remarks and references to Appendices
LA BOISSELLE Trenches	June 11th		Relief went on quite smoothly except for one platoon which was coming from TARA redoubt; this started late & held up everyone until 1 a.m. At the last moment we were ordered to detail 100 men for a digging fatigue, and 10 men for carrying; these men did not get home until 7 a.m. We are back in the same billets in ALBERT, the only exception being that A Coy now has 2 Pltns in USNA and 1 Plt in TARA redoubts, and D Coy is in billets. Casualties: 1 Sick	OVILLERS Trench Map Appendix "C"
ALBERT	12th		A quiet day. The men had a long lie in. 200 men of D & B Coy & 100 of C Coy on fatigues at night; another wet night and the men got soaked. Casualties: 1 Sick	
"	13th		Wet morning again. The Batln are allotted to us from 7am-5pm (60 men for bay) and everyone had a wash. A quiet day, but almost every man out on carrying & digging fatigues at night. The G.O.C. Bde held a conference of the G.O., 2nd-in-Command, Adjt, & all Coy Cmdrs at 3pm. Casualties: nil	

Army Form C. 2118.

WAR DIARY
or
INTELLIGENCE SUMMARY.
(Erase heading not required.)

Instructions regarding War Diaries and Intelligence Summaries are contained in F.S. Regs., Part II and the Staff Manual respectively. Title pages will be prepared in manuscript.

Place	Date	Hour	Summary of Events and Information	Remarks and references to Appendices
ALBERT	June 14th		Wet again, but cleared up later. Everyone on carrying again all night. No work done during the day, except for inspection. All this incessant night work in the wet is ruining the men's clothes and boots. As the French Govt have adopted "Summer Time", we all had to alter our clocks at 11pm & put them on one hour to midnight.	ALBERT Sheet & OVILLERS French Map
"	15th			Casualties: 2 Sick
			G.O. required in morning for a Conference at Bde. B Coy relieves A Coy in VSMA and TARA redoubts in afternoon. Finer weather. Conference at Bde Hd-Qrs. Fatigues as usual, and everyone working overtime as the day approaches. G.O. & Adjt went to 8th Div lines in order to obtain a good view of the Boche lines.	
"	16th		Finer weather. Coy Comdrs went up to look at Boche positions. Much finer. Working parties as usual — every man out. Feverish preparations continue, and matters are being hurried, almost to quickly for thoroughness.	Casualties: nil
"	17th		Fine. G.O. saw all Coy Comdrs at 12 noon. All Coy Comdrs, G.O. & Adjt at Bde H-Q at 5pm to hear a lecture. But the lecturer never arrived. The G.O.C. went through his Rde H W2544/1454 700,000 (5/15. D.D.)& Ls H plans S.S. Forms C.2118. all G.O's & Adjts. 450 men on fatigue.	Casualties: nil

Army Form C. 2118.

WAR DIARY
or
INTELLIGENCE SUMMARY.
(Erase heading not required.)

Instructions regarding War Diaries and Intelligence Summaries are contained in F.S. Regs., Part II. and the Staff Manual respectively. Title pages will be prepared in manuscript.

Place	Date	Hour	Summary of Events and Information	Remarks and references to Appendices
ALBERT	June 18th		Fine & warm. Church parades in morning (voluntary). Only 250 men on fatigue to-night and D Coy were given a rest. All leave stopped. Bde orders for the attack received. Casualties: nil	ALBERT SLOP & ONILLERS Trench Map
"	19th		180 men of D Coy on fatigue all morning. A, B & C Coys on fatigue to-night on digging & carrying fatigues. Coy Comdrs & other officers visited the trenches in order to inspect the German lines to select points to advance on. The attack which was to have taken place on some day about now, appears to have been postponed, but feverish preparations continue. Weather much finer & our all the Btn surplus kit & stores (& officers' surplus above 35 lbs) packed up, labelled & sent to be stored under the Town Major at FRANVILLERS, with a guard of 2 old cooks. Casualties: nil	
"	20th		Btn orders for the forthcoming attack commenced. C Coy & D Coy on day fatigues, and only A Coy out at night. Drew S.A.A., Bombs, yellow identification marks, water bottles etc etc from Bde Store. Orders received that we are to relieve the 22nd M.F. to-morrow night. All bombs inspected & detonated. Casualties: nil	

WAR DIARY
or
INTELLIGENCE SUMMARY.
(Erase heading not required.)

Army Form C. 2118.

59

Place	Date	Hour	Summary of Events and Information	Remarks and references to Appendices
ALBERT	June 21st		Relief of the 22nd M.F. postponed. 11 officers, 22 N.C.O's & 528 men required at 4 pm to-night in specially told-off parties to carry gas cylinders up to our trenches. Major BLORE from the Division & all the officers to be engaged in this work met at 4 pm & fully explained everything to them. Instructions for the attack completed & sent out (copy attached – Appendix D). Casualties: nil.	ALBERT Sheet OVILLIERS French Map Appendix "D"
"	22nd		The special party carrying cylinders were shelled in the front trenches, and one man killed – buried by a "minnister". The C.O. went to a conference at Bde. at 1.30 p.m. and saw all Coy Comdrs at 5 p.m. Saturday June 24th is to be "U" Day. When the bombardment commences, and the 3rd T.S. (22nd M.F.) is being relieved on night 23/24. (It seems likely by parties of the 20th, 21st, 23rd & 18th M.F., also a coy to be sent to relieve from which they will [?] up [?] [?] news that the men are extremely cramped and crowded for 5 days. No definite orders as yet received. Called at [?] for all packs, which are being stored to-morrow. [?] & [?] 8 M.G.O's & 160 men for carrying up gas cylinders & [?]	

Army Form C. 2118.

WAR DIARY
or
INTELLIGENCE SUMMARY.
(Erase heading not required.)

Place	Date	Hour	Summary of Events and Information	Remarks and references to Appendices
ALBERT	June 23rd		The Bn was put in without incident last night. The morning spent in issue of all special stores, required for the advance, to Coys — i.e. picks, shovels, bombs, bomb buckets & carriers, wire cutters, sandbags etc etc. ALBERT is being evacuated at 12 midnight, and the 22nd M.F., at present French kept in the line, are being relieved by detachments from several Btns.. Each Btn is now taking over the area from which it will finally deliver the assault. Our Btn sends 5 Pltns (D Coy + 1 Pltn A Coy) into the trenches, 1 Plt A Coy in TARA, C Coy in W.29.c.d, B Coy & ½ A Coy in the Sunken Garden under Major BURGE. Lt-Col LYLE is to command the mixed coys in the Que. All mules, packs horses stored in ALBERT, and officers kits at FRANVILLERS. All cookers & water carts withdrawn to transport lines. The 5 newly joined officers return to transport also — plus one more officer, joined to-day. Capt NICHOLLS is posted at BRESLE at 11 am for special work in charge of reinforcements. Everything is now issued & all coys are complete. A lecture by Gen ROBINS of 6 Divn, at which 10 Officers attended. Orderly Room papers & boxes sent back to transport. Btn all clear of ALBERT by 12 midnight. See Appendix. Casualties: 1 Sick E.	ALBERT Sheet & OVILLERS at present French kept 60

2353 Wt. W2344/1454 700,000 5/15 D. D. & L. A.D.S.S./Forms/C. 2118.

23rd Worcester Regt
(1/r Brigade South Afr)

Army Form C. 2118.

WAR DIARY
or
INTELLIGENCE SUMMARY.
(Erase heading not required.)

VOL 6   61

Place	Date	Hour	Summary of Events and Information	Remarks and references to Appendices
Trenches South	June 24th		June 24th was originally selected as V Day, the first day of the preliminary bombardment. The date was postponed to 29th. Bombardment of Battalion was established as follows, 2½ Companies in the line & 1½ Companies in Reserve in the trenches East of ALBERT. Nothing of note occurred to report. The Companies.	OUILLERS Sheet
	25th		Position of Battalion continued unaltered. Quiet day except for Battalion.	
	26th		V Day. 1st first day of bombardment. The trenches sustained some considerable shelling on the right and very considerable on the left. "C" Company in the trenches had a direct hit on a dug out killing one man Hewitt & wrecking the dug out & telephone communication. Two officers & one other person.	

8353 Wt. W2544/1454 700,000 5/15 D. D. & L. A.D.S.S./Form/C. 2118.

Place	Date	Hour	Summary of Events and Information	Remarks and references to Appendices
	29th		Strike unaccompanied by for was repeated by Lieut LEECH from the left creek of our front line trenches. Movie- the LA BOISELLE Y. Sap. No movements of any kind were took place. The wind was unfavourable for Gas. Gr. This day the trenches were very quiet.	OVILLERS FRENCH SHEET
	28th		About 6 P.M. a Gas attack was launched which proved very successful. On the enemy system any B & C Companies moved out into advent 2 trenches behind ALBERT.	
	29th		B. & C. Companies returned to trenches and in each case carried out under Capt Gould, invested by Capt Bullen. Lt Helm & 2 Lt Campbell and 4.5 O.R. 2nd Lt Campbell was wounded and missing. 9/Lt P. Hall of C. Company also took charge of a carrying party for the R. F's who went out and out the enemy wire. 9/Lt Hall was killed when leaving his men out over the parapet. If he Sergt (the Sergt Bearden) immediately took command of the carrying party and successfully carried out the work detailed and brought all his men safely back.	

Army Form C. 2118

WAR DIARY
or
INTELLIGENCE SUMMARY
(Erase heading not required.)

Instructions regarding War Diaries and Intelligence Summaries are contained in F. S. Regs., Part II. and the Staff Manual respectively. Title Pages will be prepared in manuscript.

Place	Date	Hour	Summary of Events and Information	Remarks and references to Appendices
TRENCHES	30	11 PM	B & C Companies took up their allotted positions for the following morning attack, with D Company in support for left and 2 Platoons of A on St. ANDREWS AV. Just before Midnight 6 S.M. Berkeley B.W. was wounded by Shrapnel. The front line & support line were bridged and hand carts out through our wire opposite all bridges. The 2nd Batt. Middlesex they run on our left and the 18th Batt. Middlesex (Pioneers) was on our right.	OUVILLERS SHEET

C. W. Prestidge
Captain & 2 3rd North'd Fus.
L. Syracuse position

SECRET.
Reference 1/40,000
ALBERT (Combined)

COPY NO. 7.

The 102nd (TYNESIDE SCOTTISH) BRIGADE.

OPERATION ORDER NO... 26

1.. The 102nd (Tyneside Scottish) Brigade will relieve the 101st Infantry Brigade in the trenches in accordance with the attached Table "A".

2.. Billeting parties of Units proceeding to ALBERT and DERNANCOURT will precede their units by at least 6 hours, and report to Town Major, who will allot billets.

3.. All movements will take place between the hours of 8 p.m. and 4 a.m.
All transport will also move between these hours.

4.. Battalions taking over sub-sectors of the line will notify the O.C. Battalion whom they relieve, whether or not they are complete.

5.. Battalions will hand over to Battalions of the 103rd Infantry Brigade who take over billets from them, all R.E. Stores, which have been drawn for instructional purposes.
Receipts for all stores handed over are to be obtained and duplicate copies of receipts forwarded to Brigade Headquarters.

6.. 102nd (Tyneside Scottish) Brigade Headquarters will close at FRANVILLERS at 8 a.m., 4th JUNE, 1916, and reopen at BELLE VIEW FARM, E.5.c. at the same hour.
The General Officer Commanding, 102nd (Tyneside Scottish) Bde. will take over Command of the Sector of the line at that hour.

7.. Acknowledge.

Major.
BRIGADE MAJOR.
102nd (TYNESIDE SCOTTISH) BRIGADE.

1st JUNE, 1916.
Issued at 10 a.m.

Copy Nos 1 - 3 retained.
    4   20th N.F. (1st Tyneside Scottish)
    5   21st   "   (2nd   "   "   )
    6   22nd   "   (3rd   "   "   )
    7   23rd   "   (4th   "   "   )
    8   102 Machine Gun Coy.
    9   O.C., 102 Bde. Trench Mortar Batteries.
   10   34th Division ....)
   11   101st Inf. Brigade ....) for information.
   12   103rd   "   "   ....)
   13   War Diary

SECRET. Ref: _____ (Trench Maps) 'AELLE A' Issued with Operation Order No. 28.

DATE.	UNIT OF 102nd Bde. Relieving.	UNIT TO BE RELIEVED.	DESTINATION.	Guides from Unit to be relieved – meet relieving unit.		REMARKS.
				TIME.	PLACE.	
JUNE Night 1/2nd	21st N.F. (2nd TYNESIDE SCOTTISH).....	10th LINCOLNS.	Battn. Hd.Qrs. 2 Companies DERNANCOURT. 2 Companies BECOURT WOOD.	8:30 p.m. 10 p.m.	Rly.Crossing E.20.b. Rly.Crossing E.3.b.	* 20 buses will be provided for conveying this party to LA HOUSSOYE. - do -
Night 2/3rd	21st N.F. (2nd TYNESIDE SCOTTISH).....	11th SUFFOLKS.	Right Sub-Sector of trenches.			All arrangements to be made by C.O's concerned.
"	20th N.F. (1st TYNESIDE SCOTTISH)	16th ROYAL SCOTS.	ALBERT.	10 p.m.	Rly.Crossing E.3.b.	
"		101 MACHINE GUN COY.....	ALBERT – 2 Sections in line.	10 p.m.	- do -	All arrangements to be made by C.O's concerned.
Night 3/4th	22nd N.F. (3rd TYNESIDE SCOTTISH).....	11th SUFFOLKS.	Battn. Hd. Qrs. & 2 Coys. DERNANCOURT. 2 Coys. BECOURT WOOD.	10 p.m. 10 p.m.	Rly.Crossing E.20.b. Rly.Crossing E.3.b.	All arrangements to be made by C.O's concerned. The 20th N.F. (1st Tyneside Scottish) will be clear of billets in ALBERT by 2:15 a.m.
"	20th N.F. (1st TYNESIDE SCOTTISH).....	15th ROYAL SCOTS.	Left Sub-sector of line.			
"	23rd N.F. (4th TYNESIDE SCOTTISH)	20th N.F. (1st TYNESIDE SCOTTISH).	ALBERT.	1:45 a.m	Rly.Crossing E.3.b.	
"	102/1 TRENCH MORTAR BATTERY. 102/2 TRENCH MORTAR BATTERY.	101/1 TRENCH MORTAR BATTERY. 101/2 TRENCH MORTAR BATTERY.	ALBERT & front line.	11 p.m.	Rly.Crossing E.3.b.	Relief of guns and personnel in the trenches to be complete before daylight on 4th June, 1916. All arrangements to be made by O.C's concerned.

ROUTES :-

To ALBERT – Direct Road.

To DERNANCOURT – Via road leading South from main AMIENS/ALBERT Road at Cross Roads E.7.c.1.9

* As the same buses will be used for both parties, an Officer guide will accompany leading bus back to LA HOUSSOYE to pick up second party.

1:6:1916.

BRIGADE MAJOR, 102nd (TYNESIDE SCOTTISH) BRIGADE Major.

SECRET.

Reference APPENDIX "A" ----- 34th Division Operation Order No. 12

WORKING PARTIES TO BE RELIEVED BY 103rd INF. BRIGADE.

DATE.		Now found by	Relieving Unit.	Time.
Evening 3rd/4th JUNE, 16.	One Company, less Specialists (strength not less than 200 Other Ranks) DERNANCOURT, for work under C.E. of Corps.	23rd N.F. (4th TYNESIDE SCOTTISH)......	103rd Inf.Bde.	12:30 a.m.
--do--	1 Officer, 50 Other Ranks, D Dump, DERNANCOURT, for work under C.E. of Corps.	23rd N.F. (4th TYNESIDE SCOTTISH)......	103rd Inf.Bde.	12:30 a.m.
--do--	One Company, DERNANCOURT, for work: 150 men under officer i/c IIIrd Corps Heavy Artillery Signals, remainder under 34th Divisional Signal Company.	23rd N.F. (4th TYNESIDE SCOTTISH)....	103rd Inf.Bde.	12:30 a.m.
--do--	Two Companies; RUE DE BAPAUME, ALBERT, for work under C.R.E. The O.C. Relieving Detachment to report to O.C. 18th Northd. Fusiliers on arrival, by whom the Detachment will be administered.	22nd N.F. (3rd TYNESIDE SCOTTISH)......	103rd Inf.Bde.	8 p.m.

SECRET.
Reference Map. 57D S.E.4
1/10,000.

COPY NO.... 6

The 102nd (TYNESIDE SCOTTISH) BRIGADE.
OPERATION ORDER NO. 27

1. The following reliefs will take place on JUNE 6th/7th, 1916, :-

   (a) The 22nd N.F. (3rd Tyneside Scottish) will relieve
   the 21st N.F. (2nd Tyneside Scottish) in the Right
   Sub-Section. Relief to be carried out between the
   hours of 6 p.m. and 10 p.m. on the 6th inst.

   (b) The 23rd N.F. (4th Tyneside Scottish) will relieve
   the 20th N.F. (1st Tyneside Scottish) in the Left
   Sub-Section. Relief to be carried out between the
   hours of 12 midnight and 4 a.m. (7th inst).

   After relief the 21st N.F. (2nd Tyneside Scottish) will move to
   BECOURT CHATEAU and become "C" Battalion.
   The 22nd N.F. (3rd Tyneside Scottish) thus becomes "A" Battalion.

   After relief the 20th N.F. (1st Tyneside Scottish) will move to
   billets in ALBERT and become "D" Battalion.
   The 23rd N.F. (4th Tyneside Scottish) thus becomes "B" Battalion.

   All further details to be mutually arranged between Commanding
   Officers concerned.

2. GUIDES from the 20th N.F. (1st Tyneside Scottish) will meet the
   23rd N.F. (4th Tyneside Scottish) at RAILWAY CROSSING,
   W.20.c.6.8 at 12 midnight.
   GUIDES from the 21st N.F. (2nd Tyneside Scottish) will meet the
   22nd N.F. (3rd Tyneside Scottish) at BECOURT CHATEAU at 6 p.m.

3. Machine Gunners and Signallers of the 23rd N.F. (4th Tyneside
   Scottish) will relieve the Machine Gunners and Signallers of the
   20th N.F. (1st Tyneside Scottish) between the hours of 3 p.m.
   and 6 p.m. on 6th inst.
   Machine Gunners and Signallers of the 22nd N.F. (3rd Tyneside
   Scottish) will relieve the Machine Gunners and Signallers of the
   21st N.F. (2nd Tyneside Scottish) in the forenoon of the 6th inst.

4. Completion of reliefs will be reported to Brigade Headquarters
   by telephoning the word "PANSY" - followed by the time at which
   the relief was completed.

5. Relieving Battalions will report whether they are all complete.
   If not, the number of absentees is to be given.

6. Acknowledge.

6:6:1916.
Issued at 10:30 a.m.

Major,
BRIGADE MAJOR,
102nd (TYNESIDE SCOTTISH) BRIGADE.

Copies to -
1 & 2 retained.
3 20th N.F. (1st T.S.)
4 21st " (2nd ")
5 22nd " (3rd ")
6 23rd " (4th ")
7 34th Division.
8 102/1 T.M. Battery.
9 102/2 " "
10 102 Machine Gun Coy.
11 102 Bde. Bombing Officer.
12 O.C. Chateau.
13. 101st Inf. Bde.
14 103rd Inf. Bde.
15 23rd Inf. Bde.
16 64th Inf. Bde.
18 18th Northd. Fus.
19 207th Field Coy. R.E.
20 209th " " "
21 Right Group R.F.A.
22 Left Group R.F.A.
23 Signals.
24 Town Major, ALBERT.
25 War Diary.

Barrier at 4 pm   Sigma Sgt Rogan & Sgt Redley
4.20 pm Lewis gunners
4.40 pm Bk Bombers

① Gas Plt- leave here for USMA at 8.30 pm   Sunday 8.45 pm

A   1st plt   10.45 at Garnier
     2nd   10.55
     3rd   11.5
     4th   11.15
C   1st   11.25
     2nd   11.35
     3rd   11.45
     4th   11.55

B   ?
     Rations

B Coy / Kerry plur

Battalion Orders
by
Lieut. Col., W. Lyle, Cmdg., 23rd. Battalion Northumberland Fusiliers.
4th. Battalion Tyneside Scottish).

B.E.F. June 6th. 1916.

Orders for Wednesday, June 7th. 1916.

Orderly Officer..................2nd. Lieut. Daggett.
Next for duty..................2nd. Lieut. Whitaker.

1. LEAVE. Leave may now be granted to any town in Great Britain, with the exception of HINDLEY, BLACKPOOL, and CARDIFF: these towns are only to be considered infected for soldiers not recently vaccinated or re-vaccinated.

2. BOMBS. Before detonators are put into bombs, the fuse attached must be carefully examined to see that it is not cracked or otherwise effected also that the fuse is properly crimped into the detonator.

3.

K.A.N. ANDERSON.

CAPTAIN AND ADJUTANT.

OPERATION ORDER.
BY LIEUT. COL. LYLE CMDG. 23RD. BATTALION NORTHUMBERLAND FUSILIERS.

JUNE 6th. 1916.

1. The Battalion will relieve the 20th. Northd. Fusiliers in the left sector of the line tonight (June 6/7th.)
2. Guides will meet Companies and specialists at the barrier on the ALBERT-BAPAUME main road as under:-

Signallers,(Hd. Qr. & Coy.), Reg. Sgt. Major.	4 p.m.
Lewis Gun Detachments	4.20p.m.
Battalion Bombers (under Lieut. Oliver)	4.40p.m.
1 Platoon "D" Company	8.45p.m.
"A" Company 1st. Platoon.	1045p.m.
" " 2nd. "	10.55p.m.
" " 3rd. "	11.5 p.m.
" " 4th. "	11.15p.m.
"C" Company 1st. "	11.25p.m.
" " 2nd. "	11.35p.m.
" " 3rd. "	11.45p.m.
" " 4th. "	11.55p.m.

"B" Company under arrangements made by Capt. Todd.
"D" Company will relieve during the afternoon.
3. Each Company will relieve the corresponding Company of the 20th. N.F.
4. On Completion of the relief the word "FINIS" should be wired to Headquarters, and the number of men absent, if any, should be added.
5. All bombs, S.A.A., Stores, rockets etc. must be taken over and receipts given.
6. Any stores and Officers Kits left behind, should be stacked at the Quartermaster's Stores at the latest, by 9 pm.

K.A.N. ANDERSON.

CAPTAIN AND ADJUTANT.

Operation Orders by Lt. Col. W. Lyle. Comdg. 23rd Btn. North'd Fusiliers
                                                            June 10th 1916.

1. The Battalion will be relieved by the 20th NF tomorrow night 11th June 1916.
2. The relief will be carried out in accordance with the attached table "A".
3. Guides will be provided to meet the following incoming parties as under:

TIME	PLACE	TO MEET	GUIDES PROVIDED
3 p.m.	BAMMER	Snipers & Intelligence Officer	Lt. Patterson
4 p.m.	do.	Lewis Gun Teams	One Guide per Company
5 p.m.	do.	Signallers	Head Signaller
6 p.m.	do.	Bombers	One Guide per Company

4. Billeting Parties (1 Officer and 2 NCOs per Company and Reg. Sergt. Major for Headquarters) will leave the trenches between 11 a.m. and 12 noon.
5. All Officers kits, Company Stores etc. which are to be taken out, must be deposited at the Cook house dump by 6.0 p.m. at latest; each Co. will detail a small party to remain with these kits until the Transport calls for them.
6. Advance parties of the 20th NF will arrive about 3.0 p.m.
7. Receipts are to be obtained for all stores, SAA, bombs or handcarts etc.
8. Companies will report relief to Battn. Headq. enters by telegraphing the word "LEMON".
9. Lewis Gunners and Bombers, although relieved in the afternoon, will remain with their Companies until the latter are relieved.
10. Hot tea will be ready for the men on arrival in billets.
11. Companies will march out by platoons.
12. A Company will leave dixies for 3 platoons at the cookhouse. The rations for these platoons will be dumped at the cookhouse by 7.30 p.m.

                                        K. Anderson
                                        Capt & Adjt

War Diary

SECRET.   Copy No. 6 D

OPERATION ORDER
by
Lieut. Col., W. Lyle., Cmdg., 22nd. Battalion Northumberland Fusiliers.
(4th. Battalion Tyneside Scottish)

June 21st, 1916.

REFERENCE (LA BOISSELLE 1:5000
          (and
           57d. S.E.   1:20000

1.
INFORMATION

a) In conjunction with the rest of the 4th. Army, an attack on the German positions is to be made by the 3rd. Corps.
The operations up to and including the day of the attack are to be spread over six days; these days are designated as U, V, W, X, Y and Z days, the infantry assault taking place on Z day.
The 34th. Division on the Right and the 8th. Division the left constitute the two leading divisions in the attack by the 3rd. Corps; the 12th. Division is in Corps Reserve.
The limits of frontage allotted to the 34th. Division are shown on map "A" (to be seen at Battalion Headquarters)
The dividing line between the 34th. and 8th. Divisions is X.14.a.5/6 - X.14.b.7/6 - X.5.d.0/5.

OBJECTIVES.

b) The objectives allotted to the 34th. Division are:
   1st. OBJECTIVE   The German front line system comprising four successive lines of trenches and extending in depth to the line marked GREEN on Map "A"
   2nd. OBJECTIVE   The enemy's intermediate line marked YELLOW on Map "A"
   3rd. OBJECTIVE   The consolidation of a zone of defence to the East of CONTALMAISON and thence facing East and extending Northwards to the outskirts of POZIERES. This objective is marked VIOLET on Map "A"

INTENTION.

c) The 34th. Division will attack on a frontage of two Brigades; the 101st. Infantry Brigade on the Right, the 102nd. Infantry Brigade on the Left, and the 103rd. Infantry Brigade in Divisional Reserve.
The 101st. and 102nd. Infantry Brigades will attack and consolidate objectives 1 and two on the respective frontages allotted to them. The dividing line between the Brigades is X.20.a.4/2 - CONTALMAISON VILLA. The 103rd. Infantry Brigade will attack and consolidate objective Three.

BOMBARDMENT.

d) The infantry attack is to be preceded by a five days' bombardment i.e. U, V, W, X and Y days. The assault is to be made on the morning of the 6th. day; i.e. Z day.
During this period fire will be kept up day and night by guns of all calibre, and heavy, medium and light trench mortars. Machine Guns will co-operate at night to prevent the enemy repairing his trenches or wire.

GAS

e) Gas will be liberated at various points along the front on the night V/W, and smoke will be liberated along the whole Army front at 7.30a.m. on Y day.

SMOKE.

f) If the wind is favourable, a smoke barrage will also be formed immediately before the assault, along both the Northern and

(2)

Southern faces of LA BOISSELLE Salient.

g) The assault by the 102nd. Brigade will be delivered as under:-

21st. Northd. Fusiliers - Right assaulting column
22nd. Northd. Fusiliers - Right Reserve
20th. Northd. Fusiliers - Left assaulting column
23rd. Northd. Fusiliers - Left reserve.

The direction is as shown on Map "A"
The assault will be delivered at zero hour (to be notified later) on Z day.)
At O - 6 minutes a hurricane bombardment will be opened on the whole German position. The bombardment of the LA BOISSELLE Salient will be continued until O plus 10 minutes, by which time both attacking columns should be well past the flanks of the salient.

2.

a) The Battalion will be formed up on night Y/Z preparatory to the assault as follows:-

"C" COMPANY.   "B" COMPANY.

2 Platoons (Front Line Trench)   2 Platoons (Front Line Trench)

2   do.   (2nd. Line Trench)   2   do   (2nd. Line Trench)

"D" COMPANY.

RHIDE St. (3rd. Line Trench)

"A" COMPANY. (Less 2 Platoons)

ST. ANDREWS AV. (4th. Line Trench)

2 Platoons "A" Company at a point to be notified later in or near COWRIE STREET.

b) The 1st. Line however will not leave our trenches until the 20th. N.F. are clear.
Scaling Ladders and sand-bag steps have been placed in position in the trenches of assembly and all trenches have been bridged at 25 yard intervals.
Each line will therefore advance direct from its assembly trenches, at 150 yards distance from the line in front, and will cross any intervening trenches by means of these bridges.

c) ALIGNMENT.

In order to ensure that a good start is made, on night Y/Z, O.C. "C" Company is responsible that a tape is laid in NO MAN'S LAND, just outside our wire, as the correct alignment on which the leading line is to be formed up; short direction tapes will also be placed in the centre and at each flank to indicate the direction of the advance.

d) The Battalion, less two platoons "A" Company will, at zero hour, move forward in rear of the 20th. N.F., to the assault of the German position, objective Two, (as shown on Map "A"), in the same formation in which it assembles, as shown above, with a distance between lines of 150 yards and with a distance of 150 yards between our 1st. Line and the last Line of the 20th. N.F.

(3)

3. BATTALION OBJECTIVES.

"C" Company will capture and consolidate its objective as shown on Map "A" from the left of the Brigade front to point X.10.c.6/8 inclusive. Particular attention being paid to the consolidation of the Corps Strong-points. O.C. "C" Company is responsible that communication is established with the 33rd. Infantry Brigade at point X.4.c.0/2 and will report at once to Battalion Headquarters.

"B" Company will capture and consolidate its objective as shown on Map "A", from point X.10.c.0/7 exclusive, to the extreme Right of the CHALK PIT inclusive. O.C. "B" Company is responsible that communication is established with the 22nd. N.F. (3rd. R.B.) at X.10.c.0/2 and will report at once to Battalion Headquarters. O.C's "B" and "C" Companies will select and make good such strong points as they consider necessary, in addition to the consolidation of the whole objective. Particular attention must be paid to the refusing of flanks in the event of troops operating on the Right and Left being delayed.

"D" Company will advance on the whole Battalion objective and will carry forward "C" and "B" Companies, if they are held up; they will assist in the consolidation of the objective from the Brigade Boundary on the left to the extreme Right of the CHALK PIT on the Right; and will, on receipt of orders from Battalion Headquarters, when the 103rd. Infantry Brigade have consolidated their advanced position, withdraw to the line marked R-R on Map "A", where they will at once consolidate and make strong points to form support to the Right Sector.

"A" Company (less two platoons) - forming the 4th. Wave- will advance and assist to carry forward the waves in front, in the event of any being held up. On arrival at hostile line running through X.3.d.5/2 - X.3.d.7/8, "A" Company will consolidate the Special Corps Strong-point shown on Map "A" in addition to point X.3.d.5/2 and the trench running through it. "A" Company will when joined by the two remaining platoons form a support to the left sector of the line. "A" Company is also responsible for clearing hostile communication trench "D" up to and including X.3.d.7/8.

The remaining two platoons of "A" Company under command of 2nd. Lieut. WILLIAMS, will form the Infantry party supporting and assisting the half Company of the Brigade Bombing Company detailed to clear the LA BOISSELLE Salient from the North. (~~scratched out~~)

Headquarters.
(1) Previous to the assault on night Y/Z in the Left Company, front line, Signal office.
(2) During the Advance with "A" Company, between the Communication Trench "D" and the Trench Railway.
(3) During the first phase of consolidation at X.10.a.6/1.
(4) Final position - X.3.d.7/8.

4. R.E. COMPANY. & BRIGADE MACHINE GUN COMPANY.

A half Company R.E. and 4 Vicker's guns from the Brigade Machine Gun Company are allotted to the Battalion and will be hurried forward as soon as the Battalion has reached its final objective in order to help in the defence and consolidation of the position.

The R.E. Company will carry up barbed wire and other R.E. material.

(4)

5.

ADVANCE Once the attack is launched it must be pressed forward at all costs until the final objective of the Battalion (objective two) is reached.

The extreme importance of a resolute advance must be clearly impressed on all ranks, and the advance must continue regardless of whether other Units on our flanks are held up or delayed.

The aim of each wave must be to support and where necessary carry forward the wave in front, until the ultimate objective allotted to the Battalion is reached.

The 20th. N.F. (1st. T.S.) will halt on reaching objective one, but all ranks must be warned that the 23rd. N.F. (4th. T.S.) are not to halt until the final objective of the Battalion (objective Two) has been reached.

The frontage to be covered by each line in the advance is approximately 450 yards, therefore as soon as the attack is launched each line will extend to 2 paces interval.

The pace of the advance will be regulated by the Artillery which will lift from line to line as stated in Appendix "C" Once the Artillery fire has lifted it will not be brought back again; hence in order to gain the maximum support from the guns, the leading line must approach as closely as possible with safety, under cover of the barrage and deliver the assault at once after the barrage has lifted.

Company Commanders will select from Map "A" and from the model at Brigade Headquarters the points which they consider should be made strong-points, and will write orders for their Companies detailing parties for all necessary work of consolidation.

On arrival at objective the German Wire must not be indiscriminately cut, but as far as possible is to be used in wiring the front of the consolidated position.

6.

DRESS & EQUIPMENT. Every man will carry:-
Rifle and Equipment (less pack)
2 extra bandoliers of S.A.A.
2 Mill's Grenades (1 in each side pocket)
1 Iron ration and rations for the day of assault.
Haversack and waterproof cape
Four sandbags.
2 Gas Helmets and 1 pair Spiwer Goggles.
Either a pick or a shovel. (excepting bombers and signallers)
Full water-bottle.
Mess tins to be carried in haversack.
Bomb Buckets, Bomb waistcoat carriers and wire cutters will be distributed under supervision of O.C. Companies.
Bombers to carry equipment ammunition only.

7.

Distinguishing Mark.

All ranks will wear an equal-lateral-triangle of yellow cloth 10" sides, attached to the back, base upwards.

8.

IRON RATIONS. All ranks are reminded that iron rations are not to be eaten without definite orders from an officer. If it is necessary to use Iron Rations only one ration for every three men is to be opened. If more are found to be required a second tin can then be opened. The number of Iron Rations used to be reported every six hours.

9.

WATER. It is extremely difficult to carry up water and all ranks must be clearly warned that drink water is to be economised as much as possible. All officers are responsible that this is done.

(5)

10. BOMBS. Immediately on reaching the objective the two bombs carried per man will be dumped by platoons in some central position to form a Reserve.

11. WIRE BREAKERS. Wire breakers are only to be used by troops in the front line and then only before other troops have passed through.

12. STRETCHER BEARERS & WOUNDED. Before the assault is delivered the Battalion Aid Post will be established in the Front Line near KEATS REDAN. All Stretcher Bearers will report to the Medical Officer on night Y/Z time to be notified later.
During the advance stretcher bearers will remain under the M.O. All ranks must be clearly warned that men are on no account whatever to assist wounded.

13. SIGNALLING & COMMUNICATION See Appendix "D"

14. ADVANCED BRIGADE HD. QRS. At the beginning of the action Advanced Brigade Headquarters will be at a dugout at W.24.b.5/1.
When the second objective has been reached Brigade Headquarters will move on to BOISSELLE VILLAGE – Point X.14.d.8½ 1/5.

15. SANITARY.
a) Food or water found in the German Lines must not be eaten or drunk untill passed by the Medical Officer
b) Latrines are to be constructed as soon as possible on reaching objective. (c) Sanitary men from each Company will
c) take forward disinfectant, to be drawn from M.O.

16. PRISONERS Prisoners of War will be passed back as the situation allows to Brigade Collecting Station established at the Headquarters of the Right Battalion (CHAPES SPUR) where they will be handed over to the guard.

17. BRIGADE DUMPS. Brigade Dumps are situated as follows and are marked by a yellow flag 15" square.

No. 1 & 2	ST ANDREWS AVENUE
3	do (in rear of left Btn. Headquarters)
4, 5 & 6	ST ANDREWS AVENUE (between KIRCKALDY St & DUNFERMLINE ST)
3a	ST ANDREWS AVENUE (between 3 & 4)
7	PERTH AVENUE.
8 & 9	GOWRIE STREET (Southern End)
10	PITLOCHRY STREET.
10a	Near No. 10.
11 & 12	ATHOLL STREET.

These contain, bombs, S.A.A., Rations and water, ready for carrying.

18. LIASON OFFICERS Capt. T.B. COULL is detailed as Liason Officer to the 23rd. Infantry Brigade and will report on Y day to that Brigade Headquarters.
20 officers only are to go into action on Z day with the Battalion. O.C. Companies have been informed of the names of the officers selected. The remainder will act as first reinforcements and will join the Transport on Y day.

12.

MISCELLANEOUS. (I). No paper or orders are to be carried by officers or men taking part in the attack except the new 1/5000 German Trench Map, and the 1/20,000 Map Sheet 57C.S.E.   All messages and reports will refer to one or other of these maps.
(II). Hand Grenades are difficult to replenish; they must not be thrown indiscriminately.
(III). Captured machine Guns must be collected or damaged.
(IV). Pipers will accompany their companies.
(V). All maps etc. referred to in these orders are to be seen at Battalion Headquarters.

APPENDIX "D"

SIGNALLING AND COMMUNICATION.

1. Detailed orders re the duties of Signallers in the advance have already been issued by the Battalion Signal Officer.

2. Brigade Forward Exchanges are being established in our front line Battalion and Brigade Headquarters on moving forward will be connected to this exchange from a lateral buried wire along our front line trench. Laddered lines will be laid across NO MAN'S LAND, the lines being continued forward up the enemy's Communication Trenches.

   VISUAL SIGNALLING. To supplement further telegraphic communication visual signal stations will be established.

   102nd. Infantry Brigade   near DRESSLERS POST.

   FLARES.
   Flares will be issued as an additional means of communication but must only be lit in the most advanced line, held by the Battalion, and as soon as any troops pass through the Battalion and continue the advance, these flares must at once be put out.
   Vigilant Periscopes for use as mirrors will also be issued; these are to be used as an additional means of indicating to aeroplanes the extent of our advance.

   METHOD OF LIGHTING.
   Flares should be placed 5 yards apart and lit in batches of three as under :-

   Light 1 Flare and wait 15 seconds.
   Light second flare do   do
   Light 3rd. flare.

OPERATION ORDERS
by
Lieut. Col., W. Lyle, Cmdg., 23rd. Battalion Northumberland Fusiliers.
B.E.F. 23/6/16.

1. The following moves will take place on night 23/24 June,
2. The 22nd. Northd. Fus. at present holding the line will be relieved by:
   (a) "C" Company, 18th. N.F. who will take over the crater area from INCH STREET inclusive to DUNFERMLINE STREET SOUTH inclusive.
   (b) 5 platoons of the 23rd. Northd. Fusiliers will take over the front and support lines from DUNFERMLINE STREET SOUTH exclusive to KEATS REDAN inclusive,
   (c) 5 platoons of the 20th. N.F. will hold from KEATS REDAN exclusive to ARGYLE STREET.
   (d) 5 platoons of the 21st. N.F. will be relieving portions of the 101st. Brigade south of the crater area.
3. Ref. para. 2(b) above:
   "D" Company and 1 platoon "A" Company under Capt. Whitehead will take over and hold this area; 2 platoons in the front line, 1 in REED STREET and 2 in ST ANDREW'S AVENUE.
4. The remainder of the Battalion will be distributed as under:-
   1 platoon "A" Company in TARA REDOUBT.
   "C" Company in the defence work in FIR WOOD (W.29.c &d.)
   "B" COmpany and Headquarters and 2 platoons "A" Company in SUNKEN GARDEN.
5. "D" Company and 2 platoons "A" Company will march by platoons at 5 minutes interval, the leading platoon leaving "D" Company billets at 11.40p.m.   off
   The rear platoon of "A" Company will branch/to TARA REDOUBT.
   Guides from the 22nd. N.F. will meet platoons at the Barrier commencing at 12 midnight.
6. Signallers for "D" Company and Headquarters under 2nd. Lieut. MacDonald and Lewis Gunners will take over at 6.0p.m.
7. On completion of the relief, O.C. "D" Company will wire the word "CATS" to Headquarters.
8. Lieut. Col., W. Lyle, will be in Command, of the line with Headquarters in ST MONAN'S STREET as before.
9. Major Burge will be in command of "B" & "C" Companies and ½ "A" Coy.
10. "B" and "C" Companies and Headquarters and 2 platoons "A" Company will move into their new positions at 9.0p.m., all moves to be completed by 10.0p.m. at latest, and to be reported present to present Battalion Headquarters.
11. O.C. Companies are responsible that all necessary equipment, S.A.A. 2 bombs per man, bombs for bomb buckets and waistcoats, yellow triangles, pins, picks, shovels, iron rations etc. are all correct and in possession of Companies. A report to this effect to be rendered by 4.0p.m.
12. O.C's "A" & "B" Companies are responsible that all stores etc, etc., required for the men in the SUNKEN GARDEN are stacked in the GROTTO by 4.0p.m.
13. Rations will be issued at the normal time and "D" Company and 2 platoons "A" Company will carry up the men's rations for the 24th. Inst.
14. The N.C.O's and men for "Smoke" Duties under Lieut. LEECH will report to him at 10.0p.m., and will live in TARA REDOUBT with the platoon of "A" Company.
15. Every mans pack, clearly labelled (excepting transport men) containing his bonnet, ground sheet and great coat and other surplus personal belongings will be stacked at the Divisional Store at BRASSERIE RUE CORBIE (E.4.a.2/8) not later than 6 p.m. O.C. Companies are responsible that this done and will render a report to that effect. Men on headquarters to stack packs with their Companies.
16. All Officers valises and company boxes etc. will be sent to Brigade Store at FRANVILLERS, and must be at Qr. Masters Stores by 3.30p.m. Each article to be clearly labelled by a wooden label.
    Coy. Orderly Room Boxes will be taken back to transport for storage at the same time.
17. The Mess Cart will visit each company Hd. Qrs at 9.p.m. to receive surplus mess stores.
18. The 5 new supernumerary officers will report to Transport Lines by 9.0 p.m. this evening and will remain there until further orders.

K.A.N. ANDERSON.

CAPTAIN AND ADJUTANT.

COPY NO. 6

SECRET.

102nd. (TYNESIDE SCOTTISH) BRIGADE.

Operation Order No. 34.

1. The following moves will take place on the night of the 23/24th. June.

2. Six Platoons of the 21st. N.F. (2nd. Tyneside Scottish) will take over and hold front line and support line from the junction of X.20.4. & X.20.5. to INCH STREET exclusive from the 101st. Brigade.

3. "C" Coy. 18th. N.F. (Pioneers). will take over and hold the crater area from INCH STREET inclusive to DUNFERMLINE ST. SOUTH, inclusive.

4. Five Platoons of the 23rd. N.F. (4th. Tyneside Scottish), will take over and hold the front and support line from DUNFERMLINE STREET SOUTH exclusive, to KEATS REDAN inclusive.

5. Five Platoons of the 20th. N.F. (1st. Tyneside Scottish) will take over and hold the front and support line from KEATS REDAN exclusive to ARGYLL STREET exclusive and be responsible for the defence of ELIE ST. and BRAY STREET, to PORT LOUIS exclusive, and RYECROFT STREET to ARGYLL ST. exclusive.

6. With the exception of the move of the five platoons of the 21st. N.F. (2nd. Tyneside Scottish), who relieve a corresponding portion of the 101st Inf. Bde. and the extension of the present line to ARGYLL ST. exclusive, all the above moves are to relieve the 22nd. N.F. (3rd. Tyneside Scottish)

7. The distribution at 4 am. on the morning of the 24th. will be as follows:-

   21st. N.F. (2nd. Tyneside Scottish), Six platoons holding the front and support line from the junction of X.20.4. - X.20.5. to INCH ST. exclusive. Battalion Headquarters and remainder at BRESLE.

8. C.Coy. 18th. N.F. (Pioneers) holding the Crater area.

9. 23rd. N.F. (4th. Tyneside Scottish).
   - 5 Platoons in the line.
   - 1 Platoon in TARA REDOUBT.
   - 4 Platoons in the defence work in FIR WOOD, W.29.c. and d.
   - 6 Platoons in SUNKEN GARDEN.

10. 20th. Northumberland Fsirs. (1st. Tyneside Scottish).
    - 5 Platoons in line.
    - 3 Platoons in USNA REDOUBT.
    - 4 SUNKEN GARDEN.
    - 4 Platoons and Battn H.Q. in USNA-TARA line North of W.24.b.5.1.

11. 102nd. Machine Gun Coy. in the line from DALHOUSIE ST. to BRAY ST. ALONG ST. ANDREWS AVENUE.

12. The O.C. 23rd. N.F. (4th. Tyneside Scottish) to take over command of the front system of trenches on completion of relief, and establish his Headquarters at the present Headquarters of the Battn. in the line - ST. MONANS STREET .

13. Guides from the 15th. ROYAL SCOTS will meet the incoming platoons of the 21st. N.F. (2nd. Tyneside Scottish) at BECOURT CHATEAU at 10 pm. on the 23rd. inst.

    Guides from the 22nd. N.F. (3rd. Tyneside Scottish) will meet the Platoons of the 20th. N.F. (1st. Tyneside Scottish) at 10 pm. at the BAPAUME BARRIER.

P.T.O.

Guides of the 22nd. N.F. (3rd. Tyneside Scottish) will meet the platoons of the 23rd. N.F. (4th. Tyneside Scottish) at 12 midnight, and "C" Coy 18th. N.F. (Pioneers) at 11 pm. at the BAPAUME BARRIER.

The 22nd. N.F. (3rd. Tyneside Scottish) on relief will proceed to BRESLE. The Billeting party will proceed to BRESLE tomorrow 23rd. inst. and will report to the TOWN MAJOR who will allot accomodation.

14. The special carrying parties, detailed in Operation Order 32, para 20 will proceed to SUNKEN GARDEN and will remain there till the night of W/X, when they will move up into the line, and report to LT. BOWKETT, Commanding 102nd. Light Trench Mortar Battery.
The Brigade Bombing Company will also proceed to the SUNKEN GARDEN and move into the line on W/X night, the O.C. 20th. and 21st. N.F. (1st. and 2nd. Tyneside Scottish), making the necessary accomodation for them.

15. Signallers will be relieved between the hours of 12 - 3 pm., Lewis Gunners between the hours of 3 - 6 pm. All further details to be
16. arranged by O.Cs. concerned.

17. Completion of relief to be reported to Brigade Headquarters by telegraphing the word "TYPE", and the hour on which relief was completed.

18. The Advanced Brigade Report Centre will be at W.24.b.5.1. from 7 pm on 23rd. inst.

19. On the night W/X the tails of all Battalions will close up and be EAST of the TARA-USNA line.

X20. 22nd. Northd. Fuslrs. (3rd. Tyneside Scottish) will move from BRESLE to SUNKEN GARDEN on W/X night and to the position in line on X/Y night.
No troops are to be quartered in the town of ALBERT after 9 pm. on the 23rd. inst. For this purpose the SUNKEN GARDEN is not included in the town of ALBERT.
Shelter to a limited extent will be provided under Divisional arrangements for troops in the SUNKEN GARDEN.

21. ACKNOWLEDGE.

23/7/13.

Major.
BRIGADE-MAJOR.
102nd. (TYNESIDE SCOTTISH) BRIGADE.

Issued at 6 a.m.

Copies to:-

1 & 2 Retained.
3. 20th. N.F. (1st. T.S.).
4. 21st. N.F. (2nd. T.S.).
5. 22nd. N.F. (3rd. T.S.).
6. 23rd. N.F. (4th. T.S.).
7. 34th. Division.
8. 102nd. T.M.Battery.
9. 102nd. M.G.Coy.
10. 102 Brigade Bombing Officer
11. 101st. Bde.
12. 103rd. Bde.
13. 23rd. Inf. Bde.
14. 18th. N.F. (Pioneers).
15. 208th. Field Coy. R.E.
16. 179th. Tunnelling Coy.
17. Left group R.F.A.
18. Signals.
19. Town Major, ALBERT.
20. 102 Bde. Transport Off.
21. War Diary.
22. Town Major, BRESLE.

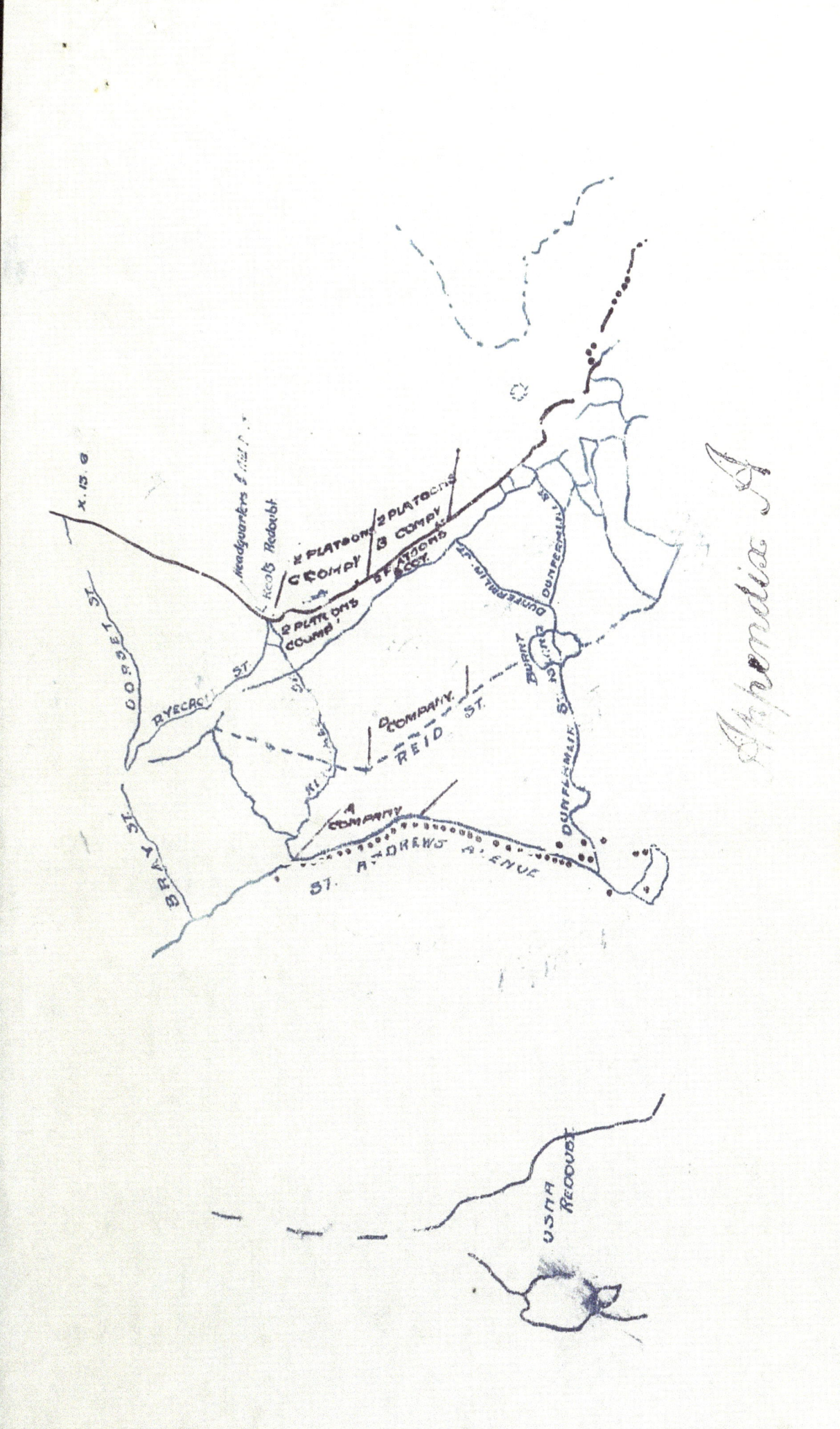

REF ALBERT - SHEET 1:40,000 (CORRECTED) Table 'A'.

			PLACE.	TIME.	Remarks
Relieving Companies of 20th N.F.	C/of 23rd N.F. & others	Destination on completion of relief.	Guides to meet 20th N.F. (two station guides, one each for Lewis Guns Detachments)		
D Coy. and 2 Platoons D Company.	A Coy. and 2 Platoons D Company.	A Coy. 2 Platoons USNA. 1 Platoon TRIH. 1 Platoon ALBERT. B Coy. and 2 Platoons Coln.	Beuvry	8.00 p.m.	6 Guides required, proceed via PERTH on lorry.
A Coy.		ALBERT.		9.00 p.m.	2 Guides required, leaving Bn.H.Q. PETIT MESNIL, to conduct relieving platoons. St Q. returns Platoons as before. Relieving 2 platoons rec'd tomorrow.
C Coy.		To be notified (ALBERT) later.	2 Guides at USNA Redoubt. 1 Guide at TRIH Redoubt. 1 Platoon BARRIER.	8.45 p.m. 9.05 p.m. 9.15 p.m.	4 Guides required. Pro-1 on 1 Coy. DIG at ANDREWS WAY.
D Coy. (in Reserve)		To be notified (ALBERT) later.	BARRIER.	9.30 p.m.	2 Guides to meet relieve the 2 Platoon at present in ALBERT D Coy. at present in garrison until A Coy 2 Platoons arrive.

Platoons of the incoming Battalion will march at 5 minute intervals. Two Redoubts will thus be occupied by one platoon until A Coy's Platoon arrives using Section will be to 2 Platoons short of its normal garrison until A Coy's 2 Platoons arrive.

APPENDIX "O"

Reference Map "D"

With the exceptions mentioned below no Artillery will fire West of:-

BLUE LINE after	0
PINK) YELLOW)	0.3 x
GREEN 8th. Division front	0.5
" 54th. " "	0.17
BROWN LINE after	0.30
Mauve LINE "	0.45
ORANGE LINE "	1.17
LIGHT BLUE "	1.35
CRIMSON	2.35

x A Barrage to be arranged by the G.R.A. will be retained on the enemy's front line on the front X.21.c.1.5. - X.20.b.7½.2 until 0.2, and on the enemy's support line on the front X.21.c.5.0. - X.21.a.2.0. until 0.5.

102nd Bde.
34th Div.

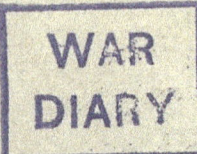

Brigade was temporarily transferred
to 37th Division 6th July -
Rejoined 34th Division 22nd August.

23rd BATTALION

NORTHUMBERLAND FUSILIERS

JULY 1916

54/02

23 North'd Fus

Army Form C. 2118

WAR DIARY
or
INTELLIGENCE SUMMARY
(Erase heading not required.)

July 1916   Vol 4

Place	Date	Hour	Summary of Events and Information	Remarks and references to Appendices
Trenches	July 1st		Z Day. The preliminary bombardment which had commenced on the 24th June and had continued throughout with varying intensity developed from 7 A.M. to 7.30 A.M. on this date to an immense bombardment concentrated on the German trenches. At 7.30 A.M. the hour previously decided upon to launch the attack, the Battn proceeded to carry out its allotted task in the general scheme which was as follows:— The 102nd Brigade had been given as their objective a position of the first system of German trenches with a frontage of 1400 yds from X.13.a to X.20.a. on which Battalions formed to attack LA BOISELLE from both flanks. "C" Company 18th Northd Fus: being detailed to remain and shell the British front line trenches immediately opposite LA BOISELLE SALIENT, for a distance of 450 yds. The 1st and 4th Battns Tyneside Scottish were detailed to attack from the left commencing with the trench running North from the ALBERT—BAPAUME road to the embankment in square X.14.a. and the 2nd and 3rd Battalions the German trenches on the right immediately S.E. of LA BOISELLE on a frontage of about 500 yds. At 7.30 A.M. the artillery barrage lifted and the 1st and 2nd Battns advanced left and right of LA BOISELLE respectively over our own front line trenches to attack.	Shet 57 D S.E.

7a

WAR DIARY or INTELLIGENCE SUMMARY

Army Form C. 2118

Place	Date	Hour	Summary of Events and Information	Remarks and references to Appendices
Trenches	July 1st		Each line advanced without the least hesitation, and through out seems "NO MANS LAND". The Battalion suffered very heavily indeed in all ranks. The losses principally being due to Machine gun fire. It was here that the following Officers lost their lives, namely; Lieut. Col. W. Lyle who was last seen alive with walking stick in hand, amongst his men about 200 yds from the German Trenches. Major M. Bruge who fell before he had gone many yards from our lines. Capt. J. G. Todd commanding B Coy who fell immediately he reached our wire. Capt. J. B. Buley commanding A Company was killed before he had gone 100 yds. Capt. H. A. Bolton, Lt. A. F. Shapley, Lt. S. Macdonald, Lt. J. M. Pattinson, 2nd Lt. L. Williams also fell mortally wounded before reaching the German line. In addition Lieut. W. B. Lytter who was reported to have reached the German Trenches and to have been seen there badly wounded, is now missing and believed killed. 2nd Lieut. R. Macdonald last seen wounded is now missing and believed killed. The German first line was taken and the second line was also reached but owing to the heavy casualties it was impossible to hold on to these lines. It parts of our men hung on for a time on to a portion of their first line trench a little to the North of the ALBERT-BAPAUME ROAD	SHEET 57.D S.E.

Army Form C. 2118

WAR DIARY
or
INTELLIGENCE SUMMARY
(Erase heading not required.)

Instructions regarding War Diaries and Intelligence Summaries are contained in F. S. Regs., Part II. and the Staff Manual respectively. Title Pages will be prepared in manuscript.

Place	Date	Hour	Summary of Events and Information	Remarks and references to Appendices
TRENCHES	July 1st		Two Platoons of "A" company. 4th Battn Tyneside Scottish were detached to support the Brigade Bombing Company which was detailed to clear the LA BOISELLE SALIENT. At 7.35 A.M. the 4th Battn: Tyneside Scottish and advanced from their positions in the trenches as follows:— FIRST LINE. 2 Platoons "B" Coy. on the Right. [Men extended to 2 Platoons "C" Coy on the Left. 2 Paces Interval] SECOND LINE. Remaining 2 Platoons "B" Coy on the Right. 150 YDS DISTANCE. Remaining 2 Platoons "C" Coy on the Left. THIRD LINE. 4 Platoons of "D" Company, at 150 yds distance. FOURTH LINE. Remaining 2 Platoons of "A" Company. At 150 yds distance. Each line immediately it advanced to and over the front line parapet came under a very heavy fire from the German Artillery and Machine Guns firing from the direction of OVILLERS and LA BOISELLE. Many casualties were at once incurred many men of our front line even being hit whilst getting over our front line parapet. Each Company was played over into "NO MANS LAND" by its fifers who continued to play until either killed or wounded.	SHEET 57D S.E

Army Form C. 2118

WAR DIARY
or
INTELLIGENCE SUMMARY

(*Erase heading not required.*)

Instructions regarding War Diaries and Intelligence Summaries are contained in F. S. Regs., Part II. and the Staff Manual respectively. Title Pages will be prepared in manuscript.

Place	Date	Hour	Summary of Events and Information	Remarks and references to Appendices
Trenches	July 1st		The Germans however launched a very strong counter attack against this party who fought gallantly, but every 1st Army greatly outnumbered were obliged to fall back and take cover in "NO MANS LAND" where they lay all day and waited ready to go forward again to with the next attacking force. It's struck came on and as no further attack was to be made that day these men under cover of darkness made their way back into our lines in an exhausted condition. Through the want of food and water and received there until the following morning. Many heroic deeds were performed during the day and though only about 100 came to special notice there were undoubtedly very many gallant deeds performed which will never come to light. Our Stretcher bearers were conspicuous by their daring in bringing in wounded men in daylight under fire. The dressing station and its trenches used were even congested with casualties and only by continual and very exhausting work by Capt. G.W. Muirhead and M.O and his staff were they able to gradually relieve this pressure which was not until the following day.	SHEET 57D.S.E
	July 2		At 9 o'clock in the morning after all the men in the Battn had been collected they were formed up behind the USNA-TARA line for a roll call to be taken and only about 100 men answered their names. During the course of the day about 20 men were sent out day into its rest until the evening when they were formed up into parties for carrying

Army Form C. 2118

WAR DIARY
or
INTELLIGENCE SUMMARY
(Erase heading not required.)

Instructions regarding War Diaries and Intelligence Summaries are contained in F. S. Regs., Part II. and the Staff Manual respectively. Title Pages will be prepared in manuscript.

Place	Date	Hour	Summary of Events and Information	Remarks and references to Appendices
Trenches	July 2		rations and ammunition to our attacking troops. The only two officers who turned up for Roll Call were 2/Lieut Graham and 2/Lieut L Daggett who were very exhausted and had had a most harrowing time, from them it was learnt of the gallant and unflinching way in which all our Officers, N.C.Os and men went over in this great attack without the slightest hesitation and men went on the bombardment increased co-operating with the infantry on to our enemy's advance but we continued no further and moved on no further attack and advance but we continued no further conversation. Major MacIntosh and Capt. Whitehead were seen by a few Officers being carried out and although badly wounded were in excellent spirits and both expressed the wish to be back with the Battalion again soon. The Brigadier was delighted with the fine performance and bravery shown by the Batt'n.	
	July 3		About 10 o'clock in the morning a bombing party under Capt Templeman assisted by Capt Cadell & 2/Lieut Collings went into LO BOISELLE they took Cherry to join up the Right of our Battalion with the flank of the next Batt'n on the Right a distance of about 500 yds. No opposition was encountered and the connection was established when the party returned having suffered no casualties.	
	July 4		The Batt'n was formed up in the morning about 10 o'clock and marched off to billets in MILLENCOURT.	

Army Form C. 2118

WAR DIARY
or
INTELLIGENCE SUMMARY
(Erase heading not required.)

Instructions regarding War Diaries and Intelligence Summaries are contained in F.S. Regs., Part II. and the Staff Manual respectively. Title Pages will be prepared in manuscript.

Place	Date	Hour	Summary of Events and Information	Remarks and references to Appendices
MILLENCOURT	July 5"	11 A.M.	The Battalion paraded with the remaining Battalions of the Brigade and were inspected by Gen. Tonkins and Gen. Ingouville Williams and Staff who congratulated the Brigade upon their magnificent conduct and gallant attack on LA BOISELLE.	
	July 6"	3 P.M.	The Battalion left MILLENCOURT in buses and proceeded to billets in LA CAUCHIE arriving shortly after midnight.	
LA CAUCHIE	July 7"		Maj. C.P. Pask. Second in Command of the 18" (Pioneer) Batt. N.F. took over command of the Batt. from Capt. Longhurst and the work of reorganization was commenced. In the evening Lt. Hamman and a party of 90 men formed a carrying party for "Pat Props" to the front line at BIENVILLERS.	
	July 8"		The work of reorganization was continued, the appointment of different officers to take command of Companies was as follows:- 249th. Dagget A.Co. — 212th. Morris B.Co. — Capt. T.B. Coull C.Co. — 2nd Lt. Collips D.Co. The the afternoon the following officers went to the trenches at HENNECAMP to go over the line with a view to taking over at some early date, Capt. Longhurst, Capt. Coull, 2nd.Lt. Collips.	
	July 9"		Every man in the Battalion was Bathed and were also put through handling of arms and Bombing and cleaning up generally from special attention to the equipment which had suffered during the advance with the rain and mud, many were fitted with new uniforms.	

Army Form C. 2118

WAR DIARY
or
INTELLIGENCE SUMMARY
(Erase heading not required.)

Instructions regarding War Diaries and Intelligence Summaries are contained in F. S. Regs., Part II. and the Staff Manual respectively. Title Pages will be prepared in manuscript.

Place	Date	Hour	Summary of Events and Information	Remarks and references to Appendices
LA CAUCHIE	July 10th		Received word about the Brigade moving and Lt. Hearn was detailed to proceed to WARINCOURT to take up duties as Town Major but returned in the evening, many Officers and men are away on different courses Machine Gun, Bombing, Signalling etc. Packing up and preparations for the move were commenced.	
	July 11th		The Battalion left billets about 8. P.M. with all transport and marched to WARINCOURT where they are billeted in canvas huts.	
WARINCOURT	July 12th		All men were bathed and training of all specialists was proceeded with at Regimental bombers were opened and greatly appreciated. Word was received from the Brigade that both 3rd and 4th Battalions were going to be inspected the following morning at 12 o'clock by our new Divisional General, Lieut. General Count Gleichen D.S.O. etc. Inspection was postponed till 3.30 in the afternoon when the two Battalions were formed up together with transport and were inspected.	
	July 14th		The Battalion moved from parade ground at 4.15 P.M. to billets at BEAUFORT a distance of about nine miles, the billets were good and no men fell out on the march.	
BEAUFORT	July 15th		The Battalion paraded and moved off at 9. A.M. and proceeded to VILLERS BRULIN covering those by 1. P.M. without any men falling out & were able to rejoin.	
VILLERS BRULIN	July 16th		The Battalion paraded & moved off at 9. A.M. and marched to DIVION and distance of about twelve miles, only one man fell out who was brought on by the ambulance.	
DIVION	July 17th		Medical inspection was held and a programme of work was commenced including Physical Drill, Bombing, Machine Gun and Handling of arms. All men were bathed.	

1875 Wt: W593/826 1,000,000 4/15 J.B.C. & A. A.D.S.S./Forms/C. 2118.

WAR DIARY or INTELLIGENCE SUMMARY

Army Form C. 2118

Place	Date	Hour	Summary of Events and Information	Remarks and references to Appendices
DIVION	July 18th		The work of refitting etc was proceeded with and the programme of work was gone on with. The County reported to the Battalion and was posted to "B" Co. at end of Howard has been awarded to C.S.M. F. HOLT for gallant conduct in the Field July 1st	
	July 19th		Programme of training proceeded. The following have been awarded the Military Medal for gallant conduct in the Field July 1st 2/Lt 7/106 L/Sgt. R. DAVISON. "C" Co. 2/3 572 Pvt. C. MADDISON. "C" Co. 2/3 965 Pvt. A. A. BELL "A" Co. 2/3 341 Pvt. S. GIBSON. "D" Co.	
	July 20th		Training continued, all gas helmets were withdrawn from the men. Information was received from Brigade Headquarters that the G.O.C. 1st Army would inspect the Brigade on Saturday 22nd inst:	
	July 21st		A C.O.'s inspection was held prior to the inspection on the following day and faults that were found were remedied.	
	July 22nd		The morning was devoted to preparing for the inspection. The Battalion paraded at 1.40.p.m. and marched off to the inspection ground, where the G.O.C. 1st Army addressed the Brigade and presented the Ribbons to the Officers & O.R. for deeds of valour performed on July 1st. The Battalion Transport was inspected by the Brigadier in the morning in our own Transport Field.	
	July 23rd		Church services were held in the morning. The sad news of the death of our late Divisional General was reported and parties were arranged to go to the funeral but unfortunately no buses could be arranged to take the parties	

WAR DIARY or INTELLIGENCE SUMMARY

Army Form C. 2118

Place	Date	Hour	Summary of Events and Information	Remarks and references to Appendices
DIVION	July 24th		The training and programme of work was continued. Official order was received as follows:- The Brigadier announces to the Brigade with profound regret that their former gallant chief, Major-General C.E. Pereville Williams C.B., D.S.O., 34th Division was yesterday killed in action.	
	July 25th		At 7. P.M. this morning the following Officers C.O., Capt. Longhurst, Capt. Coull, 2nd Lt. Baggett, and Lt. Cowman left on buses together with other officers from the other Battalions to go round and take over the line of trenches held by the 21st Battalion London Regiment and 24th Batt. London Regiment situated about two miles east of CARENCY, map reference:- from S.2. B.3. 6 to S.14. B.8.4. all Partichers were taken over and arrangements for the relief settled and a thorough tour of the line made, the party returned by bus arriving back to DIVION about 7. P.M. During the day a draft had arrived from the base of 109 men. The Battalion paraded and the 23rd Battalion was handed over to Major Porch who was to command the two Battalions while in the trenches forming the two sub Composite Battalions. The Brigade moved into reserve billets at arriving at MESNIL BOUCHÉ about 2. P.M. another draft of 175 arrived from the base.	36 S.W. 3. 1/10000 1.45 P.M.
MESNIL BOUCHÉ	July 27th		The Composite Battalion left the reserve billets at 6 P.M. and proceeded via VIQUERS AU BOIS to the trenches and the relief was completed by 12. ℗ midnight.	

Army Form C. 2118

WAR DIARY
or
INTELLIGENCE SUMMARY
(Erase heading not required.)

Instructions regarding War Diaries and Intelligence Summaries are contained in F. S. Regs., Part II. and the Staff Manual respectively. Title Pages will be prepared in manuscript.

Place	Date	Hour	Summary of Events and Information	Remarks and references to Appendices
MESNIL BOUCHE	July 27th		The Sector as already stated was sub-divided into three. On the Right a Lowhowitz Battalion commanded by Major Farquhar Cunningham of Tyneside Scottish composed of 1st & 2nd Battalions took over from ERSATZ ALLEY to ARNO. The 3rd & 4th Battalions under command of Major E.P. Porch from ARNO to ROBINEAU being the Centre Battalion and a Lowhowitz Battalion consisting of two battalions of the Tyneside Irish from ROBINEAU to the left of the sector, forming the left battalion. The relief was completed without any casualties. A draft of 45 from the base arrived and handed to OC Details.	
TRENCHES	July 28th		Very quiet day nothing of any importance occured, the weather being very fine and warm. The trenches were visited by the Brigadier in the morning. Casualties: Nil.	
	July 29th		Beyond a certain amount of sniping from the craters, the enemy are very quiet. The weather continues to remain warm and fine which is fortunate. Casualties: Nil.	
	July 30th		In many bad repair and require a lot of attention. General Count Gleichen inspected the trenches and visited the whole sector. In the evening one of our men was wounded in the hand by a piece of our own shell which fell short.	
	July 31st		Sniping by the enemy continues otherwise everything very quiet and the work of repairing the trenches is got on with. 4 to 5 crew drafts of men have worked very well. Casualties: Nil.	

[signature]

WAR DIARY
or
INTELLIGENCE SUMMARY
(Erase heading not required.)

Army Form C. 2118

Instructions regarding War Diaries and Intelligence Summaries are contained in F.S. Regs., Part II. and the Staff Manual respectively. Title Pages will be prepared in manuscript.

Place	Date	Hour	Summary of Events and Information	Remarks and references to Appendices
Senlis	July 1		machine gun ammunition &c were returned through our advancing troops. The 2 Lewis guns who turned up for Roll call were at first down and 1/0 NCOs had returned and had not a single horsefor form. I am there it is now & serious of the gallant and insubordinate way in which the 2 new Lewis NCOs and men went over the parapet without the slightest hesitation, and urging the bombardment movement supporting and the infantry on. Another amongst the bombardment salvoes did not accomplish any further advance. Very heavy attacks and Capt. McCleod was severely wounded by a British shell which was carried by British shell on our side. The Brigadier was antecedent not to lose his Battalion in any more unless ordered by the Bde.	
	July 3		About 10 o'clock in the morning a bombing party under Lieut Leyshon assisted by Capt Croal + 2 /Lt Othrig went into the trench & the Germans lost no time in getting away. We found about 14 dead in the next Bosh on the Right in advance & about 500 yds. The operation was unresisted and the remainder rejoined our numbers.	
	July 4		The Battn was formed up in the morning about 10 o'clock and marched off to billets in MILLENCOURT.	

Army Form C. 2118

WAR DIARY
or
INTELLIGENCE SUMMARY
(Erase heading not required.)

Instructions regarding War Diaries and Intelligence Summaries are contained in F.S. Regs., Part II. and the Staff Manual respectively. Title Pages will be prepared in manuscript.

Place	Date	Hour	Summary of Events and Information	Remarks and references to Appendices
MILLENCOURT	July 5	11 P.M.	The Battalion paraded with the remaining Portion of the Brigade and were inspected by Gen. Rawlinson and Sir Hy. Rawlinson and Sir Hubert Gough who congratulated the Brigade upon their magnificent and gallant assault on LA BOISELLE.	
	July 6	3 P.M.	The Battalion left MILLENCOURT on buses and proceeded to billets in LA CRUCHIE arriving shortly after midnight.	
LA CRUCHIE	July 7		Major E.P. Roch-Grant assumed command of the 13th (Reserve) R.W.F. but was removed of the battn. frequent daylight and the work of reorganization was commenced. In the evening the townsmen and a party of men found a working party for "Pont Rouge" S.E. of DRANVILLERS.	
	July 8		The work of reorganization was continued, the appointment of Company officers to Coys. remained of Companies was as follows :- 2nd Lt. Deggett A.Co. - 2nd Lt. Elborn B.Co. - Capt T.B. Coull C.Co. - 2nd Lt. Woolrep D.Co. In the afternoon the following officers went to the trenches at HENNECAMP to go over the line with a view to taking over at once, each Capt. left together with Coll: in Comd; at once on the Battalion was bussed up that night, thinking of excess that suffered during the advance with the guns and west, many were fitted with new uniforms.	
	July 9			

1875 Wt. W593/826 1,000,000 4/15 J.B.C. & A.   A.D.S.S./Forms/C. 2118.

WAR DIARY or INTELLIGENCE SUMMARY

(Erase heading not required.)

Army Form C. 2118

Instructions regarding War Diaries and Intelligence Summaries are contained in F.S. Regs., Part II. and the Staff Manual respectively. Title Pages will be prepared in manuscript.

Place	Date	Hour	Summary of Events and Information	Remarks and references to Appendices
LA CAUCHIE	July 10th		Received word about the Brigade moving and Tn. Hdqrs was ordered to proceed to WARINCOURT to take up duties as Town Major but returned in the evening. Many Officers and men were away on different courses etc. when the men were somewhat irregular. Packing up and preparations for the march were commenced.	
	July 11th		The Battalion left billets about 6 P.M. with all transport and marched to WARINCOURT where they are billeted in canvas huts.	
WARINCOURT	July 12th		The town was bathed and consisted of all theoretical and practical use of Regimental duties were opened and greatly appreciated. Word was received from the Brigade that Batt. 23rd of the Battalion was going to be inspected the following morning at 12 o'clock by our new General General together found Lieut. Fletcher D.S.O. &c. Inspection was performed till 3.30 in the afternoon when the two Battalions were formed up together with transport and were inspected.	
	July 13th		The Battalion moved from parade ground at 4.15 P.M. to billets at BEAUFORT, a distance of about nine miles. The billets were good and were full up on the arrival.	
BEAUFORT	July 14th		The Battalion paraded and moved off at 9 A.M. and proceeded to VILLERS BRULIN, arrived there by 1 P.M. without any one falling out except one B.E. Engineer.	
VILLERS BRULIN	July 15th		The Battalion paraded in march off at 9 P.M. and marched to Division.	
	July 16th		About twelve miles, only one man fell out who was brought on by the ambulance.	
Division	July 17th		Medical Inspection was held and a programme of work was commenced including Physical Drill, Bayonet attacks &c. and Monday of town billets were batted.	

102nd BRIGADE
ATTACHED 37th DIVISION till 21.8.16.
34th DIVISION from 22.8.16.

1/23rd BATTALION

NORTHUMBERLAND FUSILIERS.

AUGUST 1 9 1 6

Volume VIII   37 Division

WAR DIARY
INTELLIGENCE SUMMARY
(Erase heading not required.)

Army Form C. 2118

23rd Lt Tyneside Scottish Q
Aug 1916

Place	Date	Hour	Summary of Events and Information	Remarks and references to Appendices
TRENCHES	Aug 1st		The sector under the command of Lt. Col. Porch was visited by the C.O. and Company Commander of 1st Tyneside Irish in view of their taking the sector ~~over~~ on the following afternoon. "A" Company had one man killed through standing up in a sap, otherwise everything was quiet. Casualties 1.O.R. killed	30 B.S.G.
"	Aug 2nd		The relief took place during the afternoon without a casualty. A & D. Coys. going into the BAJOLLE LINE and C. & B. Coys. into Cellars at CARENCY	Casualties 1 O.R. Killed
RESERVE TRENCHES DALYS	Aug 3rd		the Headquarters were at DALYS near HOSPITAL CORNER. Slight shelling near CARENCY and beyond Batt. H.Q. otherwise very quiet, about 270 O.R. and six officers were out on working parties.	Casualties NIL Casualties 1.O.R. Killed
"	Aug 4th		More shelling round Batt. H.Q. and working parties continue. All the Officers at VILLERS AU BOIS joined their respective Companies. Lt. Kearby returned to "B" Company. Lt. Thompson assumed command of "B" Company.	Casualties 3 O.R.S. 1 O.R. Wounded
	Aug 5th		Some shelling around Batt. H.Q. and Hospital Corner. It lorry was started on from Major for future trenches in the followers of Capt. +C Arnold, who is posted to the command of D Co. 1 O.R. casualty moving nightly.	Casualties NIL Casualties 1.O.R. Wounded 2.O.R. Killed
	Aug 6th		30 H.E. shells fell around H. Qs. and hospital lines during the morning without trouble.	

1875. Wt. W.593/826 1,000,000 4/15 J.B.C. & A. A.D.S.S./Forms/C. 2118.

WAR DIARY or INTELLIGENCE SUMMARY

Army Form C. 2118

(Erase heading not required.)

Instructions regarding War Diaries and Intelligence Summaries are contained in F.S. Regs., Part II. and the Staff Manual respectively. Title Pages will be prepared in manuscript.

Place	Date	Hour	Summary of Events and Information	Remarks and references to Appendices
	Aug 7		Army very strong. 2/Lt McIntosh was appointed Intelligence Officer vice Commr. Naval working parties at night. Casualties 2 O.R. Sick	2/N.F S.E.
RESERVE TRENCHES			Received a draft of 54 O.R (all Northern Cyclist Battn.). The Batt. was to be relieved by the 25/26th Batt. N'ldr Fus. in the evening — we however had to send in two Cos B+C of the 22nd N.F. B+C + D into the line in the left sector and Lt.Col. Iceton with the 22nd N.F. B+C A+D into the line in the left sector and Lt.Col. Iceton with VILLERS au BOIS. Companies after returning from working parties proceeded to Billets in VILLERS au BOIS. Relief complete 2.30 p.m. CASUALTIES 1 O.R. Sick	2/N.F
VILLERS AU BOIS.	Aug 8		Received another draft of men. 40 in number all privates. These were posted to A.B.C+D Cos. The Company of the 24/27 N.F. in the left sub-sector of CARENCY II got another Coy. of our Battalion took over from this company "Grants" and had to be relieved. C div. of our Battalion took over from this company on Company out the relief the last platoon of "C" Co. came under some shelling and one man was killed and two wounded.	Casualties 1 O.R Killed 2 O.R. Wounded 2/N.F.
	Aug 9		Weather still continues warm and fine. Companies in line are going on alright. B Co. commenced strengthening the company. Men were all at Baths during the day. Everything quiet. Casualties NIL	2/N.F.
	Aug 10		Company training during day (B) and for about ¼hr March. Word received that 2nd Lt. N.F. in CARENCY III Section in under guard and went relieving. B Coy came detailed to go into that Section in support. All four companies are now	2/N.F.

Army Form C. 2118

WAR DIARY or INTELLIGENCE SUMMARY
(Erase heading not required.)

Instructions regarding War Diaries and Intelligence Summaries are contained in F.S. Regs., Part II. and the Staff Manual respectively. Title Pages will be prepared in manuscript.

Place	Date	Hour	Summary of Events and Information	Remarks and references to Appendices
In the line. AU BOIS.	Aug. 11.		Only Batt. HQrs and several detached men on Curries are now in VILLERS AU BOIS. Weather continues warm and fine. Casualties 1 O.R. Wounded.	36 B S.E
	Aug. 12.	4 P.M.	The only occurrence of any note was a small "Strafe" by the Germans with minenwerfer on the front occupied by "C" Coy. The front line trench was knocked in over a few of the new men shelters a little and slightly wounded. When the whole thing was over the new men are behaving splendidly. Casualties 1 O.R. Wounded.	
			The C.O. and Adjt. visited the Companies in the line. Everyone going on quite well. The new men are quite happy now. Our Artillery gave a small 'Strafe' and the Germans replied with "Minenwerfers" which did very little damage. Operation Orders received for relief of Bde by 27th Bde. Casualties 5 O.R. Wounded.	
	Aug. 13.		Orders issued to Companies for move from Trenches into Billets in ESTREE COUCHIE on the 14th inst. Very quiet during day. Weather very warm. Casualties. 1 O.R. Killed.	
	Aug. 14.		Companies sent Advance Parties out to new Billets about noon. The Field Kitchens were brought to the Camp formed in VILLERS AU BOIS and they performed Teas for the men when they arrived from the trenches. "B" Company arrived first about 9.40 P.M. and after resting about half an hour marched off to Billets in ESTREE COUCHIE. "A D" Company arrived together and after having tea left about 3.15 A.M. C Company were very late owing to stoppages on Communication trench and did not arrive until	

Army Form C. 2118

WAR DIARY
or
INTELLIGENCE SUMMARY
(Erase heading not required.)

Instructions regarding War Diaries and Intelligence Summaries are contained in F.S. Regs., Part II. and the Staff Manual respectively. Title Pages will be prepared in manuscript.

Place	Date	Hour	Summary of Events and Information	Remarks and references to Appendices
ESTRÉE CRUCHIE	Aug 15th	6.15 A.M.	Billets mended. The men marched very well considering the number of days they had in the trenches. No one fell out. Casualties 1 Sick. (O.R.)	Adj. Sick. 36 B.S.E.
		5 P.M.	The Battalion paraded at 5 P.M. and marched off to Billets in FRÉVILLERS arriving there about 9.15 P.M. No one fell out. Billets are fairly good, several requiring attention. Casualties 1 O.R. killed.	
FRÉVILLERS	Aug 16th		The C.O. met all Officers at Head Quarters at 10 A.M. and discussed generally the organisation and training of the Battalion. Company parade grounds were fixed upon. Instructors for Company were sent to Bde. H.Qts at FRESNI-COURT at 2.30 P.M. on BOMBING, SIGNALLING, LEWIS GUN & TRENCH MORTAR duties. Casualties NIL	
	Aug 17th		Sent 4 Officers and 160 O.R. to Bde. H.Qt. for demo. Also sent a working party consisting of 2 Officers and 25 O.R. to COVIGNY FARM for special digging. This party marched to 24th North'd. Fus. for rations. Companies were paraded under Company arrangements on own Parade grounds. Casualties 2 O.R. Sick.	
	Aug 18th		The 4 Officers sent to Bde. H.Qts on Consolidation work returned in order to enable the Batt. to carry out another working party of 3 Officers and 75 other ranks for digging at COVIGNY FARM. Remainder of Companies busy on Infantry training. Casualties 1 Officer Sick.	

Army Form C. 2118

WAR DIARY
or
INTELLIGENCE SUMMARY
(Erase heading not required.)

Instructions regarding War Diaries and Intelligence Summaries are contained in F. S. Regs., Part II. and the Staff Manual respectively. Title Pages will be prepared in manuscript.

Place	Date	Hour	Summary of Events and Information	Remarks and references to Appendices
FREVILLERS	Aug. 19th	6 P.M.	Working Party sent to CUVIGNY FM. This party reports at 10 P.M. and leaves at 6 P.M. Companies on ordinary training etc.	Casualties I.O.R. Sick
	Aug 20		Demonstrations furnished for Church Services in Morning. The C.O. saw Brigadier Commander at Bath. He O.K'd in the afternoon and discussed programme of Training. Received notification from Brigade that Lieut (Act. Captain) R.F.N. Anderson and Lieut. J.S. Nelson had been awarded the Military Crosses. Also that 28/462 Pte. D.W. Shanks, 23/1639 Pte. A.S. Rolfe, 23/1444 L/Cpl. A. Butterwell, 23/445 Pte. J. Martin, 23/759 Cpl. A. Mortledge, 25/432 Pte. W. Nuttall had been awarded the Military Medal. Sent more men away on courses. Programme of training for the following week and ammunition as copy of brigade	
	Aug 21st		Working parties at CUVIGNY FM cancelled and all men recalled. Received operation orders from Bde No. 69. The Battalion is to be attached to the 9th division for marching and carrying parties and will be billeted in the CHATEAU de la HAIE, Companies as follows. 2 Companies BOIS de la HAIE, 1 Company VILLERS AU BOIS. 1 Battalion BAJOLLE LINE. Advance parties were to be sent to their respective places by 12 NOON — orderly received orders to cancell operation order No 69 and prepare to move to 34th Division. Further advance parties and compacting parties off and preparing to move. A party of	Casualties 10 P.S. Sick 8 P.M.

WAR DIARY
or
INTELLIGENCE SUMMARY
(Erase heading not required)

Army Form...

Instructions regarding War Diaries and Intelligence Summaries are contained in F.S. Regs., Part II. and the Staff Manual respectively. Title Pages will be prepared in manuscript.

Place	Date	Hour	Summary of Events and Information	Remarks and references to Appendices
FREVILLERS	Aug 21		The transport moved off at 10 P.M. to HOUDAIN and joined other portions of the Brigade transport which proceeded by road under the Bde Transport Officer to ERQUINGHEM AREA ARMENTIERES. Baggage wagons were sent to join 39 DIVSL train. The Battalion & its contents at BERLIN at 10 P.M. the morning	JGn
	Aug 22		orders changed for the entraining of Battalion — they will now entrain at CALONNE RICOUART at 10.57 A.M. The remainder of the transport and all Horses left FREVILLERS at 6 A.M. and proceeded to where they entrained. The Battalion paraded at 6.30 A.M. and marched to station where entrained with the 3rd Tyneside Scottish. (22" N.F.). There was plenty of accommodation in the train. Detrained at LA GORGUE and were met with Staff entrained with the	CASUALTIES NIL
ERQUINGHEM.	Aug 23		Buses which conveyed the Battalion to ERQUINGHEM. All the Officers and men with the exception of Head Quarters were billetted in Laundries. Good accommodation then men all at baths during day. Operation orders received to proceed to billets in	Ref Sheet 36 N.W. EDIT. 6. B. Casualties NIL JGn
RUE MARLE	Aug 24		RUE MARLE — ae ae eae (D) Battalion in Bde. reserve. The Battn paraded at 8.30 P.M. and marched off to new billets by Companies. 2nd Lt. H.N. Foley reported for duty with Battn and was posted to D Co. Companies cleaned up billets and commenced with Company training.	Casualties 3 O.R. Sick JGn Casualties

WAR DIARY or INTELLIGENCE SUMMARY

Army Form C. 2118

(Erase heading not required.)

Instructions regarding War Diaries and Intelligence Summaries are contained in F.S. Regs., Part II. and the Staff Manual respectively. Title Pages will be prepared in manuscript.

Place	Date	Hour	Summary of Events and Information	Remarks and references to Appendices
RUE MARLE	Aug. 25th		Sent 8 men to DIV¹ H⁴ Qtrs for duty with pigeons. M.O. inspected all men of A & B Coys for "Scabies". A heart Medical assembled at Batt⁴ H⁴ Qtrs at 11 A.M. detg 5 of our men. Specialists paraded under reserve officers and carried on with training. Reserve coys for working parties for the following morning —	Ref Sheet 36 N.W. sheet 6B
	Aug 26th		Consisting of 2 Officers & 100 O.R. B&C Coys. Casualties NIL. Sent 50 O.R. H Qtrs and for working parties. Sent working parties off in morning. A & D Cos paraded for training under Coy Commanders. C & D Coys were inspected by M.O. for "Scabies etc". The Batt⁴ Bombing Platoon was assembled and commenced training under Batt⁴ Bombing Officer. B & C bombers each sent 1 Off and 50 O.R. in working parties in the evening. Casualties 1. O.R. Sick.	S.A.A.
	Aug 27th		Denominations paraded for various Church Parades. A & D Cos each sent 1 Officer & 50 O.R. on working parties. Sent two "odd men to be permanently attached to the R.E. for work in communication trenches. Casualties 1. O.R. Sick	S.A.A.
	Aug 28th		A & D Cos sent usual working parties in the morning. B & C Cos sent 1 Off & 40 O.R. each for work in the evening; also 1 Off and 15.O.R. each for a special party. Received instructions to Conference when to proceed to & fall in in case of an alarm. Casualties 4 O.R. Sick	S/L

Army Form C. 2118

WAR DIARY
or
INTELLIGENCE SUMMARY
(Erase heading not required.)

Instructions regarding War Diaries and Intelligence Summaries are contained in F. S. Regs., Part II. and the Staff Manual respectively. Title Pages will be prepared in manuscript.

Place	Date	Hour	Summary of Events and Information	Remarks and references to Appendices
RUE MARLE	Aug. 29		Manual workings in the morning for B+D bns in the trenches. Supplied working party of 1 Off. + 25 O.R. each for work near Bath. Wr Qrs. A court martial assembled at Bn. Hd Qrs. to try several men of the 3rd Tyneside Scottish (22nd N.F.). Major S.R. Macintosh was gazetted as 2nd in Command of the Battalion. Working party of 1 Off. + 30 O.R. in the evening for T.M. Battery. Rainy weather. Casualties 2. O.R. Sick 8/M	
	Aug. 30		A+D Cos on working parties. Very rainy day. The C.O. met all Company officers at Bath Wr Qrs. and discussed all points orders and orders to also speaker orders for the relief in the following day. B+ C. Cos supplied a small working party in the evening. Casualties 2. O.R. Sick 5/M	
	Aug. 31		Fine weather today. All the remaining men of Battalion who had marched to huts were sent during the morning and afternoon. The C.O. visited trenches in the morning & our a/c. 20th N.F. and to discuss details regarding relief. Signals, Observers, Snipers and Lewis gunners paraded at 2.15 P.M. and proceeded to trenches where the took over from the 20th N.F. Companies paraded at 8.0 P.M. and proceeded to trenches in order A. B. D. C. and took over from the 20th Northd Fus. in B. D. Sectrs of the Line. The Battalion is now "B" Batln. Relief complete at 11 P.M. B. D. + C. Cos just had 1 Casualty. One is Sick. After the relief at noon & working front. Casualties 3. O.R. Sick 5/M Wounded	

C.M. Ritch. Lt. Col.
Comdg. R 3rd Northd Fus.

WAR DIARY or INTELLIGENCE SUMMARY

Army Form C. 2118

23rd Bn. (Scottish) Tyneside Scottish

Instructions regarding War Diaries and Intelligence Summaries are contained in F.S. Regs., Part II. and the Staff Manual respectively. Title Pages will be prepared in manuscript.

(Erase heading not required.)

Place	Date	Hour	Summary of Events and Information	Remarks and references to Appendices
TRENCHES	Sept 1st 1916		The enemy sent over a good number of 5.9 shells and French Mortars into the sectors held by B & D Cos. A little damage was done and our two casualties occurred. The line is held in the "Picket" System. A, B & D Cos holding three defended fortunes. The undefended portions between each Company are in a bad state of repair. Patrols have been placed in these areas. The forts held by D Co. that in the Salient near CHARDS FARM. C Company one on Reserve on the S.S. Line and one meant for French Mortars. C Company one on Reserve on the S.S. Line and one meant for working and carrying parties. One platoon of C Co. is attached to D Co. and in close support at CHARDS FARM. D Co. is in the line with the exception of in close support. D Co. have 3 platoons in firing line & 1 Platoon in close support. Nothing unusual occurred during the day. Companies were busy repairing trenches etc. Patrols are sent out each night and every fortune. Casualties 3 O.R. wounded	Map Sheet BOIS GRENIER 36. N.W. Sect. 6
	Sept 2nd		Quiet day. Mutual artillery activity. Working and Wiring Parties at night — also Patrols. Nothing unusual occurred. Casualties 2 O.R. Wounded 1 O.R. Sick	
	Sept 3rd		The Undefended portions of the line have to be cleaned of obstruction and occupied. The men are carried on with and temporary saddled with frontage and given up. Rations are counted each night now by the Battalion occupying the Battalion line. Casualties 1 O.R. wounded 1 O.R. Sick	

WAR DIARY or INTELLIGENCE SUMMARY

Army Form C. 2118

Place	Date	Hour	Summary of Events and Information	Remarks and references to Appendices
TRENCHES.	Sept. 6th to 7th.		Usual mortar activity. Nothing of special note occurred. A great deal of work is being done and patrols sent out every night. Sent two officers Casualties: 4th N.I.L. 5th 2 O.R. wounded, 6th N.I.L. 7th 2 O.R. Sick. On the night of the 6th/7th we were relieved by the 20th M.F. great relief.	
RUE MORIE BRETA 11th	Sept. 7th to 11th.		On completion of relief A Coy. went to Subsidiary Line, B Coy. into Billets in Rue Morie. C Coy. into SPRING POST and LOVESEE Sectn. D Coy. into the garrisons of LILLE POST. During the period out of the trenches all the men were up the baths. Courses of instruction in the New Sound Bore. Responsibilities were given to Officers & N.C.O's for keeping also M.O. and Q.M. in Command. Working parties were supplied each day. In the nights of the 11th/12th 2/Lt Cutts who was in charge of a working party was shot through the heart by a stray bullet. He was buried the following day at ERQUINGHEM Company burying. CHURCH H.4.d.30.8.5. (Sheet 36 N.W. Part 6 c.). Casualties 8th N.I.L. 9th 2 O.R. Sqnd. mine tannan during period of "rest". Killed 11th 1 Officer (2/Lt Cutts) Killed, 10 R Sick. 10th 1 O.R. Bne. 11th 1 O.R. 10th (2/Lt Cutts) Killed, 10 R Sick.	
TRENCHES.	Sept. 12th to 15th.		On the night of the 12th 12/ 11.30 we took over the same sectn. of the trenches from the 20th N.F. Artillery fairly quiet all day. Some Patrols are sent out every night. Slow shelling the day and Patrol are out every nights. A good amount of	

Army Form C. 2118

WAR DIARY
or
INTELLIGENCE SUMMARY
(Erase heading not required.)

Instructions regarding War Diaries and Intelligence Summaries are contained in F.S. Regs., Part II. and the Staff Manual respectively. Title Pages will be prepared in manuscript.

Place	Date	Hour	Summary of Events and Information	Remarks and references to Appendices
TRENCHES	12th 13th 14th Sept. 19th		went on alive front out every night. Recontg. 12th NIL. #3rd 2.O.R. Sick. 14th NIL. 15th I.O.R. Sick. No. 2.O.R. wounded. 1.O.R. Sick. 17th I.O.R. wounded. 18th NIL.	
	20th to 24th		On the night of the 19th/20th the 26th N.F. took over from us in the line. Emit relief — matters being nosing to a double relief of the LILLE POST GARRISON. Conforms on nothing first every day and night. All available men put through the Gas Chest night the New Box Respirator. Casualties NIL. 20th I.O.R. Sick. 21st & 22nd NIL. 23rd I.O.R. Sick. 24th 10 R.O.S.R.	
	24/25		On the night of the 24/25th we took over from the 26th N.F. in the usual order. The haveots carry out a raid — did not write forward. The purpose of the raid was to secure an identification. Volunteers in being called for formed Company. Casualties NIL. Scheme for Raid prepared (see appendix No.7.) went automatic.	
	26th 27th		Enemy very quiet — a few rounds of machine gun fire so sent over during the night. Our station for our raid no fresh for the night of the 26/27. Zero how 10.5 P.M. I.O.R. killed. 2.O.R. wounded. 26th 3.O.R. Sick. 27th. 2.O.R. wounded. Casualties 2.O.R. Sick	

WAR DIARY
or
INTELLIGENCE SUMMARY
(Erase heading not required.)

Army Form C. 2118

Place	Date	Hour	Summary of Events and Information	Remarks and references to Appendices
TRENCHES	28 to 29		Plenty of work going on in the trenches — they are being greatly improved. The Artillery, Machine & Stokes Mortars are keeping the enemy wire for miles. Weather has been great all the last 24 hours. Casualties 2P.	
		NIL	2P — 2.O.R. Inch. 2P — 1.O.R. Romder	
	30.		Nothing unusual happened during the day. The weather which was in two parties were in position by 9.30 and went out from our trenches at that time. At Zero hour the right hand under Lt. Crosby moved to 2/Lt. Bronch and 15 O.R. entered the enemy trenches. They suffered one prisoner of the 18th Bav. Regt. and killed another Bosche. This right wing party were very successful and got back with their prisoner without a casualty. The left working party were held up by severe in which was had not had time to penetrate into the enemy trenches. This party under 2/Lt. Freeman amounted to 2/Lts large and 15 O.R. returned also without a casualty. The following D. message from Army was received. " June 2.10 p.m. 1st Oct. 1916. "I ollowing message from 2nd Army Corps. June 12.30 p.m. begins D.D.O. Following received from Second Army begins D.D.O. The Army Commander wishes to congratulate all concerned on the results of last nights	

INTELLIGENCE SUMMARY

(Erase heading not required.)

Army Form C. 2118

Place	Date	Hour	Summary of Events and Information	Remarks and references to Appendices
Izencho	30th Sept		contd. APA. The identifications gained are very valuable, and the damage inflicted on the enemy is very satisfactory at this stage. From Bndo. P.P.A. The Corps Commander desires to add his congratulations. The Artillery co-operation in the raid was very good, as the enemy shell fire did not seem so rough about ours during the raid. Signatures. I.O.? Ruther (?) Col. Stenhouse. Major. For Br Col. Army 23rd Watts. Fine.	

WAR DIARY

Army Form C. 2118

23rd Battn. North'd Fus. (4th Tyneside Scottish) Volume 10

INTELLIGENCE SUMMARY
(Erase heading not required.)

Instructions regarding War Diaries and Intelligence Summaries are contained in F.S. Regs., Part II and the Staff Manual respectively. Title Pages will be prepared in manuscript.

Place	Date	Hour	Summary of Events and Information	Remarks and references to Appendices
TRENCHES B2 Sect. PLOEGSTEERT	Sept 1st		Today is our seventh day in the trenches — everything quiet. In the afternoon advance parties were sent out to take over billets from the 23rd N.F. Some battalion took over from us that night. Quiet relief which was complete by 9.30 P.M. All our companies are now in RUE MARPLE arr. the Batt. in "D" Batt. I.O.R. Sok. *Granvelles*	REF. SHEET 36 N.W. L-DIT 6.c. (BOIS GREN-IER)
	Sept 2nd		In the morning A.Co. rugby Battn. — the remainder of the companies cleaned up. B Co. rugby Battn. at 1 P.M. in afternoon. In the evening large working parties were called for. Very wet day and uncomfortable for parties. H. Cowley & 2/Lt. Romach were recommended by C.O. for Military Cross on connection with the raid on the night 30th Sept / Oct 1st. Sergt. Redshaw of "A" Co. was recommended also for the D.C.M. The following men were recommended for the Military Medal. 64/Pte. Milburn, 27/23 Pte. Summers. 231 L/Cpl. Laws, 593 Pte. Watson, 201118/Pte. Dransfield. 3375 Pte. Harmer.	
	Oct 3rd		Very wet day again — large working parties out. Had two special wiring parties out in the morning preparing some entanglements for "Special" Raid.	

WAR DIARY or INTELLIGENCE SUMMARY

(Erase heading not required.)

Army Form C. 2118

Place	Date	Hour	Summary of Events and Information	Remarks and references to Appendices
ROE MARLE AREA	Oct. 4th		Very wet day. — Had large working parties out. Were again out in the morning preparing some entanglements. "Special" Raid Captain Baggett was recommended by the C.O. for the Military Cross. A Sergeant found them also commenced. Casualties 1 O.R. Sick. J.C.	
	Oct. 5th		Large working parties were out. 2nd Lieut King reported and was taken on the strength of the battalion and posted to "A" Coy. O.R.s who had not been inoculated within the last twelve months from "B" & "C" Coys were inoculated. Sergt Reitham, L/Cpl W. Carr, Pte J.H. Watson, Pte J. Milliean & Pte W. Furness were awarded the Military Medal. Casualties 1 O.R. Sick. J.C.	
	Oct. 6th		Fine weather today. "A" & "D" Coys supplied working parties — "B" & "C" Coy rested. The Divisional Gas officer inspected the Box respirators of "B" Coy. He specially and Pte Howe were each awarded a "Card of Honour" in recognition of their good work done while taking part in the Raid on the night of Sept 30th. Casualties 1 O.R. Sick. J.C.	
	Oct. 7th		Very wet day — Had large working parties out. The C.O. met all company commanders at 6 p.m. and discussed the Defence Scheme. The C.O. presented the "Card of Honour" to Pte Transfers + Pte Howe. Casualties 1 O.R. Sick. J.C.	
	Oct. 8th		Very quiet day. The 23rd N.Z. took over, on the right of 8th/9th Batt. from the 20th N.Z. in B2 Sub-sector of the line. The riflemen, snipers & Lewis gunners proceeded to take over at 2.30 p.m. The relief of the battalion was complete by 9.20 p.m. the battalion is now "B" battalion. Casualties 1 Officer Sick J.C.	

WAR DIARY
or
INTELLIGENCE SUMMARY

(Erase heading not required.)

Army Form C. 2118

Instructions regarding War Diaries and Intelligence Summaries are contained in F.S. Regs., Part II. and the Staff Manual respectively. Title Pages will be prepared in manuscript.

Place	Date	Hour	Summary of Events and Information	Remarks and references to Appendices
TRENCHES	Oct 9th		Some day — The enemy were fairly quiet. A little more activity with machine guns during the night of 9th/10th. Our trench mortars sent over a few rounds at 4.15 p.m. Casualties 1 O.R. wounded, 1 Officer Sick.	ffh.
	10th		Very fine weather — Enemy were fairly quiet during enemy he put a few minenwerfer into Charles farm doing practically no damage. Our artillery retaliated. Enemy machine guns were fairly active at night. Lieut Cowley was awarded the Military Cross for good work during the raid on the 30 Sept. Casualties 1 O.R. sick.	J.F.G.
	11th		Weather is still fine but a strong breeze blowing. Enemy is still quiet — he sent one minenwerfer into Charles Farm during the morning. Our heavy trench mortar fired four rounds at German Dorna between 12.30 p.m. and 1 p.m. The Corps Commander visited this area during the morning. General improvement on trenches and work in dugouts is being carried out at 6.30 p.m. One man was shot through the heart at Eyeworts Corner. Casualties 1 O.R. killed 1 Off. + 2 O.R. Sick	Lt.
	12th		Weather still fine but with a strong wind blowing. Enemy fairly quiet. He put over a few shells into the subsidiary line near Rifle Road heaviour. At 7.30 p.m. the 20th Bedn. North 2nd raided the German lines opposite our right company front. The raid was carried out by 2 Lieut Wilmot and 30 O.R. They entered the Boche trenches, killed several Germans and brought back a good many identifications. The raiders lost	

WAR DIARY or INTELLIGENCE SUMMARY

Army Form C. 2118

Place	Date	Hour	Summary of Events and Information	Remarks and references to Appendices
TRENCHES B2 SUBSECTOR	12th Cont.		Three of ranks wounded. The trenches retaliated on our front lines with two trench mortars and artillery and caused several casualties. 2nd Lieut King being killed. The had was quite successful. Casualties 1 Off. Killed 1 O.R. killed 8 O.R. wounded.	J.F.C.
	13th		Very quiet day. The Brigadier General visited the lines during the morning. Enemy aircraft traversed along the front at night with his machine guns firing. Parties were out at night. One of "C" Coy's wiring party was killed by machine gun bullet. Casualties 1 O.R. Killed.	J.F.C.
	14th		Very quiet day. On the night of 14/15 the 20th N.F. relieved the 23rd N.F. The 23rd N.F. then became "C" with "A" Coy at Rifle Post, H.Q. "B" Coy and 2 platoons in Orchard, "C" Coy in billets at Rue Allée and 3rd "D" Coy and 2 platoons of "B" Coy in the Subsidiary Line between Wellington Avenue and Rue Royal. Batten H.Q. went to foot of Haystack Avenue. Casualties 1 O.R. sick.	J.F.C.
SUBSIDIARY LINE	15th		"D" Coy had working party of 1 Officer and 35 O.R. out in morning at Carol Orch. & Bac Sn Kaven. "C" Coy had a party of 20 O.R. out during the evening. Very quiet day. Casualties 1 O.R. wounded 2 O.R. sick.	J.F.C.
	16th		Damp day. Everything quiet. Working party out at night.	Casualties NIL
	17th		Another damp day. Routine unexceptionable for men. Three working parties at night.	Casualties NIL
	18th			

Major R. H. Gibson, temporary 2i/c in command of the Battn was posted as temporary 2nd in Command to the 21st Northumberland. (2nd Tyneside Scottish.)

Major C R

WAR DIARY or INTELLIGENCE SUMMARY

Army Form C. 2118

(Erase heading not required.)

Place	Date	Hour	Summary of Events and Information	Remarks and references to Appendices
SUBSIDIARY LINE	18th		Battalion again took over temporary 2nd in Command of Battn. Very wet night and usual working parties. Casualties. 2. O. R. Sick.	B.M.
	19th		Dull & damp day, usual working parties. Casualties. NIL	B.M.
	20th		Very fine day – cold. A relief was made by the 21st N.F. (2nd Tyneside Scottish) from the R.W.F. de BOIS Salient. Very little alteration was given. Casualties 1 O. R. Sick.	B.M.
	21st		Fine cold day. Working parts sent in as morning. In the enemy we relieved the 26th N.F. (1st Tyneside Scottish) in the B.2. Sector of the hun front line. Boundaries were disposed of as follows. A. Coy. Keyes Out Sector. D Coy. Hunter Subsector. B Coy. Left Sub Sector. (CHARDS FARM) C. Coy. ORCHARD. Word received that we have hypothene scheme for another next in trenches I. 22. a. Casualties 2. O R Sick.	B.M.
B.2. SECTOR FRONT SYSTEM	22nd		Fine cold day again. Drainage is very bad in the left subsector – very wet in some places up to the mid. Several places in the front line are enfiladed by the enemy & have sustained a few casualties. One became C. Coy have very few men available for return carrying which entails several journeys for stores whereas in the past. Enemy are very active now every night with rifle and Machine gun Fire. Casualties 2. O. R Wounded. 1. O. R. Sick	B.M.

1875 W. W393/826 1,000,000 4/15 J.B.C. & A. A.D.S.S./Forms/C. 2118.

WAR DIARY
or
INTELLIGENCE SUMMARY
(Erase heading not required.)

Army Form C. 2118

Instructions regarding War Diaries and Intelligence Summaries are contained in F.S. Regs., Part II. and the Staff Manual respectively. Title Pages will be prepared in manuscript.

Place	Date	Hour	Summary of Events and Information	Remarks and references to Appendices
B2 Sector	Oct. 23rd 1916.		A ceremonial parade was held at CROIX DU BAC in the morning where General Plumer, commanding 2nd Army, presented Military Cross Ribbons to Lieut. F.S. Nelson and hero of St. George to Miss Nelson to 2/ 6/8 Bronds L Mathieson and Military Medal Ribbon to 23/444 Sergt. H. Bakewell. 1 officer + 10 O.R. were sent from C. Coy Portland this parade. Another enemy strafe during the evening and considerable strafing at night time. Enemy still active. Casualties. 1. O.R. Killed. 1. O.R. wounded Sgt. Thos. Olivier & Men. Col. J. Reid of the Grenade Section Bromville were also present the above Parade at CROIX DU BAC.	
	Oct. 24th.		Wet day. In the afternoon our Artillery and Trench Mortars had a "strafe". Our Heavy Trench Mortars fired 3 rounds all of which fell in our own lines — fortunately no one was hit (much to the chagrin of the Boche). The enemy retaliated with Minnenwerfers all of which fell into our lines — some doing considerable damage. Enemy very active during night with Rifle & Machine gun fire. Casualties NIL	
	Oct. 25th		Damp day. Our Artillery and mortars had another afternoon strafe (Our Heavy Mortar did not fire — to everyone's satisfaction.) The enemy retaliated with Minnenwerfers in rear of CINDERS FARM also Artillery. A quiet during the evening. The troops no showing considerable the enemy. Casualties NIL	

WAR DIARY or INTELLIGENCE SUMMARY

Army Form C. 2118

Place	Date	Hour	Summary of Events and Information	Remarks and references to Appendices
	Oct 26th		Dull day – brightened at towards evening. We had a "strafe" in the morning and a "strafe" in the afternoon with French Mortars and Artillery – very little retaliation with exception of 2 or 3 Minenwerfers into CHORD'S FORM. At about 5.30 P.M. the bombers had an organised strafe with "Minnie" and Artillery on to the left of CHORD FORM Sap 1, and on to the Edr. in our immediate left. Very little damage was done from Sector. "Rumour" has it that the Boche vacated the "Irish" Rede (Tyneside), who are on our left – definite news not yet known. Casualties. 1. O. R. died. [signature]	
	Oct 27th		The rumour that the Irish Brigade had been raided was correct – they suffered a few casualties from the bombardment and 1 Lewis Gun and Team were taken prisoners. We were relieved by the 20th N.F. (1st Tyneside Scottish) in the evening and became "D" Battalion in Billets in Rue Marle. [struck through] Casualties 1. O.R. sick [signature]	
RUE MARLE	Oct 28		Quiet and quick relief. The Battalion in the Green 24 hours rest. Bde. had to outfit a small working party the following day. Casualties. 2. O.R. sick [signature]	

Cleaning up of Billets – Baths etc. Working parties in the evening.

WAR DIARY
or
INTELLIGENCE SUMMARY

(Erase heading not required.)

Army Form C. 2118

Place	Date	Hour	Summary of Events and Information	Remarks and references to Appendices
	Oct 29th		Enemy working parties out do the morning. We supplied a "Special party" in the evening of 2 Officers + 106 O.R. for carrying typo cylinders into the School of trenches on our left. This work was done without mishap. Casualties NIL	
	Oct 30th		Enemy working parties out during day. Rainy weather. Sent several parties out over slopes of the line for wiring and work in the trenches. The enemy have been very active with Artillery and Minenwerfer and have done a great deal of damage. Casualties 4 O.R. sick	
	Oct 31st		Quiet day. Enemy working parties out in the morning. And supply of several parties again in the evening for work in CHORD FORM trenches. Party finished work at 12.30 am Casualties NIL	

C. March. Lt Col
Commdg. 2.3rd. (Northern Fine)
(4th Tyneside Scottish)

WAR DIARY or INTELLIGENCE SUMMARY

Army Form C. 2118

VOL No II

23(S)Bn Northd Fus
(S) Tyneside Scottish

Place	Date	Hour	Summary of Events and Information	Remarks and references to Appendices
TRENCHES B.2.S-Sector ARMENTIÈRES	Nov 1st 1916		We relieved the 20th Northd Fus. (1st Tyneside Scottish) in the B 2 Subsector in daylight. The relief was carried out without a hitch and completed by 11 P.M. The Battalion is now "B" Both and disposed as follows. "A" Coy Regtl Colors. "B" Coy, Hinter Subsector. "C" Coy Left Sector (CHARD FORM). "D" Coy in reserve at the ORCHARD. Very quiet day. Enemy Machine Guns very active in the evening.	
	Nov 2nd		2/Lt. J.S. Cope was hit through the wrist by a machine Gun Bullet whilst manning my own. Casualties 1 Officer wounded. Dull and wet in the morning. Our Trench and Stokes Mortars had a ½ hour strafe about noon — did some good work. They also had another ½ hour in the afternoon. Very little retaliation was given — unfortunately on the retaliation that was given we had 1 N.C.O. killed and 3 O.R. wounded. The CHARD FORM Sector is in a very bad state owing to the heavy state of Nomansland several days ago. Special working parties supplied by "D" Battalion and in every night. In several places there is practically no parapet at all — but days enemy. The morning is also very bad in other sector. Enemy aircraft were no unusual with during the night or day. Casualties 1 O.R. killed 3 O.R. wounded. 5 O.R. wounded.	JSC JSC
	Nov 3rd		Dull weather. CHARDS Sector being gradually improved. Enemy Mortars were cutting more active but our Trench and Stokes Mortars were very little retaliation of our day. Supply/Rahm and Sergt. J.W. Robertson were detained by Bole Hat ats transport to Corps Ammunition Reserve where a special parade was assembled. The Duke of Connaught inspected these front. In the evening a patrol movement	
	Nov 4th			

Army Form C. 2118

WAR DIARY
or
INTELLIGENCE SUMMARY
(Erase heading not required.)

Instructions regarding War Diaries and Intelligence Summaries are contained in F.S. Regs., Part II. and the Staff Manual respectively. Title Pages will be prepared in manuscript.

Place	Date	Hour	Summary of Events and Information	Remarks and references to Appendices
TRENCHES	Aug 4th		consisting of 3 Officers and 9 or N.C.O's. (2/Lt Pinnington & 2/Lt. J. S. Cannan and 2/Lt. J. H. & along were the Officers) They proceeded up to the enemy wire at the point where our proposed raid is to come off. After a thorough reconnaissance of the wire right up to the enemy parapet the party withdrew. When they had withdrawn some distance of about 50 yds from the enemy first system of wire they encountered by a Hostile Patrol and a Bombing fight ensued. The enemy's attack broke our patrol up and they became scattered. On reaching our lines one of the German Patrol (who had apparently lost his direction) was found amongst our prisoners. It was also found that 2/Lt V. Pinnington was missing — the other two Officers slightly wounded and 3 of the N.C.O's wounded. A strong Battle Patrol under 2/Lt Cannan was organised and sent out to search for 2/Lt Pinnington — this patrol searched the ground thoroughly where the fight had taken place, also right up to the German wire but no trace could be found of the missing officer. Casualties. 2/Lt Pinnington. (Missing believed wounded) 3. O. R. wounded.	
	Aug 5th		The Battn. his section is in a very bad state owing to a severe bombardment by Minnenwerfer shells (round the afternoon of the 4th). A great deal of work requires to be done in this sector now. There are not sufficient men in the front line or detailed for the front line to carry on with the necessary work there with the result that it becomes more uninhabitable every day. Drainage is bad and in bad	

Army Form C. 2118.

WAR DIARY
or
INTELLIGENCE SUMMARY.
(Erase heading not required.)

Place	Date	Hour	Summary of Events and Information	Remarks and references to Appendices
Lombres	Mon 5th		weather it will be difficult to find a place which does not take one out the whole day. Too much time and too many men are detailed for work on day - onto in the reserve line and 3orks. There are many places in our sector where there is no accommodation for Officers or men. The only place where Officers can sleep or get their food in our were shelters, which would not keep even men out, very much a chill. Cpl. Coulter 2.O.R. wounded. 2 O.R. sick.	JR
	Tues 6		At 2 A.M. the Bde. on our Right had a raid. To cover a diversion the enemy lines of posts and wire were subjected to a fairly heavy artillery fire with the result that retaliation was sent in tons. Several large and a great number of smaller minenwerfers were first into no amount of shennings and killing we were forced to hand over our "C" Battalion and Companies were disposed of as follows: A Co. RUE FLEURIE & LA VESÉE Road. B.Co. LILLE POST. C.Co. ORCHARD and SUBSIDIARY LINE. "D" Co. SUBSIDIARY LINE. Bn. HQtrs. are in RUE FLEURIE. Very hot day. Small working party was sent out during the day. CASUALTIES. 2.O.R. killed, 2.O.R. wounded.	JR

WAR DIARY or INTELLIGENCE SUMMARY

Army Form C. 2118.

Place	Date	Hour	Summary of Events and Information	Remarks and references to Appendices
RESERVE TRENCHES. B.2. Subsector	Nov. 8th 1916		Very wet day. Several working parties out in the evening. Enemy recovered about 5 P.M. in the 6th — in a shell hit the temporary HQrs in the CHARD Sector which we had just vacated that day — the shell killed 3 Officers and badly wounded 4 of the 20th N.F. **Casualties** Nil.	
PLOEGSTEERT	Nov 9th	8 P.M.	Normal working parties out. Overnight parties employed on RUE MORLE. Salvage of wood finished today — probable stock of wood on 12th inst. Demolition	
	Nov 9th	9 am – 10	Normal working parties out. Further normal reconnaissance. **Casualties** 1 O.R. wounded 3 O.R. Self [?]	
	Nov 11th		A few minor alterations and additions were made to orders of March. The templates [orders?] for Mount & Artillery Cooperation were issued by Brig. Gen. J. P. Lamont, Cmg. S.Bde. **Casualties** 1 O.R. wounded, 3 O.R. Sick. S/Lt.	
B.2 Subsector to Armentiers	Nov 11th		The men retired by the 22nd N.F. (3rd Tyneside Scotch) and C. Bn. went in from and relieved the 25th N.F. (1st T.S.) in the B.2 Subsector and thereon B. Bn. Old Companies were disposed of as follows: Regl. details, B Coy Centre, C Coy L. left, D Coy L. (Reserve) A Coy. Very quiet relief when no casualties by 2 P.M. The enemy were very quiet all day. **Casualties** 2. O.R. Sick.	

Army Form C. 2118.

WAR DIARY
or
INTELLIGENCE SUMMARY.
(Erase heading not required.)

Instructions regarding War Diaries and Intelligence Summaries are contained in F. S. Regs., Part II. and the Staff Manual respectively. Title pages will be prepared in manuscript.

Place	Date	Hour	Summary of Events and Information	Remarks and references to Appendices
Chamber Trenches	Nov 12th		Very quiet day. In the evening an enemy party numbering 2/Lt G. B. Herman and 2/Lt G. Daly arrived and made preparations for the raid which is shown by Brigade Operation Order No 72. Orch.	Brigade O.O. 72. Copy No 6 over G.N/S/1.
	Nov 13th	4.30 A.M.	Our raiding party entered the enemy lines as per Bde. O.O. No 72 and successfully carried the operation out, unfortunately no prisoners were obtained and we sustained a few casualties. A description and report of raid see Appendix G.N/S/1. 13/11/16. Bingham now out & got back with one two. The enemy retaliated with minenwerfers which fell about and with shrapnel and "whizz-bangs". The following telegrams received. "The Brigade Commander warmly congratulates all concerned in last night's raid which affects great credit on all those who took part." Telegram from 34th Division. "The G.O.C. congratulates all those concerned in the minor enterprise carried out this morning A.A.A. He considers the arrangements and execution reflects great credit on officers and men A.A.A. Ends A.A.A.	G.N/S/1.
	Nov 14th		Quiet day — usual working parties. From D. Bn for men in trenches. Memorandum of sympathy very great. Casualties 7. O. R. wounded. 50.R. Sick. Orch. Casualties: 2. O. R. Sick. Orch.	

2353 Wt. W2544/1454 700,000 5/15 D. D. & L. A.D.S.S.Forms/C 2118.

WAR DIARY or INTELLIGENCE SUMMARY.

(Erase heading not required.)

Army Form C. 2118.

Instructions regarding War Diaries and Intelligence Summaries are contained in F. S. Regs., Part II. and the Staff Manual respectively. Title pages will be prepared in manuscript.

Place	Date	Hour	Summary of Events and Information	Remarks and references to Appendices
TRENCHES	Nov 15th 1916		Enemy Shelling a little more active. A great number of 5.9" shells were sent into LILLE POST and PARADISE ALLEY and one bursting shrapnel (Cs.B.) over heavily shelled. The Coy Hd Qts and Kitchen were "blown in" fortunately no casualties occurred. These old emplacements may in a dry-out which is fairly sunk and isolated — or which has not been occupied for months. The routine as now being carried out by those who built emplacements in reserve trenches and posts so is more is the way to build a "decent" dug Hd Qts in reserve trenches and posts no matter what the OVER FROM BATT. Casualties 3 O.R. Sick #2	
	Nov 16		We were relieved by the 20th N.S. (1st Gwents Scottish) and moved back to billets in RUE MARLE. One coy "D" Battalion All day with the exception of "D" coy who were late in being relieved, proceeded into Baths in the afternoon. No inspection or parade. Casualties 1 O.R. wounded B/52 2/Lt D.C. Young rejoined for duty.	
RUE MARLE	Nov 17		Every available man out in working parties with exception of "D" Coy who went to Baths. Very cold day — keen frost. The undermentioned received the Military Medal for conspicuous gallantry on patrol on the 12/13 inst. 17/1065 Pte. R. Fletcher 20074 B/Lt. R.Y. Smith 283/415 Pte. J. Fairweather. The following man received	

2353 Wt. W2544/1454 700,000 5/15 D. D. & L. A.D.S.S. Forms/C. 2118.

WAR DIARY
or
INTELLIGENCE SUMMARY.
(Erase heading not required.)

Army Form C. 2118.

Place	Date	Hour	Summary of Events and Information	Remarks and references to Appendices
BOESINGHE	July 17th		No drilling paraded for general employment on the Battalion at 16 July 1916. 23/514 Sergt. H. Nelson. 23/1308 Rfn. H. Young. Casualties 5. O.R. Sick GSR.	
	18th		Slight Enemy shelling night and very cold day. Enemy working parties out	
	19th.		Showery day; nil activity further out. Sent an officer to the 1.2" Machine gun bn for instruction in Vickers guns. An officer from this Coy was sent to attend same in exchange. Casualties 1 Officer wd 3 O.R. Sick GSR 2 O.R. Sick GSR	
	20th		Usual working parties out. A shrapnel 5.8 O.R. concentrating of warmth of men also "Egrenelle Switch" carried — The majority fallen were wounded in the 1st July. Casualties 5. O.R. Sick GSR	
	21st		The tick over from the 20th S.W.F in the B.2 Sector of trenches, carriers were disposed of as follows. A Company (Elfrecht — CHORDS) D Co. Centre Sector, C Co. Right Sector, B Co. Reserve (ORCHARD). An excellent morning for the relay — very misty. 2/Lt. Foley, H.N. who had taken on duties as Intelligence Officer was shot through the head and killed by a rifle bullet. Casualties 1 Officer Killed	

WAR DIARY
or
INTELLIGENCE SUMMARY.
(Erase heading not required.)

Army Form C. 2118.

Place	Date	Hour	Summary of Events and Information	Remarks and references to Appendices
Rue du Bois ARMENTIERES	Nov 22		Fine day – very quiet. Temperature dropped upon work on flood shelters. Casualties. 1 O.R. killed 4 O.R. Batt Hq.	
	23		Fine day. Enemy artillery and heavy Minenwerfer active in the afternoon. A great number of rifle grenades and Pineapples were sent over. Following men received for W.S.R. Red Hot city figures:- "The following officers have been awarded the military cross:-" Lt. Lieut. H.N. FOLEY B.A.A. and Lieut. H.N. FOLEY B.A.A. and Lieut. 3811 Sergt. E. RUSSELL — please has been awarded the D.C.M. R.P.D. 3811 Sergt. E. RUSSELL — please convey Divisional and Brigade Commanders congratulations in relation to deserved officers and to Sergt Russell." Casualties. 3 O.R. Cub. E.R.	
	24		Quiet day. Slight damage was caused from patrol by enemy shelling in the previous night. The CHPRD behind front line is in a bad condition, in places it is knee deep in mud and badly knocked about. Enemy quite active during the evening with Rifle & Machine gun fire. Every night from "Stand to" to "Stand down" about 12 hours attending patrols have to placed out in "No Mans Land" in an defensive measure against surprise movements by the enemy. It is very exhaustive + unacceptable work for the men in such shiny weather currents of typing down in one spot for 2 hours at a stretch. Casualties. 1 O.R. killed & 2 O.R. Sick. E.R.	

WAR DIARY or INTELLIGENCE SUMMARY.

Army Form C. 2118.

(Erase heading not required.)

Place	Date	Hour	Summary of Events and Information	Remarks and references to Appendices
TRENCHES	Nov 25th		Raining day. Very uncomfortable for the men. Quiet day. Casualties. 2. O.R. Killed.	
	26th		The Bn/o Commander presented the following N.C.O's and men with Medal Ribbons:- Sergt. B. Nurse, D.C.M. Sergt. Nicholson. Military Medal. Pte. L. J Selater. M.M. Pte. J. Monmouth. M.M. A/L/Sergt. W. Sun. M.M. Pte. Linnox. W. M.M. Pte. J. H. Nolan. M.M. In the morning the 2nd N.F. relieved us in the trenches and we became "C" Battalion. Companies were disposed as follows. H. Qrs. Subsidiary Line. "B" Co. RUE TREFEVRIE. C.H. LILLE POST "D" Co. ORCHARD & Subsidiary Line. Head Quarters a SPRING POST. Quiet relief. Enemy aeroplane shewed his wit. 1 alert over Pt 60. Killed alow and over 1 Shrapnel. Two Platoons of "D" Coy found with Ervin and moving and return after "Stand Down" in the morning.	Casualties. 3. O.R. Sick. 0/R
	27th		All "D" Co. out on working parties.	Casualties. NIL 0/R
	28th		Usual working parties. Very cold weather.	Casualties. 2. O.R. Sick.
	29th		Usual Working parties and fatigue- very cold day. The Bn. Commander visited our	Casualties 4. O.R. Sick. a 24th &
	30th		of the Companies in the morning with the C.O.	1. O.R. Sick 30th

C. Ritch Lt. Col
Cmdg. 23rd Northern Fusiliers

SECRET

OPERATION ORDER No. 72
by
BRIGADIER-GENERAL T.P.B. TERNAN, C.M.G. D.S.O.
commanding 102nd.(Tyneside Scottish) Brigade.

Copy No 6

Ref. Map
BOIS GRENIER
1:10,000 Ed.2c

10-11-16

INTENTION.	1. A raid will be carried out by 2 officers and 30 O.R. 23rd. Battn. Northd. Fus.(4th. Tyneside Scottish) on the enemys trenches on the front I.22.a.68.80. to I.22.a.8.9. on the night Nov. 12/13th. 1916. The point of entry will be I.22.a.75.82.
OBJECTS.	2. The objects of the raid are to inflict loss on the enemy, obtain prisoners and identifications and if possible capture a machine gun.
ZERO HOUR.	3. Zero hour (hour at which the bombardment commences NOT the hour at which party enters enemys trenches) will be 4.30 a.m. Nov. 12/13th.
WIRE-CUTTING.	4. A gap in the enemys wire will be cut by X/34 T.M.B. from I.22.a.75.82. to a point 10 yards to the West. O.C."B" Battn. will be responsible for keeping this gap under intermittent Lewis Gun fire each night. Patrols, except those of the actual raiding party, are not to be sent out in this neighbourhood where they would prevent Lewis Guns from firing on the gap. To deceive the enemy as to the point of entry, wire will also be cut by X/34 T.M.B. at I.16.d.10.25. and existing gaps at I.21.c.62.15. and I.21.b.45.50. will be kept open. O.C."B" Battn. will keep the first and O.C. "A" Battn. the last two mentioned gaps under intermittent Lewis Gun fire each night.
PATROLS.	5. All officers and O.R. of the raiding party are to go over the route across No Mans Land towards the objective at least once prior to the raid and daily reports are to be sent to Brigade H.Q. by O.C. 23rd. N.F.(4th. T.S.) as to the state of the enemys wire at point I.22.a.75.82. On the night Nov. 12/13th. a standing patrol of 1 officer and 6 men with a Lewis Gun will be posted about I.16.c.65.45. as soon as light permits until the raiding party has gone out. The patrol will be relieved every 2 hours.
ARTILLERY & TRENCH MORTARS	6. The Heavy and Field Artillery and Medium Trench Mortar programmes are attached.
STOKES MORTARS.	7. The 102nd. Light T.M.B. will bombard the enemys front parapet from I.21.b.4.2. to I.21.b.56.22. from Zero to +0.5 minutes. Rate of fire as rapid as possible.
MACHINE GUNS.	8. The O.C. 102nd. Machine Gun Company will arrange for the 4 Vickers Guns in the left section front line to traverse the hostile parapet, the 2 guns on the right from I.22.a.3.6. to I.21.b.5.3., the 2 on the left from I.16.d.1.2. to I.16.d. 35.60. from +0.5 to +0.40 minutes. An officer to be in charge of each inner flank gun and personally superintend the firing. In addition the O.C. 102nd. Machine Gun Company will arrange to search with fire from Zero to + 0.40 minutes, (1) LARGE FARM and road running SOUTH from it. (2) PARADISE ROAD (3) Communication trench from I.22.b.38.50. to I.22.b.6.3. (4) The WEZ MACQUART-LILLE road. Fire NOT to be directed in any case short of the line LARGE FARM-WEZ MACQUART CHURCH.
COMPOSITION OF PARTY.	9. The raiders will be divided into 3 parties, (a) party. 2nd. Lieut. FALCY with 12 N.C.Os. and men (b) party. 2nd. Lieut. COMMON with 10 N.C.Os. and men (c) party. 1 Sergt. and 8 men In addition 2 sappers with explosives will accompany the raiders.
ASSAULT.	10. The raiding party will leave our trenches at Zero minus 30 minutes and form up in No Mans Land as close to the hostile trenches as will be consistent with safety when our artillery barrage is on the enemys front line. The raiders will commence to creep forward at Zero and will rush the hostile trenches at +0.5 minutes.

Page 2.

ACTION IN HOSTILE TRENCHES.
11. (a) party will work to the left along the enemys front trench and block it at I.22.a.8.9., 3 men to be on the parapet.
(b) party will work to the right along the front trench and block it at I.22.a.68.80., 3 men to be on the parapet.
(c) party will remain at the point of entry on the parapet and will be available to re-inforce either of the above parties, to collect prisoners, assist wounded and cover the withdrawal.

RECALL SIGNAL.
12. At +0.15 minutes the recall signal will be given by the O.C. raid: this will consist of blasts on French horns and will be repeated by the other officer and senior N.C.O.
As a supplementary recall signal a cluster of 2 GREEN and 1 RED Very lights will be fired from our lines at +0.15 minutes.

Return.
13. The raiders will return to our lines along the road to I.16.c.56.75. or if this is not possible to about I.15.d.6.3. near the head of AVONDALE ROAD. Green Very lights will be fired from the latter point from +0.15 minutes onwards at 30 seconds interval.

AEROPLANE CO-OPERATION
14. With a view to checking hostile artillery retaliation the 42nd. Squadron R.F.C. will be asked for an aeroplane to fly over the hostile lines during the period of the raid and drop parachute flares over any hostile batteries that may be active.

COUNTER-BATTERY ACTION.
15. Should counter-battery action be desired by the O.C. 6 Battn. application will be made through the artillery liason officer to the O.C. Left Group Divisional Artillery.
The direction of the active hostile batteries should be stated if possible.

REMOVAL OF PAY-BOOKS &c.
Faces and hands will be blackened
16. All pay-books, identity discs, regimental badges and marks from which the enemy could obtain an identification will be removed from the raiders prior to leaving our trenches.

WOUNDED.
17. Any man wounded in the German trenches is to be brought out at once.

REPORTS.
18. The Brigade Intelligence Officer will report to the O.C. 23rd. N.F. (4th. T.S.) on Nov. 12th. prior to Zero and arrange for a rapid transmission of information to Brigade Headquarters

SYNCHRONISATION OF WATCHES.
19. Watches will be synchronised at 12 midnight Nov. 12/13th. O.C. 23rd. N.F.(4th. T.S.), O.C. Left Group Divisional Artillery, O.C. 102nd. Machine Gun Company, O.C. 102nd. Light T.M.B. will each detail an officer to report at Brigade Headquarters at that hour to receive the correct time.
20. ACKNOWLEDGE BY WIRE.

Major,
acting Brigade Major
102nd. (Tyneside Scottish) Brigade.

Issued at   p.m.

Copies 1&2 retained
3 20th. N.F.(1st. Tyneside Scottish)
4 21st. N.F. 2nd.   "   "
5 22nd. N.F. 3rd.   "   "
6 23rd. N.F. 4th.   "   "
7 102nd. Light T.M.B.
8 102nd. Machine Gun Company
9 O.C. Left Group Divisional Artillery
10 O.C. 208th. Field Co. R.E.
11 H.Q. 34th. Division
12 G.O.C. 101st. Inf. Bde.
13 G.O.C. 103rd. Inf. Bde.
14 O.C. 18th. Battn. Northd. Fus. (Pioneers)

TABLE "A".

To accompany Operation Order No. 72.

LEFT GROUP DIVISIONAL ARTILLERY PROGRAMME.

Zero to + 0.2 minutes.
    B/180 (4 guns) - Support trench I.22.a.6.5 - 80.65.
          (2 guns) - Sweep front line I.22.a.98.95 - 68.78.
    C/180 (5 guns) - Support trench I.22.a.80.65 - I.22.b.05.80.
          (1 gun) - Point of Communication trench I.22.a.85.80.
    D/180 .... - Support trench I.22.b.05.80 - I.22.a.6.5.
    C/175 .... - SNIPERS HOUSE. I.16.d.05.15. I.22.a.60.65.
                 I.16.d.0.1.

+ 0.2 to + 0.5 minutes.
    B/180 .... - Front trench I.22.a.65.80 - 75.85.
    C/180 (5 guns) - Front trench I.22.a.75.85 - I.16.c.95.00
          (1 gun) - Point of Communication trench I.22.a.85.80.
    D/180 .... - as before .
    C/175 .... - as before.

+ 0.5 minutes.
    B/180 .... - Stop.
    C/180 .... - Stop.
    D/180 .... - Stop.
    C/175 .... - Stop only on SNIPERS HOUSE, continue on other
               targets.

+ 0.5½ to + 0.30 minutes.
    B/180 .... - Support trench I.22.a.6.5 to 80.65.
    C/180 .... - Support trench I.22.a.80.85 to I.22.b.05.80.
    D/180 .... - Points I.22.a.5.8. I.22.b.20.85. I.22.a.40.48.
              I.22.a.95.98.
    C/175 .... - SNIPERS HOUSE - I.16.d.05.15. I.22.a.60.65
              I.16.d.0.1.

RATES OF FIRE - Zero to + 0.15 minutes. 3 rounds per gun per
                                        minute.
               + 0.15 to + 0.30 minutes.. 2 rounds per gun per
                                        minute.

X/34th M. T. M. B. programme.
    Zero to + 0.30 minutes.
       I.16.d.10.25. I.16.d.5.8. I.21.b.5.3. I.22.a.1.4.

HEAVY ARTILLERY PROGRAMME.
    Zero to + 0.30 minutes.
    12" How: .. as many rounds as possible on WEZ MACQUART and
              I.16.d.60.58.
    6" How: .. As many rounds as possible on LARGE FARM,
              ESTAMINET de la BARRIERE, pt. I.22.a.40.45 and
              I.22.b.00.35.
    60 pdrs. .. to stand by for counter battery work from Zero till
              no longer required.

APPENDIX G.N/S/1.

REPORT ON A RAID ON THE ENEMY'S TRENCHES AT POINT
I.22.a.7.5. ON THE NIGHT OF 12/13th NOVEMBER 1916.

13-11-16

Zero hour was fixed for 4.30 a.m. 13th inst.

The party consisted of two Officers and 31 other ranks and was subdivided into three parties as follows:-
- (a) 2nd Lieut. Falcy and 12 men.
- (b) 2nd Lieut. Common and 10 men.
- (c) Sergeant Russell and 8 men.

The wire had been very well cut by X. T.M.Battery prior to the night of the raid and a clear gap was provided.

The night was very misty and very favourable for approach and the moonlight through the mist was exceptionally favourable for near objects.

The artillery bombardment and barrage was admirably laid and the raiding party were led to within 30 yards of point of entry under cover of the preliminary five minutes bombardment of the close support and front trench.

When the bombardment had ceased and was to be converted to a barrage the leading section (A) under 2nd Lieut. Falcy rushed forward through the gap in the wire and found the borrow pit immediately below the parapet to be about 15ft broad and 5ft deep and full of water. The whole party got across somehow and after climbing over the parapet, worked along the salient in the enemy's lines to the left. They came under very considerable fire from the German Artillery immediately they reached the top of the parapet, the three leading men were wounded by shell fire. 2nd Lieut. Falcy and one slightly wounded man pushed forward followed by the remainder who were not hit, and encountered four or five Germans in the trench in front of them. 2nd Lieut. threw 3 bombs and emptied his revolver into this party as they retired, and one at least is known to be wounded. This sector of the German lines is a small salient with various branches, and 2nd Lieut. Falcy and his men lost sight of the enemy round a bend and took the wrong arm of a "V" which they reached in pursuit. The wounded man who accompanied this party became faint, The ten minutes allotted for action in the trenches had already expired and 2nd Lieut. Falcy collected his men, picked up some rifles abandoned by the enemy and began to withdraw his party. They were hampered by the state of the trenches and by the wounded men who blocked the trench whilst being evacuated. The whole party including one badly wounded man who was unable to walk, got across the water again and 2nd Lieut. Falcy after seeing all clear personally carried the man who was unable to walk back across NO MANS LAND.

The casualties incurred were due to the barrage which was laid on their own front line by the Germans directly our party reached their lines. Possibly one gun shot wound may have been caused by the few remaining Germans encountered but they did not appear to fire any shots.

(b). Party under 2nd Lieut. Common followed immediately behind (a) party, got through the water and proceeded along the trench to the right. On reaching the first communication trench, 2nd Lieut. Common then proceeded to search all dugouts back to the point of entry. They were empty and consisted of small shelters with wooden frames and floors very similar to our own "Dog Kennel" pattern but rather higher than ours.

Some waterproof capes and a Sniper's helmet was all that had been left behind. The communication trench was merely a succession of trench boards at and for some distance from junction with front line. (Continued).

(Continued) No. 2

(c) Party under Sergeant Rusell got through the water and laid down on the parapet near point of entry to assist remove prisoners, wounded or to reinforce as required and to cover the eventual withdrawal of (a) and (b). This party helped to remove the wounded under heavy fire and extremely difficult local conditions caused by flooded borrow pits and damaged parapet.

It would appear that the Germans intended to leave their front line undefended to the right and south of the point of entry; also that they delayed as long as possible in the salient to the left and north of the point of entry: it was here that some few rifles and also some rows of bombs were found abandoned; 4 rifles were brought back, others which could not be carried were thrown into the water.

The German trenches on both sides were very badly damaged considerably more so than our worst sections, which the raiding party all noticed and commented on with satisfaction.

Although no prisoners were captured owing to opportunities to escape in the salient which was not one continuous trench it is certain that very considerable damage was inflicted.

The artillery bombardment must hace caused casulaties especially in view of the damaged trenches and hastily abandoned rifles.

From independent expressions by officers and men I have every reason to believe that 2/Lt. Falcy, 2/Lt. Common and Sergeant Russell led their men with courage and ability and also that all their men behaved very well.

GN/S/1

REPORT ON A RAID ON THE ENEMY'S TRENCHES AT POINT
I.33.a.7.5. ON THE NIGHT OF 12/13th NOVEMBER 1916.

Zero hour was fixed for 4.30 a.m. 13th inst.

The party consisted of two Officers and 31 other ranks and was subdivided into three parties as follows:—
    (a)   2nd Lieut. Falcy and 12 men.
    (b)   2nd Lieut. Common and 10 men.
    (c)   Sergeant Russell and 8 men.

The wire had been very well cut by X. T.M. Battery prior to the night of the raid and a clear gap was provided.

The night was very misty and very favourable for approach and the moonlight through the mist was exceptionally favouravle for near objects.

The artillery bombardment and barrage was admirably laid and the raiding party were led to within 30 yards of point of entry under cover of the preliminary five minutes bombardment of the close support and front trench.

When the bombardment had ceased and was to be converted to a barrage the leading section (A) under 2nd Lieut. Falcy rushed forward through the gap in the wire and found the borrow pit immediately below the parapet to be about 15ft broad and 5ft deep and full of water. The whole party got across somehow and after climbing over the parapet, worked along the salient in the enemy's lines to the left. They came under very considerable fire from the German Artillery immediately they reached the top of the parapet, the three leading men were wounded by shell fire. 2nd Lieut. Falcy and one slightly wounded man pushed forward followed by the remainder who were not hit, and encountered four or five Germans in the trench in front of them. 2nd Lieut. threw 2 bombs and emptied his revolver into this party as they retired, and one at least is known to be wounded. This sector of the German lines is a small salient with various branches, and 2nd Lieut. Falcy and his men lost sight of the enemy round a bend and took the wrong arm of a "V" which they reached in pursuit. The wounded man who accompanied this party became faint. The ten minutes allotted for action in the trenches had already expired and 2nd Lieut. Falcy collected his men, picked up some rifles abandoned by the enemy and began to withdraw his party. They were hampered by the state of the trenches and by the wounded men who blocked the trench whilst being evacuated. The whole party including one badly wounded man who was unable to walk, got across the water again and 2nd Lieut. Falcy after seeing all clear personally carried the man who was unable to walk back across NO MANS LAND.

The casualties incurred were due to the barrage which was laid on their own front line by the Germans directly our party reached their lines. Possibly one gun shot wound may have been caused by the few remaining Germans encountered but they did not appear to fire any shots.

(b). Party under 2nd Lieut. Common followed immediately behind (a) party, got through the water and proceeded along the trench to the right. On reaching the first communication trench, 2nd Lieut. Common then proceeded to search all dugouts back to the point of entry. They were empty and consisted of small shelters with wooden frames and floors very similar to our own "Dog Kennel" pattern but rather higher than ours.

Some waterproof capes and a Sniper's helmet was all that had been left behind. The communication trench was merely a succession of trench boards at and for some distance from junction with front line.   (Continued).

(Continued) No. 2

(c) Party under Sergeant Rusell got through the water and laid down on the parapet near point of entry to assist remove prisoners, wounded or to reinforce as required and to cover the eventual withdrawal of (a) and (b). This party helped to remove the wounded under heavy fire and extremely difficult local conditions caused by flooded borrow pits and damaged parapet.

It would appear that the Germans intended to leave their front line undefended to the right and south of the point of entry; also that they delayed as long as possible in the salient to the left and north of the point of entry; it was here that some few rifles and also some rows of bombs were found abandoned; 4 rifles were brought back, others which could not be carried were thrown into the water.

The German trenches on both sides were very badly damaged considerably more so than our worst sections, which the raiding party all noticed and commented on with satisfaction.

Although no prisoners were captured owing to opportunities to escape in the salient which was not one continuous trench it is certain that very considerable damage was inflicted.

The artillery bombardment must have caused casulaties especially in view of the damaged trenches and hastily abandoned rifles.

From independent expressions by officers and men I have every reason to believe that 2/Lt. Falcy, 2/Lt. Common and Sergeant Russell led their men with courage and ability and also that all their men behaved very well.

Vol 12

23 (S) Bn
Northd Fusiliers
(4th Tyneside Scottish)

War Diary — December
1916

Scan. VOL XII

Army Form C. 2118.

WAR DIARY
or
INTELLIGENCE SUMMARY.

4TH BATT'N TYNESIDE SCOTTISH.
23RD BATT'N NORTHUMBERLAND FUS[ILIERS]

(Erase heading not required.)

Place	Date	Hour	Summary of Events and Information	Remarks and references to Appendices
TRENCHES B.2.S Sector PLOEGSTEERT	Dec 1st		We relieved the 20th N.F. (1st Tyneside Scottish) in B2 Subsector of trenches. Quiet relief — most needed when tormented us. Relief completed by 12.30 PM. Companies are disposed of as follows:– B Coy. Left Sector (CHARDS) A Coy. Centre Sector, D Coy. Right Sector, C Coy. ORCHARD. (Reserve) Cold day. Wiring was carried on with in the evening. Casualties 1 O.R. Sick off.	
	Dec 2nd		Weather still remains cold — very quiet day. The Coy that does C Coy in the ORCHARD is to be changed — in future they must occupy some of the Convent day into which our troops ventilated in PARADIS ESTAILEY. Casualties 3 O.R. Sick off	
	Dec 3rd		Cold still day. Our trench Howard General Haldane paid a number of trenches off for more cutting purposes. Very little retaliation was given in few trenchable being sent back. Companies in the line are carrying on with general work of repairing breastworks, parapets, trenches traverses, drainage etc. Casualties 3. O.R. Sick.	
	Dec 4th "5"		Quiet day. Casualties 1 Accidentally wounded 1 O.R. Sick off. Showery weather – our trench Mortars cut the enemy wire round the retaliated with several Minenwerfer. O Company & retaliation for their Mine	

Army Form C. 2118.

4TH BATTN TYNESIDE SCOTTISH
23RD BATTN NORTHUMBERLAND FUSILIERS

WAR DIARY
or
INTELLIGENCE SUMMARY.
(Erase heading not required.)

Instructions regarding War Diaries and Intelligence
Summaries are contained in F. S. Regs., Part II.
and the Staff Manual respectively. Title pages
will be prepared in manuscript.

Place	Date	Hour	Summary of Events and Information	Remarks and references to Appendices
TRENCHES	DEC 5th		The 12" & 6" Howitzers fired several rounds. The C.O. went on leave and Major O.R. Inghram assumed command of the Battalion.	
	6"		The Division on our left were apparently rather nervous as within 3 hours they sent two flares up. Weather. Casualties. 1 O.R. Sick.	8th
			The 20th N.F. relieved us and we have left this number "D" Batalion. We 20 N.F. are at present training for an trip and have detached companies behind in billets. Remainder of them strongly fortifying the line and "C" Coy were detached for manning the ORCHARD & "B" Batt. The remainder of the Companies & B.H.Q. are in Billets in RUE MARLE. The majority of the men proceeded to Souths in the afternoon. Small working parts set in the evening. Casualties 1 officer Wounded (S Conc).	
	7th		Long working parties out. Weather. Casualties. 4 O.R. Sick.	NIL
	7.8. 9th		Moved enemy Retirement. Casualties 1 O.R. Sick.	
	11		"D" Coy relieved "C" Coy in the ORCHARD. During the night the 20 N.F. carried out a successful raid. Casualties 1 O.R. Sick.	
			We were relieved by the 27th Batt N.N.F. 7 a.m. (4.T.T.) "D" Batt and one	

2353 Wt. W2544/1454 700,000 5/15 D. D. & L. A.D.S.S. Forms/C 2118.

Army Form C. 2118.

WAR DIARY
or
INTELLIGENCE SUMMARY.
(Erase heading not required.)

4TH BATTN TYNESIDE SCOTTISH.
23RD BATTN NORTHUMBERLAND FUSILIERS

Instructions regarding War Diaries and Intelligence Summaries are contained in F. S. Regs., Part II. and the Staff Manual respectively. Title pages will be prepared in manuscript.

Place	Date	Hour	Summary of Events and Information	Remarks and references to Appendices
FORT ROMPU	11th Dec.		Proceeded into Billets in FORT ROMPU. The men and several officers are in Huts. Batt. Head Quarters and 2 and Coy. Head Quarters are in Billets. D'lem men late in being relieved.	
	12th		Supplied a working party for R.E.'s of 1 Offr. + 30 O.R. very wet morning	
	13th		Casualties 3 O.R. Sick	
			Every available man out on Morning Parades. Casualties 2 O.R. Sick	
	14th		Every man out as yesterday. Casualties 3 O.R. Sick	
	15th W.		Two days rest. Arranged inter-bay football matches in the afternoons. Carried out a programme of training in the mornings. Casualties 5 O.R. Sick	
	17th		Saturday's morning practice. Every man out. Casualties NIL	
	18th			
	19th		Whilst in the trenches by Fld. Gen. Sir D. Haig, Commander in Chief. Commenced preparations for moving in Command still. Nine football in the afternoon which the men greatly appreciated.	
	20th		The men had their Christmas Dinner today as they will be in the trenches on Xmas day. 3 O.R. Sick 1 Yr. The dinner consisted of Roast Beef, Onions, potatoes, beans & cabbage, followed by Xmas pudding and Fruit & Nuts. Everyone had an enjoyable time. Casualties 2 O.R. Sick + 1 Acct. Injured	

2353 Wt. W2544/1454 700,000 5/15 D. D. & L. A.D.S.S./Forms/C.2118.

Army Form C. 2118.

WAR DIARY
or
INTELLIGENCE SUMMARY.

4TH BATTN TYNESIDE SCOTTISH
23RD BATTN NORTHUMBERLAND FUSILIERS

(Erase heading not required.)

Place	Date	Hour	Summary of Events and Information	Remarks and references to Appendices
FORT ROMPU	Dec 21st		In the morning attention was given to the alterations & chairs etc and arrangements for the inspection the following day. In the afternoon a football match was played. In the evening all the officers assembled together at Batt Headquarters and had their Xmas dinner. Casualties. 2 O.R. Sick.	
	22nd		The Battalion turned up with the remainder of the Brigade along the FORT ROMPU-FREVINGHEM Road, facing North. The inspection by Gen Sir J Hay was at 12.15 P.M. After the inspection the men marched past. Casualties. 4 O.R. Sick.	
B 2 Sect Subsect Sauchies	23rd		Coll. morning of the 23rd we took over the B 2 Subsect of trenches (our 1st line) from Lt Col Vander Hunter & 10 (3rd Tyneside Irish). Quiet all day. Very misty and damp morning. Bumps now Infantry if any following - C Coy Left Subs (CHAPELLE) B Coy Centre Subs - A Coy Right Centre. D Coy Reserve (ORCHARD).	
ARMENTIERES			Casualties. 5 O.R. Sick	
	24th		Dull weather. Marked advance. A few minnenwerfer shells fell in our lines during my little charge. Casualties. 2 O.R. Sick.	
	25th		Weather cold and wet. Fairly heavy reply with minenwerfer shells to our trench mortar battery shots. Some damage done to timber in Chard farm locality. Right quar. Casualties. 3 O.R. Sick.	

WAR DIARY or INTELLIGENCE SUMMARY.

Army Form C. 2118.

4TH BATTN TYNESIDE SCOTTISH.
23RD BATTN NORTHUMBERLAND FUSILIERS

Place	Date	Hour	Summary of Events and Information	Remarks and references to Appendices
Subsect Trenches Brewery Spurs Posts C Battn	26		Changeable weather. Quiet day. Silenced machine gun fire at night. Casualties 1 OR Sh.	
	27		Relieved by 20 NF (1st Bn) long relief not complete till 2pm. Became 'C' Battalion. Casualties 10 OR Sh. One platoon & four Lewis guns sent to reinforce B Bn.	
	28		Quiet day. Working parties found. Taking all men except gunners by night. 1 Lee Bn 1 Platoon and 1 Lewis gun again sent to Enemy Avenue post in front line abreast of Lille Rd. This order to apply always to 'C' Battn. Casualties 2 OR Sh.	
	29		Moderate aerial activity. Three heavy battery planes came over our lines, driving on animal of our own aeroplanes. Great anti-aircraft firing. All quiet. Casualties 2 OR Sh.	
	30		Quiet day. Same working parties provided. Casualties 4 OR Sh.	
B Subsector Trenches	31		Relieved 20 NF (1 1/9). Sharp & good relief, complete by 12.45 a.m. Up to an artillery strafe, the enemy fired a large number of heavy minenwerfer shells and 77 cm shells. Seven minenwerfer shells fired as far Lille Rd in succession were blind. Considerable damage done to our Works. Casualties 2.30 a.m	

Craintilow M.L.

VOL XIII

WAR DIARY
or
INTELLIGENCE SUMMARY.

Army Form C. 2118.

23rd Northumberland
4th Tyneside Scottish

VOL 13

Place	Date	Hour	Summary of Events and Information	Remarks and references to Appendices
B2 Sub Sect, Sector D, TRENCHES, ARMENTIERES	Jany 1917 2nd		Mutual artillery and trench mortar activity during day. Hostile M.G. & e.o. regained short after dusk. Casualties: 1. O.R. wounded. Regimental.	SHEET 36 N.W. Edit 6.C.
	2nd		A concentrated artillery shoot was put along the whole Coy front, very severe gun firing. Enemy retaliated with Minnys, Bangs, shrapnel etc. Casualties 2. OR Sick.	
	3rd 4th		Mutual activity throughout day. Casualties - 5 O.R. Sick. No men relieved by the 20th N.F. and became "D" Battalion in RUE MARLE. The 21st N.F. who were to make an assault on the night of the 6/7th Jany are training for same in RUE MARLE - in order to keep the ground of "C" Battn intact, our "A" Co. have been taken for the RUE FLEURIE Guard. Casualties. NIL	
RUE MARLE	5th 6th 7th 8th		Almost every available man was out on Working Parties. Casualties 1.OR Left Bn. Working Parties out both days. Lt Whittaker who was wounded on July 1st 1916 rejoined for duty and was posted as Lt. D. Co. Casualties 6th 3. OR sick, 7 Sick, 8th 2. OR Sick, B2 on the morning of the 8th we relieved the 20th N.F. (1st T.S.) in the B2 Sector	

Army Form C. 2118.

WAR DIARY
or
INTELLIGENCE SUMMARY.
(Erase heading not required.)

Place	Date	Hour	Summary of Events and Information	Remarks and references to Appendices
B2 SUB SECTOR TRENCHES	Jan 8		The dispatching of the tone has now been altered. - Parts of 4 Companies are now in the Front line occupying them an reserve. Companies were distributed as follows. Left, A. Co, Centre left D Co, Right Centre C Co, Right B Co. Quiet day. Casualties. 1. O.R. Sick.	82
	9th		Mutual activity throughout the day. Enemy trench fires a number of minenwerfer shells during considerable damage in places. Casualties. 5. O.R. Sick.	82
	10th		Received a draft of 60 men. None of them have shed any active service experience. Mutual activity again. In the evening an enemy minenwerfer left the enemy apparently thought we were attempting a raid as he opened a heavy fire with rifles and minenwerfer. We fired several shells into his own men. Casualties. 1. O.R. Killed. 1. O.R. Sick.	82
	11th		Our artillery fired into enemy entrenched with "minenwerfer" and did considerable damage to trenches & other parts of the "CLIFFORD FARM" Salient. Casualties 1. O.R. Wounded. 2. O.R. Sick.	82
	12th		In the morning up the 12th we were relieved by the 20th O.R - (1st T.S). Quiet relief.	82

WAR DIARY or INTELLIGENCE SUMMARY

Army Form C. 2118.

(Erase heading not required.)

Place	Date	Hour	Summary of Events and Information	Remarks and references to Appendices
	Jany 12th		Companies were disposed as follows:— A Co. Subsidiary line. B Co. ORCHARD. C Co. RUE FLEURIE. D Co. Ecole Pr[ote]s. Scheme as at present under preparation for a big move which we have taken steps to [learn?]. Casualties. 1 O.R. wounded. 1 O.R. sick.	G.M.
	13th		Supplied working parties. A draft of 100 Other [Ranks] mentioned were have arrived. All were have been transferred from the R.F.A. to the Infantry. Some of them are not very enthusiastic about it. Another draft of 58 men have also arrived — all trained men. Several of our best men were now mentioned on July 1st 1916, were amongst them. Casualties. 2 O.R. Sick.	
	14th		Usual working parties. Very cold weather. Frost nearly. Casualties. NIL.	
	15th		Usual working parties. Cold weather still prevails. Casualties. NIL.	
	16th		In the morning we were relieved by the 25th Northumberland Fusiliers (2nd Tyneside Irish) and we proceeded to Billets near LE QUINQUEREM. Casualties. 4 O.R. Sick.	
	17th 18th 19th 20		Spent training in trench[es?] the arrival in billets details of each Coy in and Battalion chosen in each Company. Each Company was ordered on an average 3 Officers and 60 men. The march in to the billet[s?]	

2449 Wt. W14957/M90 750,000 1/16 J.B.C. & A. Forms/C.2118/12.

WAR DIARY or INTELLIGENCE SUMMARY

Army Form C. 2118.

(Erase heading not required.)

Place	Date	Hour	Summary of Events and Information	Remarks and references to Appendices
FRAQUINGHEM	21"		we cannot get as far by the division. Casualties 1st NIL. 18th 4. O.R. Sick. Casualties 19th NIL. 20" NIL	B.M.
	22"		Reaching parties furnished today, night parties over ground which has been dry not the snow which on the nights attacked	B.M.
			Casualties 1 O.R. Sick.	
	23"		The greater part of three days were taken up in practices by the Battn which is due to take place on the night of 24/31. 1917. A very keen and hard frost	
	24"		was prevalent as far throughout this period. The ground is covered with snow which fell several days ago. There will present a great difficulty in getting over "NOMANS LAND". Very great interest is being shown by all C.C. Commands in this event which is the first of its type.	
			In the night of the 24", a practice was held in the dark.	
			Casualties. 22nd 1. O.R. Sick. 23rd NIL. 24". 2. O.R. Sick.	B.M.
	25"		Keen frost still prevails. The G.O.C. inspected the Bombers a.o.o. Cos the Specialists and parades in the morning. The C.O. tried a provisional in the afternoon and the Specialists & Officers who were leading first in the morning. Casualties - 2 O.R. Sick.	
	26"		In the afternoon was received a move to prepare to make advance. Every thing was pushed up and in the evening the Battalion left ERQUINGHEM south in	

2449 Wt. W14957/M90 750,000 1/16 J.B.C. & A. Forms/C.2118/12.

Army Form C. 2118.

WAR DIARY
or
INTELLIGENCE SUMMARY
(Erase heading not required.)

Instructions regarding War Diaries and Intelligence Summaries are contained in F.S. Regs., Part II. and the Staff Manual respectively. Title Pages will be prepared in manuscript.

Place	Date	Hour	Summary of Events and Information	Remarks and references to Appendices
MONT DES COTS.	JANY 26th		Buses. After a cold tiring journey the Battalion arrived at MONT DES COTS about 1 P.M. the transport did not arrive until about 6 P.M. Companies are billetted mostly in Barns the weather was frost still serious. Practically missed the district. Casualties: 3. O.R. Sick	SHEET 27. Exhibit 2. C[?]
	27th		A great deal of trouble has arisen regarding new billets. Instances apparently have arisen into the many new men and in the 10th Lincolns Billets. Practical arrangements were made for the accommodation meanwhile. Men received that are still have training not the most and training so tomorrow again. Casualties: NIL.	C[?]
GODEWAERS-VELDE	28th.		The Battalion moved into Billets in GODEWAERSVELDE. Buses as in good Billets. Weather still severe very cold. Casualties. NIL.	C[?]
	29th.		Word received that the Raiding Party will proceed by lorries to ERQUINGHEM on the morning of the 30th Inst. and the battalion in the Buses (Buses). The remainder of the Battn. to carry on with training and will probably move in one then district until the 10th Feby. Rear Guard Staff Provost. Casualties. 4. O.R. Sick. C[?]	
	30th.	9.30.	At 9.30 P.M. the Miniers & Fatigue men & (326) left for ERQUINGHEM under Lt.Col. CR Prst. The remnant of Companies were amalgamated into 2 Companies and carried on with ordinary training. In the afternoon the Battalion struck a 5 mile route march. A Battalion officers Mess was opened. Casualties: NIL.	C[?]

Army Form C. 2118.

WAR DIARY
or
INTELLIGENCE SUMMARY

(Erase heading not required.)

Instructions regarding War Diaries and Intelligence Summaries are contained in F. S. Regs., Part II. and the Staff Manual respectively. Title Pages will be prepared in manuscript.

Place	Date	Hour	Summary of Events and Information	Remarks and references to Appendices
GODEWAERS VELDE	Jany 31.st 1917.		Battalion carried out with ordinary training. In the afternoon an hour's route march was done. Casualties: 2 O.R. Sick.	

C.R. Longhurst Major
Cmdg 23rd (S) Batten Northumberland Fusiliers
4th Tyneside Scottish

2449 Wt. W14957/M90 750,000 1/16 J.B.C. & A. Forms/C.2118/12.

WAR DIARY

OF

23rd (S) Bn. NORTHUMBERLAND FUSILIERS

(4th TYNESIDE SCOTTISH)

MONTH ---- FEBRUARY, 1917.

Army Form C. 2118.

WAR DIARY
or
INTELLIGENCE SUMMARY
(Erase heading not required.)

Vol XIV

Instructions regarding War Diaries and Intelligence Summaries are contained in F. S. Regs., Part II. and the Staff Manual respectively. Title Pages will be prepared in manuscript.

Place	Date	Hour	Summary of Events and Information	Remarks and references to Appendices
GODEWAERS-VELDE	FEBY 1917 1st		General Plumer, Commanding 2nd Army visited the Battalion in the morning and watched Humphries going through the programme of training. In the afternoon the Battalion went out for a Short Route March. Weather fine. Front still favorable. There was a C.O.S. conference at Poste 10th Corps in the afternoon. Casualties 3. O.R. Sick.	Ref Sheet 20 N.W. 27.
	2nd		Battalion went out for a short route march in the morning. Front still favorable. Casualties NIL	
	3rd + 4th			
	5th		Ordinary parade carried out during day. Casualties 4. O.R. Sick	
	6th		The Battalion proceeded to a special training area ... Casualties 1. O.R. Sick.	

Army Form C. 2118.

WAR DIARY
or
INTELLIGENCE SUMMARY
(Erase heading not required.)

Instructions regarding War Diaries and Intelligence Summaries are contained in F. S. Regs., Part II. and the Staff Manual respectively. Title Pages will be prepared in manuscript.

Place	Date	Hour	Summary of Events and Information	Remarks and references to Appendices
A. ODEWAERS NELD E.	Feb 7th		There were no Brigade Trench moves on this morning – all Battalions were not dis. The afternoon of ETROVINGHEM was very heavy an shows trimming show, and from ingentiment put not capital. Battn. Hotz marched	REF SHEET 27
	8th		Casualties 3. O.R. Sick. Column turnover carried out. Casualties 10. O.R. Sick.	am
	9th		Evening turnover. It late moved Feb 1st 1466 returned for duty. Casualties NIL	am
			Casualties NIL	So
	10th		Special lecture were given on Bayonet fighting etc by an Army Instructor Lent Lieutenant of Army Staff also called at morning troop were off. Casualties NIL	m
PARMENTIERS TRENCHES S.E. B.2 Sub-Sect-C	11th		On the night of the 11th/12th we carried out a raid against the enemy trenches S.E. of ARMENTIÈRES. The raiding party consisted of 12 officers and 257 O.R's. Zero hour was fixed for 10.30 P.M. The raiding party under command of... [complete] [illegible] was subdivided in 4 parties as follows: A. Co. under Capt Cox Brigitt M.C. assisted by 2/Lt. J.B. Denman & 2/Lt. S. Milley and 67 O.R.S. B. Co. under Lieut. W H Thompson assisted by 2/Lts. Morris & Mening & 60 O.R.S. C. Co. under Lieut. J.S. Heron assisted by 2/Lts. Malin, & Algie & 64 O.R.S. D.Co. under 2/Lt. J.R. Freeman assisted by 2/Lt. S.C. Kavanagh & 66 O.R.S. Lt Col C.R. Pinch assumed command of the operations. At Zero hour the parties moved	See APPENDIX #N/5/2

WAR DIARY or INTELLIGENCE SUMMARY

Army Form C. 2118.

Instructions regarding War Diaries and Intelligence Summaries are contained in F.S. Regs., Part II. and the Staff Manual respectively. Title Pages will be prepared in manuscript.

(Erase heading not required.)

Place	Date	Hour	Summary of Events and Information	Remarks and references to Appendices
PRMENTIERES	17th Feby. 1917	11th	formed to their respective gaps in the enemy wire. The left party "A 60" met with great resistance and suffered very heavy casualties. 2/Lt. J.S. Common who got into the enemy trenches was severely wounded. His orderly Pte Monmouth shewed great courage and devotion to duty, and succeeded in carrying 2/Lt Common safely from the enemy trenches twice, although once attacked in "No Mans Land" by a strong party of the enemy who had got out of their trenches in the hope of succesfully despatching our wounded party est. When attacked by this party Pte Monmouth beat them off. 2/Lt Walley effected an entrance under the enemy trenches who and turned his dugouts killing 3 Germans a little like he also shot another German with his revolver. An enemy machine gun covered a number of casualties to this party who and prevented the new portion of the party entering the enemy wire – being to the number of casualties and the enemy watching could attack left. Daggett gave orders to withdraw. These who were left continued to fight and throw bombs and gradually retire. In regaining our lines it was reported that Capt. Daggett were missing. The 2nd Party from the left "D" co met with a very strong resistance and suffered casualties in attempting to get into the enemy trenches. 2/Lt J.R. 4 men were mortally wounded and Sergt Clough wounded command of the advance party. Owing to the more heavy fighting and most of the number of casualties to be evacuated this party did not attempt to enter the enemy trenches again but evacuated all casualties. The next party on the right of "D" co which is "C" Company met with resistance not	See APPENDIX G N/S/2

Army Form C. 2118.

WAR DIARY
or
INTELLIGENCE SUMMARY
(Erase heading not required.)

Place	Date	Hour	Summary of Events and Information	Remarks and references to Appendices
ARMENTIERES	11th Feb 1917		The entrance to the mine and 2/Lt J. Morton who was in command of the Advance Party was wounded. Lt. Col. C.P. Pond accompanied this Party and he together with 2/Lt. M. Algie marked the first line of the enemy. This Party which must exhibit much skill in the German front and support trenches. 2/Lt. Algie assumed command of the support line Party and led his men straight into that line. He showed great pluck and determination and personally shot 4 Germans with his revolver — he also bombed many of the enemy who took shelter in various dug-outs. He also a bombing Parties. for shielding an ammunition store was blown up also a bombing Parties. He was assisted a great deal by C.S.M. Morris, L. and Ypfl. to Mitchell, Sappers Marrow & Brady of the 209 Field Cy. R.E. who accompanied this Party did good work in connection with blowing up the ammunition store and by 1H 0.45 2/Lt. J.B. Heron who shot very good work in the German front line. 2/Lt. S.C. Kerridge in command of a section of "D" his party established communication with the Party on "C" his left. Seven prisoners were taken by 2/Lt Algie's Party including 2 Officers. (Officers were shot by 2/Lt Algie.) The Right Party sustained heavy casualties in "No Man's Land" from a heavy & fruitless artillery barrage. Lt. W.H. Thompson effected an entrance through the enemy wire which was not cut satisfactorily. For full details of the whole raid Hence see APPENDIX 2N/5/2.	See APPENDIX 2N/S/2

Casualties: 1 Officer Missing, 1 Officer Wounded, 12 O.R. Killed, 13 O.R.s Missing
3 O.R.s Wounded, 87 O.R. Wounded.

Army Form C. 2118.

WAR DIARY
or
INTELLIGENCE SUMMARY

(Erase heading not required.)

Instructions regarding War Diaries and Intelligence Summaries are contained in F. S. Regs., Part II. and the Staff Manual respectively. Title Pages will be prepared in manuscript.

Place	Date	Hour	Summary of Events and Information	Remarks and references to Appendices
GODEWAERS VELDE.	13th Feb. 1917.		The marching party rejoined the remainder of the Battalion at Godewaersvelde. 2/Lt. J.R. Freeman died of wounds on 12" Feb. Casualties NIL. For the 14th Ordinary training was carried out.	HAZEBROUCK MAP 5.17.
	15.		Col Peck made many enquiries from slight wounds & injuries received on the raid and to C.E. S.M. Lahey the Divisional Commander inspected the Battalion at 2.30 pm the men were paraded separately. He congratulated the Battalion on their splendid performance. The Corps Commander paid a visit to the C O in the afternoon. Casualties 1. O.R. Sick	
	16.		Casualties 4. O.R. Sick	
	17.		The Battalion marched out to training area and carried out a practice attack. Casualties 2. O.R. Sick The Brigade is to move towards were commencing 19"Feb. Prepared for the move. Casualties 4. O.R. Sick	
	18.		The Battalion paraded at 8 am and marched off via CAESTRE to HAZEBROUCK at STEENBECK where they billetted overnight. A few men fell out on the line of march Casualties 9. O.R. Sick	
	19.		The Battalion of marched off in the morning via PIRE to NORRENT FONTES a large number of men fell out. Casualties 9 O.R. Sick	
	20.		The following letter was received from Corps Commander. The Corps Commander	

WAR DIARY or INTELLIGENCE SUMMARY

Army Form C. 2118.

Place	Date	Hour	Summary of Events and Information	Remarks and references to Appendices
VILLERS BRULIN.	22"		The following Honours and Rewards were notified to the Battalion:- **MILITARY MEDAL.** 107665 Sapper H. Marrows, 209 Field Coy. and Sappers & Privates of men by (both attached to this unit for march in augu 11/12 Feb 1917) following men of this unit:- 23/1525 Sergt. W. Scott, 23/691 Sergt. J. Akroft, 23/1228 Pte. M.T. Chinfield, 23/1415 Sergt. W. Bates, 31054 L/Cpl. W. Walker, 37974 Pte. W. Murdoch, 23/265 Pte. W. Stringer, 40863 Pte. B. Watermouth. The Battn. moved from CAPT LEIRS to VILLERS BRULIN. Casualties. 2. O.R's. with.	LENS SHEET 11.
	23"		The Battn. moved to huts in ECOIVRES. Very muddy tramp. The following Honours and Rewards were notified for men of this Battalion:- **MILITARY MEDAL.** 38127 L/Cpl. B. Phillips, 23/1339 L/Cpl. W. Mitchell. **BAR TO MILITARY MEDAL.** 23/415 Pte. J. Wearmouth. Casualties. 6 O.R.S. wd.	
ARRAS.	24"		The Battn. moved into huts in ARRAS and were in Brigade Reserve. Everyone much in comfortable huts. Casualties. 2. O.R.S. Sick.	

WAR DIARY
INTELLIGENCE SUMMARY

Army Form C. 2118.

Place	Date	Hour	Summary of Events and Information	Remarks and references to Appendices
NOEUX LES MINES	20		have read the report on the raid of night 11th/12th February, and desire to say that he thinks the operations were excellently planned and executed and reflect any great credit on all concerned. He wishes to congratulate Lieut Col Pard on his gallantry and leadership, and would be glad if you will communicate his appreciation of the success of the raid to all who took part in it. Sd C.W. Gwynne B.G. The following letter was also received from the Army Commander. "The operation was well planned and carried out and reflects great credit on all concerned" Sgd. Herbert Plumer, General Commanding 2nd Army 23.2.17. The Battalion moved off early in the morning and marched to DIEVAL. There was a faultline of on the march. Rainy day. Casualties: 6 O.R. Sick	HAZEBROUCK SHEET 5B & LENS SHEET 11. See APPENDIX G N/3/4 & G N/3/5 also G N/3/3. II ANZAC CORPS
	21st		The Battalion moved off in the morning to CHELERS. The Billets in this village were in a bad condition and very little assistance could be obtained from the town Mayor or the Mayor, in fact all the French people in this village seemed disinclined on making things as uncomfortable as possible and obtain as much from the soldiers as possible. Casualties. 5 O.R. Sick	

WAR DIARY or INTELLIGENCE SUMMARY

Army Form C. 2118.

Place	Date	Hour	Summary of Events and Information	Remarks and references to Appendices
ARRAS	25"		The following Telegram was received:— "The following have been awarded decorations:— DISTINGUISHED SERVICE ORDER:— Lieut Col. C.P.PORCH. MILITARY CROSS Lieut. J.B.Heron. 2/Lt. J.S.Cameron 2/Lt. W. Algie. 2/Lt. S.C. Kerridge. 2/Lt. S. Miller. 2/Lt. J. Watson BAR TO D.C.M. 21/377 Sergt. A. F. Jackson (21st N.F. attached to this unit for raid on 11/12 Feb, 1917) D.C.M. 23/1124 Cpl. S.M. L. Thorne. 23/1364 C.S.M. S. Watson. 37972 Pte. B. Craighill. Please convey Second Army, Second Anzac, Divisional and Brigade Commanders congratulations to the recipients from Corps.	ARRAS. ARRAS. 51.B. N.W.3. EOIT 6A
			Casualties NIL	O2
	26"		Practically every available man was out on working parties. A regrettable incident occurred but one of the working parties supplied by C.Os. This party were showing bombs from a store when a 4.2 not shell fell amongst them exploding. 38 casualties. 6 ORs killed. 15 of whom were either killed or died of wounds. 9 ORs died of wounds. 23 ORs wounded. Lieut. 6 OR's Wd. Casualties.	
	27"m		Large working parties out. The C.O. went round the lines in the morning. From walker appeared. Casualties. 14 from Sub. 4.O.R's wide 85 Large working parties out. Casualties. 5 ORs Sick.	
	28"			

WAR DIARY / INTELLIGENCE SUMMARY

Army Form C. 2118.

NOV. '15

23(S) Bn North'd Fus

Place	Date	Hour	Summary of Events and Information	Remarks and references to Appendices
ARRAS	March 1st 1917		Large enemy parties out all day. Weather fine.	
	2nd		We relieved the 2/2 M.F. (3rd Gwyneth Scottish) in the ROCKINGCOURT trenches. Informers were distributed as follows: A Coy Right Sector; B Coy Left C Coy Support D Coy Reserve. Pm 14 ORs was admitted on ROCKINGCOURT VILLAGE in a rattan. Casualties: L. & R.S. Lieb.	Ref Sheet 51.B. N.W.3 Coys B.A.
ROCKINGCOURT TRENCHES			There were two trades on the sector named KING & KITE. The trenches manned KING generally runs on the crest of "Monument" Spur.	
	3rd		Quiet quiet day. Normal mortar activity between artillery. 2 O.Rs Lieb. "Frot Gait" Brants on "Pineapples" and Rifle Grenades. Our Stokes Inn Mortar pounded Trenches in front action and also sent one on our enemy. 100 rifle grenades per day. Casualties 1 O.R. Lich	ROCKINGCOURT STREET 51. B. N.W.1 & 3 L.A. 5.A.
	4th		Quiet day. Two of our patrols went out at 5 Pomerance and on the enemy were found more working in front of this mine. Casualties 2 ORs Lich	
	5th	6.10 pm	A raid was carried out by the GORDONS on our immediate left. 26 seconds 1 Officer 20 O.R. prisoners. The movement of and moment by B retaliation of several descriptions. In the evening the enemy was active Rifle and M Guns had Rs on our front. Casualties 1 OR Killed 3 ORs wounded and fired a great deal with Artillery & T.M.S. 2ORs and	
	6th		Quiet day. In the evening about 7.30 Pm in enemy working party about 60 to 70 m strong attempted to water sand trenches excavated by D Co. (left sector). The new furnace A.B. bomb and Machine gun fire. The trenches of the enemy worken's were thoroughly Attend to from occasional burrying of Pm.	

WAR DIARY or INTELLIGENCE SUMMARY

Army Form C. 2118.

Place	Date	Hour	Summary of Events and Information	Remarks and references to Appendices
POCLINCOURT TRENCHES	6th		Grenades and light trench mortars which all fell just over our front line. The enemy advanced bombards and trenches throwing smoke bombs in the air. In two places on that he went and sent out an informal bombing encountered ourselves, he failing that they acted most spectaculo and knew no moral of common sense should not send a man in "NO MAN'S LAND" while every rapidly interval. In the wood worked. Giving up a barrage of trench mortars came into our front line on showers and continuous ensembles. All our men were very cool and behaved splendidly. Casualties 1 O.R. Killed. 1 O.R. wounded. 2 O.R. Sick.	
	7th		At about 2.15 p.m. in the morning a small enemy patrol again attempted to near our front line in D.L. Lots they were driven back and fired upon. Lastly the enemy were worth full. We sent patrols and safe holding advance attempted attacks by the enemy but were unable to defeat any trace of this movement etc. A most severe was our night by the R.C.M.S. (no previous attention). Casualties 4 O.Rs Sick.	
ECOIVRES	8th		We were relieved by the 25th Manitoba Bn. (2.T.I) On completion of relief the Battalion proceeded to X.Huts ECOIVRES. Very cold night. Casualties 1 O.R. Killed. 1 O.R. Wounded 4 O.Rs Sick.	
	9th		Supplied a party of 2.20 O.Rs for a working party in the morning, three hours did not show whilst the party away. A second working party of R 20 O.Rs was sent away in the evening for burying cables near ARRAS. At 11 a.m. the Battalion (less working parties) left by tram and proceeded to HOUVELIN. Two companies were billeted in HOUVELIN and the others two companies with Batth. H.Q. in ROCOURT. Cold wet evening also Second working party did not get back into billets until 5 p.m. on the 10th inst. Casualties NIL.	
HOUVELIN				

Army Form C. 2118.

WAR DIARY
or
INTELLIGENCE SUMMARY

(Erase heading not required.)

Instructions regarding War Diaries and Intelligence Summaries are contained in F. S. Regs., Part II. and the Staff Manual respectively. Title Pages will be prepared in manuscript.

Place	Date	Hour	Summary of Events and Information	Remarks and references to Appendices
HOUVELIN & ROCOURT.	10th March 1916		Spent the day in cleaning up. C.O. was at Bde. H.Q. in afternoon. Coy Commanders recce in the evening. Casualties. 1. O.R. Sick.	BDO
	11.		P.P.R. Coy in on Rifle Range. C.P.D. Coy were on working parties in morning (digging trenches) hints. Casualties. 3. O.R.'s sick.	O.R.
	12.		A Divisional Parade was held in the training area when the Corps Commander, F.M. Lt. Genrl. Sir Charles Fergusson, Bt. K.C.B., M.V.O. D.S.O. presented ribbons to Officers, N.C.Os & men of the Royals. Casualties. NIL.	BDO
	13.		During these days special training was carried out in the training area. A Series of trenches have been stitched and flagged out representing the enemy system of trenches opposite ROCLINCOURT. Specialist training has also been	
	14.		carried out so far as circumstances would allow. A strength of 48. O.R.s arrived in the 20th. The Battalion however is still under strength.	
	20.		Casualties. 13th 2nd 1. OR. Sick 16th 2nd 3 OR's Sick 19th 2nd 4 OR's Sick	BDO
			14th " 2 OR " 17 " NIL 20th " NIL	
			15th " 1 " 18 " 1. OR "	
ECOIVRES.	21.	9.0 am	The Battalion marched to X Inds ECOIVRES marching via BETHONSART–BERKETTE and thence ST POL–ARRAS road. Inds were very uncomfortable and cold. Casualties. 6 OR's Sick	BDO
	22.		Sent two large parties away for work. One party on billets in Brigade ROCLINCOURT VALLEY and the second party on St CATHERINE. Army received that the	

2449 Wt. W14957/M90 750,000 1/16 J.B.C. & A. Forms/C.2118/12.

Army Form C. 2118.

WAR DIARY
or
INTELLIGENCE SUMMARY
(Erase heading not required.)

Instructions regarding War Diaries and Intelligence Summaries are contained in F. S. Regs., Part II. and the Staff Manual respectively. Title Pages will be prepared in manuscript.

Place	Date	Hour	Summary of Events and Information	Remarks and references to Appendices
ECOIVRES.	22"		Battalion as its move into the trenches was either on the 23" or 24". but very cold day with occasional falls of snow. Casualties. 1. O.R. Sick.	Ref Sheet 57. C.
	23"		Received large scale maps of Bernet & made system of trenches also showing trenches for the Bde. Digestion (Brown line). Orders received that we proceed post RR105 on the 24" but out bile was killed from the 15" Bn. the Royal Scots. the 227 M.F. (3 M TS) on between us the left centre of the trenches. Casualties. 2.O.R.'S Sick	80. 80.
	24"		1st Instructions received for intended attack, also operation order received to prepare to attack and take the Black Line with 2.6.9" in reserve. One Battalion moved off not to RR105 in the evening. Late relief. Transport were late owing to congestion of traffic. Casualties. 4. O.R.'s Sick.	80.
ARRAS.	25" 26" 27" 28"		Very heavy machine gun fire met — Rate not in length 570 men for day but there is no probable means to the number of latched men into the number of men each doing to best trusts. Reports afterwards cannot be obtained as reserve were being controlled. The fighting efficiency of the men has been greatly reduced owing to this. Casualties. 26 Red. NIL. 27" Red 1. O.R Sick. Casualties. 26— 1 O.R. Sick 25— 3. M. Cas. 1 O.R. Wounded.	Ref. Sheet. 51 B. test N.W. 3.

WAR DIARY
or
INTELLIGENCE SUMMARY
(Erase heading not required.)

Army Form C. 2118.

Place	Date	Hour	Summary of Events and Information	Remarks and references to Appendices
ARRAS	29th MAR 1917		Sent two men out on morning party. In the evening we relieved the 22nd NF (3rd Tyneside Scottish). Relief was not completed until 11.30 p.m. The trenches are very muddy and have deep in many places. There were only 63 few Bombs in the Battalion and many bombs had leads were some anything suitably from the wet and mud of trenches. Companies were disposed as follows. B. Left Sector, B. Right Centre, D. Support, C. Reserve. The 11th Br. Suffolks are on our Right and the 9th Scottish on our left. Rainy day. Casualties. 4 ORs Sick.	R/Sketch ROCLINCOURT S13 N.W. Sheet 51.D
ROCLINCOURT TRENCHES.	30th		Artillery activity throughout the day. "BOGEY AVENUE & FATHER'S FOOT PATH" came in for a great deal of shelling. In the evening a patrol went out under Lieut. on the enemy very much on the alert. The patrol was fired upon & bombed, a number of rifle grenades were also & great matters. A great deal of work no being done in this sector and preparations for the attack are in full swing. Casualties. 1 OR killed.	BD. BD
	31st MAR		Mutual artillery activity throughout the day. The enemy have elements in good supply of gas shells of Lazy calibre. A good number of 5.9" shells were dropped into ROCLINCOURT in the evening at 8.30 pm the 1/6th Black Watch carried out a raid on the enemy lines on our left. Heavy retaliation heavily on ROCLINCOURT and on our sector of trenches. Slight shower during the day. Trenches still very sticky. Casualties 6 ORs Wounded 1 OR Sick. Lt McQueen Slightly wounded (at duty)	(4th TYNESIDE SCOTTISH) 2/3rd Northd Fus'rs Signed Longhurst Major D/O Commanding

S E C R E T.
34th Div. no. SG.34/25/2.

....
....

Herewith:-

Administrative Instructions No.1. - Part Five:-
"Police arrangements for Straggler Posts".

Administrative Instructions No.2:-

Part Ten - "Tramways"

Part Thirteen - "Control Posts (Routes etc.)

Lieut.Colonel,
A.A. & Q.M.G.,
34th Division.

30/3/17.

ADMINISTRATIVE INSTRUCTIONS No. 1.

PART FIVE.

Police Arrangements for Straggler Posts.

(1) Battle Straggler Posts are being established as follows:-

(i) 9th Division:-
G.13.d.1.9.
G.14.c.10.4.
G.16.c.3.5.
G.16.c.6.9.
G.16.c.5.7.
G.15.a.7.7.

(ii) 34th Division:-
(a) Straggler/Collecting Post.   G.9.c.6.6.

(b) Battle Straggler Posts:-
G.16.a.0.7.   )
G.15.b.4.8.   )   Strength:-
G.9.c.8.1.   )   4 other ranks
G.9.c.0.10.   )   at each Post.
G.8.b.9.6.   )

(iii) 51st Division:-
A.28.c.3.4.
A.26.d.80.25.

Disposal of Stragglers.

(2) Stragglers of the 34th Division.
All Stragglers will be directed from the various Divisional Straggler Posts to the Straggler Collecting Post at G.9.c.6.6., where they will be retained by the A.P.M. As soon as 50 have been collected, a report will be rendered to the General Staff, who will issue instructions as to their disposal.

A report will also be rendered by the A.P.M. at 9 p.m. daily of the number of stragglers at the Collecting Post for whom orders as to their disposal have not yet been received.

Stragglers of other Divisions.
Stragglers of other Divisions will be disposed of by the A.P.M. under arrangements made direct between him and the A.P.M's. of the Divisions concerned.

Re-equipping of Stragglers.

On arrival of stragglers at the Collecting Post, they will be re-equipped as necessary by the A.P.M., the equipment etc. being drawn from the Divisional Salvage Store at ST.CATHERINE.

ADMINISTRATIVE INSTRUCTIONS NO. 2.

PART TEN.

TRENCH TRAMWAYS.

SYSTEM. (1) Map "Z" attached shows Tramways in the Forward Area constructed and still under construction. The German tram system is also shown as far as it is known.

(*) to be issued later to G.O.C.R.A., and Infy.Bdes. only.

PERSONNEL (2) 2nd Lieut.J.S.CLEMENTS, 18th N.F. (Pioneers), is appointed Officer i/c Divisional Trams, (D.T.O.); a permanent staff is allotted, consisting of 20 o.r. 18th N.F. for Base Traffic Control, Maintenance Party, and repair of trucks.

The address of the D.T.O. will be c/o 18th N.F. (Pioneers); should he find it necessary to alter his location, he will report his new position by wire to D.H.Q.

BASES. (3) There are two Tram Bases in the Forward Divl. Area, situated as follows:-
No.1. Les Quatre Vents, G.10.b.2.2.
No.2. LILLE Road, G.9.b.40.99.

1 N.C.O. and 2 men will be located at each Base from the permanent Staff (para 2 above).

OPERATING. (4) Until the tactical situation admits, the tramways will only be worked by night.

Application for truckage will be made direct by Infantry Brigades and R.A. to the D.T.O., who will allot trucks as available, and inform Units the time their stores should arrive. Demands for truckage should be submitted by 12 noon on the day for which the trucks are required.

Units using the trams will arrange to provide pushing parties of 4 o.r. for each truck; this personnel will also be used for loading and unloading the trucks allotted to the Unit furnishing them.

OCTOBER TRAMWAY. (5) (a) The OCTOBER Tramway running from G.16.b.6.4. to G.11.b.5.5. (9th Divisional Area) will be extended as shown in Map "Z", as soon as the situation admits. This extension will be undertaken by this Division, and the existing tramline handed over by the 9th Division as soon as the C.R.E. reports that he is in a position to start the work.

(b) The D.T.O. will arrange to get into touch with the D.T.O., 9th Division, and report on the following points:-

(i) No. of o.r. required to run the existing OCTOBER Tramway.
(ii) No. of trucks which will be taken over.
(iii) Position at which he or the officer detailed to help him (para 6 below) will establish himself as soon as the tram is taken over.
(iv) Whether a telephone system is established along the Tram.

/6....

EXTRA PERSONNEL
REQUIRED FOR (6) (a) The O.C. Divl.Train will detail one officer
OCTOBER TRAM. to assist the D.T.O. as required from Zero Hour onwards. The officer selected should be instructed to communicate with the D.T.O. and his name is to be reported to Divl. Headquarters.

(b) The C.R.E. will arrange for any other personnel required.

CLOSING OF (7) As soon as the OCTOBER Tramway is in working
DIVL. TRAMWAYS. order the present Divisional Tramways based as in para 3 above will be closed, the G.O.C., R.A., and C.Os.C. Infantry Brigades being notified previously of the hour and date.

ADMINISTRATIVE INSTRUCTIONS NO. 2.

PART THIRTEEN.

CONTROL POSTS (Routes etc.)

(1) Control Posts have been established in the Corps Area at all road junctions, Cross Roads, and points which are likely to cause blocks in the circulation of the Traffic: those found by the Division are situated as follows:-

```
No.1.Post.    ...   B.14.c.4.5.  )
"  2  "       ...   B.14.d.7.1.  )
"  3  "       ...   B.22.a.2.2.  )  ST.POL -
"  4  "       ...   B.22.d.7.6.  )
"  5  "       ...   B.22.d.8.8.  )  ARRAS Road.
"  6  "       ...   B.23.c.8.1.  )
"  7  "       ...   B.29.b.7.4.  )

No.1.Post.    ...   L.10.b.3.7.  )  LOUEZ.
"  2  "       ...   L.11.a.3.7.  )  ST.AUBIN.
"  3  "       ...   L.11.a.5.6.  )   -do-
"  4  "       ...   G.1.d.5.0.   )  ANZIN ST.AUBIN.
"  5  "       ...   G.7.a.4.7.   )   -do-
"  6  "       ...   G.8.c.4.8.   )
"  7  "       ...   G.8.d.5.0.   )
"  8  "       ...   G.9.c.7.2.   )  ST.CATHERINE.
```

Captain G.Swinburn, 24th Northd.Fusiliers, Divisional Traffic Officer, is in charge of these posts.

In addition to the above, a half-troop of cavalry and half a Platoon of cyclists have been attached to the Division to assist in Traffic Control. In the case of the Division leaving the Corps area, these latter details will be handed over to the relieving Division.

TRAFFIC ROUTES.

(2) (a) Are shown in Appendix "T".

(b) The new road from G.8.b.5.0. to G.9.c.7.2. is for one way traffic only from East to West.

(s) The ARRAS - ST.POL Road will be closed to all traffic from Zero Hour to "Z" plus 48 hours, except for Motor Ambulances vide Administrative Instructions No.1., Part Two, para (iii).

(d) In the case of an advance, the ARRAS - BAILLEUL Road is allotted to this Division, and will be opened as early as the situation admits for horse transport both ways, and eventually for motor transport both ways. The A.P.M. will be responsible for the traffic control of this road.

GENERAL INSTRUCTIONS.

(3) (a) Attention of all ranks is drawn to Third Army Traffic Orders of January 1917, copies of which have been issued to all concerned, and to Divisional Routine Order No.167 dated 3/3/17, which reads as follows:-

/Contd....

Divisional Routing Order No. 167 - "MARCH DISCIPLINE".

"In order to allow fast-moving overtaking slow-moving traffic, and to admit of traffic regulation at Cross Roads, the following distances will be maintained between Units on the march:-

	Yards.
Between Companies	200
" Battalions	400
" The Transport of individual Units.	100
" The Transport of Brigade Groups.	1000
" Batteries of Artillery.	200. "

(b) These instructions are to be strictly adhered to, and to admit of supply services running smoothly on roads which are bound to become very congested.

(c) A telephone system has been established between various selected Posts in the Corps area, and is linked up with the Town Major ARRAS, Canadian and VI Corps.
This system is divided into seven sections, each in charge of an officer.
These officers are authorised to stop or divert traffic as may be found necessary, and all ranks are warned that any orders issued by these officers must be complied with without query.

(d) Traffic routes are being marked in ARRAS, and transport officers etc. should take steps to acquaint themselves with the traffic control in that place.
The A.P.M. can give any information required.

(e) On all traffic routes only cars and despatch riders will be allowed to overtake traffic, except with the direct orders of the Traffic Officer of the section. Lorries must conform to the pace of the slowest vehicle.
Double banking must not be allowed under any circumstances.

(f) Horses are not to be exercised on Traffic Routes; mounted men are to move off main roads, field tracks being used whenever possible.

APPENDIX "T".

AMMUNITION.

Division.	Position of wagon lines.	Routes to Battery positions.	Route of Return.	Remarks.
Right.	LARESSET.	ST.POL - ARRAS Road, DEAD MAN'S CORNER - Road junction G.15.d.15.25.	Same.	An interval of 50 yards will be maintained between every 10 vehicles.
Centre.	E.17.	ACQ - ECOIVRES - BRAY - CHAUSEE BRUNEHAUT - ANZIN - thence to ST.CATHERINE for ROCLINCOURT VALLEY batteries or to MADAGASCAR.	ST.CATHERINE or MAISON ROUGE - ANZIN - same as outward journey.	
	West of BRAY. (Camp "C")	BRAY - CHAUSEE BRUNEHAUT - same as for the E.17 wagon lines.	Same as for E.17 wagon lines as far as applicable.	
Left.	ACQ.	Same as for centre division wagon lines in E.17.	Same as for E.17 wagon lines.	

SUPPLIES.

Division.	Railheads	Refilling Points.	Routes.	Remarks.
Right.	TINCQUES.	ARRAS Road E. of HAUTE AVESNES.	ARRAS Road - DEAD MAN'S CORNER - ST.NICHOLAS - Br.Factory.	Return same Route.
Centre.	AUBIGNY.	ARRAS Road W. of HAUTE AVESNES.	ARRAS Road - DEAD MAN'S CORNER - ST.NICHOLAS - CHALK FARM.	Return same Route.
Left.	AUBIGNY.	Between ECOIVRES and MAROEUIL.	ECOIVRES - MAROEUIL - ANZIN - ST.CATHERINE - LILLE Road - ROCLINCOURT.	Return same Route.

W.D. 4N/5/6

SECRET.   OPERATION ORDERS No. 41   Copy No 8.
                                    by
LIEUT. COL. C.P. PORCH, D.S.O., CMDG. 23rd NORTHUMBERLAND FUSILIERS,
            (4TH BATTN. TYNESIDE SCOTTISH)

Reference.
Trench Map,   March 31st 1917.
ROCLINCOURT
Z51b N.W. 1.

1. Co-operation of Artillery etc.

For information re :-

    Enemy.
    Disposition & role of our own Forces.
    General and special of the plan
     of operations.
    Preparatory Measures.
    Co-operation and role of -
     Artillery,
     Trench Mortars,
     Machine Guns,

attention is called to 23rd N.F. (4th T.S.) instructions parts 1 & 2, which must be thoroughly understood by all Company, Platoon, and Section commanders.

2. Places of Assembly.

The 23rd N.F. (4th T.S.) will assemble in dugouts in WEDNESDAY AVENUE on Y/Z night.   Time and order of march will be notified later.
Battalion Headquarters will be in MONDAY AVENUE one hundred yards South of its junction with WEAK END Tram Line and Trench.

3. Formation & Direction.

On Z day at Zero plus 3½ hours the Battalion will commence to move to the BLUE LINE in Artillery Formation in lines of Half Companies in Column of Sections.   The frontage will be three hundred yards, with one hundred yards interval between sections, and twenty five yards distance between the lines of each wave.
The left section of each line will pass "F" WORK and KITE CRATER about one hundred yards on their right.   The right sections will cross MONDAY AVENUE at BATTALION HEADQUARTERS, and thence to the left of KICK CRATER.
On and after crossing NO MANS LAND, and until arrival at the BLUE LINE, Platoon Commanders will determine and point out direction and landmarks by the aid of compass, and by the position of communication trenches such as HASELMERE WEG, and TEHRAN AVENUE.
Artillery formation will be maintained by each wave until within five hundred yards of the BLUE LINE, unless the situation at any period requires a different formation, when Platoon Commanders will act accordingly.
The Battalion is due at the BLUE LINE at Zero plus 5 hours.
The distance from WEDNESDAY AVENUE is three thousand yards.
The time allotted to cross this distance for the whole Battalion is 9½ hours.   This calculation may help Platoon Commanders who may become delayed en route and have lost distance.

(CONTINUED)

/Between WEDNESDAY

(2).

/lost distance.

Formation & Direction. (Continued).

Between WEDNESDAY AVENUE and the BLUE LINE Companies will advance in the following sequence:-

2 Platoons "A" Co. for attack on first BROWN LINE.
2   "   "B" Co. "   "   "   "   "
2   "   "C" Co. "   "   " second "   "
2   "   "C" Co. "   "   " First or Second BROWN LINE
2   "   "D" Co. "   "   " second BROWN LINE.
2   "   "D" Co. "   "   " first or Second BROWN LINE
2   "   "A" Co. for assault of HOHEN WEG, the first objective beyond the BLUE LINE. These 2 platoons will carry Barbed Wire and Angle Irons, as far as the BLACK LINE, and thence follow the Battalion to the BLUE LINE.

2 Platoons "B" Co. for assault on HOHEN WEG and RAILWAY (1st objective 4th BN. T.S.). These 2 platoons will carry S.A.A., Bombs, and water to the BLACK LINE, and thence follow the Battalion to the BLUE LINE. The dumps where these stores will be drawn will be notified later.

4.

At Zero plus 6 hours 30 minutes the 4th Bn. TYNESIDE SCOTTISH will be drawn up with the leading wave 250 yards east and in front of the BLUE LINE, and in the following formation, or ready to advance <u>in the following formation as ground permits</u>:-

"A" Co. on the Right, "B" Co. on the Left, in 2 waves, 100 yards distance between waves and a frontage of 150 yards per company.
"C" and "D" Companies in 2 similar waves one hundred yards in rear of "A" and "B" Companies respectively.
It is assumed that prior to the advance to the BROWN LINE, the Railway and Sunken Road between the BLUE LINE and the barrage 500 yards East of the BLUE LINE will have been cleared by Advance Parties of preceding Battalions.
At Zero plus 6 hours 45 minutes the 4 waves 4th T.S. will advance to attack the 2 BROWN LINES and intervening objectives. The leading wave will keep as close as possible to the Barrage throughout.
The 1st. wave 2 Platoons "A" Co. and 2 Platoons "B" Companies will sieze and consolidate the first objective, namely, the communication trench HOHEN WEG - TIRPITZ AVENUE, which crosses the Railway at B.20.c.N.K.4.6.. The right platoon of "B" Coy. will aproach the HOHEN WEG moving along the railway line and mopping up where required.
The remaining platoons 1st wave will follow the barrage across country as usual.
This first wave will remain in the first objective as a Battalion Reserve until receipt of further orders.
The 2nd wave (2 Platoons "A" Co. 2 Platoons "B" Co.)
The 3rd wave (2   "   "C" Co. 2 Platoons "D" Co.)
The 4th wave (2   "   "C" Co. 2   "   "D" Co.)
will follow the barrage until reaching the first BROWN LINE, when the 2nd wave (2 Platoons "A" Co.) and 2 Platoons "B" Co.) will seize this objective and mop up.
The 3rd and 4th waves ("C" & "D" Companies) will close up to the second wave shortly before reaching the first BROWN LINE.
The 3rd wave will cross the first BROWN LINE already occupied by the 2nd wave, and follow the barrage closely, and seize the second BROWN LINE.
The 4th wave will reinforce the wave in most need as the situation demands.

XXI (3).

/BROWN LINE.

4. (Continued).   The 4th wave will reinforce the wave in most urgent need as the situation discloses, but this wave will push on to the second BROWN LINE as soon as possible.
The 3rd Battn. T.S. will be closely following the 4th wave 4th T.S. on reaching the BROWN LINE and all platoons 4th T.S. will assemble in the 2nd BROWN LINE and consolidate there as soon as the first BROWN LINE is held by the 3rd T.S. Directly the second BROWN LINE is taken, Platoon Commanders of "C" and "D" Companies of the 3rd wave will post their covering outpost groups about 300 yards out as far as the command of the forward slope and directly sufficient men are available the GREEN LINE will be constructed. This line is all important with a view to repelling the German counter-attacks from the best situation.

5. Trench Mortars.   1 Stokes Trench Mortar will accompany the rear wave of "C" & "D" Companies from the BLUE to the BROWN LINE.

6. CARRYING Parties.   Carrying parties will be furnished as follows:-
(a). 1 N.C.O. from the Battalion.
4 men per company.
Loads as follows:-
4 men carry 2 petrol tins of water each.
4 "   "   2 sandbags loads of S.A.A. each.
3 "   "   2 boxes Mills (No.5) each.
3 "   "   2 "   "   (No. 23) each.
1 "   "   S.OSS. Rockets.
1 "   "   Very Lights.
This party (a) under a selected N.C.O. will collect their loads from one of the Brigade or Battalion dumps, which will be detailed later, at Zero plus 2½ hours, and they will follow the rear wave of the Battalion until arrival at the BROWN LINE.
(b). One half of "C" Company and one half "D" Co.

"X"   will carry one pick or 1 shovel per man in equal proportion to the BROWN LINE.
(c). 2 Platoons "A" Co. already detailed but who will carry tools in addition to angle irons and wire, i.e., 1 Platoon will carry a bundle of 4 picks or 5 shovels per man.
1 Platoon "A" Co. will carry angle irons and wire.
~~Bunchampnshums, and hmmm mhmm~~
(c). 2 Platoons "B" Co. as already detailed to carry bombs, water and S.A.A.
(b). The dump where and when "C" & "D" Co. carrying parties will collect picks and shovels will be notified later.
(c). Similarly for "A" & "B" Co. carrying parties. This party (c) carries to the BLACK LINE only.

Each man of "A", "B" & "C" Companies Carrying Parties will carry 10 sandbags in addition. Some of these bags might be utilized as shoulder pads.

7. Signalling.   Signal Stations will be established as follows:-
Telephone at Brigade Hdqrs. at THELUS Redoubt
Telephone at Battn. Hdqrs. in our own lines, and later in the BLUE LINE.
A visual Station to connect with Brigade Hdqrs. in THELUS REDOUBT, will be established in KENT CRATER.

(4).

/HENT CRATER.

7. Signalling. (Cont).	As soon as the BLACK LINE is taken an advance visual station will be established in the BLACK LINE and TENNAN AVENUE.
8. Runners. Relay Post.	As soon as the BROWN LINE is taken a runner relay post will be established in a dugout near junction of BLUE LINE and TENNAN AVENUE.
9. Dress and Equipment.	The dress will be attack order, and the haversack will contain:- Mess tin, knife, fork, spoon, iron ration, also ration for "Z" day, soap, towel, one pair socks. The great coat will be carried rolled on the belt below the haversack, and the weight of the attack order can be more evenly distributed, if the shoulder buckle is raised higher than usual, even if this entails a fresh hole in the brace.

Riflemen will carry 170 rounds S.A.A.
Lewis Gunners, except Nos. 1 & 2, 50 rds. S.A.A.
Bombers, 50 rounds S.A.A in slung bandolier.
Throwers, and bayonet, and spare men will
Bombing Section. carry one bomb in each breast pocket,
one bomb in each pouch,
one bomb in each Hip pocket.
Carriers will carry bombs in bomb buckets
in addition to one in each pocket, and
one in each pouch.
Rifle Grenadiers will carry 50 rounds S.A.A.
and grenades under conditions to be
determined later.

In addition to above each man will carry 2 bombs and 2 flares to the BROWN LINE where they will be dumped on the right of Batt'n. objective in the 1st BROWN LINE near the CROSS ROADS.

10. DISTINGUISH- ING MARKS.	A distinguishing yellow triangle will be worn pinned on to the haversack, point downwards. In each section, 3 men will be issued with coloured flags, which they will wave on having reached and having gained their particular objective.
11. BATTALION HEADQUARTERS.	Battalion Headquarters will move in SE from MONDAY AVENUE to the BLUE & BROWN LINES as these lines are captured.

12. ACKNOWLEDGE.

Capt & Adjt
23rd N.F.

(6202) W 11186/M1151 350,000 12/16 McA. & W., Ltd. (Est. 731) Forms/W 3091/3.   Army Form W. 3091.

34 Div   102/34

Cover for Documents.

Nature of Enclosures.

WAR DIARY.

APRIL 1917.

23RD N.F. (4TH TYNESIDE SCOTTISH.)

102 INF BDE

Notes, or Letters written.

1/23/N.5.
4th Tyneside Scottish.

WAR DIARY or INTELLIGENCE SUMMARY

Army Form C. 2118.

Place	Date	Hour	Summary of Events and Information	Remarks and references to Appendices
FRENCAMPS ROCLINCOURT	1st APRIL 1917		Hostile artillery activity throughout the day. ROCLINCOURT was shelled intermittently by 5.9 inch & 77 m.m. shells. Shells were heavily shelled during the day also 4 m.m. day. Slight showers occasionally. Trenches in a very muddy condition. Casualties 1 O.R. Killed & 1 O.R. wounded. 4 O.R. Sick. 10 C	REF SHEET. ROCLINCOURT. 57.B.N.W.I. Grid 6A. See O.O. No. 41. And Ad- ministration Instructions & Instruction All marked on Appendix. GN/S/6.
	2nd		Very bad weather, snow & rain. Trenches in very bad condition. Warm operation orders (No. 41) and Administration Instructions (See appendix) issued to Company. Word received that hostility no T. day. Zero day being Z day. In the evening we were relieved by the 20th N.F. (1st Tyneside Scottish) In relief we proceeded to billets in PERRPS. Very late relief (1 P.M.). Casualties 1 O.R. Sick.	
PERRPS	3rd	8 P.M.	Men called upon to supply 450 men for working parties, commencing 3.30 a.m. Several of the Companies did not arrive into billets until 3.30 m. Next morning. Men in a very exhausted condition. Had a Company Commanders meeting in the afternoon with C.O. and discussed the general points in the whole scheme. Casualties: NIL	
	4th		Men detailed to supply more working parties but on parties reporting they were not required. The Bombardment commenced at 6 A.M. Enemy could very shortly hand out the turn company served ammunition. In the afternoon the Battalion moved from	

WAR DIARY or INTELLIGENCE SUMMARY

Army Form C. 2118.

(Erase heading not required.)

Instructions regarding War Diaries and Intelligence Summaries are contained in F. S. Regs., Part II. and the Staff Manual respectively. Title Pages will be prepared in manuscript.

Place	Date	Hour	Summary of Events and Information	Remarks and references to Appendices
X Huts ECOIVRES	4th March 1917		Annex to X Huts ECOIVRES. 2/Lt halkings was left behind to look after bridging arrangements and marching out schedule party from WEDNESDAY MEN VF noted as the roundly hut for this Battalion on y night. Casualties 8 O.R's sick	
	5.		All men were resting – 2nd men went to baths. Showers, steady, stoker present that W day is to be repeated. Casualties 2 O.R's sick 1. O.R. to taken	
	6.		Showery day. 240 men went to baths. Company Commanders meeting in the evening. Casualties 4. O.R'S Sick	
	7.		Companies fitted out with attack order used in firing of rehearsed attacks. All further moves abandoned at Q.M. stores. Casualties NIL	
LOUEZ	8.		The Battalion less Officers and men who were detailed to remain behind, proceeded to LOUEZ. The men were in lorries. Ladders sent with remainder of spare stores. Casualties NIL	
	9.		In the evening the Battalion proceeded from LOUEZ into their recently shelled in the ROCLINCOURT AREA. The 21st & 22nd R.F. took up their positions on the front trenches. The 20th N.F. in support trenches and this bund in WEDNESDAY MEN VE. From A.A.C. 20.20 to G.S.O. 01; The Brigade in conjunction with troops in our right and left will attack enemy	REF SHEET 57.4 N.W. Point 6.F

2449 Wt. W14957/M90 750,000 1/16 J.B.C. & A. Forms/C.2118/12.

WAR DIARY or INTELLIGENCE SUMMARY

Army Form C. 2118.

Place	Date	Hour	Summary of Events and Information	Remarks and references to Appendices
ROCLINCOURT	8th April 1917		Remarks on the morning of the 9th. Zero hour will be 5.30 p.m. The scheme for attack is contained in APPENDIX GN/S/6. Casualties 4 M.O.S. Sick.	MAP REF Sheet 51.N.W. Edition 6.B. N[?] See APPENDIX GN/S/6
	9th	a.m. 5.30	The Artillery barrage opened up at Zero hour and after 4 min. intense bombardment the barrage lifted and the leading waves of the 2nd & 12th N.F. advanced followed in rear by the 2nd M.F. This Battalion was not due to attack until Zero plus 2½ hours. There are 4 5 habitual objectives in the attack viz: Black Line, Blue Line, Black Brown Line, East Brown Line and Green Line. The Brigade limits through these 5 objectives are as follows. BLACK LINE A.30.d.60.45.45 G.6.b.90.25. BLUE LINE B.25.d.90.70.to H.1.d.90.60. WESTERN BROWN LINE B.29.c.25.95.to H.3.a.45.55. EASTERN BROWN LINE B.29.c.70.85 to H.3.a.85.50. The limits held by the Brigade front to the attack were from A.30.c.45.20 to G.6.a.50.05. At 8.a.m this Battalion advanced to the attack from WEDNESDAY AVENUE. During the first stages of the advance up to the BLUE LINE the men were in Artillery formation after which they extended into lines. The casualties were slight up to the Blue line and the enemy barrage was not very heavy. No far orders this Battalion and the 2nd OF should form up outside the BLUE LINE and advance to the BROWN LINE. The barrage allotted the Battalion was from B.25.d.90.40. to B.25.d.90.25.	

WAR DIARY
or
INTELLIGENCE SUMMARY

Army Form C. 2118.

Place	Date	Hour	Summary of Events and Information	Remarks and references to Appendices
	April 9th 1917		The position in which the Battalion found itself was a little to the right of the front laid down owing to the troops on our left having lost direction. The 103rd Infantry Brigade on our left were held up and at the River Line with the result that this Battalion advanced with the left flank in the air. The Battalion barrage had by this time become rather scattered and we lost several men from our own shelling. A thick belt of wire was encountered in front of the Western Brown Line – this was cut. Capt. J.B. Horn M.C. did some good work and not a few examples by calmly cutting a lane through the wire whilst heavy rifle and machine gun fire of our own shells were falling on the same. Lanes were eventually cut through and the Battalion continued their advance to the Brown Lines the Western Brown Line came under captured but the enemy first put up a greater resistance and the Eastern Brown line. The artillery barrage by this time had drifted further forward and the enemy were able to re-organise and the Battalion met with heavy rifle fire prevented by careful work and reasoned under the Battalion got within charging distance of the East Brown line and finally carried this line successfully	

WAR DIARY
or
INTELLIGENCE SUMMARY

Army Form C. 2118.

Place	Date	Hour	Summary of Events and Information	Remarks and references to Appendices
	April 10th 1917		During the latter part of these operations Capt. St. J. Moran M.C. 2/Lt. S.C. Kenedge M.C. were wounded and 2/Lt. F. Ashworth was dart wounded (while he about from wounds). During the evening the front trench line was consolidated. Very cold weather — snow during night 9/10th. Casualties during 9/10th. 2/Lt. F. Ashworth. 2 O.R.s killed 19 O.R.s wounded. Capt. W.J. Moran M.C. 2/Lt. S.C. Kenedge M.C. 13 O.R.s missing 11 O.R.s gun. At dawn on the 10th reconnoitring parties went forward from the Red Brown Line & reconnoitre positions for taken up in the GREEN LINE. There now enemy parties captured in Point Battery (3 guns) 77mm and 5 gunners. This battery was situated at H.3.d.5.0 a little later another Battery was captured, this battery consisted of 4 field guns (77 mm) and no evidence at B.27.b.4.4. These guns have been claimed for with an argument that we no men of same the next to the Tyneside Scottish Sommitte, Maronick-on-Tyne. At 9 pm the battalion advanced and took up a position in the GREEN LINE. The following huts are accurate. During the day the enemy artillery was very active and caused several casualties. The men were in a very exhausted condition. Rates	

WAR DIARY
or
INTELLIGENCE SUMMARY

(Erase heading not required.)

Army Form C. 2118.

Instructions regarding War Diaries and Intelligence Summaries are contained in F.S. Regs., Part II. and the Staff Manual respectively. Title pages will be prepared in manuscript.

Place	Date	Hour	Summary of Events and Information	Remarks and references to Appendices
	11th		NIL supply very difficult. Casualties in the 15th below were received but present positions and not - ship to the left rear. There were three and the following positions taken up. One Company (A) front line B.27.d.98.40 to B.27.d.18.20. Two Companies Support in Company Reserve occupying trenches in depth with front line trenches (A). Very bad weather — heavy snow storms. Men in a very bad condition - several evacuated from exposure. Battalion 15th O.R. situation in day and made Hyatsteck at B.29.d.25.85. Casualties – 18 ORs Sick. 4 ORs Missing.	
	12th		Bullets 14th O.R. evacuated sick for front by Mule. were removed into RAILWAY CUTTING at B.26.b.90.33. Weather a little finer. Many men were sent into day into the BLUE LINE for rest. One stove thereafter in support and Reserve were relieved by two Companies 15th Bath. N.F. (Pioneers) the men relieved proceeded into Numbers nothing near BLUE LINE	
	13th & 14th		Casualties 1. Offrs Sick. 4. Kupyon 17. ORs. Fine weather — Hostile artillery shelled trenches intermittently. Patrols were sent out	

WAR DIARY
or
INTELLIGENCE SUMMARY.
(Erase heading not required.)

Army Form C. 2118.

Place	Date	Hour	Summary of Events and Information	Remarks and references to Appendices
	10th/14		under 2/Lt. Milling who went out as far as road B.28.d., South West of RONLEUX, none of the enemy were encountered. B. in the night of 14/15 we were relieved by the Naval Division and proceeded into billets in ARRAS. Late relief.	51.C NW
	15th		Corvellis. 13th HQRS Bath. 2/21 MrAult 30TRS.	Nil
OLLENCOURT	16th		Proceeded home from ARRAS to OLLENCOURT.	
	18th, 19th		Carried out training and re-equipping the Battalion. Fine weather.	
	20th		The Corps Commander and Divil Commander inspected the Battalion in the 18th.	
	21st		Corvellis. 16C NIL 17:30 OD Bath. 15. 2.ORS Mended. Arrived at 4 ORS Both 14:26 OC Both 17:01 Such Corv.	
	22nd		Marched to Redmounts South of ACQ. Fine day Corvellis 1:0ts Bath. 10th	
	23rd		Carried out a little training. In the 23rd. The Brigade Commander Brig Gen J. Sherman CMG, DSO. gave a farewell speech to this Battalion prior to leaving for England on account of age. Corvellis 22nd 2.ORS Bath 23rd 7.ORS Bath, Offr	
	24th		Marched to ARRAS - Railway Network at 3.10pm. The noun covering the battalion marched into Railway Cutting and rouched from H.14.a.0.3 to H.8.C.05.00. Officer Corvellis NIL	
	25, 26, 27th		Now still in billets stations on the south of outskirts Remained in nothing - Hostile artillery action seasonably. Except in the neighborhood of	

WAR DIARY
INTELLIGENCE SUMMARY
(Erase heading not required.)

Army Form C. 2118.

Place	Date	Hour	Summary of Events and Information	Remarks and references to Appendices
	27th		The Battalion moved from Railway cutting and marched trenches from H.16.d.70.90 to H.11.c.10.85. Casualties 13.ORs. Sh.	Ref. Sheet 51 B. N.W.
	28th		Orders received that the Battalion will do an enterprise night attack against the German positions in front of and on the CHEMICAL WORKS I.13.d. on the 29th. Immediately details of the attack were received. Company Commanders were given fifty minutes instructions as to the positions that company's would occupy. Zero hour on 29th to be at 3 a.m. By the time orders were received and arrived at same 12.30 a.m. morning of the 29th. Companies moved off to trenches near lock to meet SCOTTS H.22.d.1.2 thence via TOW PATH towards FOSSE POUX there to hard covering at H.23.d.3.2. where guides were met. Companies were immediately taken to following trenches under the guidance. CEYLON TRENCH from I.13.c.45.55. to I.19.a.75.65 (junction of CORONA & CEYLON TRENCHES) Companies formed up in their stench from left to right as follows. C.B. & A. Co's. The mortar RLs were allotted for use to north of CORONA TRENCH, D.Co. formed up in rear of CEYLON TRENCH and were detailed to move forward in rear.	

Army Form C. 2118.

WAR DIARY
or
INTELLIGENCE SUMMARY.
(Erase heading not required.)

Instructions regarding War Diaries and Intelligence Summaries are contained in F.S. Regs., Part II. and the Staff Manual respectively. Title pages will be prepared in manuscript.

Place	Date	Hour	Summary of Events and Information	Remarks and references to Appendices
Trenches in front of CHEMICAL WORKS I.13.d.	25th		The four companies went ready to attack. It was about 4 p.m. The enemy held a line See Party consisting of occupied houses, a trench and advanced posts varying from 20 to TRENCH 60 yds from the trench from which we deployed to attack. The enemy had 4 or MAP 51B. 5 machine guns in and on buildings South of the roadway on front on I.13.d.80.50.N.W. 4 from the buildings South as far as the Northern Boundary of the Château grounds attached. A trench with more than two guns in a central copse and this trench was occupied by riflemen and bombers. The Battalion came under fire immediately they left the trench to attack and those from developed an embarkation as they advanced and by the time the front wave had reached a line approximately T.19.4.10.90 North to I.13.c.90.80 the two left companies were held up by intense machine gun fire (at least 5 machine guns opened from the Château grounds) and had lost nearly all their Officers and 50% other Ranks. The Right Company (D) advanced along CORONO Trench as far as the most East of the Château during the enemy trench in the trench. In doing the trench they came under very adverse Machine gun fire and being enfilade were ordered to withdraw via CORONO Trench. The enemy	

Army Form C. 2118.

WAR DIARY
or
INTELLIGENCE SUMMARY.
(Erase heading not required.)

Place	Date	Hour	Summary of Events and Information	Remarks and references to Appendices
	29th		had close observation of the bounds & deployment throughout the night. There seems any advanced by the force intended to reach position before daylight but the 2 Companies detailed hadtack across the open went straight on without all there. Officers and 60 to ORS were casualties and the remainder stood and returned to our lines until the last night but movement in chillt dark. Germans on our occasion were observed carrying our wounded in and were not fired on. In other occasions when they deployed themselves they were fired on and in certain number are known to have been hit. Casualties	
	30		North Ledlun very active – many heavy guns. Both MG & artillery under Railway Arch at H.15.d.3.2. very heavily shelled. Casualties 28th April 2 ORS. killed. 29th killed. 2Lt. J. Crockin & 2/Lt. Taylor. 14 ORS. wounded Lt. W.M. Dodds, Lt J. Metcalfe, 2/Lt. A. Linnett, 67. ORS. missing 2/Lt. A.A. Munro, 2/Lt J. Jamieson DCM 2/Lt. H. Munro, 2/Lt. D.C. Phillips. 70. ORS. 1 OR died of wounds. 1 OR wounded & missing. 2/Lt. D. C. Phillips, Lt Col Andry, 23rd M. Hibbert Hrs 30th April NIL	

S E C R E T.   Sheet 1.
                                        Copy No. _____

                23rd Bn. NORTHUMBERLAND FUSILIERS.
                        Instructions No....1.
                        ----

1.   In conjunction with other troops on the right and left,
the 34th Division will carry out an attack on the enemy's positions
on a date to be fixed later which will be known as "Z" Day.

2.   The 34th Division is attacking with three Infantry
Brigades in the line, 101st Inf.Bde. on the right, 102nd Inf.Bde.
in the centre and 103rd Inf. Bde. on the left.

            The limits on frontage allotted to this Brigade and the
dividing lines between this Brigade and the Brigades on Right and
left, are shewn on Map A which can be seen at Orderly Room.

3.   On the front of this Brigade there are three objectives
to be captured:-

 (a) First Objective (Black Line).
            The Enemy's front System consisting of four lines of
trenches on a total average depth of 500 x.

 (b) Second Objective (Blue Line).
            A second Line consisting of two trenches about 1,300 x
East of the Black Line.
            Between the Black Line and the Blue Line there are
trenches in places which have to be crossed.

 (c) Third Objective (Brown Line).
            A third Line consisting of a double line of trench at
present partly wired, about 1,400 x East of the Blue Line.

                    PREPARATORY OPERATIONS.

4.   The wire in front of the enemy's trenches will be
systematically cut by field and heavy artillery and 3" trench mortars.

            The wire in front of our own trenches will be gradually
thinned out and removed until only one line of wire remains in front
of our front trench. This line must be removed on Y/Z night by
the "A" & "B" Battalions.

            Trench Bridges for crossing our own system of trenches
are being provided under Brigade arrangements, and also ladders for
getting out of trenches.

            Lines of direction posts will be placed in position as
early as possible under Brigade arrangements from the rear lines
of assembly - i.e. those occupied on Y/Z night by the "C" & "D"
Battalions, to our front trench.

            Instructions have already been issued as regards the
organisation and necessary preparatory work in the Brigade area.
As per Map "B" which can be seen at Orderly Room.

                    ACTION OF THE ARTILLERY.

5.   The actual operations will commence with a three days
bombardment during W, X and Y days - Z day being the day of the
actual assault.

            This bombardment will be carried out by all natures of
guns and howitzers, and medium and heavy trench mortars.

            Previous to the commencement of the bombardment, the
34th Division Artillery will have been increased to a total of
108 field guns and 36 4.5" How. There will also be 36 medium
trench mortars, 12 heavy trench mortars and an extra light trench

Sheet 2.

6. (Continued).

Mortar Battery on the Divisional front.

6. During the bombardment, the Divisional Artillery less any batteries detailed for counter-battery work, will be kept on trench battering and wire cutting, in accordance with a programme which will be issued in due course.

During this bombardment, Battalions in the line will use all means in their power to observe and examine the effect of the fire on trenches and wire, and will at once report to Brigade Headquarters any localities and wire on which the artillery bombardment appears inadequate.

7. The action is divided into three phases, the general idea of which is given below.
Detailed instructions will be issued later.

1st Phase.

(a) At Zero hour on Z day an 18 pdr. Field gun barrage will be put on the German Front Line trench for 4 minutes. During this time the leading waves of the Infantry will get out of their trenches and form up close under the barrage.

(b) At Zero plus 4 mins, the barrage will lift direct from the front trench to the second (support) trench where it will rest for 3 mins. It will then lift direct from the second (support) trench to the third trench where it will remain for 3 mins. From the third trench it will move forward as a creeping barrage at the rate of 50 yards in two mins., till it is on the Black Line.
At Zero plus 35 mins., the barrage will lift simultaneously off the whole length of the Black Line and creep forward until it reaches the line R.1.a.45.45 - B.30.c.30.60 - B.35.a.30.15 i.e., the line of the KUTCHEN WEG trench where it will remain as a protective barrage until Zero plus 2 hours 6 minutes. The period during which the barrage will be maintained on the line of the KUTCHEN WEG Trench will be 1 hour 30 mins. During this period the barrage searches forward and back again to the line of the KUTCHEN WEG Trench repeatedly.

2nd Phase.

(a) At Zero plus 2 hours 6 mins, the protective barrage on the line of the KUTCHEN WEG Trench will lift simultaneously and commence to creep by lifts of 50 yards towards the Blue Line. For the first 300 yards the rate of the lifts will be 50 yards every 1½ mins, and after, 50 yards every two mins, until it reaches the Blue Line.

(b) At Zero plus 3 hours 45 mins, the barrage will lift simultaneously off the whole length of the Blue Line and creep to 500 yards East of the Blue Line where it will remain as a protective barrage until Zero plus 6 hours 45 mins. The period during which the barrage will be maintained 500 yards East of the Blue Line, will be 3 hours 51 mins.

3rd Phase.

(a) At Zero plus 6 hours 45 mins, the protective barrage East of the Blue Line will lift simultaneously and commence to creep towards the Brown Line, the lifts and rates being as in (a) 2nd Phase.

(b) The barrage will lift off the front trench of the Brown line at Zero plus 7 hours 35 mins., and will creep as in (a) 2nd Phase to the rear trench of the Brown line where it will rest for four mins. It will then creep forward to a line 500 yards East of the rear trench of the Brown line. Subsequent action of the Artillery will be detailed later.

Sheet 3.

8. The Field Howitzers will form a standing barrage, first on the support trench of the front system and subsequently on each successive trench of the system. The lift from trench to trench will be made as the 18 pdr. creeping barrage reaches the trench.
During the pauses at the Black and Blue Lines, the Field Howitzers will search forward over all communication trenches, strong points etc., between the Black and Blue Lines, and between the Blue and Brown Lines and during the advance of the Infantry, establish barrages on each of these trenches in succession. These barrages will lift as the creeping 18 pdr barrage reaches each trench.

ACTION OF THE INFANTRY.

9. The 102 Tyneside Scottish Brigade will attack with two Battalions in the front line. The leading battalions of the Brigade will be:-

      21st N.F. (2nd T.S.) on the right, i.e. "A" Bn.
and 22nd N.F. (3rd T.S.) on the left i.e. "B" Bn.
      20th N.F. (1st T.S.) will be "C" Bn.
and 23rd N.F. (4th T.S.) will be "D" Bn.

These Battalions will be assembled as follows on Y/Z night at an hour to be fixed later, per Map "B" to be seen at Orderly Room.

"A" Bn... Front Trench and support trench.
"B" Bn... Front trench and support trench.
"C" Bn... In specially constructed assembly trench & trench Ga. The whole battalion will be concentrated in the specially constructed assembly trench 2 hours before Zero hour.
"D" Bn... WEDNESDAY AVENUE.

10. At Zero hour on Z day the "A" & "B" Battalions will advance and form up in No Man's Land as close as possible to the barrage. At plus 8 mins. when the barrage lifts from the enemy's front trench "A" & "B" Battalions will advance to the assault in the formation as already practised, as shewn on sketch "C" attached.
O.C. "A" & "B" Battalions will each detail beforehand one platoon to follow close up to the protective barrage when it lifts off the Black line to capture and mop-up the NUTH WEG trench, as soon as the protective barrage lifts off it at Zero plus 24 mins., These platoons will then establish a line of outposts in the NUTH WEG trench, each post to be consolidated. These platoons will rejoin their Battalions when the advance to the Blue line commences.

11. In order to avoid the hostile barrage as much as possible and to afford a support for the leading battalions, "C" Battalion will at Zero hour on Z day move forward from its assembly trench close in rear of the assaulting battalions, establish itself in the enemys 2nd and 3rd trenches and commence the consolidation of the 3rd trench.
"C" Battalion is on no account to become involved in clearing the captured trenches of the enemy's front system.
"C" Battalion will not be used in the actual attack on the Black line, except in case of extreme urgency, when the Battalion Commander of "C" Battalion who will probably find it necessary to delegate his authority to Company Commanders, will act on his own initiative as the situation may demand.
It must be impressed on all concerned that "C" Battalion is required intact for the attack on the Brown line, in conjunction with "D" Battalion.
Any such action taken will be reported to Brigade Headquarters as soon as possible.

12. "D" Battalion will remain in position in WEDNESDAY AVENUE under the orders of G.O.C. 34th Division as a Divisional Reserve. The orders for the subsequent move forward of this Battalion to the Blue Line, when that line has been captured, for the assault on the Brown Line, will be given by the Brigade Commander.

Sheet 4.

12 (Continued).

Unless orders are given to the contrary, "D" Battalion will move from its position in WEDNESDAY AVENUE at Zero plus 3½ hours to the Blue Line, and will time its advance so as to arrive at the BLUE Line not later than Zero plus 5 hours.

13. Os.C. "A" & "B" Battalions will as soon as possible after the capture of the Black Line, reform their Battalions for the assault on the Blue Line, and commence the consolidation of the Black Line.

14. O.C. "C" Battalion will place two platoons of his Battalion at the disposal of O.C. "B" Battalion to mop up the whole length of the KUTCHEN WEG Trench. O.C. "B" Battalion will be responsible that these two platoons "C" Battalion are formed up in front of the leading waves of "B" Battalion as close to the protective barrage as possible ready to advance and mop up the KUTCHEN WEG Trench as soon as the barrage lifts from it at Zero plus 2 hours 6 mins. These two platoons "C" Battalion will rejoin their Battalion as soon as the mopping up of this trench is finished.

"A" & "B" Battalions will be formed up as close to the barrage on the line of the KUTCHEN WEG trench as possible ready to advance at Zero plus 2 hours 6 mins.

At Zero plus 2 hours 6 mins, "A" & "B" Battalions will advance from the captured first objective (Black Line) and capture the Second objective (Blue Line).

"A" & "B" Battalions will proceed in the same formation as for the attack on the Black Line except that the two leading platoons of moppers up of each of "A" & "B" Battalions will not be required for the MUTH WEG and KUTCHEN WEG trenches as these two trenches will have already been mopped up in the first case by platoons "A" & "B" Battalions, in the second case by Platoons "C" Battalion.

Special Parties will be told off by Os.C. "A" & "B" Battalions for clearing the long communication trenches from the Black line to the Blue line in their respective areas.

The primary use of the Stokes Mortars allotted to the "A" & "B" Battalions (see para 18 below) is the clearing of the long communication trenches in conjunction with rifle grenadiers.

O.C. "A" Battalion will detail a special party of not less than 1 platoon to assist the left of the 101st Infantry Brigade, in the capture of the portion of the Blue Line near the boundaries of 101st and 102nd Infantry Brigades.

This party must push on until the trench between the SUNKEN ROAD in R.25.d. and H.1.b. and the Blue Line is reached.

Should the left of the 101st Inf. Bde. be hung up in front of the continuation of this trench South of the ARRAS - BAILLEUL Road, the party of "A" Battalion detailed to assist them will probably act most effectively by bombing along this trench to the South and bring enfilade rifle and lewis gun fire to bear on the portion of the trench South of the ARRAS - BAILLEUL Road.

O.C. "C" Battalion will detail one Company of his Battalion to remain in the Black Line as garrison and to continue the consolidation of that Line until the Blue Line has been captured.

"C" Battalion (less one Company garrisoning the Black Line) will move forward from the Black Line about 600 yards in rear of "A" & "B" Battalions.

It is not intended that it shall take part in the assault on the Blue Line unless it is absolutely necessary to do so to ensure the capture of that Line, but in order that "C" Battalion may be within striking distance it must gradually reduce the distance between itself and the Battalions in front so that if necessary it may take part in the final assault on the Blue Line.

O.C. "C" Battalion will bear in mind that it is considered possible that it is the Right ("A") Battalion which may possibly require assistance in assaulting the SUNKEN ROAD and the defences behind it.

Should it be necessary for "C" Battalion to take part in the assault on the Blue Line, this will be reported to Brigade Headquarters as soon as possible.

Sheet 5.

14 (Continued).

After the capture of the Blue line the Company of "C" Bn. garrisoning the Black Line will move forward and rejoin its Battn. Should the attack on the Blue Line fail, this Company of "C" Bn. will remain in the Black Line and hold it at all costs. It will on no account be sent forward to reinforce a further attack on the Blue Line.

15. As soon as the Blue Line has been captured, "A" "B" & "C" Battalions will be reorganised and the Blue Line will be strongly consolidated.

The attack on the Brown Line will be carried out by "B" "C" & "D" Battalions on a front of two Battalions - "C" Battalion on the right, "D" Battalion on the left, with "B" Battalion following in rear of "C" & "D" Battalions as Brigade Reserve.

"A" Battalion will take over the defence of the whole of the Blue Line on this Brigade front, and will continue the consolidation. It will on no account be utilised to assist the attack on the Brown Line, and in the event of a hostile counter attack will hold the Blue line at all costs.

"B" "C" & "D" Battalions will be formed up for the attack on the Brown Line by Zero plus 6 hours 30 mins, with the leading waves as close as possible to the barrage.

At Zero plus 6 hours 45 mins, "B" "C" & "D" Battalions will advance and capture the Brown Line (3rd Objective).

The Brigade Reserve ("B" Battalion) will not be drawn into the action unnecessarily but will advance in a central position ready to render immediate support where required.

The O.C. Brigade Reserve must use his discretion in this matter as it will be impossible for the Brigade Commander to issue orders in time for the effective use of this Reserve.

As the Brigade advances to the attack from the Blue Line to the Brown Line, O.C. Brigade Reserve will detail beforehand 1 of his Companies for the express purpose of occupying the GAVRELLE WEB to form a defensive flank to the left in case such action is necessary owing to a serious check to the Brigade on our left. The Brown Line on this Brigade front South of B.27.c.3.0. must however be captured at all costs as on the capture of this line depends the success of the Division on our right.

16. After the capture of the third objective (Brown Line), strong patrols will be pushed out Eastwards to reconnoitre the most suitable line East of the Brown Line on which to establish the best line of observation possible. This line which is roughly indicated on map A by the green line will be dug as a front line trench.

At the same time the Easternmost trench of the Brown Line on this Brigade front will be consolidated.

During the consolidation, strong Patrols, accompanied by Lewis guns must be pushed well out to the Eastward to cover the consolidation and capture any guns the enemy may have left Southwest of MAILLEUL.

Gaps will be left in our artillery barrage to enable these patrols to advance.

ACTION OF MACHINE GUNS.

17 The 103 Machine Gun Company less 1 Section have been detailed to act under Divisional Orders for the purpose of maintaining a barrage of machine gun fire in front of the attacking Infantry. This machine gun barrage will be never less than 400 yards in front of the leading waves.

The remaining section 103 Machine Gun Company (4 guns) is at the Brigade Commander's disposal.

Two of these guns will be attached to each of the "A" & "B" Battalions as far as the black line.

These Vickers guns will be moved forward to the black line under the orders of the Os.C. "A" & "B" Battalions respectively as soon as that line has been captured and will remain there and act as garrison of that line.

Orders for the further moves of these guns will be issued from Brigade Headquarters.

Sheet 6.

ACTION OF TRENCH MORTARS.

18. Four mortars 1st L.T.M.B. will fire frequent bursts on W, X & Y days paying particular attention to the PUPP's NOSE.

On Z day 1 mortar will be allotted to each of "A" & "B" Battalions and will go forward with the rear waves of these Battalions as far as the Blue Line.

These mortars will then be handed over, 1 to each of "C" & "D" Battalions and will go forward with the rear waves of "C" & "D" Battalions respectively to the Brown Line.

The remaining 6 mortars will be collected in a dug-out on Y/Z night and left under a small guard until an opportunity arises of taking them forward.

The teams of these 6 mortars will be used to supplement the Infantry parties carrying ammunition for the two mortars allotted to the leading Battalions.

STRONG POINTS.

19. A list of Strong Points, important trenches and dug-outs in the enemy's lines opposite this Brigade front is attached APPENDIX I.

Strong points that are holding up the advance will be dealt with on the following lines.

A concentrated fire of Stokes Mortars and rifle Grenades will be brought to bear on the strong points for about about two minutes. Meanwhile parties will work round the flanks of the strong point, and make a determined rush with the bayonet the moment the fire of the Stokes Mortars and rifle grenades ceases.

MOVES OF HEADQUARTERS.

20. As soon as the Black line has been captured the Headquarters of "A" "B" & "C" Battalions will move to positions in dugouts in the Black line approximately at -

G.8.b.80.65 for "A" Battalion
A.W.d.3.1. for "B" Battalion
and G.8.b.70.20 for "C" Battalion. vide
Instructions afor Training of Divisions for Offensive Action Sect XIII.

As soon as the Blue Line has been captured the Headquarters of all four Battalions this Brigade will be established in or close in rear of that line.

When the Brown Line has been captured the Headquarters of "B" "C" & "D" Battalions will be established in the Western Trench of the Brown Line.

In every case the fact that Battalion Headquarters are about to to move will be reported to Brigade Headquarters, and the exact position of the new Headquarters will also be reported as soon as Headquarters has been established there.

As soon as the Blue line has been captured, Brigade Headquarters will move to G.8.b.90.40. Any further moves of Brigade Headquarters will be notified to all concerned at the time.

S T O R E S.

21. A list of dumps in this Brigade area (British Trenches) and their contents is given in Appendix II attached.

During the advance dumps of bombs, water, S.A.A., Very Lights, S.O.S. Rockets, R.E. Material &c will be established in the captured trenches as follows :-

Black Line.
  (1) Junction of SPATZEN WEG and Black Line.
  (2) Junction of HASELMEYER WEG and Black Line.

Blue Line.
  Near junctions with TAL WEG and HASELMEYER WEG respectively.

Sheet 7.

STORES (con't).

a.
Brown LINE.
Near junction with GAVRELLE RD.

These dumps will be filled by :-

(a) Battalion Carrying Parties supplied at the rate of
1 reliable N.C.O. and 16 men per Battalion.
(b) 1 Company of each of "C" & "D" Battalions.

The Battalion Carrying Parties will each carry the following loads and will advance with the rear waves of each of their respective Battalions.
4 men each carrying 2 petrol tins full of water.
4 men each carrying 2 sandbags of S.A.A.
3 men each carrying 2 boxes Mills No. 5 Grenades.
3 men each carrying 2 boxes Mills No. 23 Grenades.
1 man carrying S.O.S. Rockets.
1 man carrying Very Lights.

Each man of the carrying party will carry 10 sandbags in addition to his other load.

When the Blue line has been captured, the carrying party of "A" Battalion will be sent back to the Black Line for further supplies.

The Carrying Party of "B" Battalion may also be sent back to the Black Line for further supplies, but there will be time for only 1 journey in this case, as the party must follow in rear of its Battalion during the advance to the Brown Line.

The Carrying Parties of "C" & "D" Battalions will carry their Stores by stages in rear of their respective Battalions as far as the Brown Line.

In addition to the Battalion Carrying Parties, Os.C. "C" & "D" Battalions will each detail one Company to carry Stores as far as the Black Line.

Each of these Companies will carry the following loads and will advance with their respective Battalions as far as the Black Line where the Stores will be dumped, the Companies then going on without the Stores.
2 Platoons carrying bombs, Water and S.A.A.
1 Platoon carrying angle irons and wire.
1 Platoon carrying bundles of picks & shovels
(4 picks or 6 shovels in a bundle).

Each man of one Company of "D" Battalion (not the Company carrying Stores) and all of the rear Companies of each of "A" & "B" Battalions will carry either a pick or a shovel.
These will be carried in the case of "A" Battalion to the Blue Line, and in the cases of "B" & "D" Battalions to the Brown Line.

The Mills No. 5 Grenades and aeroplane flares carried by each man in his pockets will be collected into dumps, by "A" Bn. on reaching the Blue Line, by "B" "C" & "D" Battalions on reaching the Brown Line but not before.

The Brigade Bombing Officer will be responsible for replenishing dump No. 5 near KENT Crater in our front line from the Brigade Dumps.

He will have a party of 2 N.C.Os and 20 men at his disposal for the purpose.

Carrying parties for the 102 Stokes Mortars Battery have already been detailed.

Carrying Parties at the rate of 5 men per Battalion will be detailed to carry S.A.A. for the 102 Machine Gun Company. Instructions as to the joining 102 M.G. Company will be issued later.

Sheet 6.

CONTACT PATROL AEROPLANE.

22.   A Contact Patrol Aeroplane 15th Squadron R.F.C. will co-operate in the attack.

The aeroplane will call for flares to be lit by sending a succession of A's on the Klaxon or by firing a white Very Light.

The Infantry on reach the Black, Blue and Brown Lines respectively will get their flares ready to be lit directly the aeroplane calls for them.

The approximate times at which the aeroplane will call for flares are:-
(1) Zero plus 1 hour i.e., after Black Line is expected to be captured.
(2) Zero plus 3 hours 10 mins., i.e., after Blue Line is expected to be captured.
(3) Zero plus 5 hours 10 mins., i.e., after Brown Line is expected to be captured.

Ground Sheets and strips indicating the code calls allotted to Battalions will be exposed throughout the operations from Zero hour on Z Day onwards at Battalion Headquarters.

The strips for making the letters are to be at least 6 feet long. Sufficient white cloth must be taken over with Battalion Headquarters to replace these strips when necessary as when dirty they cannot be distinguished by aeroplanes.

COMMUNICATION TRENCHES ACROSS NO MAN'S LAND.

23.   The communication trench across No Man's Land for this Brigade will be dug by 18th North'ld Fus. (Pioneers) and will run from SUNDAY AVENUE, via KENT Crater to the SPATZEN WEG.

PERSONNEL TO LEFT BEHIND.

24.   Personnel to be left behind when Battalions take part in the attack, vide T.S. 20/17 dated 11th March 1917 will be sent back to "X" Huts prior to Battalions occupying their places of assembly.

It must be clearly understood that 20 Officers per Battalion, not more and not less, will go forward with each Battalion.

In the case of 102 Machine Gun Company and 102 Light Trench Mortar Battery 25% of the Officers, Sergeants, Corporals and Gunners will be left behind by each Unit.

MEDICAL ARRANGEMENTS.

25.   The positions of First Aid Posts are shown on map. Regimental Stretcher Bearers will carry wounded to these First Aid Posts.
In addition to the 16 Regimental Stretcher Bearers, the Pipers will act as Stretcher Bearers for collecting wounded.

DRESS & EQUIPMENT.

26.   Attention is called to "Training for Divisions for Offensive Action" Section XXXIII. Should there be any alteration in the dress or equipment as laid down therein, instructions will be issued.

All ranks will wear a yellow cloth triangular patch pinned on to the back outside the haversack, the apex of the triangle pointing

6(Continued).   Sheet 5.

triangle downwards.

WATER.

27. Commanding Officers will take steps to ensure that the men's water bottles are full when they advance to the assault. Men must not drink water found in the German Lines until it has been passed as good by a Medical Officer, as the Germans are in the habit of poisoning wells as they retire.

28.   REPORTS.

Officers are reminded of the extreme importance of sending in a continuous flow of reports at frequent intervals as to progress or otherwise, vide S.S. 135, Section XII.

                                        Captain & Acting Adjutant,
                                        23rd Northumberland Fusiliers.

SECRET.   APPENDIX I.
                                    To Accompany
                                    Instructions No. 1.

            STRONG   POINTS.

1. BLACK LINE.

   G.6.b.8.5............TAL GABEL. At Southern Point of this triangle
                        is tramway which feeds T.M's. It is well wired
                        and strong dug-outs are indicated on air
                        photographs. A Note by Corps I, says:-
                        "The supply of several Trench Mortars depends
                        "on this triangle of trenches. All three
                        "angles should be dealt with simultaneously"
                        N.E. of it is :-

   A.30.b & d........   The WERK ULM and the DITTARSECKER GRABEN,
   G.6.b & d.   forming the backbone of the front line system,
                        well wired, and many strong dug-outs, notably
                        the triangle at top corner of WERK ULM
                        (A.30.b.3.8.)

                        Other dug-outs at

                             A.30.d.80.80.
                             A.30.d.5.4.
                             TAL GABEL (see above)
                             G.6.b.05.85.
                             G.6.b.85.85.
                             G.6.b.70.65.

                        Behind WERK ULM is an important dug-out at
                        B.30.c.80.45 and near that dug-out a dump at
                        B.30.c.7.5. South of TAL GABEL, the trench is
                        doubled down to BAILLEUL ROAD in S.W. Corner
                        of H.1.a.

2. BLUE LINE.

   H.1.b & d.......... The Railway cutting is known to contain cook-
                        houses and many dug-outs along most of this
                        stretch. H.1.d.5.6. is where buried cable
                        enters cutting and a dug-out about this point
                        was formerly a Battn. H.Q. (BOIS DE LA MAISON
                        BLANCHE). This region is heavily wired with
                        a double system of wire, one along the
                        cutting and one along the trench on the
                        Western Side of it.

   B.25.b. & d........ The KLESMAN STELLUNG is very strongly wired
                        from Railway Embankment up to the TRIANGLE
                        below DEUTSCHES HAUS, (DEUTSCHES HAUS B.19.d.8.60.
                        is a junction of buried cables and believed to
                        be Regimental Battle Headquarters).
                        The TRIANGLE has 3 smaller triangles one to the
                        North, one N.E. (B.19.c.) and one South
                        (B.25.a & b). This part of KLESMAN STELLUNG
                        system is on high ground (100 & 105 contours)
                        and dug-outs are suspected at:-
                             B.19.c.40.55.
                             B.19.c.25.60.
                             B.19.c.08.12.
                             B.20.a.85.70.
                             B.25.b.10.04.
                             B.25.b.60.10.
                             B.25.c.40.80.
                        In addition, B.25.b.35.30 is an important trench
                        junction and at B.25.d.7.4. is believed to be a
                        S.A.A. and Bomb Store.

APPENDIX I (Continued)

2. XXXXXXXXX

3. BROWN LINE.

(Maison de la Cote - Point du Jour, B.20.d. to H.v.a.)

The enemy during the past two months has done a great amount of work on this line. It runs along the top of the 100 metre contour the whole way; it consists of a double line of trenches with four connecting links between the two extreme points. The interval between the two lines varies from 300 yards to 100 yards.

The rearer of the double line has a system of dug-outs throughout its length built in pairs. They are situated at each side of a traverse on the Eastern side of the trench.
The second line has only two large dug-outs in it so far - one at the Northern End (B.27.a. 88.10) and one at the Southern end (H.9.a.80.08). The Northern one has tracks leading to it from N.W. and S.E.

The GRAVELLE WEB (B.27 - H.3) divides the system into two parts. Work on the Northern Part seems not to have been begun before the end of January (see air photograph 1075, 23.1.17). Between that date and February 14th (A.P.1833) a large dug-out in the second line was constructed at B.27.a.88.10 and at least one of the present three large earthworks on the front line (see A.P.1814, Feb.11th). During this time too, the tramway from the ST LAURENT - GAVRELLE Road (which previously ran as far as H.3.a.5.7. and there ended in a loop), was continued on along the Northerly track in B.27.c. towards BAILLEUL Railway cutting. (A.P.1075 Jan. 23rd. 1840 Feb. 11th and 1465 Mar. 4th).

From the general situation of these dug-outs and the command they have of the valley running down towards the SCARPE across the Divisional front, they may be machine gun emplacements.

The same system of defence is being continued on the right of POINT DU JOUR down to ATHIES.

The Map co-ordinates of these dug-outs, noted from aeroplane photographs are :-

B.27.a.18.10.   B.27.c.80.75.   B.27.c.50.8.
H.3.a.45.94.   H.3.a.45.60.   H.3.a.45.20.
H.3.a.80.15.   H.3.a.40.00.

23rd.N.F.
26.3.'17.

APPENDIX II
To accompany "INSTRUCTIONS No.1".

Contents of Dumps.

No. of Dump.	Mills No. 5	S.A.A.	No. 20 R. Grenades.	Iron Rations.	Biscuits
1.	140 boxes	150 Sand-bags	40 boxes	-----	----
2.	140 boxes	150 Sand-bags	40 boxes	-----	----
3.	---	---	---	150 Sand bags	75 Tins with 300 Sandbags.
4.	---	---	---	150 Sand bags	75 Tins with 300 Sandbags.
5.	---	---	---	---	---
	90 boxes	90 Sand-bags	20 boxes	---	---
6.	90 boxes	90 Sand-bags	20 boxes	---	---
8.	90 boxes	90 Sand-bags	20 boxes	---	---
9.	90 boxes	90 Sand-bags	20 boxes	---	---
11.	90 boxes	90 Sand-bags	20 boxes	---	---
12.	90 boxes	90 Sand-bags	20 boxes	---	---
TOTAL	820 boxes	900 Sand-bags	160 boxes	300 Sand bags	150 Tins with 600 Sandbags.

	Water	Very Lights	Flares	Rockets & Sticks.
1.	---	8 boxes 8 Pistols	1 box	40
2.	---	8 boxes 8 Pistols	1 box	40
3.	90 Tins.	---	---	---
4.	90 Tins.	---	---	---
5.	---	4 boxes 4 Pistols	---	20
6.	---	4 boxes 4 Pistols	1 box	20
7.	100 Tins	---	---	---
8.	---	4 boxes 4 Pistols	1 box	40
9.	---	4 boxes 4 Pistols	1 box	40
10.	100 Tins	---	---	---
11.	---	4 boxes 4 Pistols	1 box	20
12.	---	4 boxes 4 Pistols	1 box	20
TOTAL	380 Tins	40 boxes 40 Pistols	6 boxes	300

Brigade Dump Comprises Nos. 1 to 4 inclusive
Right Bn. Dump Comprises " 5 to 8 do
Left do do " 9 to 12 do

T.M.G. will be placed in Dug-outs selected by D.S.B.O.

Sheet 1.

23rd Bn. NORTHUMBERLAND FUSILIERS.

INSTRUCTIONS No...2.

These Instructions are in continuation of 23rd Bn. Northumberland Fusiliers Instructions No. 1 for the main operations to be undertaken by 34th Division in conjunction with other troops on right and left against the third objective, Brown Line.

1. SIGNAL COMMUNICATION.

(a) **Cables.** O.C. 102 Signal Section will arrange for two cables to be run out from the end of the buried cables in our line, and later to the Blue and Brown Lines. These cables will be laid along the communication trench across No Man's Land near KENT Crater, SPATZEN WEG, TAL WEG and GRAVELLER WEG.

The dug-outs to be used as Battalion Headquarters in the Black, Blue and Brown Lines will be connected to these cables by the 102 Signal Section. Brigade Headquarters, on moving to the Black Line, will use the wires laid for the use of "A" Bn. in the first instance. Artillery liason lines will be laid in addition by R.A. personnel.

(b) **Telephones.** Each Battalion will retain at least four of its stock of telephones with Battalion Headquarters, two of these may be used by linesmen.

(c) **Visual.** A Visual Station will be established as soon as possible after Zero hour on Z Day in KENT Crater. O.C. 102 Signal Section will arrange for this Station to be connected by telephone to Brigade Headquarters.
This Station will be in visual signalling communication with an advanced visual station to be established as soon as the Black Line has been captured near the junction of SPATZEN WEG with the Black line. This advanced visual station will receive all messages for Brigade Headquarters sent from forward Battalions by visual. Messages will be telephoned from this station to Brigade Headquarters as long as the cables to be laid along SPATZEN WEG are intact, otherwise by visual to KENT Crater.
                                                                    visual
The following personnel will be detailed to work these stations
        102 Signal Section   1 N.C.O. to command
                                                  advanced station.
        Each Battalion   2 Signallers.

Sergt. STRAKER will detail two Signallers for this work from Headquarters Section from among those who will be left behind.

The men selected will assemble at Brigade Headquarters at 12 noon on Y day, where they will be supplied with signalling shutters, lamps, flags, and telescopes.

The code calls for use of these visual stations will be in both cases that allotted to Brigade Headquarters - viz;- A Q.

A Divisional Visual Signalling Station for use of 101 and 102 Brigades will be established at G.O.C.G.4. as soon as the Black Line in the front of the 101 Brigade has been captured. Sergt. STRAKER will also detail one signaller to be attached to this station. Details as to time this man will report will be issued later.

(d) **Wireless.** No Wireless Sets are allotted to this Brigade.

(e) **Amplifiers & Power Buzzers.** One amplifier will be placed at 101st Infantry Brigade Advanced Report Centre G.O.C.5.7. to receive messages for this Brigade in addition to messages for 101st Infantry Brigade.

Two power Buzzers are allotted to this Brigade and will form 1 station and go forward with the Headquarters of "A" Battalion under the supervision of the Battalion Signalling Officer as far as the Blue Line.

These instruments will be worked by Battalion Signallers.
The code call of the amplifier at 101st Infantry Brigade Headquarters to which messages for this Brigade will be sent, is A C.

As Battalions 101st Infantry Brigade will also be sending to this Station it will be necessary for the power buzzers allotted to this Brigade to send only during alternate periods of 5 mins.

Sheet 2.

1. SIGNAL COMMUNICATION - Cont'd.

   (e) Amplifiers & Power Buzzers Cont'd.

   The periods during which power buzzers of this Brigade will send will be the even five minutes i.e., from 0 to 5, 10 to 15 etc, minutes after each clock hour.
   Messages once started on power buzzers should however be finished irrespective of the time.
   Power buzzers when in use on the Black Line will use only 10 volts, but when on the Blue Line 20 volts will be necessary.
   Power buzzers will always be got ready to send at each position of "A" Battalion Headquarters, but will not be used as long as the telephone wires to Brigade Headquarters are intact as otherwise they "jam" the messages sent by buzzer over the wire.

   (f) Pigeons. 2 pigeons will be issued to each of "A" & "B" Battalions on Y/Z nights and will be taken forward with Battalion Headquarters.
   These birds must be kept for important messages when other means of communication fail.
   All pigeon messages will be addressed by Battalions to Divisional Headquarters as well as to Brigade Headquarters.

   (g) Runners. All runners with messages for Brigade Headquarters will be specially instructed to take these messages direct to THELUS REDOUBT until word has been received that Brigade Headquarters has been moved from this position.
   As soon as the Brown line has been captured a runner relay post will be established from 1st Brigade Signal Section in a dug-out near the junction of the Blue Line and TAL WEG.
   As soon as Headquarters of "A" "B" "C" & "D" Battalions move forward from the Blue Line, all messages for Brigade Headquarters will be sent to this post where they will be taken over by the Brigade Runners for transmission to Brigade Headquarters which will then be in the Black Line.

2. CONSTRUCTION OF STRONG POINTS.
   The following localities have been selected for the construction of strong points in the enemy's trenches in the area allotted to this Brigade:-

   (a) Supporting the Black Line   G.C.b.3.4.
                                   A.36.d.4.2.

   (b) Supporting the Blue Line   B.25.d.9c.25.
                                   B.25.c.3.5.

   (c) Supporting the Brown Line   B.27.c.5.0.
                                   B.26.c.6.6.

   The strong points supporting the Black and Blue lines will not be constructed unless the attack should fail to reach the Brown Line.
   These strong points will be constructed under Divisional arrangements by the R.E. & 18th North'ld Fus. (Pioneers), and will each accomodate 1 platoon and 1 or 2 machine guns.
   As soon as these strong points have been constructed they will be garrisoned by the nearest troops for the time being and their occupation and strength of garrison reported as soon as possible to Brigade Headquarters.

3. COMMUNICATION TRENCHES.
   The long communication trench known in different parts by the three names - SPATZEN WEG, TAL WEG, and GAVRELLER WEG will be repaired by parties of R.E. and 18th North'd. Fus. (Pioneers) under Divisional arrangements.
   Under instructions from Divisional Headquarters this trench will be called TRUMAN AVENUE and marked with boards.

4. NOTICE BOARDS.
   Boards marked Black Blue and Brown and Green Line respectively will be carried by Battalion Carrying Parties and put in position by the troops in occupation of the trench.

Sheet 2.

5. DISTINGUISHING FLAGS.
Distinguishing flags coloured half red and half yellow to be issued at the rate of two per section will be carried forward in the attack to indicate the positions reached by our troops. These must on no account be stuck in the ground and will mean nothing except when waved. These flags will only be shewn by troops in the front line.

6. DRESS & EQUIPMENT.
In continuation of para 26 Instructions No. 1, the greatcoat will be carried rolled and attached to the waistbelt underneath the haversack. The waterproof sheet or cape will not be carried unless specially ordered. If it is carried, it will be carried on the top of the haversack under the flap. *The mess tin & cover will be put inside the haversack.*

7. MAPS.
The instructions in first para of Section XXXIII of S.S. 135 regarding letters, papers, maps, orders, sketches, etc., will be strictly adhered to.

Every Officer will carry the following:-

(a) 1/5,000 New Operation Map of German Trenches.
(b) Sheets 51B N.W.1 and 51B N.W.3 1/10,000

A new edition of the maps 51B N.W.1 and 51B N.W.3 is being issued shortly.

8. ACKNOWLEDGE.

Captain & A/Adjutant.
23rd Northumberland Fusiliers.

Distribution:-

Copies Nos. 1 and 7 Retained.
2. "A" COMPANY
3. "B" COMPANY
4. "C" COMPANY
5. "D" COMPANY
6. WAR DIARY.

S_E_C_R_E_T.   COPY No. 6

AMENDMENT No. 2
to
102nd (TYNESIDE SCOTTISH) BDE. INSTRUCTIONS No. 3.
(for the main attack on the 3rd Objective (Brown Line).

1..   **Delete** the whole of para. 13 and **substitute** :-

"4 tanks will co-operate in the attack of the 34th Division.

At Zero hour on Z day these tanks will leave their starting point A.29.c.1.1. and move just North of KITH Crater to the Black line.

On arrival at the Black line they will advance in line with the Infantry as far as B.25.c.1.0. At B.25.c.1.0. 2 tanks will bear to the left keeping North of SCHWEINER WEG to B.25.d.4.5., skirt round bank at this point and proceed Southwards down the Valley West of the railway.

The other 2 tanks will make for the road about H.1.b.2.5, and then proceed South down the Valley.

All 4 tanks will co-operate with the Infantry in the Valley until the Blue line is captured, after which they proceed to H.7.b.4.3.

At Zero plus 6 hours 40 minutes, the tanks will advance from H.7.b.4.3. with the Infantry having as their objective the trenches around H.9.a.4.8.

                                                    Major.
10? B.H.Q.   BRIGADE MAJOR.
7 : 4 : 1917.   102nd (TYNESIDE SCOTTISH) BDE.

Distribution as for O.O. No. 103.

S E C R E T.   Sheet 1.   Copy No. ___1___

23rd Bn. NORTHUMBERLAND FUSILIERS.

Instructions No. 3.

(FOR THE MAIN ATTACK ON THE THIRD OBJECTIVE (BROWN LINE).)

1.   **ACTION OF THE ARTILLERY.**

The attack of this Brigade will be supported by the Centre group, 34th Divisional Artillery, comprising

    3, 18 pdrs Batteries Army F.A. Brigade No. 1
    3, 18 "   "   "   "   2
    6, 4.5" Field Howitzers Batteries have been grouped to cover the whole Divisional Front.

2.   The action of Centre group, 34th Divisional Artillery, is described in 23rd Northumberland Fusiliers Instructions No. 1., paras 5 to 8 inclusive.

3.   With reference to para 7 - 3rd phase (b) last line - the action of the creeping barrage after lifting off the rear trench of the Brown Line on this Brigade front will be as follows:-

The barrage will creep back at the rate of 100 yards in 4 mins. to a line 300 yards East of the rear trench of the Brown Line where it will remain for 40 minutes. At the end of this period, certain batteries will be detailed to search the Eastern slopes of the Spurs East of the Brown Line. The fire of these searching batteries will be directed well east of the Green Line and will leave the Spurs leading to the East clear, so that patrols may be able to get out through the barrage to consolidate positions on these spurs.

4.   At the time laid down for the Infantry to commence each stage of the attack, a salvoes of shrapnel will be fired by every 18 pdr employed on the creeping barrage, with this exception, the ammunition used for the creeping barrage will be 50% shrapnel and 50% H.E.

5.   **GAS.**

With reference to Gas, the following code words will be used :-

    D R E S D E N   =   Discharge postponed
    B E R L I N (time) = Discharge will take place at (time)

6.   **ACTION OF 4" STOKES MORTARS.**

8, 4" Stokes Mortars will be placed in position near BOGEY AVENUE at A.30.c.7.9. and will be used as follows:-

(a) If the wind is favourable 4 mortars will fire
    40 P.S. (gas) shells each against WERK ULM A.30.b.05.50.
    to A.30.b.3.3. Times of discharge will be
      (i) 15 mins. before artillery bombardment begins
         on April 4th.
      (ii) Zero minus 50 hours.
      (iii) Zero minus 45 hours.
      (iv) Zero minus 35 hours.
      (v) Zero minus 8 hours.
(b) 8 mortars will fire 240 smoke shells on the line
    A.30.a.8.1. - A.30.c.5.5. from Zero to plus Z
    0.8 mins. on "Z" day. These will only be fired if
    the wind is between West and North by West.

SECRET.   Sheet 1.   Copy No. 7

23rd Bn. NORTHUMBERLAND FUSILIERS.

Instructions No...4.

1. The following is the situation and march programme for this Battalion from today 4th inst., until further orders:-

    night 4/5th   "X" Huts.
    day   5th   "X"   "
    night 5/6th   "X"   "
    day   6th   March to Bivouacs in LOUEZ.
                  Time of march will be notified later.
    night 6/7th   Bivouac in LOUEZ
    day   7th   Remain in LOUEZ until move to position of
                  assembly in trenches.

2. On the 6th inst., all packs will be handed in at the Quartermaster's store by Companies commencing with

    "A" Company at 8.45 a.m.
    "B"   do   9.15 a.m.
    "C"   do   9.30 a.m.
    "D"   do   10.00 a.m.

    All kit which is not carried in the fighting order already detailed will be left in the packs. Balmorals will be left here.

    When packs are handed in, Companies will also hand in all Cap Badges and 1 set of numerals from great coats. These will be put up in sandbags. Officers valises will be taken to LOUEZ if required and returned to the Store on the 7th.

    Companies will at the same time hand in one blanket per man to the Q.M. Store, 1 blanket per man will be taken to LOUEZ by transport or on the man under orders to be issued later.

    All ranks remaining behind on "Z" day will remain at "X" Huts on the 6th inst., and will not proceed to LOUEZ.

3. On the night 7/8th the Battalion will move into its position in WEDNESDAY AVENUE as follows:-

    By Platoons at 100 yards distance, "A" Company leading
    "B" "C" & "D" Companies in succession.
    The leading Platoon of "A" Company will be at the starting point ST. AUBIN CHURCH L.11.a.5.5. at 8.45 p.m.
    The route will be North of the River Scarpe to ANZIN G.7.b.8.4. HILL STREET - main road to G.8.c.15.55 thence by cross country track known as overland route to SUNDAY AVENUE.

    One Officer per Company will reconnoitre this road by day and one Officer per Company by night.

    The distance from the starting point to the LILLE ROAD G.9.b.2.5. is 3½ miles. The leading Platoon "A" Company is due to reach this point at 10.45 p.m.

4. Before leaving LOUEZ all ranks will be completely equipped and carrying all special stores including "P" Bombs, Grenades, Flares etc. as already detailed, with the exception of spades, picks and sandbags which will be issued in the trenches.

    Greatcoats will be carried rolled on the belt.
    Orders re ground sheets will be issued later.

                                                Captain & A/Adjutant.

Copies to:-

    As per Instructions Nos. 1 to 3.

Army Form C. 2118.

WAR DIARY
or
INTELLIGENCE SUMMARY.

23rd Northumberland Fus
(4th Tyneside Scottish)

(Erase heading not required.)

Place	Date	Hour	Summary of Events and Information	Remarks and references to Appendices
TRENCHES Opposite CHEMICAL WORKS. I.13.d.	May 1st 1917		Hostile artillery stay active and afforded very much on the alert. Whenever any activity was shown on our front the enemy placed a barrage of shrapnel (both H.E. & Shrapnel) along road running through Railway Arch 14-15 d. 3.2. Also Artillery Headquarters were informed. About 3 a.m. a heavy barrage was put along this road by the enemy. A short of gas cylinders lying within 20 yds of the Railway Arch were burst open by this barrage with the result that several men were gassed (some shell [?]). It is not yet known whether the gas was our own or German. Arches initially entirely though out the day. On the evening we were relieved by the [?]. [?] handed the Battalion marched into a camp at [?].	REF SHEET 51.B.N.W. By [?] 51.C.F. LENS 11
			Casualties. 14 sick O.R.	
	2nd		The Battalion proceeded on trains to SOMBRIN. Spent billets and training grounds	
			Casualties 4/4	
	3rd 4th 5th 6th 7th 8th		Carried out training and re-equipping of the Battalion. Many [?] weather. Several games were played. News received that the Battalion on proceeding shortly now.	
			Casualties. 40R sick	
	9th		The Battalion marched to IVERGNY on the 8th June left and to BOUQUEMAISON on the 9th. Remarks. Casualties 4/4	

2353 Wt. W2544/1454 700,000 5/15 D. D. & L. A.D.S.S. Forms/C. 2118.

Army Form C. 2118.

WAR DIARY
or
INTELLIGENCE SUMMARY.
(Erase heading not required.)

Instructions regarding War Diaries and Intelligence Summaries are contained in F. S. Regs., Part II. and the Staff Manual respectively. Title pages will be prepared in manuscript.

Place	Date	Hour	Summary of Events and Information	Remarks and references to Appendices
PITTEFAUX				REFT. 97620 LENS. 11
	11th 12th		1st Battalion marched to PITTEFAUX when it remained in army reserve for three weeks. Pretty village, good billets. 9 am weather, first training and Rifle Ranges. Casualties 2 O.R. sick.	
	13th 14th		Did not training in war near billets. 9 am weather with occasional showers of rain. Casualties 3 O.R. sick to 12th. 2 O.R. sick on 14th.	
	15th 16th 17th 18th		Training was carried on with on area and range. Fine weather continues. Casualties 1 O.R. sick on 15th. 3 O.R. 16th. 1 O.R. 17th. 3 O.R. 18th.	
	19th 20th 21st 22nd		Church Parades and Cricket Matches were played in afternoon & evening. Training was continued, and special attack practice over flagged areas, in four of an inspection to take place shortly. Casualties 1 O.R. sick 21st. 2 O.R. sick 22nd.	
	23rd 24th 25th		Further training & practice on area and special field practice on range. Casualties NIL	
	26th		Inspection in afternoon by Divisional General at 4 p.m. Push-in close order was afterwards while doing the practice attack, in very hot weather. Casualties NIL	
	27th		Church Parades and cricket Matches. Casualties. NIL	
	28th 29th +30th		Two easy days in view of moving away, packing up and clearing away. Reg: Transport left at 7am in 29th bound for ARRAS and to arrive there by 30th inst. Casualties 1 O.R. sick.	

Army Form C. 2118.

WAR DIARY
or
INTELLIGENCE SUMMARY.
(Erase heading not required.)

Instructions regarding War Diaries and Intelligence Summaries are contained in F. S. Regs., Part II. and the Staff Manual respectively. Title pages will be prepared in manuscript.

Place	Date	Hour	Summary of Events and Information	Remarks and references to Appendices
ST NICHOLAS NEAR ARRAS	1917 May 30th		Battalion left AUTHEUX at 7.30am and marched to CANDAS where they entrained and arrived at ARRAS station about 2.0 P.M. and marched through the town up to tents situated to the N.E. of ARRAS. Weather continues to be very warm, and accommodation very small through lack of shelter.	Casualties
	31st		Rearrangement of shelters & more tents given to us. We still watch ARRA being shelled, mostly by night. Notice of Bath given to the Battalion. Casualties 1 OR. sick.	

G.N.B.M.
Lt. Col.
Cmdg: 23rd Northb'n Fus:
4th Tyneside Scottish

Army Form C. 2118.

WAR DIARY
INTELLIGENCE SUMMARY
(Erase heading not required.)

VOL. XVIII
2/3/5 B. Royal Fusiliers

Place	Date	Hour	Summary of Events and Information	Remarks and references to Appendices
ST NICHOLAS near ARRAS.	June 1st		"A" & "C" Coys. marched over to training area in afternoon to carry out a practice attack for future operations. By 2pm at 2.30pm returned about 7pm. Camp readied to hostile aircraft few are	
	June 2nd		The camp viewpoint back in ARRAS & the neighbourhood. 10R risk. Heavy carried out in camp for an hour in morning & then in the evening the Battalion marched to the training ground about 6pm & Coys carried out the attack over the ground & returned to camp about 9.20pm. 9th Bouffers & 10R side. Church parades in the morning. Great in the afternoon. Southern very quiet	
	June 3		"D" Company today in the forward area was shelled. 9th pm. 2 wounded. 2 O.R. sick. 10R had 4 sent to 10R wounded. 2 O.R. sick. Preparing for move into the trenches for the day. Battalion marched off at 3.30pm from ST NICHOLAS & to relieve the 16 Royal Scots in support on the right of brigade section of the front. found. Casualties 1 O.R. Sick	
TRENCHES IN FRONT OF GREENLAND HILL	June 4		Relief carried 2.30 AM. A, C & D Coys in support to 1st 2nd & 3rd Tyneside Scottish respectively. Slightly shelled during day 10A 10 effect. Zero hour was 8pm. Hostile barrage very prompt quickly heavy in front line. No enemy attack by	

WAR DIARY
INTELLIGENCE SUMMARY

(Erase heading not required.)

Place	Date	Hour	Summary of Events and Information	Remarks and references to Appendices
TRENCHES.	JUNE 25th (Contd)		enemy batteries during the day, the number of these replies was so far successful. Although so far successful altogether nil.	
	JUNE 26		formed out 'pockets' of Boche were fifty together nil. About 3 AM A Coy under Capt. Nash were called upon to advance & to clear a 'pocket' of Boche. Broken rifle broken support up near the Sunk. The Shropshire but owing to machine gun fire were caught in the open & were rather badly stricken. Colour Serjt. Moran having gone out front. Major S. Ridley M.C. was badly stricken. and many C.Sgt. C.B. Park D.S.O. & Major S. Ridley M.C. while he and the party were wounded by a shell, formerly, rather were severely wounded. No counter attacks. There were intermittent shelling during the day & in the evening the enemy after putting down barrage in our front line supports made a determined counter-attack. The true division of attack were known but was our barrage (artillery)' by our heavy machine gun rifle fire; the time from 1 A.Coy. V/c. D. Coy was called upon to deliver & back up the attack. Thrown alright 11 pm. We learnt casualties officers and men that 13th M.H., 13 pltn. Killed. Connelton, Bride Park D.S.O., & Major S. Ridley M.C. & 20 O.R. Wounded; 3 O.R. Died. Capt. H. Whiteread.	

Acting Officer Commanding the Batn.

WAR DIARY / INTELLIGENCE SUMMARY

Army Form C. 2118.

Place	Date	Hour	Summary of Events and Information	Remarks and references to Appendices
TRENCHES.	June 7th		The day passed quietly except for slight shelling most of which fell behind the line we were holding. S.A.A, bombs, R.E. material etc. were carried up by our parties for use on the front line. Casualties: 1 Off. killed, 1 Off. W., 11 wounded, 5 sick.	
"	June 8th		Appr. a quiet day. The Battalion moved back into the FAMPOUX – GAVRELLE line reserve where the commencement of the 101st Inf. Bde. 3 Offrs at 2 O.R. sick. The men were able to have well earned rest. Party carrying moved up carrying S.A.A., R.E. material etc. to Reformed Trenches by 101 Bde. wounded. Casualties – Nil.	
	June 9th			
	June 10th		Still quiet, nothing then worth reporting. Casualties – Nil.	
	June 11th		Bn. 21st N.F. the battalion was relieved by the 21st N.F., the Battn. from reserve and took Reserve line in the Sunken Rd. 11.7 a.m. Bn South of O.R.	Sheet 51B NW. 23000
SUNKEN ROAD H.7.a.	June 12th		Arrived safely in trenches about 2 a.m. & rather during the day. The whole battalion was out of the working parties during the day. Major C.R. LONGHURST took over command of Battalion. Casualties – Nil.	

WAR DIARY
INTELLIGENCE SUMMARY

Place	Date	Hour	Summary of Events and Information	Remarks and references to Appendices
	June 13th		Resting. Army rations. Platoon practice at night. 4 O.R. sick.	
TRENCHES	June 14th	12th	Resting. Army day. Coy marched off at 9.30 p.m. to relieve 1st 21st N.F. — The Lieut in charge of 102 Bde front. Two Coys A & D were in the firing line. C Coy was in support to GRENELLE TRIE, other Bn. HQ was established	
	June 15th		Relief complete by 2.30 a.m. 1 O.R. wounded. 2 O.R. sick. Quiet day except for shelling of Comm. Trenches. All men employed in working on trenches, wiring & patrolling. Patrols were taken out by 7th, D Scott & Spirit. C Coy working on SOUCHEZ front line.	
	June 16th		1 O.R. wounded, 2 O.R. sick. Quiet shelling. 1 C.T.s that tunnels. Some trespassers were 1.C. of patrols. D Coy had a Lieut & men [illegible] out by shell. Moment [illegible] out by night [illegible] for [illegible]	
	June 17th		Quiet. Moved day. Relieved by 2nd N.F. at night. 10 R. Wound 3 O.R. sick. Relief [illegible] carried out without relief. The [illegible] at	
SUNKEN Rd H.7.a.	June 18th		to the Sunken Rd H.7.a. Canonte at B.A.M. — men rested during day. Turn out on working parties. 1 O.R. Sick.	

WAR DIARY or INTELLIGENCE SUMMARY

Army Form C. 2118.

Place	Date	Hour	Summary of Events and Information	Remarks and references to Appendices
	Dec 19th		Major Inglehart preceded a train to Paris. Casualties: 1 O.R. Accidental. Major Horsburgh men in in working parties.	
	20th		Was relieved by 6th Bn Dorsets in Sunken Rd at 7 o'clock in evening and proceeded for the night to camp at 97. Nicholas. Heavy rainfall during relief. Arrived in camp at about 8 pm.	
	21st		Entrained in lorries at 9 am and proceeded to billets at Marchand. Officers' billets very inferior. Owing to arrive at sight officers with a draft of 92 new men and 23 returned casuals. Capt. J. S. Nolan McVittie over command of the Battalion. Whitacre as acting 2nd in command. Men's billets good.	
	22nd		Started thorough cleaning of equipment. Cleaned the Cricket ground. Football in afternoon. Casualties: W.O.R. Sick in 20th, NIL 21st, NIL 22nd.	
	23rd		Commenced Programme training. Inspection of companies by Coys in afternoon. Casualties: NIL	
	24th		Entered Programme. Company training & afternoon.	
	25th		Entered Programme. Coy Staff & Platoon Exercise in range. Cricket in afternoon. Fetes by Brigade Staff to Platoon Circles at 6 pm.	
	26th		Service in evening. General visited France Guard. W.O.R. Sick 25. Sports in afternoon. Casualties: 1 O.R. Sick	
	27th		Lecture in evening. Sports in afternoon. Casualties: 1 O.R. Sick	
			Continued programme of training. Cricket match with 25th HLI in afternoon. Casualties NIL	

Army Form C. 2118.

WAR DIARY
or
INTELLIGENCE SUMMARY.
(Erase heading not required.)

Place	Date 1917	Hour	Summary of Events and Information	Remarks and references to Appendices
MONCHEAUX	June 28		Programme of training continues. Lecture by Brigade Staff Officer Commander. Heavy thunderstorm at night which caused report. Generators for the hothouse. Gate note no 29th R.E. Camelling 207 Seh Gov.	
	29		Carried on training. S.O.C. Brigade visited trenches. Mine, burst note no 11 × N.F. Salient. Night operation "outposts" carried out.	
	30		Carried on training. Relieved 1 P.R. Rifle Camelling. Remainder moving relieving 2nd Major Regiment. Took over Command of the Battalion. Camelling. R.P. Scott.	

O.

S. Salson Copthaf
for Major
Cmdg 23rd Welsh Fus
(4th Tyneside Scottish)

Army Form C. 2118.

WAR DIARY
or
INTELLIGENCE SUMMARY.
(Erase heading not required.)

23(S)B. Yorks [illegible] Vol. XIX

Place	Date	Hour	Summary of Events and Information	Remarks and references to Appendices
MONCHEAUX	3rd July/15		Trained and bivouac.	
	4th		Orders received for move. The Battalion was to move from TINCQUES Station in two parties, one in the 4th Instant the other on the 5th Inst. 'A' Company went in the 4th, and the remainder of the Battalion with transport moved on the 5th Inst.	
	5th		The Battalion detrained at PERONNE and proceeded by march route to ROISEL. This village is very badly damaged, not a single house left standing.	
			Casualties 1st Coy. 2 OR Sick. 2nd Coy. NIL.
			3. OR. " 4. " 8. OR. Sick
			5 " NIL
	6th		The Battalion rested and cleaned up generally. In the myfl [illegible] an working party was supplied for moving some of the wood defences of the HARRICOURT Sector.	
	7th		Casualties 6. OR. [illegible] K.OR. Sick. 7. " NIL	
	8th		On the night of the 7/8 July the Battalion relieved the INNISKILLING DRAGOONS and the 58 C.I. Horse of the 4th Dismounted Brigade on the P3 Subsector of the trenches. The Battalion frontage is as follows. [illegible] Boundary. L.11.5.51 SHEET 62cSE.
TRENCHES			LEFT BOUNDARY. F.29.d.25.15.
HARRICOURT			Dispositions are disposed as follows. NE
			Two Companies in front line and 1 Coy on Reserve in the INTERMEDIATE line. The shooting front off the firing front line extension is L.5. d. 70.70.	

A5834 Wt.W4973/M687 750,000 8/16 D.D.&L.Ltd. Forms/C.2118/13.

WAR DIARY
or
INTELLIGENCE SUMMARY.

Army Form C. 2118.

(Erase heading not required.)

Instructions regarding War Diaries and Intelligence Summaries are contained in F. S. Regs., Part II. and the Staff Manual respectively. Title pages will be prepared in manuscript.

Place	Date	Hour	Summary of Events and Information	Remarks and references to Appendices
TRENCHES HARGICOURT	8/9		The bombing in recess is situated at L.10.a.1.6. Battalion Headquarters is situated at L.10.a.60.60. in Quarry. The 19th Battalion Durham Light Infantry are on the left of the Battalion and the 22nd Manchester Regt (3rd Gronnell Scottish) and on the right of the Battalion. The front system is composed of posts. The Major bombing have the following posts in their sector E.44 Post and No. 5. 1 Lt 7 Posts inclusive (Right to left.) The most advanced post in the Battalion sector is UNNAMED FARM (L.6.a.2.2.) The most valuable front in the Battalion sector is UNNAMED FARM (L.6.a.2.2.) This position came in for a great deal of shelter and machinegun fire. Casualties 5/9 NIL.	SHEET 62.C N.E
	10th		Indiscriminate shelling in both sectors all day. Posts damaged a great deal. A great deal of work has been done along with the posts improve a large amount of wire flung out. Bombers and machinery all night and garrisons one memo. The Smiths men support from Triangle recess to work in the front system. Casualties 1 O.R. Wounded.	
	11th		Very heavy shelling and machinegun onto left sector in vicinity of UNNAMED FARM and posts 8, 9, 10 & 11. In the evening in parts of above SD of the enemy were seen collecting in trench in front of Monmouth Farm. Alarm was carried out and every precaution made against a hostile attack. Nothing materialized. Casualties. 2 ORS Wounded. 1 OR Sick. MM	

A 9534 Wt. W4973/M687 750,000 8/16 D. D. & L. Ltd. Forms/C.2118/13.

WAR DIARY or INTELLIGENCE SUMMARY

Army Form C. 2118.

Place	Date	Hour	Summary of Events and Information	Remarks and references to Appendices
TRENCHES HER SI COUR?	12th July 1917		Enemy still continues to shell heavily south and near Minnenwerfers into the northern thanks of both Hedgehogs. On the evening our wire kept quiet and more made. C. Co. remained in left sector. A. Co. relieved D. Co. in the left sector. Front & supply carried out during night. Casualties: 2 O.R.s wounded. 1 O.R. Killed.	
	13/7 14		Intermittent shelling all day. Patrol went out in the evening. Several went round on right. At about 1.55 p.m. on the morning of the 14th inst a German came forward who evidently had lost his way near Tadpole from way on the left trenches front. He mentioned that an enemy raid was set for 3 o'clock (German time, that is 2 a.m. English). At about 2 a.m. the enemy opened a heavy barrage of Artillery and Minnenwerfers and a raiding party attempted to enter No. 9 Post (unnamed form) & No. 11 Post. At N.9 post he was easily held up and met one of the enemy succeeded in entering the trench. The enemy at this point immediately suffered heavy casualties. At 10.11 post the enemy succeeded in effecting an entrance - he intercepted the garrison and one of our men and times from were taken. The lift N.3 sector showed a shell which fell at British Head Quarters caused 4 Casualties. Casualties 13th 4 O.R.s Killed. 6 O.R.s Wounded. 1 O.R. Died of Wounds 14th 1 O.R. Killed. 6 O.R.s Missing. 17 O.R.s wounded. 2 O.R.s Ra?	STREET 62S N.E.

Army Form C. 2118.

WAR DIARY
or
INTELLIGENCE SUMMARY.
(Erase heading not required.)

Place	Date	Hour	Summary of Events and Information	Remarks and references to Appendices
TRENCHES.	15th July 1917		Since being relieved the enemy have not shelled us much. In the night of the	
HARGICOURT.	15/16th		The 20th Manch Fus. (1st Grenade Battn) relieved the Battalion and we proceeded into Tregnier Reserve. Two Companies were disposed as follows:- A. Co. in Reserve in the Klenidale line in B.1 Sheet. C. Co. in B.2 Sheet and D. Co. in B.1 Sub Sector. Battalion Head Quarters are situated in RUELLES WOOD. L.9.d. (Sheet 62' N.E.) Quiet relief. Casualties. 1. O.R. Wounded. 1. O.R. Sick	
	16th to 24th		Every available man in the Battalion was out on working parties during this period. The greater percentage of the men were employed for mining in front of the posts in front of B.3. Subsector occupied by 20th O.F. (1st Grenade Battn). Very hot weather. Casualties. 15th.	
			16th. NIL.	
			17th. 1.O.R. Killed. 7. O.R. Wounded. 18th. NIL.	
			1.O.R. Sick. 20th. NIL.	
			19th. NIL.	
			22nd. 6. O.R. Sick. 23rd. 3. O.R's Hospital.	21st. NIL.
			(Gas)	24th. NIL.
25.			On the night of the 25/26 July 1917 the Battalion was relieved by the 11th Dn. Suffolks Regt. Quiet and easy relief. The Battalion marched into Billets (sheds in huts, tents, etc.) at HANCOURT (Q.8.d.) SHEET 62 Casualties. NIL. C. EDFJ	

A 3834. Wt. W4973/M687. 750,000. 8/16. D.D. & L. Ltd. Forms/C.2118/13.

WAR DIARY
or
INTELLIGENCE SUMMARY.

Army Form C. 2118.

(Erase heading not required.)

Place	Date	Hour	Summary of Events and Information	Remarks and references to Appendices
HANCOURT (Q.8.d.)	July 24th to 31st 1917		The Battalion carried out with training throughout this period. There are good training grounds, Rifle ranges, Bombing Pits etc. The afternoons were principally devoted to recreational training. A chief feature in the training is "Baseball". Several nights were devoted to practice flights etc. Sports were on 24, 30 & 31st Casualties 26" NIL 27" 1.OR Sick 25" 2.OR Sick 24" 2.OR Sick 30" 2.ORS Sick 31st 3 ORS Sick 33 Officers 580. ORs	

Strength of battalion on 31/7/17.

R. Longhurst Major
Cmdg 28th Northumberland Fus.
(1st Tyneside Scottish)

Army Form W.3091.

Cover for Documents.

Natures of Enclosures.

23rd Bn. Northumberland Fusiliers

Brigade Operation Orders

During August and September 1917.

Notes, or Letters written.

246

Army Form C. 2118.

Volume I

AUGUST 1917.

23rd NORTH'D FUS.
4th Sponsored Leaflet.

Vol 20

WAR DIARY
or
INTELLIGENCE SUMMARY.
(Erase heading not required.)

Place	Date	Hour	Summary of Events and Information	Remarks and references to Appendices
HANCOURT (Q.8.d.)	Aug 1st 1917		One Company commenced extensive digging for the Divisional Commander. Very wet day. Casualties NIL	SHEET 62 2SE. C. EDIT 1.
	Aug 2nd		In the night of the 2/3rd we relieved the 24th Bn Northd Fus on the A.2 Subsector of the 34th Div Front. Late relief. The Battalion frontage extends from GRAND PRIEL FARM (L.29.d.central) on the right to the N.W edge of Peel WOOD.C.31.d. two Companies of 5 platoons each occupy this frontage. The remaining three platoons of the third Battalion are in support. 4 or 5 shell-holes are shell craters to be in defence. The shooting line is approximate. ASCENSION FARM (L.30.c.72). The posts occupied by the left company are in a delapidated condition and owing to recent heavy rains are in a very shocking and wet condition. Barrage very fast. Very wet day. Patrols sent out during night. Casualties 1 OR Sick	For dispositions see attached Sketch G.W.M (Draft attached hereto) S.R.
TRENCHES.				S.R.
	Aug 3rd		Hot day. Very quiet. Patrols sent out on the evening, no enemy encountered. Casualties 2/Lt A.L. Leigh accidentally wounded. 1 OR Sick.	S.R.
	4th		Showers throughout the day. Received a draft of 11. ORs. One working on posts during afternoon and night. Two patrols sent out. No firm and leading front, no enemy encountered. Quiet day. Casualties 1 OR Wounded	S.R.

Army Form C. 2118.

WAR DIARY
or
INTELLIGENCE SUMMARY.
(Erase heading not required.)

Instructions regarding War Diaries and Intelligence Summaries are contained in F. S. Regs., Part II. and the Staff Manual respectively. Title pages will be prepared in manuscript.

Place	Date	Hour	Summary of Events and Information	Remarks and references to Appendices
TRENCHES A 2 Sub Sector	5th		Quiet day. Patrols sent out in the evening, no enemy encountered. Slight shower throughout day. Casualties NIL	8pm
	6th		Quiet day. In the evening a patrol under 2/Lt R P Hornsby went in the direction of BIG BILL (G. 26 a) when they encountered an enemy patrol which was dispersed with Lewis gun and rifle fire. Whilst this encounter a reconnaissance of BIG BILL was carried out. In returning to our lines 2/Lt Hornsby and 2 ORs were wounded with machine gun fire. The officer was wounded whilst carrying a wounded NCO to safety. 23/8/17. 2/Lt J N Allison about endeavour gallantry in carrying in 2/Lt Hornsby under fire. Casualties. 2/Lt R P Hornsby wounded. Lt J.O. Evans Lieut. & ORs wounded.	8pm
	7th		Patrols sent out in the evening, No enemy encountered. Quiet day. Casualties. 1 OR sick.	8pm
	8th		Quiet day. In the evening two strong fighting patrols sent out. One patrol to BIG BILL and the other towards our support received shell holes in G. 27.C. These patrols worked in conjunction with the artillery. None of the enemy were encountered – both BIG BILL & the Shell holes were found to be unoccupied. Casualties. NIL.	8pm
	9th		Quiet day. Normal work being carried on in the trenches. A patrol went out in the evening towards the shell holes in G. 27.C. but they were again found to be unoccupied. Casualties. 1 OR sick.	8pm

A.5834 Wt.W4973/M687 750,000 8/16 D.D. & L. Ltd. Forms/C.2118/13.

WAR DIARY or INTELLIGENCE SUMMARY

Army Form C. 2118.

Place	Date	Hour	Summary of Events and Information	Remarks and references to Appendices
TRENCHES A.2 Sub-Sector	10th Aug '17		On the night 10/11th the Battalion was relieved by the amalgamated Battalions of the 24th and 27th Northumberland Fusiliers. On relief the Battalion marched to huts in HANCOURT & dropped 84 O.R.s received. Casualties 1 OR Lt. 2/Lt S.F. Byrne Lieut.	
HANCOURT	11th 12th & 13th Aug		Carried out training schemes. Lt.Col. C.R. Pooch D.S.O. rejoined for duty on the 11th and assumed command of the Battalion. On the 24th & 29th N.F.s amalgamating the nuclei were sorted to other various Battalions in the 102nd Brigade Sheffield Brigade. This Battalion received 5 Officers and 44 O.R.s making the strength of the Battalion up to 35 Officers and 688 O.R.s. B Lt. the front Coy was again formed. Casualties 11th Aug NIL, 12th NIL, 13th 5 O.R.s Lieut.	
	13/14 Aug		On the night of the 13/14th August we relieved the 11th Batt Royal Sussex Regt and resumed "D" Battalion in the "B" Sub. 34th Divisional Front. Companies were disposed of as follows. A Lt. QUARRY. F.27c. B.t. & Bn. H.Q.s HERVILLY. C Lt. QUARRY – L.10.a.55. "D" Lt. HARDY ROAD F.22.Q. Casualties 1. OR Lieut.	
	15th		On the night 15/16th Aug the 23rd N.F. relieved the 20th N.F. (1st Tyneside Scottish) on the left Sub-Sector of "B" Sector of Trenches, 34th Divisional Front. Companies took over as follows. A Lt. VALLEY, HUSSAR, RIFLEMAN, & BATTERIES Posts. B Lt. B1a and LITTLE BENJAMIN POSTS. D Lt. were in support in shelters F.22.c.	See Ref Sheet 3/N/M/1

Army Form C. 2118.

WAR DIARY
or
INTELLIGENCE SUMMARY.
(Erase heading not required.)

Instructions regarding War Diaries and Intelligence
Summaries are contained in F. S. Regs., Part II.
and the Staff Manual respectively. Title pages
will be prepared in manuscript.

Place	Date	Hour	Summary of Events and Information	Remarks and references to Appendices
TRENCHES Left Brigade D. Subr.	15th Aug 1916		D.L. and Batt. HqRs were established in QUARRY F.27.c. Bruit not take relief.	B.M.
HARRICOURT	16.17.18 Aug		The posts, especially Mr. BENJAMIN'S, were in a very bad condition. A great deal of work was carried out and drainage commenced. By the 18th Inst. the posts were in a fairly dry condition. Several shelters were built. Every night patrols were sent out. Those of the enemy were encountered. Casualties 16th Aug 3 O.R's Inst. 18th Aug 2 O.R's Inst. 17th Aug 2 O.R Maconday Inst.	B.M.
	19th		In the night of the 19th/20th the battalion was relieved by the 22nd N.F. (9th Tyneside Scottish) and marched into billets in HERVILLY. Very late relief. Casualties. 2 O.R's Killed on return. 2 O.R's wounded. 1 O.R Inst.	B.M.
HERVILLY	20.21.22		Supplied a few working parties. Orders received that the Battalion is to take a front in an attack against the enemy. The 104th Infantry Brigade are to attack and capture the Hindenburg Line occupied by the enemy from F.30.c.79.95 to G.17.d.63.97. This Battalion is to move forward at Zero Hour and occupy the enemy front line "RIFLE PIT TRENCH". The occupation of this trench is to form the left defensive flank. Also, if the enemy will occupy Rifle Pit trench and dig it out and put same in a defensible state, they will also construct 3 strong points. On the 22nd Inst. 19 hrs were practised in the method of occupation afterwards and the various groups of working men engaged. Casualties. 20th Aug 1 O.R Inst. 21st Aug 2 O.R Inst. 22nd Aug 1 O.R Inst.	REF SHEET. NAVROY. ED.I. 1/20/100 See O.D. No 64 Pt II Marked and Patrol Rech. S.W/M/II Sh. GILLEMONT FARM PART I SHEET PART I 1F 57 S.E. 57 D S.W. 62 C N.E. & N.W. B.M.

Army Form C. 2118.

WAR DIARY
or
INTELLIGENCE SUMMARY.
(Erase heading not required.)

Instructions regarding War Diaries and Intelligence Summaries are contained in F. S. Regs., Part II. and the Staff Manual respectively. Title pages will be prepared in manuscript.

Place	Date	Hour	Summary of Events and Information	Remarks and references to Appendices
INTERMED-IATE LINE "D" Subs 31 - 9 N.	23rd		On the night 23rd/24th Aug. The Battalion relieved the 20th N.F. in the Intermediate Line. B. Subs of trenches. Companies were as follows :- F.27.c. B Coy. QUARRY. (L.10.a.5.5.) C Coy FERVACQUE TRENCH (near VILLERET). D Coy HARDY BANKS. (F.22.c.) Quiet relief. Casualties. 1 O.R. Sick.	
LEFT SUB-SECTOR OF "B" Subs of TRENCHES HARGICOURT	24th		On the night 24th/25th. The Battalion relieved the 22nd N.F. (3rd Tyneside Scottish) in the LEFT SECTOR of B. Subs of trenches. Companies were disposed as follows. A. Coy. QUARRY (F.27.c.). B. Coy. RIGHT Left Sector of trenches (ARTAXERXES & RIFLE MAN POSTS only). VINLEY & HUSSAR Posts were taken over by the 11th Batln. Royal Sussex Regt who are now the Left attaching Battalion of the 101st Bde. The relief was to commence at 4.30 pm on the morning of the 26th inst. C. Coy were in Sellers in Bank. F.22.c. & D. Coy were in LEFT Sector of trenches battln in back rows very active. Casualties. 1 O.R. wounded.	
	25th		Heavy shelling by our artillery and by enemy throughout the day. Patrols were sent out during the evening and patrolled round midnight. An enemy recruiting party were sent out at Midnight to protect the 11th Suffolks while forming up in No Mans Land. Casualties. 3 O.R.s wounded. 1 O.R. Sick. G.S.W.	

WAR DIARY or INTELLIGENCE SUMMARY

Army Form C. 2118.

Place	Date	Hour	Summary of Events and Information	Remarks and references to Appendices
LEFT SUB-SECTOR OF "B" Sector HARRAICOURT	Aug 26th 1916.	4.30 A.M.	At Zero hour (4.30 a.m.) The "D.I." Bde commenced their attack and "A" Co. of the Battalion moved out from RIFLEMAN POST in a South Easterly direction along RIFLE PIT Trench. Some Germans were taken prisoners without any fighting taking place. "A" Co. got in touch with the 11th Battn. Suffolks at point in Sunken Road where RIFLE PIT Trench joins same (F.30.c.38.58). The consolidation and digging out of this trench was strenuously commenced with. A fairly heavy damage was put down by the enemy and RIFLEMAN and HUSSAR Posts came in for a fair amount of shelling. During the actual advance and occupation of RIFLE PIT Trench by "A" Co. only 3 slight casualties occurred. At Zero + 2 hours two platoons of "C" Co. were sent out to mine in front of RIFLE PIT Trench. Enemy snipers were very active from portion of MALAKOFF Support trench NORTH of Second Hegelein in A.25.d. There were no reinforced mining by day very difficult to do and caused the majority of our casualties. It being felt was very difficult to the junction of trench and Sunken Road. At 6.30 a.m. a considerable number of the enemy were seen assembling at the Southern edge of QUENNET COPSE, this party was broken up by our battery fire. At 7 a.m. our trenches were subjected to shelling by the enemy - the shells containing lachrymatory fumes. Ho ill effects were caused. At 2.30 P.M. RIFLEMAN POST was shelled - very little damage done. Heavy rain and thunderstorm in the evening. RIFLEPIT Trench in very muddy condition. Casualties. 2/Lt. T.A. ABBEY & 2/Lt. H. HANNINGTON wounded. 3 O.R.s. killed. 16 O.R.s. wounded. B.M.	

WAR DIARY or INTELLIGENCE SUMMARY.

Army Form C. 2118.

Place	Date	Hour	Summary of Events and Information	Remarks and references to Appendices
"B" Subst of TRENCHES HARICOURT	26/27 Aug 1914		"B" Coy of the Reinst reoccupied RIFLE PIT Trench from 5.30 P.M. 26. But at 8.30 P.M. a hostile counter attack approached & be beaten back against No1. Rifle front. Enemy first seen F.20.c.4.5. advanced in party of the enemy about 30 strong advancing along the South side of Sunken Road moving from MALAKOFF. Support trench to our front. Report. Two and Lewis gun fire was opened upon our front and the enemy party was broken up and hurriedly retired. During the _____ remainder of the night everything was quiet. Two platoons of "C" Coy relieved "B" Coy in RIFLE PIT Trench at 9 P.M. and continued work in digging of trench. Enemy snipers were very active. At 1 A.M. Two Platoons of "A" Coy relieved "C" Coy and carried on with work. By 5 P.M. RIFLE PIT trench was made into a continuous trench throughout. Very heavy rain in the evening and during night. Trenches in very wet and dirty condition. Casualties. 2 O.R.S. Wounded.	
	Aug 28		Very windy day, very little artillery activity during the day. Between 9 P.M. and 10.30 P.M. ARTAXERXES POST and HUSSAR ROAD were heavily shelled with 9.5.7 shells. 3 Casualties were sustained. Our artillery was very active during this period also. Work on RIFLE PIT Trench and wiring in front of same was carried on with. Trench still in dirty condition. Casualties 2 O.R.S. Wounded. 3 O.R.S. Sick. 8 P.M.	
	Aug 29		Slight shelling on the morning onto our front. Heavy enemy shelling on to the Bulloirs in morning. In the evening the Battalion was relieved by the 26th Batt. 5t Welsh F and	

Army Form C. 2118.

WAR DIARY
or
INTELLIGENCE SUMMARY.
(Erase heading not required.)

Place	Date	Hour	Summary of Events and Information	Remarks and references to Appendices
SUNKEN ROAD L.22.c L.28.a	Aug 29th 1917		In relief the Battalion proceeded to shelters and dug-outs vacated by 26/N.S. in the Sunken Road L.22.c - L.28.a. Reconnaissance patrols carried out relief. Casualties:— Killed 1. OR. Wounded 3. ORs.	REF. SHEET. 62.C EDIT. J.
	Aug 30th		In the evening a large working party of 6 Officers & 150. ORs were sent out on a special digging task. The work consisted of dugouts & New Post and communication trenches. Worked very well. Showery day. Casualties NIL.	
	Aug 31st 1917		Showery day. Spent cleaning up of equipment, clothes and shelters etc. In the evening a large party were sent out for digging communication trenches etc. Casualties NIL.	

Strength of Battalion on 31st Aug. 1917.

OFFICERS: 38
O.R's: 650

[signature] Lieut Colonel
Cmdg. 23rd Battn. Northumberland Fusiliers
(4th Tyneside Scottish).

SECRET.   Copy No.. 9

GENERAL INSTRUCTIONS No.. 1
for
OPERATIONS AGAINST COLOGNE RIDGE.

Ref. Map
GILLEMONT FARM
1:10,000

1..   The 34th Division is to capture the COLOGNE RIDGE from about
        the junction of RAILWAY and JUNCTION Trenches to MALAKOFF FARM
        joining the flanks of the captured position to the present Outpost
        Line,

        (a) On the right by a trench to be dug from junction of
            RAILWAY and JUNCTION trenches to about G.7.d.15.70.

        (b) On the left by making good RIFLE PIT Trench from
            RIFLE MANS POST to Sunken Road at A.30.c.35.80 and
            connecting this point by a trench to MALAKOFF trench
            at A.30.c.70.75.

        These operations will be known as Phase 'A'.

2..   At some time after the conclusion of Phase 'A' it is intended
        to prolong our line from the junction of RAILWAY and JUNCTION
        trenches to the South so as to deny to the enemy observation of
        the Valley North of VILLERET.

        The right flank of the captured position would then probably
        be protected by a series of posts to be made on the general line
        G.13.b.9.8 to No. 2 VILLERET Post.

3..   The objects of the operations are to deprive the enemy of
        his advantage in position, and gain a line to the East which will
        enable us to obtain observation into BUCKSHOT RAVINE and the low-
        ground North of RUBY WOOD.

4..   Phase 'A' is being out under the orders of G.O.C. 101st Inf.
        Bde. who has the following troops under his Command for these
        operations :-
                    4 battalions 101 Inf. Bds.
                        20th N.F.
                        23rd N.F.
                        207th Field. Co. R.E.
                        101st L.T.M.B.
                 2 mortars 102 L.T.M.B.
                        8 guns 101 M.G. Co.
                        3 Coys. 22nd N.F. : as carrying parties.
                        1 Coy. 21st N.F. :

        All orders for the action of troops 102nd Inf. Bde. under
        the Command of G.O.C. 101st Inf. Bde. for the operations are
        being issued direct to units concerned by G.O.C. 101st Inf. Bde.

                                                5.. The operations

5.. The operations of Phase 'A' will consist of -

(1) a main attack under a creeping artillery barrage.
(2) a flank attack.

(a) The main attack is to be carried out on a four battalion frontage -

15th Bn. Royal Scots on the Right to be known as 'A' Bn.
16th Bn. Royal Scots .. Right Centre ... ... 'B' Bn.
10th Lincolnshire Rgt...... Left Centre ... ... 'C' Bn.
11th Suffolk Regiment .. .. Left .. .. 'D' Bn.

20th Bn. N.F. is to be known as 'E' Battn. and under present arrangements is to form a reserve to 101st Inf. Bde.

(b) The objectives of the main attack are :-

First Objective - (Black Line)
From RAILWAY Trench at G.7.d.85.95 - POND Trench to L.6.a.75.30 including Triangle East of POND COPSE - SUGAR trench - MALAKOFF Trench as far as its junction with MALAKOFF Support Trench.

Final Objective - (RED Line) -
BAIT Trench from its junction with POND Trench (G.1.d.5.0.) Northwards - thence along Eastern edge of SUGAR FACTORY to TRIANGLE TRENCH at A.25.d.1.2. - thence along MALAKOFF SUPPORT Trench to its junction with MALAKOFF Trench.

(c) The line to be consolidated is RAILWAY TRENCH - POND TRENCH to its junction with BAIT TRENCH thence along the RED LINE.
Posts are also to be established on the general line G.7.d.95.50 - G.8.a.05.40 - G.1.d.7.2 (and East of BAIT TRENCH if necessary) to get the required observation.

(d) The flank attack is to consist of making good RIFLE PIT trench as in Para. 1 (b) above.

6.. Strong points out of direct observation of the enemy and sited to suit the contour of the ground are to be made near the following localities -
G.7.b.4.5. - G.1.d.2.3. - G.1.b.0.1. - L.6.a.8.8.

7.. ENFILADE TRENCH, HIP LANE and PIN LANE are to be made into Communication trenches.

8.. The assault is to be carried out at Zero hour on 'J' day. 'J' day will be 26th AUG. 1917. Zero hour will be notified later.

9.. The operations are to be preceeded by a 2 days artillery bombardment on 'H' and 'I' days.
A Chinese attack is to be carried out on the front G.7.b.70.55 to L.6.c.8.3. about one hour after dawn on the morning of 'I' day.

10.. 100 Machine guns are taking part in the operations.
The whole of the 102 M.G. Coy. will be under Divisional control. O.C. 102 M.G. Coy. will receive orders for the action of the 102 M.G. Coy. in the operations direct from Div. M.G. Officer.
All ranks will be warned that our machine guns will be firing over the heads of the assaulting troops and in case of hostile counter attack, but that in no case will the bullets be less than about 100 feet above the heads of the front line troops.

/ 11 (a) Visual

11. (a) Visual Signalling Stations are to be established as follows -

   103rd Inf. Bde.

   At Forward Command Post G.13.d.6.5. working to Battalion Headquarters at L.23.b.5.5.

   At Battalion Headquarters L.23.b.5.5. and L.23.d.4.5. working to Adv. Bde. H.Q. at L.28.b.2.2.

   At Adv. Bde. H.Q. L.23.c.5.8. working to Divisional Station at K.36.b.3.5.

   101st Inf. Bde.

   At Right Battalion Headquarters L.11.b.4.6. to Adv. Bde. H.Q. L.10.a.7.7.

   At Left Battalion Headquarters L.5.b.3.3. to Adv. Bde. H.Q. L.10.a.7.7.

   At Adv. Bde. H.Q. to Divisional Station L.9.c.6.4.

   (b) Amplifiers are to be installed as follows -

   one at L.11.b.4.6. for 101 Inf. Bde.
   one at L.23.b.5.5. for 103 Inf. Bde.

   (c) Wireless -
   Threabtrench sets are to be established as follows -

   one at 101 Inf. Bde. Adv. H.Q. .. L.10.a.7.7.
   one at 103 Inf. Bde. Adv. H.Q. .. L.28.b.2.2.
   one at COOKERS QUARRY.

   (d) Units will detail runners as laid down in para. 7 of Sec. XI S.S. 135. Training of Divisions for Offensive Action.

12. (a) Contact aeroplanes cooperating with the Division during the operations are marked with 2 Black bands under the Port Lower plane and the Black bands are prolonged to the rear by Black streamers.

   (b) The infantry is to be prepared to light red flares when called for by the aeroplanes by a succession of A's on the Klaxon horn or by firing of White Very lights.
   Flares will be lit by front line troops in the final objective by order of Company and Platoon Commanders and by posts and standing patrols in advance of the final objective.

   (c) Battalion Headquarters will use their ground signal panels and lamps for communication with aeroplanes. Attention is directed to Appendix 'B' of S.S. 135 "Instructions for training of Division for Offensive Action" in this connection.

   (d) Every man taking part in the operations will carry two flares.

13 .. Instructions as to

13.. Instructions as to the numbers of officers and other ranks of units 102nd Inf. Bde. who will not take part in the operations will be issued separately.

14.. Battle Headquarters during the operations will be as follows:

    102nd Inf. Bde. .. H.Q. HERVILLY.
    21st N.F. .... .. H.Q. HERVILLY.
    22nd N.F. .... .. H.Q. HERVILLY.

    101st Inf. Bde. .. H.Q. L.10.a.4.5.
    15th Royal Scots . L.11.b.6.5. (EGG)
    16th Royal Scots . L.11.b.3.7.
    10th Lincolns. L.5.b.3.2.
    11th Suffolks. L.5.b.3.2.
    20th N.F. .... L.11.b.3.7.
    23rd N.F. .... F.27.c.6.7.

    103rd Inf. Bde. ... H.Q. L.28.a.5.5.
    24/27th N.F. ... L.23.b.50.35.
    9th Bn. N.F. ... L.23.b.50.35.
    26th Bn. N.F. ... L.23.d.45.85.

15.. The Headquarters 102nd Inf. Bde. and 21st Bn. N.F. (less 1 Co.) will be in Divisional Reserve together with other troops.

16.. ACKNOWLEDGE.

                                              Major
                                  BRIGADE MAJOR
22 : 8 : 1917.   102nd (TYNESIDE SCOTTISH) BDE.

Distribution -

    Copies Nos. 1 & 2 retained.
       No. 3 21st N.F.
          4 Staff Captain.
          5 102 Signals.
          6 102 Bde. Transport Officer.

          7 20th N.F. .... :
          8 22nd " .... :
          9 23rd " .... :
        10 102 M.G. Coy ... : for information.
        11 102 L.T.M.B. ... :
        12 H.Q., 34th Div. :
        13 H.Q., 101st Bde. :
        14 H.Q., 103rd Bde. :

Operation Order No. ... (Draft)   Copy No.
                                                                   Aug. 22nd

1st Bat. 11th Suffolk Regt.
Reference Trench Map Sheet 57C S.E.
                (1:10,000 sheet)

(I)   The 101st Brigade will capture the high ground
occupied by the enemy from F.30.c.89.95 to G.7.d.63.97.

(II)   The Left Battalion (11th Bn.) of the 101st Brigade – the
11th Suffolks – frontage of objective will be:-
                    F.30.c.59 to F.29.d.85.20
its flank bounded by Sunken Road exclusive.
Objectives: RIFLE PIT trench, South of Sunken Road,
MALAKOFF trench, MALAKOFF FARM, MALAKOFF Support
trench, and will form up MALAKOFF Support to RIFLE
PIT trench, with a fire trench making the junction with
RIFLE PIT trench North of the Sunken Road.

(III)   The 23rd Northumberland Fusiliers (L.T.M.) will
co-operate on the left flank of these operations as follows:-
At Zero – 30 minutes "A" Company, 23rd N.F. will assemble
in the hollow road with 2 platoons North & 2 platoons
South of RIFLEMAN Post & at Zero hour will advance
along RIFLE PIT trench & join hands with the moppers
up of the 11th Suffolk Regt. South of the Sunken Road.
        This trench will then be prepared as a fire &
communication trench facing N.E.
        They will be divided by Platoons into groups of
6, carrying 2 picks & 4 shovels per group. Thirty six yards
apart, each group working from Right to Left.
        "A" Company will detail 4 Lewis Guns and teams
as covering parties whilst the work is in progress.

(IV)   "B" Company will furnish a wiring party of
2 Officers & 30 men in relays, first relief to leave
HUSSAR Post at Zero + 2 hours if the situation permits & will
wire from the Sunken Road, F.36.c.40.50 towards
RIFLEMAN Post.
        Picks & shovels & wire & pickets for these parties will
be arranged at a dump which will be specially
pointed out beside ARTEXERXES Post & will be collected
en route to work.

(V)   On the night 25/26th August VALLEY Post & HUSSAR Post will
be occupied by details from the 11th Suffolk Regt. & on
arrival of these parties the "B" Company will vacate
VALLEY Post entirely & will vacate HUSSAR Post, with the
exception of 1 Lewis Gun & team of 6 men who will remain
at the N.E. portion of this post until further orders.
        The Platoons of "B" Company thus relieved will be formed
into immediate local Supports & remain covered in
ARTEXERXES Post & HUSSAR Road until new post in
RIFLE PIT trench are ready for occupation.

VI. Platoons of "A" & "C" Coys. where not engaged in digging, or wiring will be prepared and organized for immediate Support or Counter-attack.

Each platoon will move preceded by its hand bombing section with rifle grenadiers, riflemen, & Lewis Gun section in the above order.

Hand & rifle.

The bombing sections will carry 50 rds. S.A.A. & 6 bombs per man, the balance of their pouch ammunition will be stored and re-issued on return from the trenches under Coy. arrangements, grenades for this purpose will be drawn by Companies in present lines at HERVILLY 23rd inst at 12 noon.

VII. O.C. 'A' Coy. will arrange rum & tea for their working party to be issued at the CLOSE SUPPORT Cookhouse in HUSSAR ROAD, F.29.A.80.30. & at ZERO – 1 hour, & tea for breakfast to be carried to the platoons whilst at work about 8 a.m. if the situation permits.

VIII. The following personnel will be detached from Coys., & will be accomodated at Bn. H.Q, F.27.c.7.7.

1 Sergeant.	
2 Corpl. or L/Cpl.	
2 Rifle Bombers.	From each
2 Scouts & Snipers.	Coy.
4 Lewis Gunners	

also Coy. Sergeant Major   "A" Co. & "C" Co.
      4 Signallers   – "A" Co.
      3   "   – "C" Co.
      4 Runners   – "A" Co.
      4   "   – "C" Co.
      1 Gas Instructor   – "A" Co.
      2 Lewis Gun Instructors – "C" Co.

These details will not be included in parties of Bn. H.Q. which may be required for forward duty.

IX The Battalion will move into the LEFT SECTOR. from the INTERMEDIATE LINE on the night 25/26th August 1917. Time will be notified later.

Coys. will relieve the 22nd N.F. (3rd T.S.) as follows:-

"A" Co. ---- In reserve at BANBURY BARRACKS.
"B" Co., ┐ 1 Platoon & Coy. H.Q. ARTAXERXES POST.
        │ 1   "   HUSSAR POST.
        │ 1   "   RIFLE PIT POST.
        ┘ 1   "   VALLEY POST.
"C" Co. ---- In Support. Road near HARDY BANKS.
"D" Co. ---- 1 Platoon LITTLE BENJAMIN POST.
             2   " & B.G. BENJAMIN POST.
             1   " & Co. H.Q. in HUSSAR ROAD.

Operation Order No. 64 (Part II)
(Continued)

X First Aid Post & an advanced Batt. H.Q's for urgent reports will be in HUSSAR Road, adjoining "D" Company H.Q's
The Batt. H.Q's for normal trench routine will remain as before.

XI The following Dumps will be established in the Left Sector prior to Zero hour on X day. (Y day).

(a) "K.N" Dump at ARTAXERXES Post which will be separate from the forward Company Dump & will contain:—
120 Shovels. 60 picks. 200 Iron Rations 55 Petrol tins, wire & standards
This will be stocked under Brigade Transport Arrangement.

(b) HUSSAR ROAD ration dump containing grenades, S.A.A., Flares, Sandbags, wire cutters etc. a detailed list of which will be handed to O/C "D" Company who will check same & post a sentry on this Dump.
The Regimental Transport Officer will arrange to stock this Dump.

A. R. Liddell
Lieut & Asst. Adjt.
for Capt & Adjt.
23rd N.F. (4th T.S.)

OPERATION ORDER No. 55   Co...
                    25th Bde. 23rd ...

RELIEF ...Bde...less 23rd N.F. (4th F.S.)
will be relieved in the Reily. H.Q. 8 Corps.
...of Brigade by the night 24/25th
Aug... On relief 103rd Infantry Brigade
will be in Divisional Reserve.
         23rd N.F. (4th F.S.) will relieve 12th N.F.
(3rd N.F.) in the Left Sub-sector & will come
under orders of N.O.C. 103rd Inf. Brigade
...through ... 25th August 1918.

DISPOSITIONS

A Co. will remain in BANBURY BARRACKS
at F.97.a.7.

B Co. will relieve B Co. 22nd N.F. in the
Right sector of front line. A guide
from B Coy 22nd N.F. will await B
Co. 23rd N.F. at BATHS. F.27.c. B Co.
will move off at dusk.

C. Co. will relieve B Co. 22nd N.F. in BANKS
F.27.c.

C Co. 23rd N.F. will send one platoon to
relieve B Co. 23rd N.F. in HARICOURT
QUARRY L.10.a. by 8pm. This
platoon to form a nucleus garrison
until relieved by a Coy 103rd Bde.

C Co. 23rd N.F. will leave one platoon in
FERVAQUE TRENCH as nucleus garrison
until relieved by one Company
Royal Scots. & will send 4 guides
(1 per platoon) to be at Road Bend
Central at 9pm. to guide in
incoming Company.
The remaining 2 platoons of C. Co. 23rd N.F.
will proceed ... ... C.O.

2. DISPOSITIONS. 22nd N.F. in BANKS F.27.c.
   (Cont) Immediately the 2 platoons of "D" Co.
          23rd N.F. acting as nucleus garrisons
          are relieved they will rejoin their
          Coy. in the BANKS, F.27.c.

   "D" Co.   will relieve "A" Co. 22nd N.F. in
             the left sector of the Front Line, & will
             move off at a time to be given verbally
             by the C.O. this morning.

3. ADVANCE PARTIES of 1 officer & 1 N.C.O. per Coy
   will proceed to take over from Corp.
   22nd N.F. which they are relieving.

4. TRANSPORT ARRANGEMENTS. One limber will
   move Mess Boxes, Trench kits etc. of
   "B" & "C" Coys. from their present positions.
   One man to be left in charge of each
   of these mess boxes etc. until collected by
   transport. Coy. Lewis Guns will be carried
   by the men.
         D Co will arrange for moving
   their own mess box, trench kits, etc.
         T.O. will arrange to collect H.Q.
   Mess Boxes etc. at 8 p.m. for transport
   to F.27.c.7.7.

5. RATIONS for 25th inst. will be taken to new positions.

6. COMPLETION OF RELIEF will be notified to Bn HQ.
   by writing the words "Please expedite reply."
   (not in B.A.B).

Issued at 12.30 p.m.

To Note
1. A. Co   6. T.O
2. B. Co   7. R.S.M
3. C. Co   8. 22nd N.F.
4. D. Co   9. File
5. Q.M.

A. Liddell
2/Lt asst. adjt.
for Capt adjt
23rd N.F.

SECRET

T.S. 66/199

Headquarters,
    20th N.F.
    21st "
    22nd "
    23rd "
    102 M.G. Coy.
    102 L.T.M.B.

1..   Reference General Instructions No. 1 for Operations against COLOGNE RIDGE - Para. 9 - the Chinese attack will commence at 5.20 a.m. tomorrow, morning, 25th August.

24:8:1917.
102 B.H.Q.

P.T.O

Major
BRIGADE MAJOR
102nd (TYNESIDE SCOTTISH) BDE

II.

O.C. "B" & "D" Companies.

Ref: minute I. The front line should be
held as lightly as possible & supporting
platoons under cover.

Observations of hostile retaliation should
be made for future guidance.

Please note & return. Correspondence.

24/7/17.

J.H. Stevenson Capt & Adjt
23rd NF

T.S. 66/108

SECRET

Headquarters
    21st N.F.
    22nd "
    23rd "
    102 M.G. Coy.
    102 L.T.M.B.

1...   Reference 102nd Brigade General Instructions
        No. 1 for Operations again COLOGNE RIDGE - Para. 9 -
        the preliminary bombardment is to commence today 24th
        inst.

2...   O.C's battalions in the line will each detail
        at least one officer to observe the effect of our
        artillery fire on the enemys trenches and wire and
        will at once report to Brigade Headquarters any
        localities and wire on which the artillery and trench
        mortar bombardment appears inadequate.

102 B.H.Q.
24:9:1917.

                                            Major
                                        BRIGADE MAJOR
                                102nd (TYNESIDE SCOTTISH) BDE.

SECRET

AMENDMENT No. 1
to
GENERAL INSTRUCTIONS No. 1
For OPERATIONS AGAINST COLOGNE RIDGE.

1.. Para. 5 (c) - line 5 -

    For G.7.d.95.50   Read   G.7.d.65.95.

2.. Para. 10 -

    delete lines 2, 3 and 4 -

    and substitute :-

        2 Sections 102 M.G. Co. have been placed under the orders of G.O.C. 101st Inf. Bde. for the defence of B.2 and B.3 Subsectors.

        102 M.G. Co. less 2 Sections mentioned above will be under Divisional control.

        O.C. 102 M.G. Co. will receive orders for the action of those guns under Divisional control direct from Division Machine Gun Officer.

3.. Para. 11 (a) under 103rd Inf. Bde. -

    Erase 'At Forward Command Post' to L.23.b.5.5.

    and substitute - " At Battalion Headquarters L.11.d.5.7. working to Brigade Visual Station at L.18.d.3.8."

4.. Para. 11 (b) - line 3 -

    For L.23.b.5.5.   read   L.11.d.5.7.

5.. Para. 14 -

    For   24th/27th N.F. L.23.b.50.35

    Read   24th/27th N.F. BERNES.

    and for   9th Bn. N.F. L.23.b.50.35

    Read   9th Bn. N.F. BOUVINCOURT.

24:8:17.
102 B.H.Q.

                              Major
                          BRIGADE MAJOR
                102nd (TYNESIDE SCOTTISH) BDE.

Addressed all recipients of General Instructions No. 1

SECRET

AMENDMENT No. 2

to

GENERAL INSTRUCTIONS No. 1

For OPERATIONS AGAINST COLOGNE RIDGE.

1.. Delete the whole of para. 8 and substitute :-

'G' day will be AUG. 24th 1917.'

'H' day will be AUG. 25th 1917.'

'I' day will be AUG. 26th 1917.'

The assault is to be carried out at Zero hour on 'I' day. Zero hour will be notified later.

2.. Para. 9 - line 2 -
For "H and I days" read "G and H days".

3.. Para. 9 - line 4 -
For "I day" read "H day".

4.. ACKNOWLEDGE.

10? B.H.Q.
24:8:1917.

Major
BRIGADE MAJOR.
102nd (TYNESIDE SCOTTISH) BDE.

Addressed - all recipients of
General Instructions No. 1.

SECRET.   Operation Order No66   Copy No 1.

by
Lt. Col. E. P. Porch, D.S.O., Cmdg. 23rd Northumberland Fusiliers

Ref. Map.
Sheet NAUROY   August 29/17.
 1/20000

1. The 23rd N.F. will be relieved in the Left Subsector
    of the trenches by the 26th N.F.
    Coys. of 26th N.F. will take over from Coys. 23rd N.F.
      as follows:-
      "A" Co. 26th N.F. from "A" Co., 23rd N.F.
      "B" Co.   "   "   "   "B" Co.,   "   "
      "C" Co.   "   "   "   "C" Co.,   "   "
      "D" Co.   "   "   "   "D" Co.,   "   "
    On completion of relief 23rd N.F. will move into
    positions in SUNKEN ROAD L.22.c.

2. ADVANCE PARTIES. of 26th N.F. are proceeding to Coys.
    this afternoon & will take over all trench stores
    etc.   Receipted lists of Stores handed over
    & taken over in new positions will be sent to
    Orderly Room by noon tomorrow 30th inst.

3. GUIDES. Each Coy. 23rd N.F will send 3
    guides to Battn. H.Q. at 7.30 p.m. tonight.
    These guides will shew incoming platoons to
    their positions.   O.C. "C" Co. will ensure
    that one of his guides takes a platoon direct
    to Left Coy. Hdqrs. in HUSSAR ROAD.   The
    Advance party of 1 officer & 1 N.C.O. sent from
    each Company to take over positions in L.22.c.
    will report at CROSS ROADS, near QUARRY,
    L.10.a.5.5 at 11.0 p.m.
        These parties will act as guides & will
    take companies to their new positions.

                                ((cont))

2

RATIONS. Q.M. will send rations for Companies & Bn. H.Q. for 30th inst. to SUNKEN ROAD L.22.c. Both watercarts will be sent up with rations.

All Lewis Guns, Mess Boxes, trench kits etc. will be dumped at respective ration dumps & Q.M. will arrange to collect same and carry them to new positions.

5. COMPLETION OF RELIEF will be notified to Bn. H.Q. by wiring "NO RUM RECEIVED."

6 ACKNOWLEDGE.

Issued at 5 pm to.

1. 'A' Co.
2. 'B' Co.
3. 'C' Co.
4. 'D' Co.
5. Q.M.
6. 26th N.F.
7. R.S.M.
8. File.
9. War Diary

J. Shelon
Capt & Adjt.
23rd N.F.

REF. GN/M

WAR DIARY
or
INTELLIGENCE SUMMARY.
(Erase heading not required.)

Army Form C. 2118.

Place	Date	Hour	Summary of Events and Information	Remarks and references to Appendices
Turkey Road L.22.c. L.28.A.	Sep 1st		Showery day. Parties sent to Baths at Montigny during day, and working parties of 6 Officers and 150 ORs out at night digging new communication trench. Report received from 205 Z Coy R.E. expressing high satisfaction at excellent work done followed by similar verbal report by Brigade Commander. 2 Other Ranks Sick.	See Copy No 1. O.O. 6 Pty attached
	Sep 2nd		Five officers reports back from Courses. More parties sent to Baths during day. Relieved at night by two Companies 15th R. Scots and two Companies K.O.S.B. Easy and early relief. Proceeded by Brigade to BOUVINCOURT, our billets vacated by Corps Artillery. 2 Other Ranks Sick.	
BOUVINCOURT	Sep 3		The whole Battalion passed through the baths at BERNES, remainder of day being spent in inter-platoon football matches. A draft of six officers and 88 ORs joined unit, 47 coming from 1st N.F. and 40 from 12/13 N.F. Posted to A, B and D Companies. Notification received from Brigade of Military Cross to 2nd Lt R.R. Moriarty and D.C.M. to Corporal Aiddon D. Coy. Weather excellent, fine and warm. Sick- Nil. Billets good.	
	Sep. 4		Training carried on during morning. Inter platoon football matches continued in afternoon. Issue of clothing and general inspection of clothing, kit & equipment to complete. Sick- Nil	
	Sep 5		Training carried on in morning consisting of Bombing, and musketry, Lewis gunning etc. On the Bombing pit and rifle range near HANCOURT in the afternoon the Battalion went over the practice trenches near BEAUMETZ. C.O. accompanied Col. Allison and party at a Battalion parade strength of Battalion including new draft 44 O. 750 ORs. Sick- Nil	

WAR DIARY or INTELLIGENCE SUMMARY

Army Form C. 2118.

Place	Date	Hour	Summary of Events and Information	Remarks and references to Appendices
BOUZINCOURT	Sep 6		The Battalion practised the attack over the practice trenches, and in the afternoon the football competition was played. Weather fine but showery. Sick one OR.	
	7		Rehearsal of the attack was carried out on the practice trenches, consisting of a reconnaissance of the objective at which the Bayonet & Wire Corrangers were present. In the morning all preparations for the unit were completed and arrangements made. The Co. discovered the following were completed to the TD 98 3R9 97 B.55.30 trenches. Battalion Bomb 4070 Pte Place H. 17908 Pte Downey J. 14657 Pte Thorne A. 4254 Pte Finlen. 9/13 were awarded with the Military Medal at 4254 Pte. These men whilst digging out a man who had been completely buried by a shell continued their work until the operation was completed. See G.O. No. 4. G.O. No. 6 R.
			In the afternoon fire firing of the Platoon in Rifle Pit Trench. Platoon B Coy at night the Battalion proceeded to the trenches by No. 5 leaving by two at Templeux at 7.30 pm A, B, Coy and HQ following at 11 pm. C Coy took over No. 5 and No. 6 Posts, east of Villeret, with A, B and D companies in support in COTE TRENCH, Headquarters in dugouts in western edge of VILLERET. Relief was completed by 2 am. Sick 2 officers 1 OR.	See O.D. No. 61 attached
Trenches G.12.B.	8		During morning and afternoon preparations were made for the attack. Officers of A, B and D Coys proceeding to the front line to reconnoitre the ground. Villeret was shelled heavily all day with 4.2 shells but little dwelling on the front line posts. At 10.15 pm the Battalion took up its position for the attack in No Man's Land, the two assaulting Companies, C Coy on the right, D Coy on the left, A Coy in rear with materials for turning the captured trench, and B Coy in CLUB TRENCH acted as Carrying Storer to the attacking line immediately following. The objective being gained the assaulting Companies were formed into four objective each at 15 yrs distance. The first wave was detailed after the objective had been taken, to form a bayonet line 120 yds in front of the captured trench, the second wave to mop up the trench and dugouts, and	

WAR DIARY
or
INTELLIGENCE SUMMARY

Army Form C. 2118.

Place	Date	Hour	Summary of Events and Information	Remarks and references to Appendices
Trenches S.13.B.	9		the third and fourth waves to extricate rapidly without any casualties and were supported by 1/15 on a strong point of 1 Off and 15 OR. from B Coy. forming a protective screen. Casualties NIL. Zero hour was at 12.15 a.m. and 1st Battalion favoured the attack at that time under a barrage of 18 pdr. and 4.5 how artillery, and an artillery and over-head Machine Gun barrage. The enemy garrison were seen to retire in disorder and the trench was occupied which opposition being observed on the right with 21st NF (2nd JS) and on the left with 20th NF (1st JS). Two enemy machine guns were captured, and the Grenadiers and wiring of the captured trench at once commenced. The objective gained was RAILWAY and FIRM trench from 97.D.98.30 to 6.9.7.B.65.00. Heavy shelling was directed against YILMRET but there was little hostile activity against the captured position with the exception 7.14.9. the fire from the left flank. The wiring parties occupied a compass system of wire in front before day down. During its attack 9 of the captured position was very light but as the day proceeded hostile shelling of our casualties were explored and we had many casualties inflicted by this. Eleven prisoners were captured and many enemy were found. On the night 9/10 the enemy appeared to be massing for a counter attack. The SOS signal was put up and the enemy were caught and badly hit. During the fire barrage apparently suffering heavy casualties. Later a small an enemy sniper was seen near the CO (A Coy) were dispersed with heavy fire. During the night the C.O. (A Coy C.O. Capt DSO) was wounded by an enemy sniper and Major F. Erskine (20 NF) assumed command. Approx 50 OR killed and wounded. One J Cheese officer killed & promoted. Later in the day the bombardment of the newly captured position and trenches.	See G.S.N/9/1 sketches for details of positions.
	10/10		MILMRET continues intermittently. The men were becoming very shaky and tired. During the night fresh wiring was done, strengthening the	

WAR DIARY or INTELLIGENCE SUMMARY

Army Form C. 2118.

Place	Date	Hour	Summary of Events and Information	Remarks and references to Appendices
Trenches G.13.13	10th inst	10.00	Option that up the present night "C" Coy. less the left company frontage if the 2/5 N.F. (2nd 35) who had not attained all objectives, and was preparing to make a further attack in its early hours of following morning the night proved quiet. 2 officers were wounded and approx 20 O.Rs. were killed and wounded.	
		11th	During the day the hostile bombardment continued although it was less intense during the afternoon. At 4 A.M. 2/6 N.F. (Bn 35) made a further attack on our right, attaining all objectives. During the further advance M.G. Det sent forward to a very heavy bombardment but their casualties were slight. Became quiet. At night the battalion was relieved by 2 companies 16th Royal Scots and No Company 11th Suffolks at 10.4 Brigade ordering to trenches in advance. Relief was complete by 2 A.M. but the last company did not reach billets till 6 A.M. Casualties were approx 2 O.Rs. killed 6 wounded.	
B.FRNES.	12th		The total casualties from these operations were now found to be two officers killed eleven wounded, 13 O.Rs. killed 65 O.Rs. wounded 1 missing, one suffering from shell shock. Throughout the whole of the day the battalion remained recuperating being unengaged in anything. Three officers reported, two from hospital and one from a course. Sick. Nil.	
	13th		During the day kit inspection were held, and facilities given for cleaning up. In the afternoon there were football matches, and an inter trenching party was attended the One Acre? party. Sick. two O.Rs.	
	14th		Light training was carried out. Inter company arrangements. In the afternoon there was football company arrangements. The remainder of the byonds attended the Div. Coy's Party. Sick. One O.R.	

WAR DIARY or INTELLIGENCE SUMMARY.

Army Form C. 2118.

Place	Date	Hour	Summary of Events and Information	Remarks and references to Appendices
BERNES.	15		Light training was carried out in the afternoon. In the morning the Brigade was inspected by the Corps Commander who heavily (?)being presented to him for the Military Medal, namely the L/. Stone and Dooney. Weather fine but showery. Sick 1 O.R.	
	16		Major Bridges was ordered to the Battalion. Major Grace 20/n3 taking command. Training was carried out in the morning and sports in the afternoon and evening. Weather dull and showery. Sick NIL.	
	17		Parade for inspection prior to going into the trenches ever held. In the morning the O.C. Commander inspected the Benefit(?) lines. At night the Battalion took over the left sector of our arrangement following 26/47th F. Relief was quiet and complete by 11.30 p.m. Weather fine. Sick 3 O.Rs.	See O.O. No. 70. attached
Trenches F.24.D F.29.B F.30.C.	18		Day passed very quietly. A Rafael(?) of 1 Off. and 12 O.Rs reconnoitred the trench N. of Quenner Copse. Weather warm and bright. Casualties NIL. Sick 1 O.R.	
	19		Day again passed quietly. At night a patrol of 1 Officer and 10 other ranks reconnoitred the valley in front of BENJAMIN POST. Weather warm and bright. Casualties NIL. Sick 3 O.Rs.	
	20		Quiet day. Some enemy aerial activity, otherwise day passed without movement. A patrol of 1 Off. 10 O.Rs investigated Quenner Copse and adjacent trenches without seeing any enemy. Weather continues fine. Casualty NIL. Sick NIL.	
	21		Again the day passed quietly. Some enemy aerial activity, otherwise their activity. A patrol 1 Off. and 10 O.Rs again proceeded towards Quenner Copse without meeting any enemy. Casualties NIL. Sick 1 O.R.	

Army Form C. 2118.

WAR DIARY
or
INTELLIGENCE SUMMARY.
(Erase heading not required.)

Instructions regarding War Diaries and Intelligence Summaries are contained in F.S. Regs., Part II. and the Staff Manual respectively. Title pages will be prepared in manuscript.

Place	Date	Hour	Summary of Events and Information	Remarks and references to Appendices
Trenches F 24 D F 29 B F 30 C	22"		Slight enemy activity and much enemy aerial activity. Otherwise day passed quietly. A patrol of 1 Off & 10 OR's proceeded to Quenner Copse without meeting any enemy. Wrote for Lieut. 1 OR. Casualties NIL.	
	23"		About 5 A.M. the enemy sent over a great number of gas shells which fell in the vicinity of HARDY BANKS. No casualties ensued. A great deal of aerial activity throughout day. A draft of 76 ORs were received. In the evening we relieved the 20th N.F. (1st Tyneside Scottish) in the Centre Sector, left Brigade. The 20 N.F. at the same time occupied the positions vacated by us. Dispositions were disposed of as follows B his left front Company. C his Right front Coy. A his Support D his Reserve. Battalion HQrs were situated at L.5 b.3.2. The boundaries of the Battalion were as follows :- On the left Junction 20th N.F. (1st Tyneside Scottish) F 30.c. 85. 90. On the Right, Junction 21st N.F. (2nd Tyneside Scottish). G.1.b. 35.40. Quiet & windy night. JC Casualties. 1 OR Sick.	See OO 26.71 Attached
	24"		Quiet day. Patrols sent out in the evening but none of the enemy encountered. Enemy aircraft rather active. Four weather. Casualties. NIL JC	
	25"		Gunman carried on with work in trenches. Slight trench mortar activity on both sides. An draft Advance party of 93rd Infantry Brigade arrived. The Battalion is to be relieved on 26/27 inst. Patrols sent out in evening. No enemy encountered. Casualties. NIL JC	

WAR DIARY
or
INTELLIGENCE SUMMARY.
(Erase heading not required.)

Army Form C. 2118.

Instructions regarding War Diaries and Intelligence Summaries are contained in F. S. Regs., Part II. and the Staff Manual respectively. Title pages will be prepared in manuscript.

Place	Date	Hour	Summary of Events and Information	Remarks and references to Appendices
TRENCHES HERRICOURT	24th Sept. 1917		The Battalion was relieved by the 9th Batt. Royal Sussex Regiment very quiet and quick relief. & relief the Battalion marched to BERNES. Casualties 2/Lt D.Bell wounded. 1. OR. Ked. 5.OR.	See H.Q. 72 attached See O.S. No. 73 attached 45M/0/2.
DOINGT	25th		The Battalion entrained at noon and proceeded to DOINGT near PERONNE. a draft of 163 ORS recruit joined. 31 thereof returned to duty. Casualties NIL.	
	26.		The troops Commander Lt. Gen. Dudley Inspected matting relative to the understanding Officers & men of the Battalion — Lt. Tony Arnold. Middleton Jones. (attached M.O.) The Light Trench Mortar Battery) H.Q.E.&V. Dunn, 47494 Bds. & Ashurste. 23/822 Sergt. C.B. Commn. all Holding Middle. Casualties NIL	
BOISLEUX AU MONT	27.		The Battalion entrained at PERONNE and proceeded to BOISLEUX AU MONT arrived then returned and marched to BAILLEUL MONT. (W.2. O.R.D. Sheet 51 C.S.E. Polish 6.D) No good billets Casualties NIL Or.	See O.S. No. 74 attached
MOLLIEVILL.	28.		General cleaning up and organization. Good march. Casualties NIL. Strength of Battalion. (Fighting Strength) 29 Officers. 951 ORS OR.	

J.J. Groves Major
Cmdg. 2-3rd Norfolk Yeo.
(4th Cyclist Battn.)

SECRET. OPERATION ORDER No. 67   Copy 9

Lieut. Col. G. P. Porch, D.S.O., by Cmdg. 23rd Northd. Fus.

Ref. sheet.   Sept. 2/17.
NAUROY - 1/20000.
62 C. 1/40000.

I. RELIEF.
The 103rd Infantry Brigade will be relieved in Centre Sector, 34th Divisional Front by 101st Infantry Brigade on nights 2/3rd and 3/4th Sept. 1917.

The 23rd N.F. (4th T.S.) will be relieved by the 16th Bn. Royal Scots. Relief to be complete by 9 pm.

II. DESTINATION.
On relief the Battalion will proceed to BOUVINCOURT by busses.

III. TIME OF DEPARTURE.
Busses will be at JEANCOURT. Companies will leave present positions in following order:-
"A" Coy.
"D" Coy.
"C" Coy.
"B" Coy.
Bn. HQ

by parties not greater than platoons at 200x distances. The first platoon of "A" Co. to arrive at JEANCOURT by 9.45 pm.

IV. ADVANCE PARTY.
Each Coy. will send a N.C.O., who can ride a cycle, to report at Orderly Room at 1.30 pm. this afternoon. These N.C.O's will proceed with Lieut. Spink H.M. as Advance Party. In the evening they will guide Companies into Billets. Each N.C.O. should be given a statement shewing the number of officers & men in the Company who require billets.

V. STORES.
All Stores, French Shelters, Ablution Benches etc. will be handed over on relief. Receipted lists of Stores handed over to be forwarded to Orderly Room by noon 3rd inst.   (Con.)

3rd inst.

VI. OFFICERS VALISES ETC.
All Company & Battn. H.Q. Stores, Officers Valises, Mess Boxes etc. will be dumped outside respective H.Q. by 7.30 pm. The Q.M. will arrange to collect same & will carry them to Billets in BOUVINCOURT. All Officers Valises to be taken to BOUVINCOURT with rations for 3rd inst.

VII. COMPLETION OF RELIEF
will be notified to Bn. H.Q. by runner.

VIII. ACKNOWLEDGE

Issued at 11.45 am. to

1. 'A' Co.
2. 'B' Co.
3. 'C' Co.
4. 'D' Co.
5. M.G. Sec/n.
6. Q.M.
7. R.S.M.
8. Retained.
9. War Diary.
10.

A. Liddell
2nd Lieut. a/Asst.
for
Capt. & Adjt.
28th N.F.
(4th T.S.)

SECRET   ADDENDUM to O O 67
by
Lt Col. C.P. Porch DSO, Comdg. 23rd Royal Fusiliers
Sept 2/17

1. One Company of 15th Bn Royal Scots will take over from 'B' Coy 23rd N.F.

'A' Coy of the 16th Bn Royal Scots will take over from 'A' Co. & 2 platoons of 'D' Co 23rd N.F.

O. 'C' of 16th Royal Scots will take over from 'C' Co. & 2 platoons D. Co., 23rd N.F.

Guides at the rate of 1 per platoon & 1 for Battn. H.Q. will be at the entrance to 70th Bde. H.Q. (Nr 'A'Co's H.Q.) at 8.15 p.m. this evening to guide incoming platoons & H.Q. to their respective positions.

II. 'D' Co. 23rd N.F. will hand over this afternoon to O.C's 'A' & 'C' Coys 23rd N.F. any stores etc that will be in the sector to be occupied by 'A' & 'C' Coys 16th Royal Scots.

'A' & 'C' Coys. 23rd N.F. will render complete lists of Stores as per para V. T.O. No 67, including those taken over from 'D' Co of this Unit.

A Piddell
The & Hon. Adjt.
for
Capt. & Adjt.
23rd N.F.
(4th T.S)

SECRET.   Operation Order No 68   Copy No 7
Ref Maps   by
Special   Lt. Colonel C. P. Porch O.S.O. Commanding
G.T.S. Map   23rd Northumberland Fusiliers (4th Tyneside Scottish)
No 101 – 1/10,000
dated 4-9-1917.   6th Sept 1917.
NAUROY Sheet 1/20,000.

1. **Intention** The 102nd Infantry Brigade will capture and consolidate the enemy's positions in RAILWAY and FARM trenches between G.13.6.95.40 and G.7.6.73.50 in order to deny observation of the VILLARET VALLEY to the enemy.

2. The objectives and frontages of the 21st and 23rd N.F. (2nd & 4th Tyneside Scottish) taking part in these operations have been communicated to Company Commanders. Summary as follows:-
   23rd N.F. (4th T.S.) frontage:-
        G.7.d.98.30
     to G.7.b.65.00 } 400 yards.

   "C" Coy frontage:- G.7.d.98.30 to G.7.d.90.65
   "D"   do   ; G.7.d.90.65 to G.7.b.65.00

3. **Role** "C" & "D" Companies will deliver the assault in waves of platoons at 15 yards distance. The leading platoon of each Company will, after gaining the objective, furnish a covering party along its own Company front and 120 yards in advance. The second wave will clear dug-outs, mop up and man the trench and in the case of "D" Company establish a bombing block in the left flank.
   The third and fourth waves assist in capturing the objectives and then rapidly consolidate.
   The second, third and fourth waves will each carry tools in the proportion of 3 shovels to 1 pick.
   "A" Company will wire the Battalion front as soon as this work can be commenced.

Sheet 2.

"B" Company will carry ammunition; wire stores etc; from "E" dump near No 6 post, L.12.c.9.8 to "F" dump G.7.d.90.60.

Contents of "E" dump:-

S.A.A	12 boxes
Mills No 23 Grenades	40 "
Mills No 5 "	8 "
Very lights White 1"	1 "
" 1½"	1 "
Water (petrol tins)	20
Picks	20
Shovels or Spades	40
Barbed French Concertinas	8
Plain French Wire (Coils)	1
Long Screw Pickets	30
Barbed Wire (Coils)	20
Stokes	100
Ring Charges	200
Green Cartridges	100

Loads to be carried by each man:-

S.A.A.	1 box between 2 men
Mills No 23 Grenades	2 boxes
" No 5 "	2 "
Very lights White	1 "
Water (petrol tins)	2
Picks	4
Shovels or Spades	5
Barbed French Concertinas	1
Plain French Wire (Coils)	1
Long Screw Pickets	3
Barbed Wire (Coils)	1 between 2 men.

NOTE:-
(a) Picks to be tied up in bundles of four, shovels or Spades in bundles of five.
(b) Screw Pickets to be tied in bundles of three
(c) The end of the strand of each barbed wire coil to be tied up in a piece of sacking.

In second journey S.O.S. grenades and Red very lights will be taken in lieu of white very light

Equipment. All men will carry:-
2 - No 23 Rifle Grenades
2 Red Aeroplane flares
3 Sandbags.
S.A.A. - 170 rounds per man. with the exception of:-

Sheet 3.

    Wiring party   - 120 pounds
    Bombers   -   50   "
    Signallers   -   50   "
    Lewis Gunners -   50   "
    Runners   -   50   "

"C" and "D" Companies' second, third and fourth waves will carry a pick or shovel.

"A" Company,- Wiring material, Cutters, hedging gloves and equipment elsewhere detailed.

In addition to the above, the following stores will be carried:-

S.O.S. grenades - 25 per assaulting Company distributed amongst Officers & N.C.Os.

Very lights 1" & 1½" Red;- 25 per assaulting Company distributed amongst Officers & N.C.Os.

Very lights 1" & 1½" White. 50 per Assaulting Company. distributed amongst Officers & O/Rs carrying Very Pistols.

Very pistols - 2 p. Company and 1 p. Lewis Gun.

"P" Grenades - 12 per Assaulting Company, distributed to Platoons detailed to mop up captured German trench.

Advance Company Headquarters will be established on the Eastern boundary of VILLERET, the exact localities will be pointed out to Company Commanders on the 8th inst. Battalion Headquarters will be on the Western side of VILLERET point L.H.d.5.y. Communication between the objective when captured, and Company Headquarters and thence to Battalion Headquarters must be established by signallers as soon as the situation permits, and by runners when other communication fails. Company & Platoon Runners must be specially selected and detailed.

Forming Up. On the night of the 8/9th September the Battalion will be formed up ready to advance on a taped line, the inner ends of which will be linked up by 10.15pm. The moon rises at 10.50 pm. Zero hour will be notified later.

Sheet H.

The maintenance of absolute silence is of the greatest importance. Equipment and accoutrements must be arranged accordingly. Chewing gum will be issued as a cough preventative.

The O/C "B" Coy will detail a standing patrol of 1 Officer + 20 O.R. in two groups and two reliefs to cover the forming up. This patrol will lie down at a distance of from 50 yards on the left to 150 yards on the right in front of the taped line. This patrol will leave the new No 6 VILLERET POST first relief at 5 pm, second relief at 9.15pm. The second relief will rejoin their Company at Zero hour.

Companies will parade completely equipped and move from their localities as follows:

"D" Coy move off from COPE WOOD trench at 8.15 pm.
"A"   do   "   "   "   "   "   " 8.20 pm.
"B"   do   "   "   "   "   "   " 8.25 pm.
"C"   do   "   "   " VILLERET POST at 9.30 pm.

No 5 Platoon "B" Coy will be attached to "A" Coy for rations, discipline, accommodation and operations from 2 pm the 8th inst., until further orders.

Copies to:-
1 - Retained
2 - "A" Co.
3 - "B"
4 - "C"
5 - "D"
6 - C.O.
7 - War Diary
8 -

A. Liddell.
2nd Lieut + Act. Adjt.
23rd N.F. (4th T.5.).

SECRET.
Ref. Maps.
MIRAUMONT
Scale: 1/10,000

Operation Order No. 89   Copy No. _____

Lt. Colonel C. R. Pearce D.S.O. Comdg
23rd Northumberland Fusiliers (4th Tyneside Scottish)

7th Sept 1917

1. The 102nd Inf. Bde. will relieve the 101st Inf. Bde. in the Centre sector, 34th Div. front on the night 7/8th Sept 1917. On completion of the relief the dividing line between the Centre & Left sectors, 34th Div. front will be the junction of ONION LANE and POND trenches inclusive to Centre sector.
The 23rd N.F. (4th T.S.) with 1 Company ('C' Coy) will take over the front line from No. 5 VILLARET POST inclusive to new No. 6 post inclusive relieving a part of the 10th LINCOLNS, the remaining three Companies being accommodated in COTE TRENCH area relieving a part of the Royal Scots. Battalion Headquarters will be at L.11.d.5.7.

2. Routes. 'C' & 'D' Companies will leave BOUVINCOURT by bus at 7 p.m. to a position to be notified later where they will be met by their guides on arrival.
   'A' & 'B' Companies will leave by bus at 8.30 p.m. and will be similarly met by guides on arrival.

3. Advance Parties. One Officer & 1 N.C.O. per Company and Sergeants Straker & Craven for Headquarters will report at Battn H.Q., BOUVINCOURT at 2 p.m. to proceed to take over stores etc. from Companies which they are relieving and to allot accommodation for their Companies on arrival. Great coats for this party will be carried under Company arrangements.

4. Dress. The Battalion will go into the line in attack order with ground sheets rolled on the belt. 'A' 'B' & 'D' Companies & H.Q. will take greatcoats for the night 7/8th September. These will be collected and stored under Battalion arrangements prior to the operations on the night 8/9th September.

Sheet 2.   O.O. 59.

5. **Lewis Guns.** Lewis Guns under Company escort will go up to the line on the night 7th/8th inst. with rations. The Lewis Guns will be collected by transport at BOUVINCOURT at 4 p.m.

6. **Stores.** Trench mess boxes and Company stores and Headquarters mess & Orderly Room boxes which must be reduced to a minimum in view of the operations will be collected at 6 pm for transport to the respective Company & Battalion Headquarters.

7. **Details.** The details remaining behind & will be quartered for the night 7/8th Sept. in N° 31 billet under Capt. J.W.C. Leach and packs of "A", "B", "C" & "D" Companies and Headquarters, greatcoats of "C" Company, Officers valises and all kit for storage will be dumped there under Company arrangements before going into the line. These will be collected by the Transport Officer on the morning of the 8th inst. when these details will move into the transport lines unless otherwise ordered.

8. Completion of relief will be notified to Battalion Headquarters by "BAB" code.

9. Acknowledge.

                    A R Liddell
                    2nd Lieut & Act: Adjt.

Copies to:
1 - Retained
2 - "A" Coy
3 - "B" "
4 - "C" "
5 - "D" "
6 - QM & T.O
7 - C.O
8 - War Diary.

GSN/O/1.   23rd Northumberland Fusiliers.
           (4th Tyneside Scottish) 18/9/17

Report on operations against the enemy trenches
EAST of VILLERET on night 8/9th September 1917.

Objectives:- RAILWAY FARM TRENCHES from
   G.7.d.98.30 to G.7.b.65.00.
   This was subdivided into company objectives:-
   C. Coy   G.7.d.98.30 to G.7.d.90.65.
   D "   G.7.d.90.65   G.7.b.65.00.
   A "   was detailed to rapidly wire the front of the objective after capture.
   B. Coy   was detailed to carry stores from CLUB TRENCH to the objective.

Formations.   Attacking companies were formed into 4 waves of 1 platoon each at 15 yards distance.

Method of attack.   The first wave of each Company, after gaining the objective was to go on for 120 yards so as to form a wiring party for the consolidation and wiring of the captured position.
   The second wave was to mop up the trench and dug-outs and in the case of the left company to form a bombing work on the left flank.
   The third & fourth waves were to assist in capturing the objective and then rapidly consolidate and man the trench.

Detail of events.
1. C Coy (on right).   The Company commenced the advance at Zero hour (12.15am).   When about 60 yards from the position the enemy garrison were seen to flee in disorder.   They were followed by our first wave who fired at them from the hip with Lewis guns and rifles.   The trench was occupied without opposition and touch obtained with both flanks. 2 hostile machine guns partially buried by our shell fire were found.   The consolidation of the trench was put in hand at once.

2. D Coy (on left).   The advance was carried out according to plan and the position captured without opposition.   Ten of the enemy were made prisoners and a machine gun was also captured.
   On the left flank of the Company the enemy immediately commenced a bombing attack down the trench, but with the assistance

assistance of a bombing squad of the 20th N.F. who took the enemy in rear who was easily defeated and touch obtained with the 20th N.F. on the left.

On the night of the 9/10 the enemy appeared to be massing for a counter attack in consequence of which the S.O.S. signal was put up and our artillery and machine guns immediately replied. The enemy scattered in confusion and appeared to suffer many casualties.

Later in the night a small party of the enemy were observed near our wire and were driven off with Lewis Gun fire.

3. A bn. without great difficulty completed by 2 a.m on 7th day a belt of wire entanglement in front the battalion front. A second belt was commenced but work had to cease owing to lack of material. This however was continued on subsequent nights.

4. From 1 a.m. 9th Sept. the enemy commenced a very heavy bombardment in front of and including VILLERET. This lasted until 6 hr. This bombardment was continued on the 11th was from 3 a.m to 4 p.m.

Major
Comadg. 23rd Northd Fus.
(4th Tyneside Scottish)

12-9-17

SECRET

Ref Map Copy No...7...
NAUROY Edn. 2
1/10000

Operation Order No. 70
by
Major J.T. Gracie, Commanding,
23rd North:ed Fusiliers, (4th Tyneside Scottish)

16th Sept 1917.

1. **Relief.** The 102nd Bde will relieve the 103rd Bde tomorrow night 17/18th inst.
The 23rd N.F. (4th T.S.) will relieve 26th N.F. in the left subsector, 34th Divisional front.

2. **Dispositions.** "A" Coy will take over the right Company frontage of the Battalion with 1 Platoon in RIFLE PIT TRENCH with the extreme right boundary at Sunken Road. F.30.C.
1 Platoon at RIFLEMAN POST
1 Platoon & Coy H.Q. at ARTAXERXES POST
1 Platoon in support from "C" Coy in HUZZAR ROAD
"A" Coy will take over from "A" Coy, 26th N.F.

"D" Coy will take over the left Company frontage of the Battalion with two platoons in BIG BENJAMIN POST, 1 Platoon in LITTLE BENJAMIN POST, Coy H.Q. and 1 Platoon in support from "C" Coy in HUZZAR ROAD. "D" Coy relieves "C" Coy, 26th N.F.

"C" Coy will be in support with 1 Platoon in ORCHARD POST and Coy H.Q. in HARDY BANKS.
"C" Coy will relieve "D" Coy, 26th N.F.

"B" Coy will be in reserve with 1 Platoon in TOYNE POST and two platoons and Coy H.Q. in the SUNKEN ROAD.
"B" Coy will relieve "B" Coy, 26th N.F.

O/C "D" Coy will arrange for 1 Lewis Gun and team to take over the position between LITTLE BENJAMIN and CAT POST. He will also arrange with the Company Commander of the Company on his left for the Standing patrol between these two posts.

3. **Patrols.** Standing patrols sent out by the 26th N.F. on the night of the relief will be withdrawn on completion of the relief and will be at once replaced by Standing patrols sent out by the Companies concerned.

4. **Guides.** 1 Guide per platoon will be at the Headquarters 26th N.F. at F.27.C.7.7. at 7.45 pm.

5. **Route.** The route taken will be HERVILLY thence by the track running N.E. which joins the ROISEL – TEMPLEUX road at K.12.d.2.3. thence via TEMPLEUX to Battalion H.Q. in the QUARRY at F.27.C.7.7.
All moves will be made by platoons at 200x interval. No troops will pass over the crest at K.18.6.20.15 before 8.0 pm. The first platoon of "A" Coy will arrange to pass this point immediately after 8.0 pm.

Sheet 2.

6. **Dress.** Packs will be taken into the trenches.

7. **Advance Parties.** Advance parties as follows will arrive at Battalion H.Q., 26th N.F. F.27.c.7.7. not later than 4.30 pm. 1 Officer and 1 Gas N.C.O. per Company and 1 Senior N.C.O. per Platoon and 1 Lewis Gunner per Lewis Gun.
H.Q.:- 2nd Lieut. W. Scott, R.S.M., Sgt. Straker and 1 Gas N.C.O.

In each case the Officer detailed will be responsible for taking over all details of trench stores, aeroplane photographs and maps, all details of work in progress and all information regarding the activity of the enemy and the state of the wire.

Complete receipted lists of stores taken over will be forwarded to reach Orderly Room by 10 am on the morning of the 18th inst.

8. **Transport arrangements.** Rations for the front line Companies will be dumped at the forward dump at F.23.c.9.6 and rations for the support and reserve Companies and Battalion H.Q., will be dumped at their respective H.Q.

All Lewis Guns, trench kits, mess boxes, Orderly Room boxes will be dumped outside the Orderly Room by 6 pm, 17th inst., for conveyance to the trenches.

All Officers valises and stores to be returned to the Q.M. Stores will be dumped in the yard outside present Regimental Aid Post by 6 pm.

One water cart will supply the two forward Companies nightly and 1 water cart will supply the Companies in support & reserve and Battn H.Q. nightly.

9. **Completion** of relief will be notified to H.Q. by using "B.A.B." code.

10. ACKNOWLEDGE.

A. Liddell.
2nd Lieut. & Act. Adjt.

Copies to:-
1. "A" Company
2. "B" "
3. "C" "
4. "D" "
5. 26th N.F.
6. R.S.M.
7. War Diary
8. Retained.
9. O.O.
10. Sgt. Straker.
11. T.O. & Q.M.

Ammendment to 23rd N.F.
O.O. No. 70.

Para 5 route is ammended as follows:-

Companies will leave BERNES at the following times:-

"A" at 5.45 pm followed by
"D", "C" & "B" Coys in the order named, at intervals of 25 minutes.

Companies will march by Platoons at 200x interval to HERVILLY whence they will march by Sections at 200x interval to the point where Guides will meet them

The Platoons attached to "A" & "D" Companies from "C" Coy will join these Companies prior to starting.

A Liddell
2nd Lieut & Act. Adjt.

Copies to:-
As per O.O. 70.

SECRET.   23rd N.F., (4th T.S.),   Copy..........
Ref.Map.   Operation Order No. 71.
MAUROY Sheet,   ---------------------------
1/10000.   September 22nd 1917.

1. RELIEFS.   Reliefs will be carried out as under:-

        (a). Night 22nd/23rd Sept. 1917 - 21st N.F.
             will relieve 22nd N.F. in Right Subsector.
             On relief 22nd N.F. will take over the
             accomodation vacated by 21st N.F. and will
             be in Brigade Reserve.
        (b). Night 23rd/24th Sept. 1917 - 23rd N.F.
             will relieve 20th N.F. in Centre Sector.
             On relief 20th N.F. will move to Left
             Sector.   Front Line Companies 23rd N.F.
             will not move until relieved by Companies
             20th N.F.

             In no case will more than 1 front line coy.
             of each Battalion in the Line be in process
             of relief at the same time.

2. DISPOSIT-   Companies 23rd N.F. will take over from Coys.
   IONS.   20th N.F. as follows:-

        "A" Coy. 23rd N.F. from "B" Co. 20th N.F. in
             Support. 3 platoons in RIFLE PIT TRENCH from
             SUNKEN ROAD F.30.d.45.80 to F.30.c.4.1. One
             platoon & Coy. H.Q. in VALLEY POST.
        "B" Co. 23rd N.F. from "C" Co. 20th N.F. in left
             section of trenches. 3 Platoons in MALAKOFF
             SUPPORT TRENCH and one Platoon and Coy. H.Q.
             in MALAKOFF TRENCH.
        "C" Co. 23rd N.F. from "A" Co. 20th N.F. in Right
             Section of trenches.   One and a half platoons
             in MINNOW TRENCH.   Half platoon in BOWER
             LANE, 1 platoon and Coy. H.Q. in SUSAN trench
        "D" Coy. 23rd N.F. from "D" Co. 20th N.F. be
             situated in QUARRY L.5.b.3.3.

3. MOVES.   Companies 23rd N.F. will move from present
                   positions as follows:-

        "C" Co. Immediately it is dusk will move off and
             relieve "A" Co. 20th N.F., who, on relief, will
             move into positions vacated by "C" Co. 23rd N.F
             At 1.D.M. "B" Co. 23rd N.F. will move off and
             relieve "C" Co. 20th N.F. whose relief will
             move into positions vacated by "B" Co. 23rd N.F.
             Immediately it is dusk "D" Co. 20th N.F.
             will move off and relieve "A" Co. 23rd N.F.
             who on relief will move off and relieve "B" Co.
             20th N.F.
             "B" Co. 20th N.F. will relieve "D" Co. 23rd
             N.B.N.F. who on relief will move into positions
             vacated by "D" Co. 20th N.F. in QUARRY
             L.5.b.3.3.
             All moves will be made by platoons at 200ᵡ
             distances.

4. ROUTES.   "B" & "C" Coys. 23rd N.F. will proceed via
                   SUNKEN ROAD to Cross Roads F.29.d.2.1 thence
                   to HARGICOURT and Battn. H.Q.
                   "A" Co. 23rd N.F. 2 platoons side slip along
                   RIFLE PIT TRENCH to new positions.   1
                   Platoon and Coy. H.Q. direct to VALLEY POST.
                   "D" Co. 23rd N.F. via HUSSAR POST - VALLEY
                   POST - thence Quarry L.5.b.3.3.

(2)

5. **ADVANCE PARTIES & GUIDES.** Advance parties at the rate of 1 officer per Coy. and 1 N.C.O. per platoon, also 1 N.C.O. for Battn. H.Q. will be sent. These parties will not move off before 5 p.m. Coy. advance parties will all move via RIFLE PITTRENCH to respective positions. These parties will take over all stores, details of work etc., and in the evening will act as guides under Coy. arrangements.

In addition to our own guides 20th N.F. are supplying guides at the rate of 1 per platoon for "B" & "C" Coys. 23rd N.F. These guides will met "B" & "C" Coys. 23rd N.F. at Battn. H.Q. L.S.H.S.G., "C" Co. 8.3 p.m. and "B" Coy. at 8.30 p.m. "A" Co. 23rd N.F. will send guides at the rate of 1 per platoon to meet incoming platoons of "D" Coy. 20th N.F. at 8 p.m. on road outside VALLEY POST. "D" Co. 23rd N.F. will have a similar number of guides at same place at 9 p.m. to meet incoming platoons of "D" Coy. 20th N.F.

The following specialists will be sent ahead with advance parties:-
    1 Lewis Gunner per team.
    1 Signaller per Coy. Station.
    1 N.C.O. & 2 men for Bn. H.Q. Station
    1 GasN.C.O. per Co. & Bn. H.Q.

6. **STORES.** Receipted lists of Stores etc. handed over and taken over will be sent to Orderly Room by 10 a.m. 24th inst.

7. **STORES, RATIONS Etc.** All Coy. and Battn. H.Q. Stores, Mess Boxes etc. will be dumped at Respective ration dumps by 8 p.m. and transport officer will arrange to collect them and take them to Ration Dumps in new positions.
Rations for the 24th inst. will be dumped at new positions on 23rd inst. and Companies on arrival will arrange own carrying.
Lewis Gunners will carry their own Lewis Guns. Transport Officer will arrange for bulk water carts to be brought to Battn. H.Q. L.S.H.S.G., where petrol tins for the use of the Battn. will be filled. O.C. 20th N.F. is arranging for all empty petrol tins to be dumped at Bn. H.Q. on night of relief. On relief O.C. "D" Co. will detail 2 parties of 1 N.C.O. and 6 men to carry water to the 2 front line Coys. Transport Officer will reconnoitre routes to new ration dumps on 22nd inst.

8. **COMPLETION OF RELIEF** will be notified to Bn. H.Q. by wiring code message " PLEASE SEND CORRECT TIME."

9. **ACKNOWLEDGE.**

Issued at 6 p.m. to
1. "A" Co.
2. "B" Co.
3. "C" Co.
4. "D" Co.
5. M.O. & Q.M.
6. 20th N.F.
7. R.S.M.
8. War Diary
9. File.

Capt. & Adjt.
23rd N.F. (4th T.B.)

SECRET.   23rd N.F., (4th T.B.),   Copy......7......
Ref. Maps.   Operation Order No. 78.
BUNDY, Edn. 3b,
 1/10000
Rm. Sheet 62c, N.E.   September 25th 1917.
 1/10000.

1. **RELIEF.** The 34th Division is to be relieved by the 24th Division between 26th and 29th September, both dates inclusive, and on relief move via PERONNE and DOINGT to VI Corps Rest Area.

   The 102nd Infantry Brigade will be relieved in the Line by 73rd Infantry Brigade on night 26/27th September and march to Billets in Reserve Brigade Area.   On relief 102nd Infantry Brigade will be in Divisional Reserve.

   The 23rd N.F. (4th T.B.) will be relieved in the Centre Subsector , "C" Sector, by the 9th Bn. Royal Sussex Regt.   On relief the Battalion will march to BERLES via the following route:-
   HAMELINCOURT-CROSS ROADS L.10.a.4.7.-BEHAGNIES-HENVILLE-BERLES.

2. **DISPOSI-** Companies 23rd N.F. (4th T.B.) will by be
   TIONS.   relieved by Companies 9th Royal Sussex as follows:-

   "A" Co. 23rd N.F. (Support) by "D" Co.9th Royal Sussex
   "B" "   "   " (Left Co) " "B" " "   "   "
   "C" Co.   "   " (Right Co) " "A" " "   "   "
   "D" Co.   "   " (Reserve-) " "C" " "   "   "
                      (Quarry.)

   Not more than 1 Front Line Company will be in the process of relief at the same time.   ENFILADE Trench is allotted to this Battalion for the purpose of relief and will not be used by Right Battalion.

3. **MOVES.** On relief Companies will at once move off and 300X distance will be kept between platoons until the leading platoon reaches point about L.14.c.2.9. where the Company will form up as a whole and march to BERLES.

4. **ADVANCE** The 9th Sussex Battalion are sending one officer
   PARTIES. per Company and 1 N.C.O. per platoon on the night 27/28th September 1917.   Each Company 23rd N.F. will detail 1 N.C.O. to report to 2/Lt. H.Stanley at Battalion H.Q. at 1 p.m. 26th Sept.   This party will proceed and take over billets to be occupied by this unit at BERLES.   They will meet Companies in the evening and guide them into Billets.

5. **GUIDES.** Guides at the rate of 1 per platoon and 1 per Company H.Q. and 1 for Battalion H.Q. will proceed to 102nd Bde. H.Q. L.10.a.4.5. (QUARRY) at 7.45 p.m. and will guide incoming platoons to respective positions.   Company Commanders will ensure that guides know exactly where they have to go and will include 1 responsible N.C.O. amongst their guides.

                    (Continued)   /PATROLS.

5a. ORDER OF   Coys. 9th Royal Sussex will arrive in following
    RELIEF.   order so that no more than one font line Coy. will
                be inprocess of relief at the same time:-

                "B",   "D",   "C",   "A".

/guides.

6. **PATROLS.** All standing patrols will be handed over on relief. The 9th Sussex Regt. are sending 3 scouts on the night 25/26th Sept. to accompany Fighting Patrol sent out by this Unit on nights 25/26th and 26/27th Sept. This Fighting patrol will be found by this Unit on night 26/27th Sept. and will stay out as usual. On return this Patrol will proceed direct to billets in HERMES.

7. **STORES, DETAILS OF WORK IN HAND.** All defence schemes, aeroplane photographs, trench maps, S.O.S. and longthem range signals, S.A.A., grenades, Reserve rations, anti-gas appliances and all other trench stores will be handed over to incoming unit during dak daylight on September 26th. Receipted lists of Stores handed over will be forwarded to Orderly Room by 10 a.m. 27th inst.

All intelligence, work and wiring reports will also be handed over.

8. **MESS BOXES ETC.** Company Mess Boxes, Stores, and H.Q. Mess Stores etc. will be dumped at respective ration dumps by 8.30 p.m. and Transport Officer will arrange to collect.

Lewis Guns will be brought out and carried as far as Battalion H.Q. where Transport Officer will collect same.

9. **RATIONS.** Rations for the 27th inst. will be dumped at new Billets in HERMES.

Immediately after ten tomorrow 26th inst. Companies will arrange to send out to HERMES a proportion of their cooks. Transport Officer is arranging to have the cookers at billets, also for all C.Q.M.S. to be present at billets when Companies arrive, and these C.Q.M.S. will be responsible for having a meal and hot tea ready for the men on arrival.

10. **COMPLETION OF RELIEF** will be notified to Battn. H.Q. by wiring code message "RETURNS ALREADY RENDERED."

11. **ACKNOWLEDGE.**

Issued at 9.30p.m. to

No. 1.........."A" Co.
No. 2.........."B" Co.
No. 3.........."C" Co.
No. 4.........."D" Co.
No. 5..........T.O. & Q.M.
No. 6..........9th Royal Sussex.
No. 7..........War Diary.
No. 8..........Retained.

..............................Capt. & Adjt
23rd (S) Battn. Northumberland Fusiliers.
(4th Bn. Tyneside Scottish).

SECRET.   23rd N.F., (4th T.S.),   Copy. 9.....
           Operation Order No. 73.
           BNBN ----------------

Ref. Maps.
62c, 1/40000.
LENS 11,-1/100000.   September 26th 1917.

1. RELIEF.   The 102nd Brigade Group comprising
                      102nd Infantry Brigade,
                      102nd Field Ambulance
                  will be relieved by 72nd Brigade Group in the
                  Reserve Brigade Area (BERNES-HANCOURT-HERVILLY-
                  ROISEL etc) and will move to DOINGT on Sept. 27th,
                  dismounted personnel by bus or lorry, transport and
                  mounted personnel by march route.

2. BILLETING   2/Lieut. H.C.Stanley and 1 N.C.O. per Coy.,
   PARTY.   and H.Q., will leave BERNES on the 27th inst. and
                  proceed on bicycles to DOINGT where they will
                  report to the Town Major by 9 a.m. This party
                  will allot billets and will meet respective Coys.
                  etc. at debussing point and guide them to thir
                  billets.

3. MEALS,   Companies will arrange to give men breakfast
   CLEANING-   at 9 a.m. on the 27th inst. and a light dinner at
   UP.   11.30 a.m.
                      From 9 a.m. to 11.30 a.m. Coys. will devote
                  time to general cleaning-up of clothes, equipment
                  etc.

4. PARADE.   The Battalion will parade at 12 noon on the
                  Right side of the road, in order H.Q., "A". "B"
                  "C" & "D" Coys. head of column to be at Brigade
                  H.Q.
                      Companies will be told off into parties of
                  25. Any odd party left over in each Coy. will
                  be sent under an N.C.O. to report to the Adjutant.

5. EMBUSS-   Embussing will commence at 12.30 p.m.
   ING.

6 OFFICERS   Officers Valises, Orderly Room Boxes, H.Q. Mess
   VALISES.   Boxes, etc., will be dumped at Battn. H.Q. by
                  10.45 a.m. Coy. Mess Boxes will be carried in
                  the kitchens.

7. DEPART-   Immediately after men have had dinner, the
   URE OF   Kitchens will move off under orders of Transport
   KITCHENS.   Officer. Each Coy. will send 2 cooks with
                  kitchen who will prepare dinner on the march of
                  transport. Dinner will be served on arrival
                  of transport at DOINGT.

8. SUPPLIES"   Railhead will be ROISEL up to 29th inst.
   RAILHEADS   Railhead on 30th inst. BEAUMETZ-RIVIERE. 102nd
                  Brigade Group will draw from VIth Corps troops
                  BEAUMETZ-RIVIERE on 29th inst.

   REFILLING   102nd Brigade Group.
   POINTS.   27th inst. - as at present.
                  28th inst. - From Mechanical Transport at I.22.d.7.7
                               at 10 a.m.
                  29th inst. - Supplies will be delivered by Supply
                               Wagons at Billets in New Area.
                  30th inst. - will be notified later.

                      (Continued).   /MOVES.

(2).

/later.

9. **MOVES OF 1st LINE TRANSPORT.** 102nd Brigade Group:-

Sept. 27-29th. DOINGT.
Night 29th/30th Sept. - BAPAUME.

Above march will be under Brigade T.O.

10. **ENTRAIN-ING.** On 29th September the 102nd Bde. will move from PERONNE by train.
On arrival at VIth Corps Area this Battalion will be billeted in BAILLEULMONT.

11. **ACKNOWLEDGE.**

Issued at 6.50 p.m. to

1........"A" Co.
2........"B" Co.
3........"C" Co.
4........"D" Co.
5........T.O.
6........Q.M.
7........R.SM.
8........WARDiary.
9........Retained.

..................Capt. & Adjt.
23rd (S) Bn. Northumberland Fusiliers,
(4th Bn. Tyneside Scottish).

G24/0/2

23rd (S) Bn., Northumberland Fusiliers,
September 29th. 1917.

Bn. ORDERS.
To:- R.S.M.
DRUM MAJOR.

PRESENT-ATION.   The Corps Commander will present ribbons to various recipients of the 34th Division tomorrow morning 30th inst.
The m/m of this Battalion will parade to recive ribbons:-

  23/612 Sgt.   G.A.SPAIN.
  40549 XXX   H.V. BUSH, L/CPL.
  47164 PTE.   F. ASPINALL.

The Battalion will be represented on this parade by a composite Company consisting of

  5 Officers.
  4 Platoons each of 1 P.B.

Capt. H.D.Whittaker will take command of this party. Each Company will detail 1 officer platoon Commander and 30 selected O.R. for this parade.

DRESS.
  Officers -   Uniform, balmoral, Sam Browne belt, P.H.Helmet. No sticks and no officers will be mounted.
  O.R.   -   Uniform, Service Dress Cap, belt Rifle and bayonet, P.H. Helmet.
  Recipients.- Same as O.R. but without rifles. Recipients will not wear the ribbons to be presented on this parade until they recive it from the Corps Commander.

REVEILLE.   Reveille will be at 6.30 a.m., breakfast at 7 a.m. tomorrow morning. Great care will be taken in the selection of the men for this parade, and Company Commanders will ensure that the men are thoroughly clean and tidy.

PARADE. *facing*   The composite company will parade on the road outside Battalion H.Q. at 8.30 a.m. in following order from the right:-

  "A"   "B"   "C"   "D" Coys.

They will then be inspected by the C.O. prior to marching off to the parade ground, which is the football field, DOINGT, I.3.b.1.a.

BAND.   The pipers and drummers of this Battalion will assemble on the parade ground at 9 a.m. and will be massed for the parade under the senior N.C.O. or S.C.O. present.

MARKERS.   The R.S.M. will detail 8 markers to report to the Brigade Major at 9 a.m. on the parade ground.

       ....Capt. & Adjt.
      23rd (S) Bn. Northumberland Fusiliers,
       (4th Bn. Tyneside Scottish).

SECRET.   23rd N.F., (4th T.S.),   Copy........
                        Operation Order No. 74.

Ref. Maps.
SHE, 1/40000
LENS 11, 1/100000   September 28th 1917.

1. **MOVE.**   The Battalion will move by train on the 29th
                       inst., entraining at PERONNE FLAMICOURT, detrain-
                       ing at BOISLEUX au MONT.

2. **DEPART-**   Train will leave station at 5.15 p.m., and
   URE OF   arriving at BOISLEUX au MONT at 8.50 p.m..
   TRAIN.   On detraining the Battalion will march to
                       BAILLEULMONT by the following route:-
                       ADINFER-RANSART-BOILEUX-BAILLEULMONT.

3. **PARADE.**   The Battalion will parade, outside own billets,
                       ready to march off at 3.30 p.m., in order -

                       H.Q., "A", "B", "C", "D", Coys.

                       H.Q. will move off at 3.30 p.m. prompt, followed
                       at 100 yards distance by "A" Coy. Each Company
                       will maintain a 100 yards distance.

4. **COMPLET-**   Entraining is to be completed half an hour before
   ION OF   departure of train.
   ENTRAIN-
   ING.

5. **HEAVY**   All heavy baggage, surplus baggage, kits, etc.,
   BAGGAGE   not required on the train will be dumped at Q.M.
   ETC.   Stores tonight.   This will be taken direct to
                       Billets by lorry tomorrow.   The Q.M. will detail
                       2 guides to report to 2/Lieut.A.L.Redfe at the
                       Town Major's office, DOISNT, at at 8.45 a.m.
                       tomorrow morning 29th inst..   This unit will be
                       allowed two x thirds of a lorry to carry this
                       heavy baggage.   These guides will direct the
                       lorries to the Q.M. Stores to collect the baggage
                       from the dump.   Q.M. will arrange loading party.
                       All officers kits, one mess box per company and
                       one for Battn. H.Q. and cooking utensils for men
                       will be conveyed to the entraining stax station
                       at 2 p.m. in the afternoon.   All these stores
                       will be dumped at Q.M. Stores by 2 p.m.
                       R.S.M. will detail 2 guides to be at the TOWN
                       MAJOR'S office, DOISNT at 2 p.m. prompt to g
                       guide Rolley to Q.M. Starres to pick up mess
                       boxes etc.
                       Q.M. will arrange to send unloading party, who
                       will also act as guard, to the station with this
                       lorry.
                       4 cyclists only will accompany the Battalion,
                       and the remainder will march with transport. The
                       R.S.M. will arrange to hand over rations for the
                       cyclists accompanying the transport before 8 a.m.
                       on the 29th inst.

Issued at 5 p.m. to
   Copy 1......"A" Co.
        2......"B" Co.
        3......"C" Co.
        4......"D" Co.   ....Capt.&Adjt.
        5......T.O.   23rd Bn. Northumberland Fusiliers,
        6......Q.M.   (4th Bn. Tyneside Scottish).
        7......R.M.O.
        8......War Diary.
        9......Retained.

Page 1.

SECRET.

OPERATION ORDERS
by
Lieut. Col., C.F. Porch, Cmdg., 3rd. Battn. Northd. Fusiliers.
(4th. Battalion Tyneside Scottish)

REF. MAP
BOIS GRENIER
36.N.W.4.
Edition 6.C.
1/10,000

Holding B2 Subsector of the Line.

I.16.b.5.8. to I.21.a.8.7.

Information 1   The enemy are reported by patrols and by look-out men in the front line to be very active repairing their front line immediately opposite our sector, North and South of the LILLE ROAD.

INTENTION.   A raid will be made on the night 30th. Sept./ 1st. Oct. to engage the enemy working parties between point I.16.d.38.60 and point I.16.d.10.35 and to bring back prisoners.

Artillery & Trench Mortar co-operation.   The artillery and trench mortar batteries will co-operate under separate orders by Lieut. Col., HARDWICH, R. F. A., and will on the 4th. Sept. cut the wire at points I.16.d.38.60 and I.16.d.xx 10.35. where the infantry parties will enter the trenches.

On the night 30th. Sept./ 1st. Oct. an intense bombardment will be laid on the enemy's lines as follows:-
From Zero hour to Zero hour plus 5 minutes on the enemy's "S" Line I.16.d.5.8. to junction "S" Line and LILLE ROAD I.16.d.4.4. and from I.16.d.1.0. to I.16.d.30.85.
From Zero hour plus 5 minutes to Zero hour plus 5 minutes on the enemy's front line from I.16.d.4.7. to I.16.d.5.5. the junction of front line and LILLE ROAD and from I.16.d.0.1. to I.16.d.... .
From Zero hour to Zero hour plus 5 minutes the enemy's front line will be kept under fire at the point where it crosses the LILLE ROAD.

At Zero plus 5½ minutes the artillery will place a barrage of 10 minutes duration on the following trenches. I.16.d.60.85 to I.16.d.5.7. to I.17.d.60.65 and from I.16.d.25.0 to I.35.b.10.65 to I.27.a.5.6. SNIPERS HOUSE

The R.A. and the trench mortar batteries will after this barrage direct fire on known or suspected Machine Gun positions situated 1000 yards North and 1000 yards South of the LILLE ROAD for a further 10 minutes to cover the retirement of raiding parties.

INFANTRY
a) 2nd. Lieut. Freeman 23 N.F.
2nd. Lieut. Coyne, 23 N.F.
15 N.C.Os & men
b) Lt. Cowley,
2nd. Lt. Brough
15 N.C.Os & men

At Zero, 2 Infantry raiding parties strength as per margin, will be in position in NO MAN'S LAND, 50 yards opposite their respective points of entry.

   "A" Point   I.16.d.38.60.
   "B" Point   I.16.d.10.35.

At Zero plus 5 minutes they will advance and enter the enemy's line and work inwards along the enemy's front line for kkms for 40 yards each.
"A" party from I.16.d.38.60 moving South West towards the LILLE ROAD.

Page 2.

"B" Party from I.16.d.35.65 moving North East towards
the LILLE ROAD.
"A" party and "B" Party will each block the enemy's
front line trench 20 yards to the outer flank of their
respective points of entry.
"A" and "B" parties return by their own respective points
of entrance and will be clear of these points by Zero
plus 15 minutes.
Both parties will be constituted as follows,
2 men to block and guard outer flank of point of entry.
1 Officer and 7 N.C.Os and men to immediately raid
inwards and engage enemy encountered along the trench.
1 Officer, 5 men and 1 messenger in reserve at point of
entry to repel possible counter attack on outer flank
and also to collect prisoners or identifications as
evacuated.
The enemy will be attacked as silently as possible on
entry and prisoners taken. Opposition to be met by
bayonet men and bombers supported by bomb carriers.

A white tape will be laid at Zero - 15 minutes from Sally
Ports in our own lines at points I.16.c.9.9. and
I.16.c.7.7. to respective points of entrance in the enemy
lines. These tapes will act as guides to men on returning
across NO MAN'S LAND.
The signals to as return will be given from points 200
yards on the outer flank of each Sally Port in order to
distract enemy's attention from actual points of ingress
and egress and will consist of a bugle sounding one "G"
at intervals. Also 1 green very light fired at 30 seconds
interval.
At each Sally port a whistle will be sounded quietly at
intervals to assist actual and required direction.
"A" and "B" Parties will on return assemble in the "S"
Line between BRICK STREET and COWGATE where the rolls of
each party will be called and before moving off will
receive orders f om Advance Headquarters in the front line.

"A" and "C" Companies, 23rd. Battalion Northumberland
Fusiliers will each send 1 stretcher and bearers to
remain at the Sally Port of "A" Party until required.

"B" and "D" Companies, 23rd. Battalion Northumberland
Fusiliers will each send 1 stretcher and bearers to
remain at the Sally Port of "B" Party until required.

"A" and "B" Parties including Officers will wear uniform
without any identification marks.

Faces and hands and wrists will be blackened.

All reports including verbal messages from raiding party
leaders by their specially selected runners will be sent
to the C.O. at Advanced Headquarters at the junction of the
left and centre company sub-sections in the front line
between BRICK STREET and LILLE ROAD

Zero hour will be at 10.0p.m.

The Stokes Trench Mortars, Vickers and Lewis Guns will
from Zero - 30 minutes until Zero plus 30minutes
co-operate under orders which will be detailed them
directly later and which at present depend on
information which observers and night patrols may obtain.

................Lieut. Col., Comdg.,
23rd. Battalion Northumberland Fusiliers.

NO. 3 SCHEME.

GENERAL IDEA.

Recent patrols have discovered that the enemy is now very active in repairing his front line, parapet and wire, immediately North and South of the LILLE ROAD and also that he has strong patrols occasionally in NO MAN'S LAND and there has recently been a considerable increase in his Machine Gun and Artillery Fire opposite this sector.

It is proposed to carry out two simultaneous raids - (a) and (b) - on his working parties North and South of the LILLE ROAD after and during Artillery and Trench Mortar co-operation as follows:-

(a) party....
(b) party....

(a)   A clear passage for each raiding party to be cut at point I.16.d.32.80   and at point I.16.d.10.35 on Thursday, September 28th, and kept under Machine Guns fire on the night 28/29th. September and 29/30th. September.

(b)   On the night 30th. Sept. / 1st. October, two infantry raiding parties, strength
(a) 2 Officers, 15 N.C.O's and men and 1 Lewis Gun
(b) 2 Officers, 15 N.C.O's and men, and will form up in NO MAN'S LAND, opposite their respective points of entry to be in position 5 minutes before Zero hour.

Artillery &
Trench Mortar
Action.

In order to keep the enemy's working party in the front line and to injure and cut off possible supports, a three minutes heavy bombardment should be laid on the enemy's "S" Line from Zero - 5 minutes to Zero - 2 minutes from

For "A" Raid-
ing party.
For "B" Raid-
ing party.

(point I.16.d.5.6. to junction "S" Line and LILLE
(ROAD I.16.d.4.4.   and from
(point I.10.d.1.0. to I.16.d.30.26.

From Zero - 2 minutes to Zero hour the bombardment should be laid on the front line

"A" Party.

(from point I.16.d.4.7. to point I.16.d.7.5. the
(junction of the front line and LILLE ROAD and from

"B" Party......point I.16.d.0.1. to I.16.d.3.3.

There should be a half minute cessation of the Artillery fire at Zero hour when the two raiding parties should enter the enemy's front line, under orders detailed later to engage any of the German Working parties found within 40 yards of their respective points of entrance towards the LILLE ROAD.

At Zero plus 30 seconds the Artillery should place a protection barrage of 15 minutes duration on the following trenches,

For "A" Infan-
try party.

(I.16.d.4.4. to I.16.d.6.7. and one gun on point where the
(enemy's front line crosses the LILLE ROAD.
Also from I.16.c.95.0. to I.22.a.80.90. and on "S" Line I.22.b.1.0. to I.22.a.5.6. SNIPERS HOUSE.

INFANTRY PARTIES ACTION.

"A" party will enter at Zero hour at point I.16.d.32.80, will block the enemy's front line trench 10 yards North of point of entry and will work 40 yards South West along the front line and will engage any of the enemy encountered and will return and be clear of enemy's front line at point of entry at Zero plus 10 minutes.

The Lewis Gun attached to "A" Party will accompany this party to and from our lines on the left flank and will remain on the left of the point of entry, whilst "A" party is in the trenches.

At Zero hour "B" party will enter the enemy's line at point I.16.d.10.35. and will block the enemy's front line South of the point of entry and will work along the enemy's front line 40 yards North West from entrance

Page 2.

towards the LILLE ROAD and will engage any of the enemy's working parties encountered. They will return by point of entry and will be clear by Zero hour plus 10 minutes.
"A" and "B" parties will each be equipped and armed as follows:-

2 Officers with revolver, torch and life preserver.
2 N.C.O's with revolver, life preserver and 3 bombs.
2 men with rifle and bayonet to accompany blocking parties
4 men - bombers - with 6 bombs each and life preserver
2 men - carriers with 12 bombs each and life preserver.
6 men with rifles and bayonets and 2 bombs each as covering party on retirement, or emergency party as required.

It is assumed that the enemy will have working parties on their front line as at present.

It is hoped that a heavy initial bombardment of the immediate "S" Line for 3 minutes, followed immediately by 2 minutes on the front line will dis-organise any immediate support and will inflict casualt-ies on the occupants of the front line some of whom will retire along the front line towards the LILLE ROAD.

The 2 raiding parties will enter simultaneously North and South of the LILLE ROAD 200 yards apart and work for 40 yards inward each and should, whilst having their outer flanks at entrance guarded, engage any of the enemy who remained under the bombardment or who retired inwards towards the LILLE ROAD and thus masking Machine Gun fire from within on the raiders.

........................Lieut. Col., Cmdg.,
23rd. Battalion Northumberland Fusiliers.
4th. Battalion Tyneside Scottish.

SECRET

Copy No..

ADDENDUM No.. 2
to
102nd INFANTRY BRIGADE
OPERATION ORDER No. 155

Ref. Maps.
Sheet 6 f.C. -
1:40,000.
Sheet 11 LENS.
1:100,000.

27th SEPT. 1917.

1.. Reference Operation Order No.155 - Para. 9 - the entrainment of dismounted personnel 102nd Inf. Bde. Group (i.e. 102 Inf. Bde., 102 Field Ambulance, 1 Section 207th Field Co. R.E.) on September 29th 1917, will be carried out in accordance with the attached Table 'A'.

2.. Units will march independently to the entraining station with 200ˣ distance between Companies, etc., so as to arrive there 1 hour before the time of departure of the train. Routes to entraining station will be reconnoitred by units beforehand. Entraining to be completed half an hour before time of departure of train.

3.. An entraining state showing number of Officers, other ranks and bicycles proceeding will be handed by O.C. each unit to R.T.O. at the entraining station immediately on arrival.

4.. Units will take with them in the train only such camp kettles, Officers kit, etc. as are essential for the night 29th/30th and 30th inst. prior to arrival of transport.
Not more than 4 bicycles per unit will be taken by train, remainder will march with the transport.
The Staff Captain will be at the detraining station to meet each train and will allot lorries as may be available to carry men's packs, cooking utensils, etc. to billets.
Fatigue parties to load these lorries will be detailed beforehand by each unit.

5.. Units will march independently from the detraining station to billets.
Reports of arrival in billets and position of Headquarters will be forwarded by each unit to Brigade Headquarters.

6.. Brigade Headquarters will close at DOINGT at 5.30 a.m. September 29th and reopen at BAILLEULMONT at the same hour.

7.. The attention of O.C's Units and O.C's trains is called to Field Service Regulations, Part I, Sections 34 to 37 inclusive.

8.. ACKNOWLEDGE.

R. Lethidge
Major
BRIGADE MAJOR
102nd (TYNESIDE SCOTTISH) BDE

Issued at

Distribution -
Copies Nos. 1 & 2 retained
3 20th N.F.
4 21st "
5 22nd "
6 23rd "
7 102 M.G. Coy.
8 102 T.M.B.
9 207th Field Co. R.E.
10 102nd Field Ambulance.
11 Staff Captain.
12 102 Bde. Transport Officer.
13 102 Bde. Signal Officer.
14 H.Q. 34th Division.)
15 R.T.O., PERONNE FLAMICOURT) for
16 Town Major, DOINGT.) information.
17 Town Major, PERONNE.)

Q.10 2/33

Reference 34th Division Administrative Instructions No. 18, and subsequent Amendments, and 102nd Infantry Brigade Operation Order No. 155 and Addendums Nos. 1 and 2, the following instructions are issued for the guidance of units :-

- HEAVY BAGGAGE -

Four lorries are placed at the disposal of the Brigade for conveyance of heavy baggage to the new area. These lorries will be allotted as follows :-

LORRIES -

No. 1	..	20th N.F.	..	2/3rds.
		102 M.G. Coy.	..	1/3rd.
Nos. 2 & 3	..	21st, 22nd, & 23rd N.F.		2/3rds. each.
No. 4	..	102nd L.T.M.B. &)		
		102nd Bde. H.Q.)	..	⅓ each.

Two representatives from each unit sharing a lorry will report to 2/Lt. A.L. SCAIFE 23rd Bn. N.F. at 6.45 a.m. at the Town Major's Office DOINGT on the morning of 29th instant. The lorries will be detailed by 2/Lt. SCAIFE in accordance with the above table and he will see that each unit gets its share of the lorry accommodation and that not exceeding 2 representatives from each unit accompany these lorries. The lorries will be collected, after being loaded, by 2nd Lieut. SCAIFE and he will proceed with them to the new area.

Attention of O's. C. is drawn to the scale of allowances for heavy baggage accompanying units, previously issued.

OFFICERS' KITS & COOKING UTENSILS ACCOMPANYING ENTRAINING PARTIES.

Officers' kits, mess boxes, and cooking utensils for men will be conveyed to the entraining station by first line transport as follows :-

For first train .. To be dumped at the station at 6.30 a.m.
For second train .. A lorry will be provided. Representatives will be sent by units to act as guides, to be at the Town Major's Office, DOINGT, at 2.0 p.m.

Necessary Guards will be provided at the station. O's. C. Units are warned that only the very necessary things are to be taken on train as the accommodation is limited. The first line transport wagons are not to be detained at the entraining station as they have to return to the transport lines to re-load and resume the route march.

- CYCLISTS -

Rations for cyclists accompanying first line transport will be handed over to the Transport Officers of Units by 7.0 p.m. on the evening of the 28th instant.

The mounted portion of the Section of the 207th Field Co. R.E. will not accompany first line transport by route march.

- FIRST LINE TRANSPORT VEHICLES -

All vehicles, field kitchens, water carts, mess carts, maltese carts and Officers chargers are to report to Brigade Transport Officer at the transport lines at 9.0 a.m. on the morning of 29th instant.

28 : 9 : 1917.

for STAFF CAPTAIN.
102nd (TYNESIDE SCOTTISH) BRIGADE.

Distribution - Addressed all recipients of O.O. No. 155.

Reference Map Sheet 52c.
LENS. 11.

102nd Brigade Group, 1st Line Transport.
Orders for Route March on 29th and 30th Sept.1917.

1. The 1st Line Transport of the 102nd Brigade Group will march to the New Area in accordance with the attached March Tables Nos. 1 & 2.

2. On the morning of the 29th instant, Transport Officers of Units whose Dismounted personnel are proceeding by Rail by the 1st train, will detail sufficient Transport to convey the Officers' Kits, Mess Boxes and Cooking Utensils for the men from the present billets to the Entraining Station so as to arrive at the Station not later than 6-30am. These wagons must return immediately to the Transport Lines.

3. All Transport Vehicles at present with Units eg., Field Kitchens Water Carts, Officers' Chargers and etc are to return to Transport Lines by 9am on the morning of the 29th instant. The Water Carts of all Units are to travel filled.

4. Attention of Transport Officers is drawn to the necessity for the strictest regard to be paid to March discipline. All ranks will wear Steel Helmets. An interval of 200 yards will be maintained between Units on the Line of March.

5. On arrival in Camp at BAPAUME Transport Officers will detail 1 N.C.O. and 1 Other Rank to report to the Brigade Transport Officer who will allot the Camping ground. Transport Officers will send in by 6pm the Marching-in-State. No animals will be sent to Water until a Time Table has been issued. Each Unit will have erected a latrine for the use of the men in the Camp. This latrine to be filled in before moving off the following morning.

6. One Cyclist will be detailed by each Battalion for duty as Orderly with the Brigade Transport Officer. These Orderlies will report at the starting point.

7. Lieut. J.THOMSON, Transport Officer, 20th Bn. North'd Fus.will carry out the duties of Orderly Officer on the night of 29/30th at BAPAUME. The 21st Bn. North'd. Fus. will detail a Corporal to act as Orderly Corporal on the night of 29th/30th.

Brigade Transport Officer.

28/9/17.

102nd (TYNESIDE SCOTTISH) Brigade.

Reference Map 62c.
LENS 11.

MARCH TABLE 1.   29/9/17.

Order of March.	Starting Point.	Time to pass Start point.	Route.	Destination.
23rd Bn. N.F.	E. of Fork Roads. I.23.c.2.4. Sheet. 62.c.	9-30am.	ST DENIS. MT ST QUENTIN. BOUCHAVESNES. RANCOURT. LE TRANSLOY. BAPAUME.	BAPAUME.
21st Bn. N.F.		9-36am.		-do-
22nd Bn. N.F.		9-42am.		-do-
20th Bn N.F.		9-48am.		-do-
102nd M.G.C.		9-54am.		-do-
102nd Bde Hqrs.		10am.		-do-
102nd Field Amb.		10-3am.		-do-

TABLE II.   30 : 9 : 1917

Order of march.	Starting Point.	Time to pass Starting Point	ROUTE	DESTINATION
21st Bn. N.F.	At the fork Road South of the B in BIHUCOURT	8.0 a.m.	ACHIEY-le-GRAND	BAILLEULVE
22nd Bn. N.F.		8.6 a.m.	ABLAINZEVILLE	-do-
23rd Bn. N.F.		8.12 a.m.	AYETTE ADINFER	BAILLEUL
102 Bde. H.Q.		8.18 a.m.	RANSART.	-do-
102 Field Amb.		8.21 a.m.		-do-
20th Bn. N.F.		8.27 a.m.		BELLACOURT
102 M.G. Coy.		8.33 a.m.		-do-

WAR DIARY
or
INTELLIGENCE SUMMARY.
(Erase heading not required.)

Army Form C. 2118.

23rd Month from 1st 22

Place	Date	Hour	Summary of Events and Information	Remarks and references to Appendices
BAILLEUL-MONT.	1st to 8th Oct. 1917		Carried out general reorganisation of platoons and training. Training men and rifle and bombing ranges as detailed near. Casualties. 1st NIL 2nd 2 ORs Sick 3rd 4 ORs Sick 6th 1 OR Sick 5th 1 OR Sick 6th 3 ORs Sick	
	9th		On the night of 9th/10th the Battalion moved from BAILLEUL MONT and entrained at GODEWAERSVELDE and proceeded to POPERINGHE (near POPERINGHE) BELGIUM. After detraining the Battalion marched into PLURENDON CAMP situated near PROVEN. Casualties 9th 3 ORs Sick 8th NIL	REF SHEETS. 20 S.W. 28 N.W. 1/20,000
PROVEN	10th			
	11th	9.30	Carried out reorganisation of the Battalion and practiced attacks on "PILL 30×25". When the Battalion was formed all details and its reserve behind and only the fighting Portion in its front. One hundred and two OR and ranks were sent to the CORPS reinforcement dump on the 10th B.A. (XIX Corps). Very few from Parade grounds and meals our strength. Casualties. 9th 4 ORs Sick 11th 2 ORs Sick Dr.	
	12th		10th NIL 12th NIL The Battalion marched from hut to PROVEN STATION where they entrained and proceeded to ELVERDINGHE. After detraining the Battalion marched to WOLFE CAMP (B.22.d.3.6) Camp was in a very bad condition many of the bivouacs being quite unterable an insufficient number of same to accommodate all the men. Very wet day. Casualties NIL Dr.	
ELVERDINGHE	13th			

WAR DIARY

Army Form C. 2118.

Place	Date	Hour	Summary of Events and Information	Remarks and references to Appendices
WOLFE CAMP? B22.d.86	14th 1917	6/h	West Milly. A fleet of enemy GOTHA aeroplanes appeared over the Camp and dropped several bombs causing about 6 casualties. A great many crumbs were inflicted on another Battalion in the vicinity. This day. Casualties: 2/Lt HANNAH & 6 ORs wounded. 2/Lt CARR (attd) wounded. 1 OR died of wounds.	
	15th		Supplied a working party of 200 ORs for carrying stuck loads to the forward area. Showery day. Casualties: 1 OR wounded. 4 ORs sick.	
	16th		The Battalion was fitted out during the morning with storm shelters. The Battalion is to relieve 3 Coys of the 10th West Yorks Regt tonight with 2 Battalions and the 7th Batta. Yorks Regt with the 3 remaining Coys hereafter in the line. At 10pm the Battalion moved from WOLFE CAMP and made a halt in the STRAY FARM AREA. At 6pm the Battalion moved to the forward area and completed relief. In relief dispositions were as follows - HQ & ORDERLY ROOM at KORTEBEEK FARM PREM. V.II.c.45.55. (PILL BOX) A Company V.12.d. (Shell Holes) B. Company V.18.d. (PILL BOX and SHELL HOLES) C. Coy in EAGLE TRENCH. V.23.a. and Lt. Carpenters were subject to heavy shelling for and several casualties were incurred. Casualties - 3 ORs killed. 10 ORs wounded. 2/Lt 1st BUCKLEY DCM, was wounded. 8pm	
KORTEBEEK FARM AREA	19th		Fine day. Enemy shelling very heavy throughout day. Positions occupied by A Coy very heavily shelled and held the remnants. 2 Platoon + Coy HQrs moved into remnants of Battalion HQ ORs. S/Lt. W.G. WHITAKER who was detailed for extra duty at Battalion on post with Lewis Guns — (killed in a.r.) Casualties 2/Lt J. BURRY killed. 7 ORs killed. 26 ORs wounded. 1 OR missing. 8pm 6 ORs sick	

WAR DIARY or INTELLIGENCE SUMMARY

Army Form C. 2118.

Place	Date	Hour	Summary of Events and Information	Remarks and references to Appendices
KORTEBEEK FARM FREN.	Oct. 18. 1917		Fine day. Enemy artillery heavy and intermittent throughout day. Major J. Shardlow assumed command of the Battalion vice Major N.V. Grace who returned to his Unit (2.D.O.LI.) Enemy aircraft active, several times flying machines passed over the men encamped several times throughout the day. Casualties - 2 O.R.s Killed. 20 O.R.s Wounded.	JJH
	19.		Marked Artillery activity and aircraft. In the evening the Battalion was relieved by the 11th Notts Lincolnshire Regt. and two Companies (R+B) proceeded to SUVLA CAMP (B.23.a.3.0.) C+D Companies proceeded to STRAY FARM area with Bn HQ also in STRAY FARM. Late relief. Casualties 4 O.R.s Killed. 9 O.R.s wounded.	JJH
	20.		Quiet day. R+B Companies were under the Command of Major J.J. Grace. 2nd W.F. Companies throughout the day carried out re-organisation of platoons and cleaning up of equipment. 9/H Off Scarfe & 2/Lts J. Watson joined. Casualties 2nd Off. killed. 6 O.R.s wounded. 3 O.R.s Sick. JJH	
	21.		In the evening C+D Companies moved forward and took positions up in EDALE & WHITE TRENCHES. Bulk of O.R. men in a PILL BOX & DOUBLE COTTS. Quiet relief. Casualties 5 O.R.s wounded. 6 O.R.s Sick. JJH	
	22.		In the evening C+D Co. moved forward and took up position in TPS 21945 FARM & COM PROM'S FARM areas. 2/Lt WHITTAKER killed. 2/Lt W.G. Slaughter joined. 18 O.R.s wounded. 4 O.R.s Sick. Casualties 2/Lt W.G. Slaughter. 18 O.R.s wounded. JJH	
	23.		In the evening C+D N.F. on the Front System of Shell Holes. By 11.30 p.m. FERDAN HOUSE moved forward and relieved the Battalion (M+B Coys P+B Bns) At 11.30 p.m. FERDAN HOUSE 8 O.R. wounded. Casualties 1 O.R. died of wounds. 8 O.R. wounded. 2 O.R.s Sick. JJH	

Army Form C. 2118.

WAR DIARY
or
INTELLIGENCE SUMMARY.
(Erase heading not required.)

Instructions regarding War Diaries and Intelligence Summaries are contained in F.S. Regs., Part II. and the Staff Manual respectively. Title pages will be prepared in manuscript.

Place	Date	Hour	Summary of Events and Information	Remarks and references to Appendices
FERDAN HOUSE IPPER.	24" Sept 1917		Intermittent shelling throughout the day and from aerial activity. In the 8 evening the Battalion was relieved by the 2/5" NORTH LANCS. Late relief. On relief the Battalion marched to BOESINGHE STATION. Casualties 1. O.R. killed in action. 20 O.Rs wounded.	8ths
	25"		The Battalion entrained at BOESINGHE Station and proceeded to PROVEN where they marched into tents (PLUREDON). Lings 24 marched general Battalion. Casualties 1. O.R. wounded.	8ths
PROVEN.	26" 27" 28"		Cleaned out reorganization of platoons and clearing up. Men went to Baths. Casualties 26" 10 O.Rs Sick. 27" 8 O.Rs Sick. 28" 8 O.Rs Sick.	8ths
	29"		The Battalion marched to IPPROUTRE STATION near POPERINGHE where they entrained at 3.15 P.M. and proceeded to BRISLEUX-LOMONT arriving there at about 1.30 P.M. on the 30". Casualties 1. O.R. Sick.	8ths
	30"		Settled down in Camp. General Cleaning up & re-organisation. Casualties 1. O.R. Sick.	8ths
	31"		The Battalion is to undergo the 2 weeks Lancashire training on Nov 1st 1917. Recruits for this Arrived in the trenches early in the morning. Casualties 15 - O.Rs Sick.	8ths

D.M. [signature]
Cmd'g 2/3 Northern S'Pals
(Lt. Graeme? Batten)

WAR DIARY or INTELLIGENCE SUMMARY

Army Form C. 2118.

Volume 23
23 NF

Place	Date	Hour	Summary of Events and Information	Remarks and references to Appendices
TRENCHES COLFUL SECTOR 51B.9.W	Nov 1st		The Battalion relieved the 2nd Lancashire Fusiliers in the morning in the COLFUL SECTOR. Quick and easy relief completed by 12 noon. Splendid weather and day passed quietly. CASUALTIES NIL.	
	2nd		Another very quiet day. Weather continues fine. A patrol at night sent to sights of the enemy. Little activity. CASUALTIES NIL. SICK 3.	
	3rd		Very quiet day. Much continued fine weather. A patrol at night Enemy wire. Patrols continued seeing or hearing anything. CASUALTIES - NIL. SICK 4.	
	4th		Another quiet day. Slight enemy artillery activity. Patrol again found no signs of enemy. CASUALTIES NIL. SICK 4.	
	5th		Were relieved in morning by 21st North'd Fus. (2nd Ypres Sector). Easy and quick relief. Completed by 12.30 p.m. Proceeded to bus at CARLISLE LINES, and two companies marching forward at N.16.c. in support. CASUALTIES NIL. Weather continues fine. SICK 2.	
	6th		Day given up to rest, cleaning up, and recreation. 10,000 yards and mud appeared to men. Football competition started between companies. Work on front line and 100-OB from forward companies. CASUALTIES NIL. SICK 2.	
	7th		Weather showery. Light training and parties to the trenches in the afternoon. Received training P.O. and Lewis gun carrying party from forward companies in the evening. Showery all day. CASUALTIES NIL. SICK 4.	
	8th		Training continued. Lewis carrying party again in the evening. Good wet day. Football match in the afternoon CASUALTIES NIL. 3 Sick.	

Army Form C. 2118.

WAR DIARY
or
INTELLIGENCE SUMMARY.
(Erase heading not required.)

Instructions regarding War Diaries and Intelligence Summaries are contained in F.S. Regs., Part II. and the Staff Manual respectively. Title pages will be prepared in manuscript.

Place	Date	Hour	Summary of Events and Information	Remarks and references to Appendices
COJEUL SECTOR TRENCHES	Nov 9th		Relieved 2/8th Norths & Fus (21ts.) in the morning. Excellent relief, complete by 11.20 am. Day proved quiety. Two patrols were sent out at night, but contact with enemy not obtained.	CASUALTIES 1 SICK
	10th		Quiet day with little activity. Two patrols sent out at night, but no trace of enemy in NO MAN'S LAND, although a working party was heard. Showery day again.	CASUALTIES 1 SICK
	11th		During the early hours at about 1.30 am a party of the enemy cut a gap in our wire and attacked the officer NCO on duty in a bombardier between two posts. The officer was killed and the NCO was missing. The remainder of the night passed quietly and the day showed little activity.	CASUALTIES 1 OR Killed 1 OR missing SICK 5
	12th		Day proved quiet, with slight artillery activity on both sides. At night two patrols were sent out but did not obtain contact with the enemy. Dull day 2 howitzer.	1 OR SICK
Yorkshire (AUX)	13th		Were relieved in the morning by 21st Nyths Fus (2tts). Good relief. Complete by 2 noon. All four companies in same camp in good billets. 6 Battalion officers now commenced Cheng leave.	1 OR SICK
	14th		Day given over to cleaning up, light work, and recreational training. Dull heavy day.	3 OR SICK
	15th		Training and full kit and Stores inspection carried out. Games in the afternoon. Other leave sent out in pursuit of the enemy, whom it was...

Army Form C. 2118.

WAR DIARY
or
INTELLIGENCE SUMMARY.
(Erase heading not required.)

Place	Date	Hour	Summary of Events and Information	Remarks and references to Appendices
York Camp	Nov 15		Two tellers were preparing to retire. Dull day. 2 O.R. sick.	
	16th		Training carried out and further detailed instructions re pursuit of enemy issued. Bright day. Rifle range in full use all day. 2 O.R. sick.	
COJEUL SWITCH TRENCH	17th	2.30pm	Relieved 25th North'd Fus (2nd TS) in trenches. Good relief, complete by 2.30pm. Quiet day. Heavy patrols. 1 O.R. sick.	
	18th		Fairly quiet day. Slight artillery activity and T.M.'s on both sides. Patrols were out at night without contact with enemy. Our aeroplanes very active. 1 O.R. killed, 1 wounded. 2 O.Rs sick.	
	19th		Activity on both sides increased. Our howitzers were cutting. In the afternoon the artillery of the division and an left put up a dense smoke barrage. At night our patrols found the enemy very alert and nervous, without however obtaining direct contact with him. 10 O.R. wounded.	
	20th		At 6.20 am 500 gas drums were discharged from a position behind our front line, accompanied by heavy M.G., T.M. and artillery fire. Enemy barrage was weak and scattered. At 11am a daylight patrol found the enemy locking his front line in strong numbers and further patrols at night found him very alert, and present in large numbers. Otherwise night passed quietly. Moderate artillery and T.M. activity. Dull heavy day, observation bad. At night patrols found enemy alert. 3 O.Rs wounded. 2 O.R. sick and 1 officer	
	21st		Were relieved by 2/5 N.F. in the morning. Good relief, complete by noon. The battalion proceeded to dugouts and shelter in N.16.c. 3 O.Rs sick	
N.16.c. BRAS	22nd		Day spent in cleaning up. 153 men were out on working parties. A special lookout from 2/5 N.F. front found enemy very alert. The officer on trapping over a wire a flare who at once ignited, and a heavy enemy	
	23rd			

Army Form C. 2118.

WAR DIARY
or
INTELLIGENCE SUMMARY.
(Erase heading not required.)

Instructions regarding War Diaries and Intelligence Summaries are contained in F. S. Regs., Part II. and the Staff Manual respectively. Title pages will be prepared in manuscript.

Place	Date	Hour	Summary of Events and Information	Remarks and references to Appendices
N.16.c	Nov 23		Barrage fell in NO MAN'S LAND. The patrol then returned safely. Our party, without sustaining any casualties. 2/Lt W.J. Fearn was in charge of this patrol. 2 ORs sick	
	24th		Working parties again provided high. Having a rest today for the remainder. Weather wet and cold. 1 OR sick	
	25th		Same routine as to previous day. Letter to report orders issued to keep a good lookout as aeroplane reconnaissance reported enemy concentration. 4 OR sick	
	26th		Little to report. 155 men on working parties. One officer reported back from hospital. Coy wet day	
	27th		Relieved by 2/5 RWF (?.T.) in the morning, relief complete by 11.30 am, A and D Coys in front line, C in support B in reserve. Trenches left in bad condition. Two patrols went out obtaining certain information to enemy. 1 OR sick	
Gospel Labords of Trenches	28th		Day spent without work into continues in the fort. Some flares went up [every?] artillery [illegible] exposing in the [illegible] on own left. Patrol went out touch not met any of the enemy but sentry presence on his front but slight appeared strongly held. 1 OR sick	
	29th		Harassed artillery fire and hand grenades. A lively henry barrage fell on our front line, and on the division on our own	

Army Form C. 2118.

WAR DIARY
or
INTELLIGENCE SUMMARY.
(Erase heading not required.)

Place	Date	Hour	Summary of Events and Information	Remarks and references to Appendices
COLEUL Subsectn of p 30 trenches	Nov 30		Left Patrols as usual, obtaining useful information 30/30 150 rounds Aldrith signal but observation that Orders issued to return all special stores. Patrols again at night but no enemy seen or heard. Wet day 1 O.R. sick Lt. P. Brown sick. J.K. Mark Lt. Col. Cmdg. 4TH BATTN TYNESIDE SCOTTISH. 23RD BATTN NORTHUMBERLAND FUSILIERS	

Oaland 74
23 N F
Vol 24

Army Form C. 2118.

WAR DIARY
or
INTELLIGENCE SUMMARY.
(Erase heading not required.)

Place	Date	Hour	Summary of Events and Information	Remarks and references to Appendices
YORK LINES	DEC 1st/17		What relieved by 21st Northd Fus in the morning, and battalion proceeded to this at York Lines. Excellent accommodation, and the battalion Officers mess was reformed. Weather was cold but fine.	Casualties Nil.
	2nd		Training was commenced, and continued though morning. In the afternoon recreational training. Men much appreciate a good rest and half the battalion received leave. The Divl Cmdr inspected the QM Stores, and arrangements commenced for a Begmed QM stores.	One OR to hospital Sick
	3rd		Training continued in morning and recreation in the afternoon. Remainder of battalion to baths. Weather cold and windy.	1 OR Sick
	4th		Training continued in morning, and relaxation in afternoon. At night a battalion concert was held which was much appreciated by the men. Thorough inspection kept of all kit. Weather continues very cold.	9 OR Sick
COLFUL Subsects 57 B.S.W.3	5th		Relieved 21st NF (2nd ??) in the morning. Quiet day. Quiet day, at night two patrols went out bringing in interesting information. Night passed quietly. Weather fine and fair.	2 OR Sick
	6th		Quiet day. All stand-to at night while stripes were run across parapet and front line. All ascertain made to ...	1 OR killed In action 1 Dec 1917 2 OR Sick

Army Form C. 2118.

WAR DIARY
or
INTELLIGENCE SUMMARY.
(Erase heading not required.)

Instructions regarding War Diaries and Intelligence Summaries are contained in F.S. Regs., Part II. and the Staff Manual respectively. Title pages will be prepared in manuscript.

Place	Date	Hour	Summary of Events and Information	Remarks and references to Appendices
Trenches Copse Support	6th		Most enemy snipers paid on attack. Night however passed quietly. Two patrols were out during the night, reconnoitring enemy trenches.	Casualties
	7th		Considerable enemy artillery activity during the day. Battalion Headquarters heavily shelled. 2nd E.S. Regts. did an excellent patrol at night. A known standing patrol were in at night in the Copse Valley, with the particular object of taking any trenches of battalion for a hostile attack but they reported warnings signalling same. Night observers between patrols.	1 O.R. sick
	8th		Considerable artillery activity on both sides. At night an enemy shelling that three men of an R.E. Coy. Another division who were digging a M.G. post under the Bn's charge at Bn P.A fighting patrol found enemy working from line in strength. The standing patrol as on the 7th was out, without seeing any hostile enemy movement	5 O.R. sick
Support N 16 c	9th		Was relieved in the afternoon by 2nd B.J. (273) Bn. on completion by B.n. proceeded to bivouacs in N 16 c to R points Battalion Accommodation very bad, but weather has been fine Casualties	1 O.R. sick
	10th		From 8am to 3.30 pm the area N/16 c and Copse Valley were not heavily shelled with 59's and 42". Estimated at two hundred rounds per day.	4 O.R. sick

WAR DIARY or INTELLIGENCE SUMMARY

Army Form C. 2118.

(Erase heading not required.)

Place	Date	Hour	Summary of Events and Information	Remarks and references to Appendices
	10th contd		Put on the top still in support. Finding the unusually large numbers of men killed two large working parties put out. Wiring to be kept up during heavy fog and men had fatigues. Notice given of an impending attack and each man issued with additional SAA and bombs.	Casualties
	11th		A heavy barrage fell at 5.30 am on the right divisions HQ. Enemy attacked and met with enormous loss. All quiet on this brigade front. At night "C" Coy wired 700 yards. The support line and two companies were finding additional parties and Coys which remain much fatigued but are holding up well. Night proved quiet.	2 OR. wounded 4 Ors Sick
	12th		Men attained what rest they could. At night 'A' Coy wired 700 yards in front of support line and two other companies were carried additional wire. Very heavy snow and all the men beginning to feel the heavy strain.	NIL
	13th		Men rested during the day and at night large working parties were found. B Coy continuing and improving wire put out by previous parties. Quiet day otherwise.	1 OR Sick
	14th		Were relieved during the morning by 24/27 N.F. Good relief and men proceeded to huts at Noeuxchatel. These huts being in a poor state. Very cold weather and men consequently very cold.	1 OR Sick
Noeuxchatel lines	15th		Men noted during all day. Inspections held, and dry kit and given over to dept. and overcoat.	NIL

WAR DIARY
or
INTELLIGENCE SUMMARY.
(Erase heading not required.)

Army Form C. 2118.

Instructions regarding War Diaries and Intelligence Summaries are contained in F. S. Regs., Part II. and the Staff Manual respectively. Title pages will be prepared in manuscript.

Place	Date	Hour	Summary of Events and Information	Remarks and references to Appendices
Dec. 16 Montia Lines	Dec 16		Training carried out throughout the day. At night working parties salving gas projectors. Very cold weather. Battalion canteen open with excellent results	Casualties 1 O.R. sick
	17		Training carried on throughout the day. Consisting of rifle range, drill, inspections and lectures; by C.O. in afternoon the men rested and recreational training. Foot ball. Boxing	1 O.R. Sick
	18		Light training throughout the day. At night large working parties out, commenced S/S wire from 3000 in G.S. wagons	2 O.Rs. sick
	19		Working parties out during the morning. Men worked very cheerfully. Received artillery activity noticeable in Corps front, also congratulations from Division on working parties. During afternoon the whole battalion out on working parties. D. Co.	2 O.Rs. sick
	20		A.O.'s and Coy Cmdrs reconnoitred the Right Brigade area. A warning order having been received that we were going into this sector. 2/Lt James Thompson reported for duty	3 O.Rs. Sick
	20		Quiet day spent in resting. Four officers, one per company were sent in advance to reconnoitre night bivouac area. Left camp	Nil
Fontaine Subsector	21st		Relieved 16th Royal Scots in the morning. A great relief compared by 1pm. Fairly good trenches but water supply very bad. At night each company in station reserves the batteries, entered	2 O.Rs. Sick

WAR DIARY or INTELLIGENCE SUMMARY.

Army Form C. 2118.

(Erase heading not required.)

Instructions regarding War Diaries and Intelligence Summaries are contained in F.S. Regs., Part II. and the Staff Manual respectively. Title pages will be prepared in manuscript.

Place	Date	Hour	Summary of Events and Information	Remarks and references to Appendices
Fontaine Subsector	21st Cont.		however obtaining contact with enemy. Day proved quiet, and very little activity. Lt Watson reported for duty	Casualties
	22nd		Day proved very quiet. The same system of patrolling as previous night adopted, without any unusual result. Weather continued cold and damp, and Coy's continued different experiences with ration supply.	NIL
	23rd		Another quiet day. Continuous patrols out at night as before, but no signs of enemy seen. But usual M.G. and rear artillery activity.	1 O.R. Admitted to Hosp.
	24th		Little activity during the day. Light exchange of artillery but little damage. Enemy response to fire of our heavy artillery on trench was continuous but nothing unusual to be reported and no contact obtained. Day was uneventful but continued fine.	NIL
Hinderberg Tunnel	25th		Bn relieved during the morning by 2/2 N.F. Lord Henry Seymour Bennebury came down to see relief and was having a drink, and the whole of the Bn being relieved by daylight. Bn much appreciated the warmth and comfort of their quarters. A distribution of cigarettes was made to each man during the morning.	1 O.R. Admitted to hospital
	26th		140 men were out on working parties, the remainder resting and cleaning up. Very cold weather with heavy snowfall. 2/Lt Lawless notified to report for duty from hospital.	1 O.R. Sick

WAR DIARY
or
INTELLIGENCE SUMMARY.
(Erase heading not required.)

Army Form C. 2118.

Instructions regarding War Diaries and Intelligence Summaries are contained in F.S. Regs., Part II. and the Staff Manual respectively. Title pages will be prepared in manuscript.

Place	Date	Hour	Summary of Events and Information	Remarks and references to Appendices
	27th		Morning Parties again supplied. Very cold weather with heavy fall of snow. Lt Thompson evacuated sick. Lt Paton reported for duty.	1 Offr S.I. O.R. Sick
	28th		Day fine & working parties on account of Christmas as no work was held in the Battery. Dinners in billets Xmas Day turkey, ham Christmas pudding about 8% whisky rum & tea. Very cold weather and more snow. Appreciated by all the men.	2 O.Rs sick
To same Billets	29th		Reliefs 2.P.M.B in the line, light reliefs. Relief completed by 11.40 Activity normal but no patrolling at night owing to bright moon and snow on ground. Day quiet night quiet.	NIL
	30th		Day fairly quiet. Enemy T.M. activity seen from our right. Two patrols went out on listening post instructions. Nothing done. Any enemy movement. Each patrol reported nothing.	1 O.R. Sick 1 O.R. wounded
	31st		Considerably worried by hostile T.M. heavy retaliation. Afternoon however silenced this again. Saw a severe frost at night. Few patrols about situation quiet, and M.Gs patrols all quiet. Light artillery activity not excessive. 8th during observation normal. Capt. A M. Logg reported for duty from 3/5th N.F.	3 O.Rs sick

Lt. Col. Comdg.
4th BATTN TYNESIDE SCOTTISH.
23RD BATTN NORTHUMBERLAND FUSILIERS

WAR DIARY
or
INTELLIGENCE SUMMARY.
(Erase heading not required.)

Army Form C. 2118.

23 NF
Vol 1 25

Place	Date	Hour	Summary of Events and Information	Remarks and references to Appendices
Fontaine Sub. Sector	1918 1st Jan		Very quiet day and night. Weather still severe, a hard frost. Tried. Patrols sent out during the night reported enemy inactive, claim patrols reported situation quiet. One of our aeroplanes crashed to earth in enemy lines, occupants captured, machine destroyed by our Artillery from Slight Artillery activity.	1 O.R. to Hosp.
	2nd Jan		Relieved in the morning by the 21st N.F. (2.T.S) Carried out quickly, relief complete by 11 am. Proceeded to bivouac in "The Nut" as Support Bn. Companies distributed in various sections of support line. Accommodation fairly good, consisting of underground dugouts. Weather still cold. Capt. A. Mortlidge attd. to R.F. for 4 days.	1 O.R. to Hosp. See App. 1.
	3rd Jan		Working parties found as follows. 3 Offrs. 60 O.R. Carrying. 1 Off. 40 O.R digging. 1 Off. 30 O.R wiring. Both parties reconnoitred and dispositions made. Weather cold & frosty. I.C. front was Quiet both day & night. Casualties 1 O.R. to Hospital. Accidentally injured.	
	4th Jan		Proceed working as follows. 3 Offrs. 60. O.R! Carrying 1 Off. 40.O.R Entrenching 1 Off. 50.O.R! Entrenching. Weather conditions, cold & frosty. Situation in front Quiet. CASUALTIES. 3 O.R. to HOSPITAL. Sick.	
	5th Jan		Detail of Working Parties as follows. Entrenching 2 Offrs 70 O.R's Carrying Party 3 Offrs 60. Other Ranks. Weather conditions Still cold & frosty. Situation normal. CASUALTIES. 3 O.R. to HOSPITAL Sick.	
	6th Jan		Relieved in Support by 30th (S) Co North Fus at 11 am. Bn then proceeded to relieve 21st Bn North Fus in Central Subway of Front line Relief complete at 2:15 pm Dispositions "A" Coy Right Front. "B" Coy. Left front "C" Coy. Centre Front. "D" Coy. Support.	See App. 2.

Army Form C. 2118.

WAR DIARY
or
INTELLIGENCE SUMMARY.
(Erase heading not required.)

Instructions regarding War Diaries and Intelligence Summaries are contained in F. S. Regs., Part II. and the Staff Manual respectively. Title pages will be prepared in manuscript.

Place	Date 1918	Hour	Summary of Events and Information	Remarks and references to Appendices
Front-Line CHERISY. Spent Shed. U.1.a.40.75.6 O.31.B.70.20	6th Jan. (cont)		Situation Quiet. Activity on both sides normal. Night Patrols reported that "No Man's Land" clear of enemy. Weather still continues cold. Capt A MORTLIDGE rejoined from R.F.A. Casualties. 1 O.R. wounded. Slight (Shrapnel).	
	7th Jan.		Situation quiet. Enemy Activity normal. Patrols report no unusual movement of enemy. Battalion dispositions same as previous day. Weather changed to rain during the day, much warmer. Each company carried out wiring on their front line trenches during the night. No change in Strength. CASUALTIES. 1 O.R. to Hosp. (Sick)	
— do —	8th Jan.		Situation still quiet, no unusual activity. No Man's Land patrolled during the night, and reported all clear and no movement of enemy beyond the ordinary. Dispositions unchanged. Weather changed to frost towards severe. Wiring again carried our during the night. Capt Nelson, M.C. returned from 34th Div. Depot & reported for duty. No change in strength. CASUALTIES. 3 O.R. to Hosp. Sick	
— " —	9th Jan.		Situation still normal. Very quiet day. Bn dispositions remained the same as previous day. Weather conditions still severe, cold & frost. Snowstorm set in about 2pm & lasted until 7 p.m. Rum Issue increased to full ration. All ranks bearing the severe weather quite cheerfully. Major Murphy reported for duty on finishing tour of duty on Staff. No Change in Strength. CASUALTIES. 1 O.R. Wounded G.S.W. Back (in wiring party)	

A 7092 Wt. W128. g/M1293 750,000. 1/17. D. D & I Ltd. Forms/C2118/14.

WAR DIARY
or
INTELLIGENCE SUMMARY.

(Erase heading not required.)

Army Form C. 2118.

Instructions regarding War Diaries and Intelligence Summaries are contained in F. S. Regs., Part II. and the Staff Manual respectively. Title pages will be prepared in manuscript.

Place	Date 1918	Hour	Summary of Events and Information	Remarks and references to Appendices
Front line Trench. Ref Trench Map CHERISY. U.14.40.75 to O.31.B.70.20 Right Sector of 162nd Right Sector	10th Jan		Situation quiet. Enemy dispositions remained the same as previous day. Weather broker, snowed showers during the day & much warmer. The Bn was relieved by the 21st N.F. which were carried out complete by 1.30 p.m. The Bn on relief proceeded to SHAFT AVENUE as the Bn in Reserve to Centre Subsector. Occupied in dug dugouts in the Hindenburg trench system was provided with a improved bed, electric light in tunnel, which was much appreciated. Bread Ration increased to units in Front Line 8oz to 70%. Working Parties provided in afternoon ➔ 30 MH 140 O.R's ➔ Wiring reconnaissance of Ibsens Band Dumps provided Neuville Vitasse for bathing. NCOs and Men showing signs of Scabies due to long term of duty in trenches. Capt A HARVEY att to Centre Group R.F.A. for instruction. Strength. 2nd Lieuts J. H. Price & W. L. Bowman.	(3)
Reserved trench Shaft No 260 U.T.S. M.35 C S.O.	11th Jan		Stood To, at 6.30 a.m. Boy Comdr reconnoitred their Defence Position. Manual digging revamping parties provided. A. & C Coys trained. No unusual enemy activity. Enemy Artillery and aeroplanes inactive. Change in Strength. Casualties. 3 O.R. to Hosp. (Sick) 2nd Lieut Berg Oakley & Thompson marched on parking	
SHAFT AVENUE Shaft 260 U.T.S K. 35 c.5.0	12th Jan		Very quiet day. Manual Working parties provided. Details of Coys H Q's worked. No change in strength. Casualties. 1 O.R rank wounded (Working Party).	
-do-	13th		No important events to record. Working parties as usual. Capt Douglas proceeded on 14 days leave. Strength increase 2nd Lt Johnson returned from leave. Strength increase 70 O.R.S evacuated P.B. 2nd Lt Johnson returned from leave. Strength increase. 2/Lt Williams & Vince reported to hospital. CASUALTIES. 2 O.R to Hosp. (Sick)	

Army Form C. 2118.

WAR DIARY
or
INTELLIGENCE SUMMARY.
(Erase heading not required.)

Instructions regarding War Diaries and Intelligence
Summaries are contained in F. S. Regs., Part II.
and the Staff Manual respectively. Title pages
will be prepared in manuscript.

Place	Date 1918	Hour	Summary of Events and Information	Remarks and references to Appendices
FRONT LINE Centre Subsector Rt HEINEL TRENCH MAP SHEET 57c SW3 V18. 50 95 03s1 b 65 5	14th Jan	4.30 pm.	Relieved 21st Bt N.F in front line. Well carried out completed by 11.30 am. Dispositions. "D" Coy Right Front. "C" Coy Centre Front. "B" Coy Left Front. A Coy Support. Weather conditions. Snow in afternoon. Thaw set in during afternoon. Situation quiet. Movement of parties of enemy & enemy transport to & from this direction of FONTAINE and SUN QUARRY/CTsd. "A" Coy sent on fly gun duty during the night. (CAPT AIRVEY reported ARTILLERY. 2nd Lieut Turner marched in signalling course. 2nd Lieut Hammond from attachment to 5th Army, & 2nd Lieut Petersen to Snipering Course. Change in strength. NIL CASUALTIES. 2 O.R. ↑ Hosp. (Sick)	Appendices (4)
—do—	15th Jan		Situation quiet. Dispositions same as previous day. Serious damage to fronts line and C.T. Trenches by rapid thaw, numerous slides in intervening wires melted and available between devoted to clearing stoppages & communication. Our Weather conditions deplorable. Very warm all day, no snow visible. Strength Increase of Front Line. Strength Increase of our R Reglt approxt small from trench parties issued to garrison of Front Line. CASUALTIES. 1 O.R to Hosp. Sick on parties and ours. H A Coy.	
—do—	16th Jan		Situation normal. No enemy activity. Trenches becoming worse, especially on Right Coy front where lateral communication between posts completely impassable. R E rapped and opened working parties detailed to clear water situation. Change in Strength NIL. Casualties NIL.	
—do—	17th		Situation still normal, enemy very quiet. No improvement in state of trenches. Weather conditions improved, occasional showers during the day	

Army Form C. 2118.

WAR DIARY
or
INTELLIGENCE SUMMARY.
(Erase heading not required.)

Instructions regarding War Diaries and Intelligence Summaries are contained in F. S. Regs., Part II. and the Staff Manual respectively. Title pages will be prepared in manuscript.

Place	Date 1915	Hour	Summary of Events and Information	Remarks and references to Appendices
Support Line THE NEST Rf HENINEL TRENCH MAP UTS N°360 N.30.a to 30	17th	10 pm	Relieved by 21st N.F. owing to the state of C.T.'s the day relief was found impracticable so returned to night relief. Commenced at 5 pm, completed by 8.45 pm. All movement on Right front Company taking place above the trenches. The state of trenches bad. R.Es & pioneers still working on them. Change in strength. Increase 2nd Lt Simpson reported from Hosp. Decrease 2.O.R.K. Hosp. (Sick)	N° 5
— do —	18th		Situation quiet, some artillery activity on this H'Qrs. Weather improved, occasional showers during the day. Condition of trenches very bad, dugouts collapsed, and numerous slides. Working parties provided for Left Bn in front line. 4 Offrs + 80 O.R.'s Remainder of Bn working on own trenches. Strength. Increase M. L. Decrease (5) O.R.'s Casualties 1 O.R. killed 1 O.R. wounded. 3 O.R.'s L. Hosp. (Sick)	
— " —	19th		Situation unchanged. Usual Artillery Activity. Weather conditions improved. A dry day enabling a considerable amount of work to be done in improving the trenches. 4 Offrs + 80 O.R.'s placed on disposal of O.C. Left Bn for work. STRENGTH. Increase 4. O.R.'s rejoined from Hosp. Capt Riddell returned from leave. Decrease 2.O.R.'s L. Hosp (Sick) Cpl White wounded on 9th (Buld of wounds)	
FRONTLINE Ref HENINEL TRENCH MAP U.T.S. N° 36.0 U.I.B.50-95 O.31.B.65-25	20th	7 pm	Situation normal. Artillery quiet. Weather conditions, dry mild. Relieved the 21st N.F. in front line, commencing at 5 pm. Relief well carried out and completed by 7 pm. Position in support taken over by the 22nd Br N.F. Inspection of Bn on following. Right Front. A Coy. Centre Front. D Coy. Left Front. B Coy. Reserve Coy "C" Coy. Condition of Trenches very much improved. With exception of Left Coy Relief carried out by Grenel. STRENGTH. 1 O.R. Accidentally injured.	N° 6

Army Form C. 2118.

WAR DIARY
or
INTELLIGENCE SUMMARY
(Erase heading not required.)

Instructions regarding War Diaries and Intelligence Summaries are contained in F. S. Regs., Part II. and the Staff Manual respectively. Title pages will be prepared in manuscript.

Place	Date 1918	Hour	Summary of Events and Information	Remarks and references to Appendices
Front Line	21st Jan		Situation quiet. Weather conditions improved, dry & mild. Condition of trenches improved considerably. Outpost communication along what front, with exception of No 4 & 5 P.O's in Right Coy. Gen. Strength. Increase. NN. Decrease. 3 O.R's to Hosp. (Sick)	
"	22nd Jan		No change in Situation. Weather conditions good. Strength Increase. NN. Decrease. NN Evacuee to O.R's Hosp. Sick.	
"	23rd Jan		Situation normal. Enemy very quiet. Weather conditions as previous day.	No. 7 O.O.
SHAFT AVENUE Rq HENNEL TRENCH MAP UTS N° 360 N°35 C.50.10		5 pm	Relieved by 2/4 N.F. in good order, well carried out, completed at 7 p.m. 3/ 4 Y & R. B. I/M proceeded to Camp Huts in SHAFT AVENUE Strength Increase 1 Officer (A/Capt (Lieut) Capt Leech proceeded to Army I/C W.K.	
— do —	24th Jan		No change in situation. Working parties provided 5 off: 120 O.R. Evening Finish. Strength. Increase NN. Decrease 4 off's to Hosp. Capt Jive & Lieut proceeded on 14 days leave to U.K.	
"	25th Jan		Situation very quiet. Working parties found during the day. 4 off's 110 O.R's.	
YORK LINES FRANCE Sheet 51.B.S.W. M.21.B		8 pm	Relieved by 4th Bn R.F. Very well carried out, commenced at 5 pm. Completed 7.45 pm after relief Coys marched to YORK LINES and nothing ?? ?? switch, the march being ?? by ?? men and very tired to somewhat wet & tired through rain & heavy march during much ??	N° 8

Army Form C. 2118.

WAR DIARY
or
INTELLIGENCE SUMMARY.
(Erase heading not required.)

Instructions regarding War Diaries and Intelligence Summaries are contained in F.S. Regs., Part II. and the Staff Manual respectively. Title pages will be prepared in manuscript.

Place	Date 1918	Hour	Summary of Events and Information	Remarks and references to Appendices
YORK LINES TRENCH MAP SHEET 51.B.S.W. 2d.S.a.	25th	9 pm	Cont.d The whole of Bn were reported in Camp at 10 pm on arrival via Camp which was greatly appreciated. Accommodation consists of Nissen huts holding about 30 men. They are fairly comfortable but require repairs, a considerable amount of the cement repairs remaining. Planks were issued at the rate of 2 per man in proportion of Bell tents men available, in tents admitted to compete. STRENGTH. Increase 27 O.R. Decrease 2 O.R. Hosp Sick.	
— do —	26th		Day spent in general reorganisation of Corps of N.C.O's. Inspections of Equipment Clothing & kit. Issuing & fitting of new clothing. Bathing. Haircutting & tc. Regt. Canteen instituted & greatly appreciated as shown by takings. Ran after Mess started, and togethers. STRENGTH Increase N.2. Decrease 20.R. Hosp Sick. Weather conditions good.	
— do —	27th		Completion of reorganisation, relaxing of Equipment, clothing & kits, also inspection of same instituted. Arrangements of programme of work to commence tomorrow. Coy Comdrs & Platoon Comdrs lectured by Comdg Officer in training in general. N.C.O's and men drawing winter of 48 hrs rest. Weather conditions good. STRENGTH Increase. 2 O.R. Casuals reported. Decrease N.2.	
— do —	28th		Training commenced as 9 am to 1 pm. Bn formed up in Mass and inspected by C.O. a good turn out. Programme of work consisted of P.B.T. drill. Rifle Exercises. Mus. Winry. Bombing & swimming at the Swimming stages. Weather conditions good, clear. Enemy aeroplanes visited vicinity of Camp during the day & night & —— their night raid dropped bombs at various places near the Lines, no damage done in our camp. Strength. Increase. N.2. Decrease. 3 O.R. to Hosp. sick. Weather conditions good.	

WAR DIARY or INTELLIGENCE SUMMARY

Army Form C. 2118.

(Erase heading not required.)

Place	Date 1918	Hour	Summary of Events and Information	Remarks and references to Appendices
YORK LINES M.22.b. Raf. Sheet 51.b.S.W.	29th Jan.		Training continued. Work on same lines as previous diary. Brigade Instructing in Platoon outposts placed at our disposal. Physical & Bayonet Training, Lewis Gun Instruction & Gas Instructor Recreational Training during the afternoon. Bath nearest built around huts for practice against Enemy Gas etc. Strength increase 4 O.R's from Hosp. Decrease 1 O.R. to Hosp. Sick. Capt Douglas rejoined from leave	
-do-	30th		Continued training on previous lines. A. Coy find on Rifle Range. Company practice reached very fair. Weather conditions front Instructor in Bombing placed at our disposal. Recreational Training carried out in Ras[...] 57 N.C.O. & men allotted week on reserved theatre seats as good enough. 3 I.G. & Coys moved on leave 4 U.K. No change in strength	
-do-	31st		Training as usual. B. Coy on Rifle Range find & firing on Musketry Lewis Gun Instruction no gunnery for platoons which Lewis Gun Instructor placed at our disposal. Fund attendant. Guards on reserved theatre seats approved. Strength increase Nil Decrease 1 + O.R's to Hosp. (Sick)	

J. R. Clark Lieut & adj
Comdg 23rd Bn Norfolk A.rnl P?

WAR DIARY
INTELLIGENCE SUMMARY

Army Form C. 2118.

23 NF
Volume 26
J.W. 26

Place	Date 1916	Hour	Summary of Events and Information	Remarks and references to Appendices
YORK LINES Ref. Trench Map Sheet 51.B.S.W. M.22.6.	1st Feb.		Training continued on lines similar to previous day. "C" Coy attend Rifle Range and fired a Grouping practice; result very fair; weather conditions unfavourable for good shooting. Being cold & windy. D. Coy's training consisted of rapid wiring under supervision of Brigade bayonet. Brigade HQ also on subject walls around huts for protection against bombs & enemy officer attended conference at Brigade HQ on suggested reorganization of 13th N Brigade; decided that 20 O's & 21st Bn N.F. be discharged and personnel distributed amongst remaining Bns. STRENGTH 37 Offs 717 O.Rs. Capt. Nelson M.C. proceeded on leave to U.K.	Decrease 1 O.R. to Hos.
— do —	2nd Feb.		Training carried out until 10 a.m. Bn then divided into working parties as under. 3 A. Coys 3 Offs. 3 & 5. 75 O.Rs. paraded at 1.30 p.m. under Major Murray proceeded by train to HENINEL and for digging training. Returned to Camp 11–20 p.m. 2nd Lieut Simpson proceeded on draft to U.K. STRENGTH 37 Offs 719 O.Rs.	Increase 2 O.R. rejoined from Hosp.
— do —	3rd Feb.		Training modified owing to no working parties being furnished. No. 1 A. Coy to Rifle Range. Bn formed working parties night previous commenced at 10 a.m. & finished at 11.30 a.m. Bombers working parties furnished by 4 after bays. Received following reinforcements on our wounded scheme from 20th N.F. 5 Offs. 50 O.R's. 21st N.F. 7 Offs 150 O.R's 26th N.F. 1 Off. & 8 O.R's. Weather continues fine & cold. Lieut J. Pears reported from Base. STRENGTH 50 Offs. 1004 & O.Rs. Lieut S. Hepworth proceeded to Boulogne in connection reorganization N & B. Reinforcement from base.	Increase 13 Offs 208 O.Rs Reinforce. 1 Offs. rejoined from base 2 Hosp Sick
— do —	4th Feb.		Continuance of Training. Pte B.T. Bombing Rifle training until 11.30 a.m. Coy B. carried on building Walls round huts for protection against bombs. 1 Off 50 O.Rs on working party burying water pipes. Also carried out reorganization consequent on reinforcement received. Recreational training during afternoon. STRENGTH 50 Offs 1001 O.Rs. Weather conditions good	Decrease 3 O.R sick 1 Off Hospital 2 N.R. Casually to Hosp 3
— do —	5th Feb.		Programme of training as given. D. Coy R.B.T. Range; C. Coy R.B.T. B. Co. wiring; A. Co. Rout. March. Received draft during afternoon. 2 privately detained still good. 1 Off & 50 O.R's furnished for work. Burying water pipes. STRENGTH 50 Offs 1001 O.Rs	

Army Form C. 2118.

WAR DIARY
INTELLIGENCE SUMMARY.
(Erase heading not required.)

Instructions regarding War Diaries and Intelligence Summaries are contained in F.S. Regs., Part II. and the Staff Manual respectively. Title pages will be prepared in manuscript.

Place	Date 1918	Hour	Summary of Events and Information	Remarks and references to Appendices
York Lines, trench map 51 B SW M 12 B	6th Feb		Inspection of Bn by Comdg Officer. Even Marching order training continued until 11.30 a.m. 300 men Employment at 2 p.m. afternoon furnished for working parties on HENIN-HEMEL, Trench, turnouts on 2 b/m rationals. Visited by G.O.C Division, down accompanying Divisional Staff Officer & Commander. Remaining hours of afternoon for rest men not on working parties. STRENGTH. 50 Offrs. 1,018 O.R. No casualties.	Increase 17 O.R. from 2.5th N.F.
— do —	7th Feb		Training continued from 9 to 11 a.m. working parties furnished 6 Offrs 12 Sgts 300 men for completing work on HENIN E & L switch, proceeded 2 p.m. returned 11 p.m. Weather conditions good. Recreational training during afternoon. STRENGTH. 49 Offrs 1,022 O.R.	Decrease. 2/Lt Thompson to 14 R.S. (Sick) Joined (Sick) 2. O.R. draft 3 O.R. Casuals.
	8th Feb		Training as follows. P.T. & T. Lewis Gun Training. Bayonet Bombing. Wiring. Weather conditions fair, hundreds of men sent during the morning, arranged to 300 N.C.O. men in tickets, during the afternoon Remainder of N.C.O. men continued recreational training. STRENGTH. 49 Offrs. 1,021 O.R. (Sick) 10 R. to Hosp. (Sick) Capt W.M. Brooks proceeded on leave to U.K.	
York Lines 9th until 9.30 a.m. BLAIRVILLE remainder of day.	9th		Proceeded by Route march to BLAIRVILLE distance 6 kilos. Completed by Bayonet Contact & Divisional Cyclists en route. On arrival accommodated in huts, no overcrowding. Fresh inspection revealed very poor state of billets. Transport arrangements very good. Bn utilized a portion of meals at S.M. CHEQERS. Latrine arrangements and absentees taken of same. STRENGTH. 50 Offrs. 1,023 O.R. Increase Capt Higgins posted 2 O.R. returned to duty from Hosp.	
BLAIRVILLE 10th Feb until 9 a.m. BARLY remainder of day.	10th Feb		Marched from BLAIRVILLE to BARLY distance 17 kilometres. 1 man fell out. Bn arrived by ambulance in billets monthly drawn up for huts. Bn went cooked on the march and ready for consumption at meal. Weather conditions quite good. Capt. Matthews proceeded to U.K. on leave. STRENGTH. 50 Offrs. 1,023 O.R. No change.	
BARLY to PENIN	11th Feb	10.15 a.m.	March route from BARLY to PENIN. distance (10 kilometres) no falling out. Accommodation on arrival considered billets mostly barns, were found to be in a very dirty condition. Latrine accommodation insufficient. Village of the usual style, small and straggling considerable...	

STRENGTH. 50 Offrs. 1,021 O.R. Decrease 2 O.R.

WAR DIARY or INTELLIGENCE SUMMARY

Army Form C. 2118.

Place	Date 1918	Hour	Summary of Events and Information	Remarks and references to Appendices
PENIN Ref. Map. FRANCE 51.C. EDITION 2	12th Feb		Physical Training one hour in the morning. Coy Officers inspected billets and made a few re-arrangements. Inspected the billets contained baths, which require repair. Drill grounds inspected and found quite suitable for Coy parade drills. The Rifle range was also visited and found to be a good amount of repair and supply of targets required. Programme of work submitted to Brigade. NCO's down with heavy colds drawn & making situation comfortable. STRENGTH 50 Offrs 1021. Nochange. Capt Keech & P. McEwan reported from leave.	
do	13/2/18		Indoor training owing to inclement weather. Heavy rain all morning. Visited by Divisional & Bgde Cmdr's. Inspection of billets. Arrangements made to improve Latrine accomodation. Increment availed. Targets made for Rifle Range. Training point improved. STRENGTH 50 Offrs 1018. Decrease 5 O.R. Increase 2 OR from Hosp. 2/Lt Rifle M.C. proceeded on leave G.U.K. Capt Selek reported from leave.	
do	14/2/18		Training continued. One Coy commenced firing certain practices of M.C. Remaining Coys P.+G.T. Coy Drill Lewis Gun Training. Capt Keech proceeded to Bt. of Instruction to transfer to Home Est. 6 hrs this time. Weather conditions good. STRENGTH 50 Officers 1015. Increase 3 O.R. Hosp. Decrease 6 O.R. 3 to Hosp (Sick) 3 to U.K. for commission	
do	15/2/18		Training continued on previous days lines. Weather conditions very favourable. Bgd inspected under Bgd arrangements completed on full cleanliness drill. STRENGTH 49 Offrs 1014. Decrease 1 O.R. to Rgt Est.	
do	16/2/18		Training carried on similar lines to previous days. Company Muster carried out by Rifle Range. Weather conditions favourable. Trench out and visited during the day by Brigade Comdr. STRENGTH 49 Offrs 1012 O.R. Decrease 2 O.R.S. to Hosp. (Sick)	
do	17/2/18		Church Parade. Repairs to Rifle Range C.O. Inspected Br Billets & found them very clean. 2/Lt Regar rejoined from leave. STRENGTH 49 Offrs 1011. Decrease 1 O.R. to Hosp. Sick.	
do	18/2/18		Continued training A Coy wiring B Coy Brigade Rifle Range C Coy wiring Thursday, D Coy B. Rifle Range B Coy Bathing in the afternoon. D Coy afternoon being Gun Teams inspected by Bgde Bombs Offr. Col. H. Sir Thomas Oliver also present. A Coy carried out the G.R.A. Platoon competition during the afternoon. STRENGTH 49 Offrs 1011. Nochange.	

Army Form C. 2118.

WAR DIARY
INTELLIGENCE SUMMARY.
(Erase heading not required.)

Instructions regarding War Diaries and Intelligence Summaries are contained in F. S. Regs., Part II. and the Staff Manual respectively. Title pages will be prepared in manuscript.

Place	Date	Hour	Summary of Events and Information	Remarks and references to Appendices
PE NIN. Map Reference	19/2/18		Training carried on. Bn D Coy on Brigade Rifle Range and bathing. C Coy carried on as R of B Platoon. Calisthenics. Weather conditions good. Lent from during the night. STRENGTH. 49 Offrs O.R. 1007. Decrease 2 O.R's trans. to Hosp. Rest. 3 G. Hosp. (Sick)	
FRANCE Sheet 51.C.Sd. 2	20/2/18		Brigadier visited O.R. from Hosp. Brigade commander inspected D Coy on attack scheme and expressed his pleasure at their cleanliness & afterwards the battalion inspected the Boy Scouts and expressed his pleasure with same. Brigade Guard Mounting was held at 11 am A Coy field kits and who very keenly. Brigade Band who inspected the Bugands and admired the class. N.C.O. and returned by the bn. Brigade Bombs who inspected on the parade. States with this Coy Mess. Coy Cmdrs where occupied or employed in the parade. STRENGTH. 48 Offrs 997 O.R. Decrease 10 O.R. U.K. during demobilisation. 7 to Hosp. Sick 11 from 6 IN M.B.C. 1 from 29th Mf.E.	
do	21/2/18		Continued Bn training and result of numerous visits noticeable in A Coy. which expresses with their candidly considered incomparable in the Division quite noticeable to anyone who was present for and from 9 G. to 12 pm. for was on Parade. Working parties from 2 & 6 & 9 pm. Friendly match appointed. No sick this pictured. Hop Drains 13 G Hosp (Sick) STRENGTH. 48 Offrs 976 O.R. Trans. to D.K.P. 6 months Home Service 1 O.R. trans. to O.R. p.m.	
do	22/2/18		Training continued. Weather conditions good. Lewis Guns turned out for the hour under B.P.G. Officers. Bn drill performed during the morning & various items. Bys Offrs in the Afternoon STRENGTH. 48 Offrs 973 O.R's. Decrease 2 O.R's transf. to Hosp. Sick. G. Holiday appreciated on Genl. G.U.K. G. Simpson returned from hosp.	
do	23/2/18		Bn inspected by the Comdg Officer Brass Morning Golden. Boys drill turned out and only a number of small details require attention. Officer H.Q. Inspection. Bn marched past in Column of Coys and Platoons of Platoons. Bay Diffi scheme in the evening. STRENGTH 48 Offrs 973 No change.	
do	24/2/18		Church Parade Inspection of Rolls. Weather conditions good. Capt Coddo appointed from Ean. STRENGTH 48 Offrs 973 O.R's. Decrease 2 O.R to Hosp. (sick) Increase 2 1.C.s hosp. from 20th N.F.	
do	25/2/18		Training continued. Weather conditions good. Lewis Guns on Rifle Range. Two boys at drill. P.G.R.T. and free lectures. Bn orders received. Two boys ev. confirmed. STRENGTH 48 Offrs 971 Decrease 2 O.R's G Hosp. (Sick)	

WAR DIARY

INTELLIGENCE SUMMARY

Place	Date	Hour	Summary of Events and Information	Remarks and references to Appendices
PENIN Ref Map LENS Sheet 11. Ed. 2.	26/1/18		Carried out training on similar lines as yesterday weather conditions good. Nothing important to report. STRENGTH. 48 Offrs 974 O.R. Lecture R.S.M. Blindon and C.S.M. Jones & issued from Hosp: The Bengali was inspected by the Corps Commander who expressed his satisfaction at the turn out of the Bgn.	
— do — POMMIER	27/1/18	9 am 2 pm	Proceeded by march route to POMMIER. Distance 11 miles. Before assembled falling out on arrival. Coy accommodated in barns. Farms very clean & comfortable. STRENGTH. 48 Offrs 978 German 3. O.R. Weather conditions good.	
— do — HAMELINCOURT	28/1/18	8.30 am 2.30 pm	Proceeded by march route to HAMELINCOURT. Distance 10 miles very bad roads. 5 men fell out en route. Coy arrived accommodated in Huthmits in good repair & clean. Weather cold taking snow. STRENGTH. 48 Offrs 972 No change. SgT Potwin reported on completion of Signalling Course.	

Murray Mayo
Commandant 23rd Bn North'n Fus.

34th Division.
102nd Infantry Brigade.

23rd BATTALION

THE NORTHUMVERLAND FUSILIERS

MARCH 1918

MARCH 1918.   VOLUME N° 3.   Army Form C. 2118.

102/34

WAR DIARY
or
INTELLIGENCE SUMMARY.
23rd Bn: NORTHUMBERLAND FUSILIERS.
(Erase heading not required.)

Instructions regarding War Diaries and Intelligence Summaries are contained in F. S. Regs., Part II. and the Staff Manual respectively. Title pages will be prepared in manuscript.

WH 27

Place	Date	Hour	Summary of Events and Information	Remarks and references to Appendices
Ref Map LENS. II.	1		Battalion in Camp at CIONMEL LINES, HAMELINCOURT. — Training carried out.	GR
	2		23rd NF relived 2/6 SHERWOOD FORESTERS (78th BRIGADE) in Brigade Reserve, Right Sector, Centre Section, this Battalion occupying the Sunken Road in B.25.b. Capt S.H. MATTHEWS returned from leave. Lt N.B. PIGG, M.C. from leave. 2/Lt S. HEPWORTH from Reinforcement Camp, BOULOGNE.	GR
	3		Working parties in front line, and constructing shelters. 2/Lt E.J. ROBSON to leave.	GR
	4		Working parties to front line, and constructing shelters	GR

Army Form C. 2118.

WAR DIARY
or
INTELLIGENCE SUMMARY.
(Erase heading not required.)

Instructions regarding War Diaries and Intelligence Summaries are contained in F. S. Regs., Part II. and the Staff Manual respectively. Title pages will be prepared in manuscript.

Place	Date	Hour	Summary of Events and Information	Remarks and references to Appendices
	5		2/Lt. A. LAMBERT from leave. Working parties to front line, & constructing shelter	GR
	6		2/Lt. CHARLTON from leave. Working parties to front line & constructing shelters	GR
	7		Relieved by 10th LINCOLNS and marched to CLONMELL LINES arriving 10.30 pm. Casualties — NIL	GR
	8		Training programme carried out. 2/Lt. S. F. EGAN from hospital	GR

Army Form C. 2118.

WAR DIARY
or
INTELLIGENCE SUMMARY.
(Erase heading not required.)

Instructions regarding War Diaries and Intelligence Summaries are contained in F. S. Regs., Part II. and the Staff Manual respectively. Title pages will be prepared in manuscript.

Place	Date	Hour	Summary of Events and Information	Remarks and references to Appendices
	9		Training programme carried out. Summer time came into operation at 11 P.M.	C/R
	10		Training programme carried out.	C/R
	11		Training programme carried out. Warning order received to be ready to move into positions on receipt of word "BATTLE". 2/Lt. J. LINDSAY from Hospital. Lt. A. HARVEY from leave. 2/Lt. E. J. WILMOTT, T. C. ROBSON and P. C. ROGERS from 26th N.F. joined for duty. Capt HERON on leave.	C/R
	12		Battalion moved up to assembly positions. Bellisle under Major H. H. NEEVES, DSO, MC. at ERVILLERS. Bn. HQ. T.7.d 4.6 NE.	C/R

WAR DIARY or INTELLIGENCE SUMMARY.

Army Form C. 2118.

Place	Date	Hour	Summary of Events and Information	Remarks and references to Appendices
	13.		Heavy Bombardment kept up for 5 hours. Large No. of gas shells were. Training programme carried out except in this position.	CJR
	14.		Training programme carried out.	CJR
	15.		2/Lt. W.L. BOWMAN and W.R.T. COLE from Course. Training programme carried out	CJR
	16.		2/Lt. LEATHARD from Hospital. Training programme carried out	CJR

Army Form C. 2118.

WAR DIARY
or
INTELLIGENCE SUMMARY.
(Erase heading not required.)

Instructions regarding War Diaries and Intelligence Summaries are contained in F. S. Regs., Part II. and the Staff Manual respectively. Title pages will be prepared in manuscript.

Place	Date	Hour	Summary of Events and Information	Remarks and references to Appendices
	17.		Training programme carried out.	CJR
	18.	9/30	Battalion moved forward to front line commencing 3pm. Bad weather. Lt F. LEATHARD to Hospital. Capt DOUGLAS from course.	CJR
	19	9/15	C. J. ROBSON from leave.	CJR
	20.	11pm 9/15	Enemy aeroplanes flew over back areas dropping red lights. Lt. LINDSAY on leave.	CJR

Army Form C. 2118.

WAR DIARY
or
INTELLIGENCE SUMMARY.
(Erase heading not required.)

Instructions regarding War Diaries and Intelligence Summaries are contained in F. S. Regs., Part II and the Staff Manual respectively. Title pages will be prepared in manuscript.

Place	Date	Hour	Summary of Events and Information	Remarks and references to Appendices
	21	2 AM	Enemy bombarded our lines for about ½ an hour, chiefly support line.	
		3.30 AM	Similar bombardment.	
		5 AM	Heavy bombardment with gas shells and high explosives	
		7 AM	Intense bombardment continued. (this bombardment must be termed bombardment from 5-7 am)	
		9 AM	Atmosphere clear of gas - still heavy shelling with H.E. and shrapnel. Bombardment kept up till about 10.30 a.m. At this time no attack on our front had been made.	
		12 noon	Rifle, MG fire and bombing heard on the high ground between ECOUST and ST LEGER.	
		2 PM	Fighting on high ground between ECOUST & ST LEGER and Railway embankment in U.24.A.	
		5.30 PM	Enemy had occupied Sunken Road and Rly in U.25.A. to T.24.d	

Army Form C. 2118.

WAR DIARY
or
INTELLIGENCE SUMMARY.
(Erase heading not required.)

Instructions regarding War Diaries and Intelligence Summaries are contained in F. S. Regs., Part II. and the Staff Manual respectively. Title pages will be prepared in manuscript.

Place	Date	Hour	Summary of Events and Information	Remarks and references to Appendices
	21	6.30pm	Remaining personnel of 23rd NF with 22nd NF retired to FACTORY AN where touch was effected with the 15th RBs.	JR
	22		2/Lt Pygg and 40 men proceeded to SUPPORT LINE, CROISELLES SWITCH T.17.9.90.15. Message received that enemy were getting around right flank. A retirement took place to HILL SWITCH and at 3 pm to front line of 3rd system. This party relieved by the 31st BF at 3.30 am on 23rd and joined details at MOYENVILLE. In retirement from 3rd system 2nd Lieut Moorleage and 2/Lt Pygg lost touch with each other. Capt Moorleage with 3 officers & about 10 men remained in the 3rd system until 2nd Scots Guards until relieved on the evening of 23rd March.	JR

Army Form C. 2118.

WAR DIARY
or
INTELLIGENCE SUMMARY.
(Erase heading not required.)

Instructions regarding War Diaries and Intelligence Summaries are contained in F. S. Regs., Part II. and the Staff Manual respectively. Title pages will be prepared in manuscript.

Place	Date	Hour	Summary of Events and Information	Remarks and references to Appendices
	22		Details moved at 6 pm to huts near BUCQUOY. Rejoined by a number of Officers & OR who had just been relieved in the line, in charge of Capt MORLIDGE.	CJR
	23		Marched to BERLES-AU-BOIS. Received draft of 185 OR from 24th N.F. 2/Lt E.T. ROGERS to hospital.	CJR
	24		Marched to LIGNEREUIL. Lt TERRY returned from leave.	CJR
	25		Marched to VILLERS L'HOPITAL. Major H.M. NEEVES DSO, M.C. appointed Lieut Colonel.	CJR

A7092 Wt. W128.9/M1293. 750,000. 1/17. D. D & I. Ltd. Forms/C2118/14.

Army Form C. 2118.

WAR DIARY
or
INTELLIGENCE SUMMARY.
(Erase heading not required.)

Instructions regarding War Diaries and Intelligence Summaries are contained in F.S. Regs., Part II and the Staff Manual respectively. Title pages will be prepared in manuscript.

Place	Date	Hour	Summary of Events and Information	Remarks and references to Appendices
	26.		Marched to FREVENT and spent the night in station.	CYR
	27.		Entrained at 8AM at FREVENT. Detrained at STEENBECQUE (Ref. Map HAZEBROUCK SA) and marched to billets at HAVERSKERQUE. Some rain.	CYR
	28.		Marched to billets at RUE DU BOIS.	CYR
	29.		Marched to NEUF BERQUIN. Complimentary letters from Divisional & Brigade Commanders received (see copies attached)	CYR

Army Form C. 2118.

WAR DIARY
or
INTELLIGENCE SUMMARY.
(Erase heading not required.)

Instructions regarding War Diaries and Intelligence Summaries are contained in F. S. Regs., Part II. and the Staff Manual respectively. Title pages will be prepared in manuscript.

Place	Date	Hour	Summary of Events and Information	Remarks and references to Appendices
	30.		Marched to LA ROLANDERIE FARM, ERQUINGHEM, and relieved 9th N.F. in Brigade Reserve.	GR
	31.		Interior economy. "B" & "C" Coys took over billets in ERQUINGHEM.	GR

AW Humphrys
Lt Col
Commanding
23rd Bn NORTHUMBERLAND FUSILIERS.

WAR DIARY
or
INTELLIGENCE SUMMARY.

Army Form C. 2118.

(Erase heading not required.)

Instructions regarding War Diaries and Intelligence Summaries are contained in F. S. Regs. Part II. and the Staff Manual respectively. Title pages will be prepared in manuscript.

Place	Date	Hour	Summary of Events and Information	Remarks and references to Appendices
			Officers.	
			2/Lt. W. T. Lewis — Wounded.	
			2/Lt. H. C. Hammond — Missing believed killed	
			2/Lt. J. Wilson —	
			Lieut. J. G. Rodgers —	
			Capt. J. F. V. Wiggans —	
			2/Lt. H. Johnson — Missing	
			2/Lt. R. V. Cole — Believed	
			Capt. S. H. Bowles MC — Wounded	
			Lieut. M. Dodds —	
			Lieut. W. Watson MC —	
			2/Lt. W. Rowman —	
			2/Lt. Boyd —	
			A. Lambert —	
			Casualties	
			Lt. Col. L. Charlton — Wounded	
			Lieut. C. P. Howell —	Believed Prisoners.
			Lt. R. Jefferson —	
			2/Lt. H. A. Davies —	
			2/Lt. B. Wilmot —	
			O.R.	
			57. Wounded	
			375 Missing	

KNOWLES AID POST 15.19 y.5.b.

20/3/18.	1 P.M.	German Gotha flying direct from our back areas into enemy territory dropping red lights about every five minutes. The night very quiet indeed.
21-3-18.	2 AM.	Enemy bombardment of our lines for about half an hour.
	3.30 AM.	Similar bombardment for about the same period.
	5 AM.	Very heavy bombardment commenced, the majority of shells falling about the aid post being gas. Gas quickly penetrated dug out and gas curtains lowered.
	7 AM	Gas still very thick outside and shelling intense especially along support trench and sunken road from CROIX-CIRCUS to CROISELLES.
	9 AM	Atmosphere much clearer. Shelling now all HE and Shrapnel.
	12 noon	Rifle, Machine Gun fire and Bombing heard on the high ground between ECOUST and ST LEGER.
	2 PM.	Increased fighting in above mentioned ground where a large number of men could be seen. Much rifle fire from our men about the Railway embankment in U 24 d.

EXTRACT

Ref Map. CROISILLES (Special Sheet).

Information as to operations on the 21st 22nd and 23rd March 1918.

Date	Time	
		D Coy were reserve Coy to Left Forward Battⁿ of Right Brigade.
		Disposition. Whole company were in RAILWAY embankment between U.25.a.70.55 to U.25.b.40.25.
		Orders. Coy was to be in STAND TO position in STRAY RESERVE by 5 AM on the morning of the 21st ult.
21-3-18	5.10 AM	A very heavy bombardment was opened out along the whole front.
	6.30 PM	After consultations with Capts. Mark and Morledge it was decided to retire and form defence in FACTORY AV. This retirement took place and touch was obtained with 15th R.S. in FACTORY AV.
22-3-18		I was sent with 1 Officer & 40 men in support to CROISELLES SWITCH NORTH at T.17.a.90.15. Touch was obtained with 25th N.F. on right and 16th R.S. in trench about T.17.A.60.70. A message was received from 25th NF that the enemy were getting round their right flank.

At same time the 16th R.S. retired up SONREN.
RD running through T.17a (Hendon Rd).
put a Vickers gun into action to cover right
flank of 25th N.F. Place T.17a 80.20. I informed
Capt Morledge of the situation, a retirement
took place up Sunken Rd and another stand
was made on HILL SWITCH. Touch was obtained
with 11th Suffolks on our left. Vickers guns &
Lewis Guns were pushed out in front of the line
of HENIN HILL. Capt Morledge assumed command
A retirement took place about 8 pm to front
line of 3rd system. On this retirement I lost
touch with Capt Morledge. On arrival at
3rd System I reported to Major FRACIS 18 NF
and was put into line on the right of his
Battn with 2/Lt Bailey & 25 men.
I endeavoured to get into touch with Bgde
but failed. I was relieved by the WEST
YORKS about 3.30 AM on 23rd. 31 DIVN
relieved 34 Div. I reported to 23rd Battn
details at MOYNEVILLE about 5.15 AM.

34th Divn. No. A/222.

COPY

1. The following letter has been received from the G.O.C. VIth Corps, dated 23rd March:—

   "The heavy loss the 34th Division has suffered and the trying work that has fallen upon it during the last three days, makes it unavoidable that it should leave the VIth Corps. Will you please thank all ranks for their work during the opening stage of the great battle now in progress. The task that they had to carry out was not an easy one, and I fear that their losses have been great."

2. On my own behalf, I wish to record my high appreciation of the gallantry and the stubborn power of resistance shewn by all ranks and arms of the Division on the 21st and 22nd March.

3. When the full story of those days is known, the gallant fight of the 102nd Brigade and part of the 101st Brigade on the 21st March when outflanked and almost surrounded, the stubborn and protracted resistance of the 11th Suffolks on the left of the Division on the 21st and 22nd March and the steady disciplined gallantry of the 103rd Brigade on the 21st and 22nd March will go down to history among the greatest achievements of the War.

4.   A separate order has already been issued to the Artillery of the Division, and it is only necessary to say here that their conduct was worthy of the highest traditions of the Royal Regiment.

5.   The 34th M.G. Battalion, recently organised as it is, laid, during the 21st and 22nd March, the foundation of a tradition of its own. No higher praise can be given to it than to say that the orders issued to the Battalion, that each gun was to be fought to the last man and the last round of ammunition, were carried out in all cases, in the spirit of the order and in many cases, to the letter of the order.

6.   As admirable as the gallantry displayed in action, has been the high standard of discipline, endurance and cheerfulness shown by all during the days which have elapsed since the Division was withdrawn from the line.

During these days also, the work of the ASC carried out under great difficulties, has been beyond all praise.

It is now necessary for the Division again to go into the line, but I feel more than ever confident that no call can be made upon the 34th Division which will not be instantly and cheerfully responded to.

(Sgd) J. Nicholson
Major General
Commanding 34th Division.

29th March 1918.

Copy

The Officer Commanding
23rd Bn. Northumberland Fuslrs.

It is with great pride in my Brigade that I read our Divisional Commander's appreciation of the good work done by it.
Your Battalion did magnificently against great odds and I am full of admiration for the fine fighting spirit which it displayed.
I very much regret your losses but I am confident that the Germans suffered far more heavily at your hands.

(Sgd) M. Thomson
Brigadier-General
Cdg 102nd Infantry Brigade.

31-3-18.

34th Division.
102nd Infantry Brigade

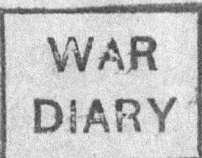

23rd BATTALION

NORTHUMBERLAND FUSILIERS

APRIL 1 9 1 8

WAR DIARY
23rd NORTHUMBERLAND FUSILIERS
VOLUME 4
INTELLIGENCE SUMMARY
APRIL 1918

Army Form C. 2118.
Vol 28

Place	Date	Hour	Summary of Events and Information	Remarks and references to Appendices
Ref Map Sheet 36 NW ¼ etc 23rd in Div Res	April 1/18		102 Bde in Divisional Reserve. Battn in Camp at LA ROLANDERIE Farm H.N.C.S.S. Company training; special training of Lewis Gunners and Signallers. 2Lt Latham returned to duty from hospital and joined "C" Coy. — Transport lines near STEENWERCK. — Brigade HQ at H.4.c 3.7.	
	2nd		B & C Coys moved to billets in village of ERQUINGHEM leaving A & D & Bn HQ at LA ROLADERIE FARM. General training programme carried out. — Lt L E Ward proceeded from VI Corps Signal School & took over duties of Sig. Off. — Proceeding 131 O.R. recruits and proba to Coys (see Part II)	
	3rd		Bn under training and reorganisation. Parades included Gas Drill, and special parades namely, Special training of Signallers, Lewis Gunners and Junior N.C.O's. Capt. A. W. McClintock (21 NF) attached and assumed duties of 2nd in Command. At 11.A.m slight effect of Mustard Gas felt being about ten minutes — also felt in vicinity probably continuing a kind of Mustard Gas.	
	4th		Training programme carried out. — Officers Reconaissance made to the HOULINES Sector and the BRIDGE HEADS in vicinity of ERQUINGHEM in accordance with plans — Scheme. Transport & Q.M. staff also reconnoitred route to new area and arranged 102 Bde. O.O. No 200 received. — Gas Helmets inspected by Bn Gas Officer. Inspection Satisfactory. Capt T. E. Heron M.G. returned from leave and took over duties of the Capt.	

PART II

2nd April.   Draft 131 ORs posted to Coys as unders.
                     A. 34   B. 32
                     C. 33   D. 32

3/9086 Pte Cannan T.S. posted to A Sqy
59094   Dean J. from Hospital

PUNISHMENTS.

38942 McLauren P.   2: 3.18 Using obscene language to a NCO.   2½ F.P. No 1
50193 Dixon   31.3.18 Absent from Parade   7 days C.B.
22962 Stony   31.3.18 R Drunkenness   F.G.C.M.

WAR DIARY
INTELLIGENCE SUMMARY.
(Erase heading not required.)

Army Form C. 2118.

Instructions regarding War Diaries and Intelligence Summaries are contained in F.S. Regs., Part II. and the Staff Manual respectively. Title pages will be prepared in manuscript.

Place	Date	Hour	Summary of Events and Information	Remarks and references to Appendices
	5/4/18		Lewis Gunners training on range near FROUINGHEM CHURCH. – Rest of Bn in reserve – first part weather fine, latter part wet – 2/Lt Falon and 3rd O.R. proceeded to join the 102 Bn's sleeping boy. At 7 pm Bn proceeded to the HOUPLINES Sector (subsection wetor) and relieved the 16th Royal Scots. – 11th Suffolks took over LATTARANDERIE FARM, Bn H.Q. near Houplines Station. – Brigade H.Q. B29.b.6.0. JUTE FACTORY. A Coy Right Front line, B Coy Support, D Coy Reserve. 2/Lt Unie, 2/Lt P Hughes & 7/Lt Henry on carried out patrols in N.M.L. Laid parties out each morning. At 1.30 am Gas projection discharged from neighbourhood of LEITH WALK. Bn. O.P. established at POPPY BANK.	
Rt mdl. HOUPLINES No ooo	6th			
	7th			
	8th			
	9th		Enemy shelled Armentieres with 2500 Gas shells; this bombardment lasting through the evening. Our area not affected, our ration wagons slightly delayed. Another S.O.S. N.S. Easter portion of Town. No enemy Enemy activity, getting more active front of line at times considerable bombardment by A & C Coy Zones – weather wet, & sharp – Active patrolling each night – troops on wire and general repairs – Very heavy bombardment of front of Division on our Right.	
	4-14am		Right commenced. At 1-10 pm received message BM 154 attack & getting underground enemy front bombarded chiefly in vicinity of CEMETERY about 2000 hops went over on sight & left – bombardment of NEWBURN LANE C.28.6.0.3 & building near SugarCtrl.1.5	

Army Form C. 2118.

WAR DIARY
or
INTELLIGENCE SUMMARY.
(Erase heading not required.)

Instructions regarding War Diaries and Intelligence Summaries are contained in F. S. Regs., Part II. and the Staff Manual respectively. Title pages will be prepared in manuscript.

Place	Date	Hour	Summary of Events and Information	Remarks and references to Appendices
	9/11/18		Enemy trench mortars were active near PANAMA CANAL & WESSEX AV. — Enemy planes active during evening. — 4 Prisoners captured in our front system — deserters near No 14 post.	C/R
		5 pm	Further aviation report to effect that enemy were in BAC ST MAUR.	C/R
	note	6 am	Dawn patrol reported no unusual movement.	C/R
		10.30 "	Very heavy bombardment in front of Brigade on our left — enemy advance had been launched in that area — nothing developed on our front.	C/R
		2 pm	Enemy shelled our BHQ heavily and buildings near river evidently searching for our batteries. — Ref Map CROIX DE BAC.	C/R
		2.50	Order received to withdraw to the ESTAIRES–LYS Line. This was carried out by the 23rd N.F. following the 22nd N.F. Withdrawal carried out in orderly manner. All stores & trench material destroyed before leaving. — Dispositions in the ESTAIRES LYS Line were as under:	C/R
			Capt Douglas	
			2Lt Cox B Coy MANCHESTER POST	
			Lt N.B. Pegg C Coy Astride Road between B & C Coys	
			Capt Mortridge D Coy BURNLEY POST	
			A Coy Astride Road in NIEPPE SWITCH	

WAR DIARY
or
INTELLIGENCE SUMMARY
(Erase heading not required.)

Army Form C. 2118.

Instructions regarding War Diaries and Intelligence Summaries are contained in F. S. Regs., Part II. and the Staff Manual respectively. Title pages will be prepared in manuscript.

Place	Date	Hour	Summary of Events and Information	Remarks and references to Appendices
	11/4/18		Enemy had crossed River LYS during the night and attacked our forward posts early, securing the buildings in PONT de NIEPPE, driving a long wedge between Reserves and front line at same time frontal attack on our position from the river side	
		4-0am	One enemy plane brought down by M.G. fire. One of ours also down. Battle continued throughout the day, but enemy kept in check at NIEPPE System, and attacks repulsed. Order was received to drop back from that salient to M. DE SEULE line. Good work by Runners getting orders to front line. Battalion H.Q. formed rearguard for the withdrawal. Bn marched back along the main BAILLEUL ARMENTIERES Rd & a Bn bivouac at junction of NEUVE EGLISE – DE SEULE Rd. Bivouac in field for NIGHT.	
	12th	6.0am	Dispositions received from Brigade H.Q. our line (practically Bn) on outskirts of BAILLEUL ARMENTIERES Rd comprised B.H.Q. at B – A Road. Disposition of Coys A Right, B Centre, C Support, D Left. Bn placed at disposal of 88 Brigade. Enemy shelled our area during the day – NEUVE EGLISE – DE SEULE (confused) as Bn – orders received to re-establish line –	
	13/4/18		Bn moved up, found line re-established. Under return to move Bn to a position parallel to and in front of DE SEULE – NEUVE EGLISE line –	

WAR DIARY
or
INTELLIGENCE SUMMARY.
(Erase heading not required.)

Army Form C. 2118.

Instructions regarding War Diaries and Intelligence Summaries are contained in F. S. Regs., Part II. and the Staff Manual respectively. Title pages will be prepared in manuscript.

Place	Date	Hour	Summary of Events and Information	Remarks and references to Appendices
Ref Map Sheet 28.S.W.			Order rec'd:- OC 13th NF (1) You will move your Battalion and occupy a position parallel to and in front of the DE SEULE - NEUVE EGLISE ROAD. (2) The following routes are available: (a) The main BAILLEUL - ARMENTIERES Road. (B) The Broad gauge and Narrow gauge Railway which run parallel to each other from S.30.a.2.3. to T.25.d.6.3. (C) The DE BROEKEN ROAD (3) Headquarters R. Newfoundland Regt. and Monmouthshire Regt. were established at B.2.c.0.7. near Water Tower. You will attempt to restore the front line which runs East of PONT D'ACHELLES to B.2.a.D.5. to T.27.d.0.5. (Sig) T. McConnor Capt. (See Major 58 Inf Bde)	
	13th 8		This was carried out and the whole of the night was spent digging a new line. Wire was erected by the RNLD Our disposition on the morning of the 13th were as under:- D Coy Left B " Support A " Centre C " Right Observation very bad	

WAR DIARY
or
INTELLIGENCE SUMMARY.
(Erase heading not required.)

Army Form C. 2118.

Place	Date	Hour	Summary of Events and Information	Remarks and references to Appendices
	13.4.18	6.15 am	Enemy commenced attack at 6.15 a.m. from direction of wood about T.3.1.6. in a N.W. direction towards front of Bde on our left. When first seen was 350 × carrying across in full pack and carrying blankets — Our rifle and M.G. fire drove him off. He again attacked but was forced to retire into wood 4 Rats at T.7.3.0. in both attacks.	
		8 am	Situation was fairly quiet except for T.M.s occasional bombs falling in T.2.5.e.	
		9.30 am	Our line held firmly — Casualties at that hour slight.	
		10.45"	Enemy active sniping & T.M. Guns heavies retaliated	
		2.30 pm	Enemy shelling with heavies on BAILLEUL_ARM Rd. & firing with M.G. from direction of B.3.6.4.d.4.c.	
		3.15"	RNFLD patrol reconnoitred through T.21.b.97.9.c.5.6 & Northd. Huns Rd. mounted.	
			T.20.a. - along "Nieuwe Eglise Rd. to left of WORCESTER Regt...	
		4.05"	Enemy shelling T.25.c.	
		5.25	In view of dispersion forces of enemy massing on my left & right of front I have withdrawn my front line posts to the line of the Railway Embankment and Cap. If the situation demands it I shall eventually withdraw to the Auncalion of my men to the same line a.a.a. Please inform N.W.B. (Cdg Dnmken coys 2nd WORCESTER on). In view of this Lt Rigg was informed to swing around his left flank to organise with Worcesters	

(Copy of Wire) —

Army Form C. 2118.

WAR DIARY
or
INTELLIGENCE SUMMARY.
(Erase heading not required.)

Place	Date	Hour	Summary of Events and Information	Remarks and references to Appendices
	13/4/18	6.25 pm	Front line attacked violently & driven back to lines in rear. A gallant defence by Lt Riggs to the last moment. Line taken up in two lines 800 x in rear of Neuve Eglise – De Seule until ordered to withdraw to HILLE through FEURRE FARM with R NFLD following Rgts	C/R
	14th		Arrived at Keersebrom S 10.a.8.8. and had breakfast at camp. Bn HQ at Hille Farm. — 102 Bde. Composite Bn formed under command of Lt Col H H Heaves DSO M.C. — Comp Bn reorganised as under:	
			22nd N F Coy — Lt Harry 23rd N F Coy — 2Lt Vivier 25th N F Coy — 2Lt Coleby 2nd Motor MG's Attached 8 Vicker's Guns "	C/R
			At 11 a.m. Comp. Bn marched to position on S.2 & 3. and dug trenches there running through S.2.c.v.d & S.3.c.v.d. — Men rested as much as possible during the night. The 5.9 H Divn passed through our lines and proceeded to retire front line. Bn HQ in cottage S.2.b.6.6	C/B
	15th		Information was received that the 59th Divn were being withdrawn after this withdrawal the 34th Div became front line, with line from BAILLEUL to LOCRE – MONT NAIR Rd junction thence South.	

Army Form C. 2118.

WAR DIARY
or
INTELLIGENCE SUMMARY.
(Erase heading not required.)

Instructions regarding War Diaries and Intelligence Summaries are contained in F. S. Regs. Part II. and the Staff Manual respectively. Title pages will be prepared in manuscript.

Place	Date	Hour	Summary of Events and Information	Remarks and references to Appendices
	15/4/18		Corps took over dispositions as under —	
			23rd NF. Front line S3.a.n.S. to S3.a.S.L. mile	S.P.
			103 Bde on left of 7th Bde on Right. 2 platoons of 28th NF close support S3.a.9.9. and 2 platoons active Res S3.a.5.6. — 22nd NF Reserve M33.a.11.59.	
	16th	3h am	Heavy bombardment of Div on Right. — 102nd Comp Bn Front all quiet. The Comp Bn was withdrawn from line & marched to camp at Farm M33.c.11.2. —	2/9
			Remained there during day & put out protective patrols — Later took over disposition in reserve —	
		7 p.m.	Owing to heavy shelling Bn HQ moved to vicinity of M33.a. — returned at 10 p.m.	2/8
		10.45 p.m	100 C.R. 23rd NF under 2/Lt Vince proceeded to ST JANS CHAPEL — attached to Dukes of Wellington's Regt.	
			Bn HQ moved to 6164 Bde H.Q.	
	17th		Heavy shelling of whole area, M32, 33, 26, 27. —	
			Later relieved 7th Bde in the line — Dispositions were	2/7
			1 Coy 22nd NF — Right	
			1 " 28th " — Left	
			1 " 25th " — Close support	
			1 " 23rd " —	S.3.C.7.4
			1 Coy 22nd " — Reserve	S.3.a.3.9

WAR DIARY or INTELLIGENCE SUMMARY

Army Form C. 2118.

Place	Date	Hour	Summary of Events and Information	Remarks and references to Appendices
	17th/18th	5 pm	The party of 23rd NF attacked Avnk of Willaughts Redoubt returned. 2 x NCO's killed, 22nd NF wounded slightly. - 2 P Poltr 23rd NF 15 R & P killed.	O/R
	18th		Relieving of Front Carried out. Strength: 22nd NF Coy. 11 Off. 359 O.R. 23rd " 9 " 225 " 26th " 8 " 400 " B. H. Q. " 6 " 71 " Total 34 Off. 1055 O.R.	O/R
	19th	11.15 am	Quiet day. Intermittent shelling by enemy over area. Major H.E. Thomas, Suffolk Regt, attached commdg 25th NF, killed by shrapnel following Reg. Gas bombardment of area S&A by our artillery - Enemy remained quiet during morning and throughout the day except for slight shelling - 18th NF onelist double apron fence along front. - 21/24 F/N Vicker's machine (640s)	O/R
	20th		Except for occasional shells in vicinity of Camp B1. H.Q. & CROIX de Poperinghe a very quiet day - There was considerable aeroplane activity on both sides. - O.O. No 201 rec'd. Relieved by 401st French Infantry Regt. 3rd Bn. Body of Major H.E. Thomas buried & cross erected.	O/R
	21st		Relief by French was completed by 2 am - on relief Bn marched via the CROIX de POP - Mc.NAIR Road to PODEFORT. Assembly point. - Breakfast there. - Here the Camp Bn was broken up & the 102 Bde reorganised into 3 Bns - Bn continued march to Transport Lines.	O/R
	22nd	10 am	The 102 Bde marched to Road Camp - JAN du BIEZEN - and took over part of Road camp. Day spent in reorganisation of a number of men bathed at du Balec under Bn arrangements. Major Walker attached.	O/R

WAR DIARY
or
INTELLIGENCE SUMMARY.
(Erase heading not required.)

Army Form C. 2118.

Place	Date	Hour	Summary of Events and Information	Remarks and references to Appendices
	23/4/18		Morning spent in inspection and training. — At 12 noon inspection by the Div. Comdr. — In the course of a few remarks the General said he had a special message of thanks to convey to us on behalf of Gen. Plumer & Lt Gen. Hamilton Gordon. He also expressed warm appreciation & said he never felt so proud of the Div. as he did at that moment. He felt absolute confidence in the Div. (see copy of message attached).	A/R.
	24/4		Training & reorganization — Special parades of Lewis Gunners & Signallers — Enemy aircraft bombing actively in neighbourhood, but no damage caused in our camp	A/R
	25/4		34th Div. in adjacent camps. Training programme carried out during morning opened parades of Signallers & Lewis Gunners during P.M.; also Musketry in afternoon	
R/Mar		3.50pm	Situation reports overdue on the front — Ordered to "Stand to" — 6.15 p.m. and warned to be ready to move at a moment's notice — Stand down given 9 P.M.	A/R
Sheet 28 N.W.	26/4	1.30am	Major Wallace left for IX Corps Reinforcement Camp	A/R PERNES
			Warned to be ready to move. to move on notice of the Corps — Line NE of PERNES Training staff left with Transport — 8.30 marched off — Some hazy halts on road — but by casual chance arrived B.n 2h in marked Farm A 28 a 2.7	
		4.30 pm	and settled down in Camp there Orders received to move, but cancelled 4.30 p.m.	A/R
		5.30	Ordered to Stand to to await instructions	
		6.15	Moved on Cavalry Line running through G.9. — Bn H.Q. at G.9.C. Central	A/R

Army Form C. 2118.

WAR DIARY
or
INTELLIGENCE SUMMARY.
(Erase heading not required.)

Instructions regarding War Diaries and Intelligence
Summaries are contained in F. S. Regs., Part II.
and the Staff Manual respectively. Title pages
will be prepared in manuscript.

Place	Date	Hour	Summary of Events and Information	Remarks and references to Appendices
	27/8/18	2.00am	Enemy to heavy shelling by high velocity shells. Bn A/A moved to G & P C 8'5'- Intermittent shelling during day	C/R
		4.15pm	Received orders to cease work and be ready to move.	
		9-0pm	Bn relieved 10th Lincolns in BRANDHOEK LINE	
	28/t		Quiet relief. Bn H.Q. at farm G.17.c.5.8 along with Royal Scots who were also holding a portion of the BRANDHOEK LINE - Quiet day. Coys engaged under Supervision of R.E's in constructing outpost line and BRANDHOEK Syselem.	C/R
	29/t	7.30a	Heavy bombardment-Communion on left away to our front - shelling of our own & rear area. Heavy bombardment lasted all night and gradually slackened down in morning. Work under R.E's continued daily.	C/R
	30/t		Very quiet day - enemy artillery and M Guns inactive - our aeroplanes very active throughout the day. Coys working on the BRANDHOEK line.	C/R

M.W. Jervis
Lt. Col.
Commdg
23rd North'd FUS

A7092 Wt. W128.9/M1293. 750,000. 1/17. D. D & L. Ltd. Forms/C2118/14.

102nd Infantry Brigade.

Message begins:— G.759   16th   aaa

During 7 days heavy fighting and in the case of the 34th Division eight days the enemy has used 15 divisions in vainly attempting to break through the 9th Corps front. It is true that the enemy has gained ground but he has suffered very heavily indeed in the process. The Corps Commander again wishes to congratulate all ranks on their fine fighting qualities and on the tenacity all have shown in the defence. He also wishes to thank the staffs of Formations and the Signal Service for their untiring devotion to duty. Added all divisions.

G.O.C. 9th Corps.

Ends.

102nd Infantry Brigade.

Message begins:— G.760.   16th   a a a.

Following received from Corps. a.a.a.

The Corps Commander in addition to his congratulations on the qualities displayed during eight days heavy fighting by all ranks of the 34th Division and attached troops wishes specially to congratulate them and the 147th Inf Brigade on the complete repulse of the enemy attack on their front this afternoon aaa

Aaad 34th Div. Repeated 149th Div.

G.O.C. 9th Corps

Ends

Lieutenant-Colonel Reeves.
  Commanding Composite Battalion
    102nd Infantry Brigade

  For information. All ranks are to be informed.

(Sgd) J Trowbridge
Major
Brigade Major
102nd Infantry Brigade

17-4-1918

102nd Inf. Bde.

Following received from Corps:-

G.782.   Day of month - 17th.

The Commander-in-Chief has just been at Corps H.Q.. He would have liked to see all ranks now fighting on the 9th Corps front and to tell each one of them of his personal appreciation of the magnificent fight they have made and are making. He would have liked to shake hands with each individual and thank him for what he has done. He has no time for this but has asked me to give everybody this message.

Addressed all British Units and Formations 9th Corps.
From G.O.C. 9th Corps.

G.790.   Day of month - 17th.

The following message from General Plummer Commanding Second Army has been received.
Begins. I wish to place on record the gallant devotion to duty displayed by all units of the 9th Corps during the recent fighting. At the end of eight, and in the 34th Division, nine days fighting of the severest type the troops have maintained their positions all along the front against a much determined attack made by greatly superior numbers. I congratulate all ranks most heartily on their splendid performance and know I can rely on them to maintain their front with unceasing determination.   Ends.

The Corps Commander in forwarding this message wishes to add his own congratulations and to say how much he appreciates the gallantry shown by the troops under his command during the recent fighting.

Addressed all Divisions repeated Second Army.
From G.O.C. 9th Corps.

(Sgd) H.C. Marsh Capt
for Lt.Col. G.S.
34th Division

18th April 1918.

O.C.   B.M.C. 6.
102nd Bde Composite Battalion
    For information and communication to all ranks.
        (Sgd) J.B. Trowbridge Major
            Brigade Major
            102nd Infantry Brigade.

18-4-1918

First Army GS 1152.
Second Army No. G.56
XV Corps 128/18 G.

XV. Corps.

I wish to express my appreciation of the great bravery and endurance with which all ranks have fought and held out (during the last five days #) against overwhelming numbers.

It has been necessary to call for great exertions and more must still be asked for, but I am quite confident that, at this critical period when the existence of the British Empire is at stake, all ranks of the First Army will do their very best

First Army HQ
18-4-1918

(Sgd.) H.Horne General
Commanding First Army.

Four days 9th-12th April in the case of troops transferred to Second Army on 12-4-18 from First Army.

2

Second Army.

A Copy of an Order which I have issued is attached.

I should be glad if you would convey this message to the XV Corps and all troops who were transferred with it on the 12th April.

(Sgd) W.H.Anderson MG
for General
Commanding First Army.

B.M. C.3.

O.C.
102 Bde Composite Battalion

For information and communication to all ranks.

(Sgd) H.Trowbridge.
Major.
Brigade Major
102nd Infantry Brigade

18-4-1918.

34th Div. No A/222

The G.O.C. has received the following message from the C.R.A. 38th Divisional Artillery, and he wishes it communicated to all ranks of the Division.

It was received in response to a Special Order communicated to the 36th and 38th Divisional Artilleries.

(Sgd)

22/4/18.

Lieut. Colonel
A.A. & QMG, 34th Division

21st April 1918.

G.O.C.
34th Division

On behalf of the 38th Divisional Artillery and of the 36th Divisional Artillery, which have been attached during the last few days, I thank you for the very generous appreciation of their work.

If anything can inspire men to their maximum effort it is such a gallant stand as has been made by the 34th Division and attached Infantry Brigades through 13 days of battle.

I know that the Gunner Officers of 36th and 38th will always remember the 34th as a fine fighting Division.

(Sgd). J.E. Topping.
Brig. Gen.
38th Div. Artillery

Special Order of the Day
by
Major General. C. L. Nicholson. CB, CMG.
Commanding 34th Division.

22nd April 1918

General Sir H. O. Plumer, GCB, GCMG, GCVO, Commanding Second Army, and Lieut. General Sir A. Hamilton-Gordon, KCB. Commanding IXth Corps, have directed me to express to all ranks and arms of the Division their great admiration of the gallantry and tenacity shewn by all during the nine days continuous fighting in which the Division has just been engaged, and to say that the behaviour of the Division has had a large share in saving a very difficult situation. On my own behalf, I can only say that, proud of the Division as I have always been, I have never felt so proud of it, or felt such absolute confidence in it than I have done during these last few days. The behaviour of all ranks has been worthy of the highest traditions of the British Army, with the result that during the whole period, the front of the Division has never been broken and no retirement has been made until it was ordered. This is a record of which the Division may well be proud.

(Sgd) J Nicholson
Major General
Commanding, 34th Division.

Copy

Special Order of the Day
by
Major General Nicholson, C.B. CMG.
Commanding 34th Division

23rd April 1918.

The G.O.C. has received the following message from XVth Corps, and and desires that it be made known to all Ranks of the Division :-

"34th Division."

"On your transfer to the IXth Corps the Corps Commander"
"desires me to convey to you his thanks for the valuable services rendered"
"by the 34th Division during the operations of the 9th - 12th April."

"XVth Corps."   (Sd.) H Knox, Brig- General,
General Staff.

(Sgd)
 Lt- Colonel,
A.A & QMG. 34th

102nd Brigade.
34th Division.

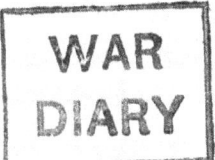

23rd NORTHUMBERLAND FUSILIERS.

M A Y   1 9 1 8

Army Form C. 2118.

WAR DIARY
INTELLIGENCE SUMMARY.
(Erase heading not required.)

MAY 1918 VOL. 5

23rd (S) Bn Northumberland Fus[iliers]

Place	Date MAY	Hour	Summary of Events and Information	Remarks and references to Appendices
SHEET 28 N.W BRANDHOEK LINE	1st		Completing work on advanced Posts & Communication, Wiring, front along along whole front. Strength: CAPT T. HERON M.C. to Hospital sick. Lt. T. DE WEED to England	
	2-		Work on line continued and reinforced. RELIEVED by 22nd N.F. Orders were received re. KAPPELTON to England moved to DEFENDED LOCALITIES G.14.b & G.9.c. (BRIGADE RESERVE) Bn. H.Qrs near G.8.a.9.2 in cottage.	
	3rd		WORKED on POPERINGHE SYSTEM under R.E. Supervision. ENEMY ARTILLERY fairly quiet. Parties to BATHS - no clean clothes available. Strength 21 off 1185 OR	
	4th		WORK ON POPERINGHE SYSTEM continued. Relief arrived in [blank] day. Reconnoitring parties 1st EAST LANCS reconnoitred position. ENEMY ARTILLERY quiet. STRENGTH (Arrivals Hd O.Rs. Drennan 2 off 24 O.Rs) 29 off 549 O.Rs.	
SHEET 28	5th		RELIEVED by 1st EAST LANCS moved to CAMP at K.12.b.6.4. BAND distributed amongst Companies. ROADS very bad. Camp pleasantly situated.	
	6th		Day spent in cleaning up & on inhum recovery. TROOPS paid.	
	7th		TRAINING & REORGANISATION in full swing. ORGANISING Bn on new WAR ESTABLISHMENT. HONORS & AWARDS: MILITARY MEDAL: No 38121 L/Sgt Rivers B.E. 40443 L/Cpl Rowlands W.E. 2364 Pte Porter H	
	8th		FULL TRAINING carried out. LEWIS GUNNERS under Bde arrangements. Rumours of big change	
	9th		TRAINING as per training diary	

Army Form C. 2118.

WAR DIARY
INTELLIGENCE SUMMARY VOL 5. CONTD

(Erase heading not required.)

Instructions regarding War Diaries and Intelligence Summaries are contained in F. S. Regs., Part II. and the Staff Manual respectively. Title pages will be prepared in manuscript.

Place	Date MAY	Hour	Summary of Events and Information	Remarks and references to Appendices
KIN B 6.4.	10th		FULL TRAINING carried out. Special Instructors chosen. LEWIS GUNNERS now practice	OSS
	11th		TRAINING as in previous day. Coy Commdrs + SPECIAL INSTRUCTORS under Bn Instruction. WARNING ORDER in new STRENGTH (numerical 11 ORs. December 18f/12 ORs) 28 9th SHs ORs	OSS
SHEET 12th	12th		MOVED to RUBROUCK AREA. MARCHING food. 2/Lt PIKETHLEY W.B. transferred to 1st NF.	OSS
HAZEBROUCK 5A.	13th		MOVED by BUS to LUMBRES AREA + MARCHED to LOTTINGHEM AREA walkin very bad. ORDERS in [ ] TRAINING BN [ ] AMERICAN UNITS now.	OSS
CALAIS. 13.	14th		COMPANIES at disposal [Coy Commdrs] Divl Commdrs inspection [original 3rd Divisional now cancelled. BN [ ] into TRAINING CADRE.	OSS
	15th		TRAINING [General Staff. Preliminary preparations for sending SURPLUS PERSONNEL to BASE.	OSS
	16th		FINAL ARRANGEMENTS for new formation complete. all amendments completed too. 102 BDE allotted to 55th AMERICAN BDE BN maintained TRAINING CADRE	OSS
	17th		SURPLUS PERSONNEL entrained at DESVRES for BASE (4 Offrs 404 ORs) STRENGTH (numerical 21 ORs December (55 Offrs 1180 ORs) 24 Offrs 151 Y.K. 1	OSS
	18th		MOVED to BLEQUIN AREA. DEMONSTRATION PLATOON attached. (1 Offr 44 ORs.)	OSS
	19th		102 Bde ADMINISTRATIVE INSTRUCTIONS issued. 4 Field Kitchens, 1 water cart, 2 L.G.S. wagons + Personnel attached to 105th Bn.	OSS
	20th		ARRIVAL [1st + 3rd INFY BNS] 110th AMERICAN INFY REGIMENT at LUMBRES STATION. Commencing of Instructions.	OSS
	21		do	
	22.d		do	
	23		do	
	24th		do	
	25th		do	

Army Form C. 2118.

WAR DIARY
or
INTELLIGENCE SUMMARY.
(Erase heading not required.)

MAY 1918   VOL 5 contd.

23rd (S) Bn Northumberland Fusiliers

Instructions regarding War Diaries and Intelligence Summaries are contained in F. S. Regs., Part II. and the Staff Manual respectively. Title pages will be prepared in manuscript.

Place	Date May 1918	Hour	Summary of Events and Information	Remarks and references to Appendices
	26th		Moved to HENNEVEUX. & attached to 103rd Brigade.	
	27th		C.O. to Boulogne to act in General Arms Capt Murray me. adm. C.O. A. & B. Coys provided officers to 108th & 9. Bn A.E.F., but instructors at a standstill owing to arrangements being incomplete.	
	28th		Training 1 morning man. for Bn Demonstration Platoon.	
	29th		Moved north to hilt bivouc between 1. 108th Inf. Bn A.E.F. command work very unsatisfactory all ranks very keen to learn, very enthusiastic.	
	30th		General training with units.	
	31st		ditto.	

[signature] Lt. Col.
Commanding 23rd (S) Bn North Fus.

102nd Brigade.
34th Division

Battalion transferred to
39th Division 17.6.18.

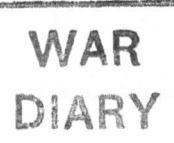

23rd NORTHUMBELAND FUSILIERS

J U N E   1 9 1 8 .

Army Form C. 2118.

WAR DIARY

JUNE 1918   VOL. 6.

INTELLIGENCE SUMMARY.
(Erase heading not required.)

23rd (S) Bn Northumberland Fusiliers

Date, Place	Summary of Events and Information	Remarks and references to Appendices
CALAIS 13 1st June	Continued Training of 28th Div: A.E.F.	VSL 30
2nd "	Lt Col R.H. Huron D.S.O. we returned from commanding 103rd Brigade. B/R Rhodes attached to 103rd Bn.	att
3rd "	Move to (Bonsin) Musut - [?] into a good billet through the Co's efforts. Ready to take on new division ? & ?.	att
4th Bonsin	Dispatched 3 Officers & 3 O.R.s to have but came of 78th Division A.E.F. of Haymen.	att
5th "	holding of district - Machine Gun companies A.E.F. had arrived	att
6th	do	att
7th	do	att
8th	do	att
9th	Prospects of same work - arrival of 309th M.G. Bn at 309th M.G. Coy A.E.F. area commandant fixing station. Bunch needed everywhere but were able to had [?]	att att att
10th	Started Regimental School. Students very back [?] promising	att

JUNE 1918 WAR DIARY VOL 6. CONTD. Army Form C. 2118.
INTELLIGENCE SUMMARY.
(Erase heading not required.) 23 - (1) Bn Northumberland Fusiliers

Hour, Date, Place	Summary of Events and Information	Remarks and references to Appendices
11th June Bouisin	Arrival of 308 M.G. Bn & 311, 312 M.G. Coys.	
12th June	Lt Col H.H. NEEVES D.S.O. M.C. to command 102nd Brigade	etc.
	School & training programme	etc.
	HONOURS & AWARDS. Lt N.B. PIGG - 2nd BAR TO M.C.	
	C.Q.M.S. W. WHITEHEAD M.M. - D.C.M.	
	Sgt C.A. COWANS M.M. - D.C.M.	
	L/Cpl R. JACKSON - M.M.	
13th June	CONTINUANCE of training	etc.
14th "	do	etc.
15th "	do	etc.
16th "	blow of first week's school. Look to Batt	
	Students assembled for no course. Cook to help	
	Kakiaka (Kowinsky) on his difficulties - working with	
	much trouble.	
17th	Departure of 34th Division - July are round.	etc.
	22nd Bn to England with 16th Division.	etc.
	Came under 116th Brigade, 39th Division. Into no	
	Training of 308th M.G. Bn from 22nd N.F.	

Army Form C. 2118.

JUNE 1918   WAR DIARY   VOL 6. CONTD

INTELLIGENCE SUMMARY.

(Erase heading not required.) 23rd (S) Bn Northumberland Fusiliers

Hour, Date, Place	Summary of Events and Information	Remarks and references to Appendices
17th June Bermerain	HONOURS & AWARDS 2/Lt D Goward — M.C.	
	2/Lt J H Dunn — M.C.	
	Pte L.G. Johnson M.M — Bar to M.M	
	Cpl Ocxeyton, H/Cpl W.R. Mickledam, Pte P Eaton	
	Pte C.J. Barker, H/Cpl J Carr M.M.	
	Continuous Training	
18th	do	
19th	do	
20th	do	
21st	do	
22nd	7 men proceeded writes school.	
23rd	Students enrolled for three weeks School.	
	Russian Symposium for training in addition	
24th	Continuous Training. Fine lecture by Pte Bankrupt	
	On C.T. B.E.F.	
25th	Continuous Training	
26th	do Col H.H. Moore Stevens picked from	
	102nd Brigade.	

WAR DIARY

JUNE 1918   VOL. 6. CONTD

INTELLIGENCE SUMMARY.

23(S) Bn Northumberland Fusiliers

Hour, Date, Place	Summary of Events and Information	Remarks and references to Appendices
27th June Phoenix	Continuous training 20 ORs to Base - period ing. with Brand.	
28th "	do	
29th "	2 weeks field works school	
30th "	25th N.F. have gone to Wost. to take over from M, L, T Bns & Coys to training. Reshuffling training staff has rendered unavoidable but no chances further one.	

Signed Lt. Col.
Comdg 23rd (S) Bn. NORTHD FUSrs

Copy No 6.

SECRET. Page 1.

102nd. (TYNESIDE SCOTTISH) Brigade
OPERATION ORDER NO. 32.

P.f 1/5000   La Boisselle

Information.

1. (a). In conjunction with the rest of the Fourth Army an attack on the German positions is to be made by the III Corps.

The operations up to and including the day of the Infantry Attack are to be spread over six days; these days are throughout these orders designated as U V W X Y and Z days; the infantry assault taking place on Z day.

The 34th. Division on the right and the 8th. Division on the left constitute the two leading Divisions in the attack by the III Corps.

The 19th. Division is in Corps Reserve.

The limits of frontage allotted to the Division are shown on map A. to be seen at Brigade Headquarters.

The dividing line between the 34th. Division and the 8th. Division on its left is:-

X.14.a.5.5.   -   X.14.b.7.8.   -   X.5.d.0.5.

Battalion Intelligence officers will be sent to Brigade Headquarters to copy this map.

Objectives allotted to 34th. Divn.

(b). The objectives allotted to the Division are

<u>1st. Objective:</u> The German front line system comprising four successive lines of trenches and extending in depth to the enemy's defensive line marked GREEN on map "A".

<u>2nd. Objective:</u> The enemy's intermediate line marked YELLOW on map "A".

<u>3rd. Objective:</u> The consolidation of a zone of defence to the EAST of CONTALMAISON and thence facing EASTWARDS and extending NORTHWARDS to the outskirts of POZIERES.

Page 2.

Objectives allotted to 34th. Divn. Ctd.

The right flank of this zone of defence to be refused to the SOUTH of CONTALMAISON so as to link up with the right of the second objective at point X.22.b.8.2. thus forming a defensive flank to the SOUTH against an attack from the direction of MAMETZ WOOD.

The zone of defence comprising this objective is marked VIOLET on map A and constitutes the ultimate objective allotted to the Division.

Objectives allotted to 8th. Divn.

(c). The attack by the 8th. Division on our left is to be made simultaneously with the attack by the 34th. Division. All three Brigades in the 8th. Division are attacking in line each Brigade on a two-battalion front. The 23rd. Infantry Brigade is to be on the right.

The right of the 23rd. Infantry Brigade are debouching from their trenches at point X.13.b.2.6. immediately SOUTH of the junction of ARGYLL STREET with the front parapet. The Right of their advance is to be directed on the line point X.14.a.8.7. (inclusive) thence on QUARRY (inclusive) thence on the line indicated as the dividing line between the two Divisions on to point X.4.d.8.3.

The first, second and third objectives allotted to the 8th. Division together with the principal strong points that their Right Brigade intends to consolidate are shown on map A.

19th. Divn.

(d). The 19th. Division in the 1st. instance is to be in Corps Reserve and is after Zero hour on Z day to move as follows:-

A and B Brigades to the BECOURT AVENUE.-TARA.-USNA.- OVILLERS.- line as soon as the Reserve troops of this and the 8th. Divisions have vacated these trenches. C Brigade to the intermediate line NORTH of ALBERT with one or two battalions, if desired, in the trenches of the ALBERT defences.

21st. Divn.

(e). The attack by the 21st. Division (Fifteenth Corps) on our right, is to be made simultaneously with the attack by the 34th. Division.

Page 3.

INTENTION.
(34th.Dvn).

2. The 34th. Division will attack on a frontage of two Brigades, the 101st. Infantry Brigade on the Right, the 102nd. Infantry Brigade on the left. The 103rd. Infantry Brigade will be in Divisional Reserve.

The 101st. and 102nd. Infantry Brigades will capture and consolidate objectives one and two on the respective frontages allotted to them. The 103rd. Brigade is allotted the task of capturing and consolidating objective three.

BOMBARDMENT.

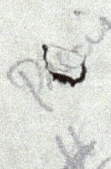

3. The infantry attack is to be preceded by a five days bombardment i.e. U V W X and Y days. The infantry assault is to be made on the morning of the sixth i.e. Z day. The artillery lifts on the day of the assault are shown on map B and appendix A, both to be seen at Brigade Headquarters. During the bombardment prior to Z day, the artillery reckon the night to be from 8 pm. to 4 am for purposes of bombardment.

During U V W X and Y days the Divisional Artillery and 2" Trench Mortar Batteries will be responsible for cutting wire on the front allotted to the Division up to the EASTERNMOST trench of the hostile front line system i.e. up to and including the enemy's line marked GREEN on map A. Wire to the EAST of this line will be dealt with by the Corps Artillery. Fire once opened will be kept up day and night. The 18 pdr. and 60 pdrs, assisted by machine guns will fire throughout the night to prevent repairs being executed or any reliefs being carried out.

After the assault the subsequent movement of the Infantry will be assisted and regulated by a system of barrages which will move back in accordance with the time-table in Appendix A and A1. and shown on map B.

The Field Artillery will lift from each line at the same time as the Heavy Artillery, but instead of lifting straight back on to the next line, as in the case of the Heavy Artillery, the Field Artillery will gradually rake back to

Bombardment contd.

to/ the next line. The speed at which this rate goes back to the next line will be calculated so that the shrapnel barrage moves back faster than the infantry can advance. As the infantry advance progresses the barrage becomes heavier until when the final objective is reached, a barrage of the whole of the available artillery is to be formed in front of it whilst it is being consolidated.

GAS.

4. Gas will be liberated the night Y/Z on the fronts
X.20.c.7.5. - X.20.a.0.5. and
X.19.b.4.7. - X.19.c.7.7. Details of liberation are given on appendix B.

SMOKE.

5. (a). Smoke will be liberated along the whole Divisional front for hlaf an hour at 7-29 am. on Y day in accordance with the instructions contained in appendix C.

(b). On the day of the assault, if the wind is favourable, a smoke barrage will be formed by 4" Stokes Mortars as follows:-

(i). Along the NORTHERN face of LA BOISSELLE salient. This barrage to be formed by four 4" Stokes Mortars - 90 bombs allowed.

(ii) Along the SOUTHERN face of LA BOISSELLE salient. This barrage to be formed by two 4" Stokes Mortars. - 40 bombs allowed. No. 5 Battalion, Special Brigade will be in charge of these mortars and will find the necessary personnel.

MINES.

6. At Zero hour On Z day two mines will be exploded under the hostile trenches at points ⟨and times⟩ which will be notified to commanding officers concerned. Both these mines will make a crater, including lip, of a maximum diameter of 100 yards.

Page 5.

PRELIMINARY MOVES. 7. Units to be attached to Infantry Brigades.

From the night X/Y, the following units will be attached to the Brigade.

    102nd. Inf. Bde.   208th. Field Coy. R.E.

                                  One Coy. 18th. Northd. Fusilrs
                                       (Pioneers).

Orders for the moves of these units to join the Brigade to which they are to be attached will be issued by Divisional Headquarters.

Closing up of Units forward area. 8. Detailed instructions on this subject will be issued later.

Areas allotted to Units. 9. Areas allotted to Infantry Brigades and affiliated Field Coys. R.E. and to the Pioneer Battalion, less company attached to the 102nd. Inf. Bde. are shown on tracing D., which can be seen at Brigade Headquarters.

Wire cutting. 10. The 102nd. Inf. Bde, is responsible for cutting the wire on its own front, so as not to show, on the night X/Y, and for preparing steps and placing ladders to help the assaulting troops to get out of the trenches. Commanding Officers must be most careful to see that this is carried out.

The gaps in our wire will be cut so as to ensure columns debouching through our wire at the angle at which they have to continue the advance.

Alignment 11. Pegs will be placed in NO MANS LAND on the correct alignment, on which the leading wave is to line up prior to their final charge on the enemy's front line. The pegs will be connected up by tape on the night Y/Z. On this night also, the flanks of gaps in our front line and support line wire will be marked by boards, the rear face of which will be painted white.
Officers Commanding units will take the necessary steps to carry out this order.

Page 5 a.

Brigade Machine-gun Coy.

During the intense bombardment of the LA BOISSELLE salient by Heavy and Medium Trench Mortars on Z day from Zero hour to 0 + 12, 4 selected guns of the 102nd. Brigade Machine gun company will maintain a heavy fire on certain specified trenches in the salient.

When the bombardment ceases these guns will also cease fire on the salient and will be utilized to cover the advance of the assaulting columns ~~will be utilized to cover the advance of the assaulting columns~~ by directing fire on the enemy's trench X.8.d.7.0. - X.14.b.7.5. - X.15.a.8.0. at 0 17 this fire will cease and these guns will move forward and join their company.

At Zero hour the guns not employed as directed above will cease fire and prepare to move forward in rear of the troops who are detailed to assault the 1st. objective, half the guns with the right assaulting column and half with the left assaulting column. The O.C.Company will previously have, after studying the map and model and the general plan of the attack detail positions to his guns so as to assist (1) In the attack on objective 1. and when that has been taken, objective(2.) utilize his guns in the attack on 2nd. objective. In this connection it is probable that hostile machine gun fire will be brought to bear on our advancing troops from a flank, and steps must be taken accordingly. When both objectives have been captured the disposition of the M.G.Company will be as follows: 12 guns in the second objective line, 4 guns in first objective line. The O.C. M.G.Co. will be responsible for maintaining his supplies of S.A.A. rations and water by using the Infantry Detachment ~~carrying party~~ attached to the company to bring the above forward from the Dumps.

Page 8.

Keeping open gaps in enemy's wire.

13. Rifle and machine-gun fire will be kept up from our trenches each night during the bombardment, to prevent the enemy repairing their wire or relieving their advanced troops.

RANGE CARDS

14. All Lewis and Vickers guns must be provided with range cards, prepared with a view to bringing fire to bear not only on the enemy's wire but also on all his communication trenches, which should be kept under fire throughout each night.

Every effort must be made to prevent the enemy relieving his forward troops during the period of the preliminary bombardment, and also to prevent him supplying them with rations.

Range cards must also now be prepared for all Lewis and Vickers guns for use on arrival at the objectives to which they are assigned.

Objectives assigned to 102nd. Bde.

15. 102nd. Infantry Brigade.

First objective. The enemy's defensive line marked GREEN on map A.

Second objective. The enemy's intermediate line marked YELLOW on map A.

The dividing line between the attack by the 101st. Inf. Bde, and 102nd. Inf. Bde. is a line from the junction between trench sector 20.4. and 20.5. (Square X.20.a.9.2.) to CONTALMAISON VILLA. The true bearing of this line is 30 degrees.

The enemy's communication trench marked C. on map A. is included in the subsector allotted to the 102nd. Inf. Bde., who will be responsible for the clearing and consolidation of this trench. Map can be seen at Brigade Headquarters. The Officer Commanding 21st. Northd. Fusiliers (2nd. Tyneside Scottish), and Officer Commanding 22nd. Northumberland Fusiliers, (3rd. Tyneside Scottish) will be careful to off parties to deal with this bit of trench, which, if

page 7.

Objectives assigned to 102nd. Bde Cont?

neglected, might lead to serious casualties in the 101st. Inf. Bde. on our right, as well as to our own Brigade.

EMPLOYMENT OF R.E. COYS. AND PIONEER BATTN.

16. R.E. Field Coys. allotted to Infantry Brigades will not accompany waves of the attack. They will be assigned the task of taking material up to, and assist in the defence of, the specially important localities shown on map A. after these have been captured.

The company of the 18th. Northd. Fusiliers (Pioneers) allotted to the Brigade, will move into the Brigade area on the X day and will relieve the party of the B Battalion in occupation of the mine area, under mutual arrangements to be made by the Officers Commanding battalions concerned, from and including INCH STREET on the right, to DUNFERMLINE STREET on the left.

The 18th. Northd Fusiliers (Pioneer) Company will rejoin their own Battalion as soon as LA BOISSELLE is cleared of the enemy.

The Officer Commanding the company will get into touch with the bombing and Infantry parties referred to in para 9 in order to keep himself well informed on the situation, and will not move from his position prematurely.

Grenades. S.A.A. Tools.

17 Officers commanding units will note that the grenades and S.A.A. at present in the Battalion wagons forming their mobile reserve are on no account to be touched until after the advance.

Battalion tools will be supplemented by those of the Brigade Reserve and the full number required to complete 1 pick or shovel per man will be made up from Divisional supply.

Officers commanding units should indent at once for the tools they require to complete and should draw them as soon as possible.

R.E. Coy. Where?

18 The R.E. Company will, on the day Y take up a position in ST. ANDREWS AVENUE, North end. When the 103rd. Brigade has passed this point on Z day, the R.E. Company will move forward, carrying R.E. Material to the front line of the Brigade.

The Officer Commanding 208th. Field Coy. R.E. will arrange that the material he is to carry forward is so placed as to be picked up and carried forward without any delay.

Page 8.

Employment of R.E. Coys. and ~~Pioneer Cp.~~ ctd.

18. ~~Each~~ The company of R.E. ~~and the company of Pioneers~~ will, on arrival at their objective in the front line, remain there under the orders of the O.Cs. as follows:-

  Officer Commanding,   ½ - 208th. R.E.Company.
  22nd.N.F.(3rd.Tyneside   ~~½ - Pioneer Company.~~
  Scottish)Battalion.

  Officer Commanding,   ½ - 208th. R.E.Company.
  23rd.N.F.(4th.Tyneside   ~~½ - Pioneer Company.~~
  Scottish)Battalion.

for work in construction of strong points.

All Officers Commanding Battalions of this Brigade will consolidate their objective as rapidly as possible.

ASSAULTING COLUMNS.

19 (a). The assault will be delivered by two columns, each column will consist of one battalion, supported by Stokes Trench Mortar and a Reserve Battn. Each column ~~platoon~~ will be formed on a front and depth of four platoons.

The task of assaulting columns will be to make good and consolidate objective one. (To Brigade Reserves will be allotted the task of gaining and consolidating objective two).

Officers Commanding units will arrange, as far as possible, for waves of the attack to follow one another over ground direct from their forming up places.

The distance between all leading lines of each of the two assaulting battalions is to be 100 yards;* the distance between other lines is to be 100 yards, *at 2 paces interval* *at similar interval*

Ladders and bridges are being placed in order to assist men getting out of trenches and crossing our trenches to their front. *In calculating the frontage of the attack Each man is to be allowed 2 paces.*

Where waves have to file down communication trenches to trenches of departure, measures must be taken to to/ Page 9.

Assaulting cols. 102nd. Bde., c'd.

ensure taht delays do not occur.

The initial advance of the assaulting battalions 102nd. Bde. will be directed viz: Right assaulting battalion - right, on a point 50 yards NORTH of X.20.a.3.5. (to avoid crater), thence on point X.20.b.39 ; - left, on a point X.20.a.3.6. thence on point X.14.d.3.3.

Left assaulting battalion: - Right on point X.14.c.3.9. left on point X.14.a.6.5., thence to QUARRY exclusive.

Action of Stokes Mortars.

(b). Every gun will be employed in the hurricane bombardment referred to in para. 27).

As soon as it is necessary to discontinue firing at LA BOISSELLE, owing to the proximity of our troops, one sect on from each of the two batteries will push forward, i.e. one section of the right battery in rear of right leading battalion, and one section of left battery in rear of left leading battalion. These sections will dig themselves in at the first objective.

½ section (2 guns) from the remainder of the battery will in each case follow the Reserve Battalion on their own flank and will proceed to the 2nd. objective.

½ section (2 guns) in each battery will remain under escort in position until sent for.

A party of one officer, one N.C.O. and 28 men of the 21st. Northd. Fuslrs. (2nd. Tyneside Scottish), will be detailed to carry up Stokes Mortar ammunition to the section accompanying right section Stokes Mortar Battery.

The Officer Commanding 20th. Northd. Fuslrs. (1st. Tyneside Scottish), will detail a similar party for

Page 10.

Action of Stokes Mortars contd.

for/
left sections. These parties should report for duty to LT. BOWASET, commanding 102nd. Trench Mortar Battery on 18th. inst., under arrangements to be made by him and O.C. concerned, and will, prior to Z day be employed in carrying Trench Mortar ammunition forward.

Bombing Coy.

(2). The Brigade Bombing Company under LT. RUTHERFORD will be utilized to deal with LA BOISSELLE. The company will consist of: - 2 Officers, 2 Sergeants, 8 Lance Cpls, 56 Privates - formed into 8 bombing parties. Each party will be numbered 1 to 8 and will consist of -

2 bayonet men, 2 bombers, 4 carriers.

Four of these parties under Officer Commanding company will move out in rear of 21st. Northd. Fusiliers (2nd. Tyneside Scottish), and will take up suitable positions for bombing down certain of the enemy's communication trenches - (which have been indicated to O.C.Company), as soon as the fire of our artillery on LA BOISSELLE has ceased viz: O 12 minutes.

The other four parties will be under the command of LT. CONNOLLY and will follow the 20th. Northd. Fuslrs.(1st. Tyneside Scottish), and will act in the same manner.

As soon as the O.C. bombing company is satisfied that LA BOISSELLE is cleared of the enemy, he will march his company back to one of the Brigade/dumps and will fill up with grenades. He will then move forward as rapidly as possible to the line held by 22nd. Northd. Fusiliers (3rd. Tyneside Scottish), and 23rd. Northd. Fuslrs. (4th. Tyneside Scottish), and will report to the two O.Os of that line for orders, dividing his company into two detachments for this work if necessary.

The O.C. bombing company will send back to the Brigade Dump his carriers, for further supplies of grenades as opportunities

Page 11.

occur/

Bombing Coy.

If he has to apply to an Infantry Battalion for men for this purpose, two privates from the bombing company must be sent back in each case to act as guides.

The C.Os. of the 22nd. and 23rd. Northd. Fusiliers (3rd. and 4th. Tyneside Scottish) Battns, will each detail two platoons, and one Lewis machine-gun to work in conjunction with the bombing company in clearing LA BOISSELLE of the enemy.

It is considered probable that after the assaulting and reserve Battalions have moved forward to their objectives, a certain number of the enemy will continue to snipe and machine-gun our men in the back, from isolated places in the German former front and support trenches.

The parties referred to above will therefore, after dealing with LA BOISSELLE remain and clear the whole of the rest of the area between the original German front trench and our first objective.

They will subsequently report to their respective C.Os. These parties will also collect any of our own stragglers and take them up with them.

(d). Flame projectors and necessary personnel are being supplied to co-operate in this attack.

BRIGADE DUMPS.

22. Officers Commanding all units must pay special attention to the Brigade Dumps, so that the Officer Commanding any party may know exactly where the dumps are.

The Brigade Dumps are situated as follows, and are marked by a board "102nd.Inf. Bde,

No. 1 and 2	ST. ANDREWS AVENUE.
3	Do. (in rear of left Btn. Headquarters).
4, 5, & 6	ST. ANDREWS AV. (between KIRKCALDY ST. and DUNFERMLINE ST)
3A	ST ANDREWS AV between 3 & 4
7.	PERTH AVENUE.
8 & 9	COBRIE STREET (Southern end).
10.	PITLOCHRY STREET.
10a	NEAR No 10
11 & 12.	ATHOLL STREET.

Page 12.

BRIGADE DUMPS ctd.
In these dumps are stored in loads ready for carrying, bombs, Stokes Trench Mortar ammunition, S.A.A., Rations, and water.

R.E.DUMPS.
23. The R.E.Dump for wire and other R.E.Material is situated in KIRKCALDY STREET.

MARKING OF DUMPS IN OUR LINES.
24. Dumps are being marked as follows:

Brigade Dumps.　　　　YELLOW flag, 18 inches square.

Divisional Dumps.　　BLUE Flag, 12inches square.

Divisional Stores.　　Sign board with Divisional sign 12 inches by 18 inches.

DIVISIONAL RESERVES.
25. Brigade Reserves will consist of two battalions and Field Coy. R.E. As soon as our front trench has been cleared by the assaulting columns, Brigade Reserves will be launched to the attack on objective 2.

Brigade reserves will closely follow the last wave of assaulting columns so that if necessary, timely assistance may be given to the leading battalions to gain their allotted objective on the barrage lifting, without affording time to the enemy to make dispositions to meet their attack.

The assaulting columns of this Brigade are

Right assaulting column.　　21st. Northd. Fusiliers
　　　　　　　　　　　　　　　(2nd. Tyneside Scottish Bn)

Left assaulting Column.　　20th. Northumbd. Fusiliers
　　　　　　　　　　　　　　　(1st. Tyneside Scottish Bn)

Right Reserve.　　　　　　　22nd. Northd. Fuslrs.(3rd.
　　　　　　　　　　　　　　　Tyneside Scottish Bn).

Left Reserve.　　　　　　　23rd. Northd. Fuslrs.
　　　　　　　　　　　　　　　(4th. Tyneside Scottish Bn)

The O.C. 22nd. Northd. Fuslrs. (3rd. Tyneside Scottish) will be careful to arrange for bombing parties to be sent on his right towards CONTALMAISON, to co-operate with the 101st. Inf. Bde. in the capture of that place.

Page 13.

Method of procedure to be adopted in the attack.

26. (a). The Right assaulting column will start from their trenches at Zero hour. The Left assaulting column will start at O-2 minutes.

Successive waves of assaulting battalions are to make direct over ground for the objective allotted, irrespective of the progress made by troops on their flanks; special bombing parties being told off to link up on the flanks with neighbouring units.

The Brigade Commander wishes it made clear to every officer and man that once launched to the attack, they are to push on to their objective without taking any notice whatever of any delays which may occur to other units of this or other Brigades on their flanks. On no account is one unit to wait for another unit to advance. <u>Positions once occupied are to be retained at all costs.</u>

The aim of each wave must be to support and where necessary carry forward the wave in front until the ultimate objective allotted to the battalion is reached.

(b). On gaining the first objective connection will be established,

(1) By the 101st. Inf. Bde. with the left assaulting Battalion of the 51st. Division, and with the right of the 102nd. Inf. Bde. at point X.18.b.7.2. The Officer commanding 21st. Northumberland Fusiliers (2nd. Tyneside Scottish) will report to Brigade Headquarters when connection has been established.

(2). By the 102nd. Inf. Bde. with the left of the 101st. Bde. at point X.18.b.2.1. and with the right of the 8th. Division at point X.9.c.4.8.

The Officer Commanding 20th. Nrthd. Fuslrs. (1st. Tyneside Scottish) will report in the same way when communication has been established with the right of the 8th. Division (23rd. Bde).

Page 14.

General procedure in the attack contd.

(c) On gaining the second objective, connection will be established

(i). By the 101st. Inf. Bde. with the left of the 21st. Division, and with the right of the 102nd. Inf. Bde. at point X.10.b.8.7.

(ii). By the 102nd. Inf. Bde. with the left of the 101st. Inf. Bde. at point X.10.b.8.3. and with the right of the 8th. Division in the cutting towards the point X.4.c.8.9. Officers commanding 22nd. and 23rd. Northd. Fusiliers, (3rd. and 4th. Tyneside Scottish) will report to Brigade Headquarters when connection has been established.

Battalions on gaining the enemy's line constituting their objective will quickly consolidate by constructing strong points protected by wire at the points previously selected. The points so selected by the Brigadier are marked on map A. If neighbouring battalions have failed to reach the objective assigned, special precautions will be taken to guard against flank attack by the construction of strong points echeloned back on either flank.

O.Cs units will, in addition, select and consolidate various other points so as to form a strong defensive line. To ensure that the work on strong points to be constructed in the line constituting the ultimate objective, of each battalion is commenced without hesitation or delay, garrisons and parties for entrenching, blocking and wiring of each post, will be detailed beforehand by O.C.s units.

Pending the arrival of wire and angle irons the men detailed for wiring must be set to work on other work of consolidation.

[margin: Also with 20th NF on right]

Page 15.

General procedure to be adopted in the attack Ctd.

(d). A battalion having gained its ultimate objective will make no retrograde movement in order to consolidate in depth the area allotted to it until,

(1) All units in the Division assigned to more advanced objectives have passed through it.

(2). And then only provided that it is clear that the next objective has been made good in its entirety.

(e). Should an assaulting battalion fail to gain its allotted objective, waves of Brigade Reserves and finally, if necessary, waves of the Divisional Reserves must be pushed forward to its assistance without hesitation so as to break down the enemy's resistance.

Waves of battalions merged into an attack of an objective short of their own, will, as early as possible, be reorganized and advance to their allotted objectives where they will consolidate.

(f). There must be a clear understanding as regards the responsibility of command so that when casualties occur loss of command may not result. This applies to all bodies of troops from sections upwards, also to smaller units which may temporarily find themselves isolated.

(g). Upon reaching their objectives the two bombs carried by each man will be dumped at a suitable spot in rear of each platoon for the subsequent use of bombers.

Trench Mortars.

27. The Heavy Trench Mortars and such Medium Trench Mortars as bear on LA BOISSELLE

Page 16.

Trench Mortars. salient, will continue to bombard the salient on Z day until O.+ 15. The exact area to be covered by this bombardment is hachured on map A. O. C.Units concerned should study this point.

From 8 minutes before Zero hour on Z day the enemy's front trench will be subjected to a hurricane bombardment from Stokes Batteries which will be continued until the fire from these guns is masked by the proximity of our infantry to the targets.

Advance of Units. 21 The hour of Zero will be notified later. The advance of the units of this Brigade will be carried out as follows:-

At two minutes before Zero hour two lines of men from 21st. Northd. Fuslrs (2nd. Tyneside Scottish) will move over the parapet or through the sallyports, if latter are suitable, and lie down outside the remains of our wire; the two lines immediately in rear will close up and occupy front trench.

22nd. Northd Fslrs. (3rd. Tyneside Scottish) will move up and occupy cover vacated by 21st. Northd. Fusiliers (2nd. Tyneside Scottish) and will follow in rear of 21st. Northd. Fusiliers. (2nd. Tyneside Scottish).

? The 20th. Northd. Fuslrs. (1st. Tyneside Scottish) will take similar action, but will commence moving *forward* at O-2.

23rd. Northumberland Fusiliers, (4th. Tyneside Scottish) which has to follow in rear of 20th. Northd. Fuslrs. (1st. Tyneside Scottish), will not move forward until the whole of 20th. Northd. Fuslrs. (1st. Tyneside Scottish) Bn. has moved out from our trenches. This must be clearly understood by all ranks

Page 17.

Trench Mortars. Ctd.

of the 23rd. Northd. Fuslrs. (4th. Tyneside Scottish) as otherwise confusion is liable to occur.

Signal Communication.

29 The position of troops will be indicated by the lighting of flares at 10 seconds interval, the flares being placed on the ground in a row of three or four paces apart.

It must be understood that the flares indicate to our artillery that there are none of our troops in front of those flares, therefore, the very greatest care must be taken to stamp them out should any of our troops move in advance of them.

Flares will only be lit by troops who are in the front line.

In addition, flares are to be lighted by the advanced troops of the Divisions every four hours starting from Zero hour. Care must be taken that these latter flares are lit at the clock hours indicated.

Mirrors (Vigilant Periscopes) will also be carried and used where flares are not available.

Contact Patrol Aeroplane

30 When the contact patrol aeroplane is present, Brigade Headquarters will put down a white ¾ circle sheet Battalion Headquarters a white semicircular sheet.

Communication with aeroplanes will also be carried out by ground signal panels.

Communication with the Kite Balloon will be carried out by lamps. The lamp must be directed on the basket and not the gasbag.

Forward Exchange

31 Brigade forward Exchanges are being established in our front line. Battalion and Brigade Headquarters on moving forward will be connected to this Exchange from a lateral buried wire along our front trench line. Laddered lines will be laid across NO MANS LAND

Signal Comm. Contd.

Visual Signalling

the lines being continued forward up the enemy's communication trenches.

32. To supplement further telegraphic communication visual signal stations will be established.

    101st. Inf. Bde.   near Adv. Report Centre.
    102nd. Inf. Bde.   near DRESSLERS POST.
    103rd. Inf. Bde.   KINFAUNS STREET.

Divisional Signal Stations will be established in E.14.a.3.6. - E.5.b.2.3. - E.16.b.2.8. Battalion Commanders to supplement the above means of communication will ensure the runners throughout their respective Battalions, being thoroughly organized.

Comm. Trenches.

33. Boards will be supplied by C.R.E. for marking UP and DOWN communication trenches as follows, ~~and O.Cs in the line~~ *the CRE* will be responsible that these boards are put up:-

    UP... BECOURT as far as Chateau.
    DOWN. BERKSHIRE, from CHAPES SPUR Cross Roads.
    DOWN. MERCIER STREET, continued along DUNDEE AVENUE, BUDDON STREET - NORTHUMBERLAND AV. The portion of DUNDEE AVENUE between junction of DALHOUSIE STREET and PITLOCHRY STREET, to junction of BUDDON STREET, to be renamed DALHOUSIE STREET. The junction of NORTHUMBERLAND AVENUE with BARRY and PANMUIR STREET. to be called CHARING CROSS.
    DOWN. GOURIE STREET from its junction with MET EUN STREET - PERTH AVENUE.
    UP. ST. ANDREWS AVENUE - ELIE STREET.

NORTHUMBERLAND AVENUE, when open, will be used as a Medical Avenue. Wounded will be evacuated down this trench. Communication trenches in

Page 79

enemy's/

Communication Trenches contd.

system will be marked as indicated on map A. Calico squares with letters are now being prepared and will be issued in due course.

ADVANCED Bde HQrs

34. Advanced Brigade Headquarters at the beginning of the action will be at a dug-out at W.24.b.5.1.

When the 2nd. objective has been reported as captured, Brigade Headquarters will move on to BOISELLE village - point X.14.d.1.9.

MODEL OF COUNTRY

35. There is at Brigade Headquarters, Albert, a model of the country which the Brigade has to pass over to reach its objectives. All officers are invited to come and inspect this model. A careful study of it will be a very great help to officers.

MAINTAINING DIRECTION

36. The question of maintaining the correct direction by units is one of the utmost importance, and the Brigade Commander wishes all officers to pay most particular attention to this point. By a careful inspection of the model, intermediate points on which to march can be selected, which cannot at present be seen by ground view.

The Officers and N.C.O.s responsible for the correct leading of their units cannot be too carefully instructed by their ~~units~~ Commanding Officers.

REPORTS.

37. The necessity for early and frequent reports to Brigade Headquarters as to the progress of their units during the advance, is impressed on Commanding Officers, in order that the Brigade Commander may be kept fully informed and be able to report to Divisional Headquarters. It is the duty of Adjutants to remind their C.Os on this point. This point is one not

/

Comm. trenches.
contd.

sufficiently appreciated, and the Brigade Commander trusts that every effort to communicate frequently either by wire, visual or runner, will be made. Brigade Commanders have to report the lines of advance (within the enemy's system of communications) to be followed by Battalion Headquarters. Officers Commanding Units will furnish this information as early as possible.

Commn. between Inf. Bdes. and 1st. line Transpt.

38. The Transport runners at Visual Signalling Station, will maintain communication between the Visual Signal Station and their respective transport lines. Should visual signalling fail, Advanced Divisional Headquarters will on receipt of a message from Brigade arrange to forward messages to the Brigade Transport Officer concerned.

MEDICAL.

39. Evacuation of wounded.

Four Regimental aid posts will be established near the following points and manned by the regimental M.Os. and regimental stretcher bearers. (All drummers will be utilized as stretcher bearers):-

(a). Road junction. ARBROATH ST. - MONYMUSK ST.
(b). Do. MERCIER ST. - MONIFIETH ST.
(c). Do. GOWRIE ST. - METHUEN ST.
(d). Do. KIRKCALDY ST. - METHUEN ST.

Evacuation of wounded from these regimental aid posts to the advanced dressing stations will be carried out by regimental stretcher bearers and by Bearer Division of the Field Ambulance.

(a). By MONYMUSK ST and CARNOUSTIE ST. to A.D.S. at BECOURT CHATEAU.

(b). By MERCIER ST. and BUDDON ST. to A.D.S. at CHARING CROSS.

(c). By GOWRIE ST. and PERTH AVENUE to (new) A.D.S. at junction of KINFAUNS ST.-PERTH AVENUE.

Page 21.

...nced Dressing Stations, wounded will be
... the Field Ambulances, and will be

...cks, greatcoats, and waterproof sheets will not
be carried in the attack. Officers commanding units
will arrange to collect all the above mentioned
articles, on or before the 22nd. inst. Packs to be labelled
with two labels showing Rank, name, initials, (number,
in the case of O.R.) Regiment and Brigade. Guards will
be provided under Divisional arrangements.

~~Xxxxxxxxxxxxxxxxxxxxxxxxxxxxxxxxxxxxxxx~~
~~Xxxxxxxxxxx.~~

These articles will be stored in the HOSPICE, ALBERT,
under arrangements to be made by the Staff Captain.

Every Infantryman will carry:-

(i) Rifle and equipment less pack.

* 2 Bandoliers of S.A.A. in addition to equipment
ammunition. - 220 rounds in all.

* 2 Mills grenades.

1 Iron ration, and rations for the day of the assault.
Waterproof cape.

* 4 sandbags in belt.

2 Smoke helmets and Spicer goggles.

Haversacks will be carried on the back; bombers will carry
equipment ammunition only. The method of obtaining
stores marked * will be notified later. Existing
Divisional Dumps are not to be drawn on without Divisional
Orders. Brigade Dumps must not be drawn upon for
preliminary requirements.

(ii). As many men as possible will be provided with wire
cutters.

Page 22.

Equipment to be carried contd.

(The numbers that will be available is dependent on the date fixed for the operations). O.C.s units should indent at once for the numbers they require.

Officers commanding units will arrange to draw grenades, sandbags and entrenching tools to complete the requirements of their units, not later than W. day.

Distinguishing mark

(iii) All ranks will wear a distinguishing mark, an equilateral triangle of yellow cloth 16 inches sides attached to the back - base upwards - which will be issued later.

(iv). Every man will carry a pick or a shovel (proportion of picks and shovels to be equal). Information re. time and place of drawing will be given by the Staff Captain later.

(v). Personnel of Field Coys. R.E. will carry explosives for hasty demolitions (i.e. for blocking trenches &c) barbed wire, French wire, angle irons and mauls.

IRON RATIONS.

41. Men must be reminded that the Iron Ration is not to be eaten without definite orders from an officer. If it is found necessary to use Iron rations, Officers Commanding are to ensure that only one ration for every three men is opened; if more are found to be required they can be opened at the discretion of the officer of the formation concerned. The number of Iron Rations used is to be reported at the first opportunity to Brigade Headquarters.

DRINKING WATER. -PRECAUTIONS.

42. All ranks must be warned on no account to eat any food or drink any water in the enemy's lines until allowed to do so by their Commanding Officers. Permission will only be given after steps have been taken by the Medical Officers to satisfy themselves that there is no danger of poison or contamination.

SUPPLIES
Water, Rations
Grenades, S.A.A.
R.E.Material.

43. The Officer Commanding 12th. Northd. Fuslrs (Pioneer Battalion) will, on Z day arrange to bring up supplies of water, rations, grenades, S.A.A. and some R.E.Material.

These supplies will be dumped by the 12th. Northd. Fusiliers at our first objective, and it will be the duty of the Officer Commanding, holding that line, to tell off parties to carry on the loads to the 2nd. objective. Subsequently, journeys will be made by the 12th. Northd. Fusiliers, and on these occasions, the same procedure will be followed, i.e. the supplies will be dumped at our first objective and will be sent up to the second objective as before, until the requirements of the 2nd. objective are complete.

The position of dumps in 1st. and 2nd.objective must be notified by the O.C. concerned to the Officer of the Pioneer Battalion in command of the carrying party.

TRANSPORT.

44. The Transport of the 141st. and 132nd. Inf. Bdes. will move to D.18.c. and D.18.b.a respectively on the night of the 12th. June.

The Officer Commanding the 103rd. and 104th. Field ambulances will send the following vehicles to the Infantry Transport lines to their affiliated

TRANSPORT. ctd.
Infantry Brigades on R/S and X/Y night respectively.

Two water carts, One Limbered wagon, one G.S. Wagon, three horse Ambulance wagons.

They will retain with each Field Ambulance one water cart and seven Motor Ambulances. The remaining transport of these units will join the 102nd. Field Ambulance at FRANKVILLERS on the dates mentioned above.

PRISONERS.
45. Prisoners of war will be passed back from Brigades as the situation allows, to a Brigade Collecting Station to be established at the Headquarters of the Right Battalion in occupation of the line (CRAPES SPUR), where they will be handed over to the guard there, found by the 103rd. Brigade.

Escorts furnished by Brigades between the fighting line and the Brigade Collecting Station will hand over the prisoners at a latter place and <u>return immediately to their own unit.</u>

LIASON OFFICERS.
46. The 102nd. Inf. Bde. will be required to detail two officers to report to Advanced Divisional Headquarters at MOULIN VIVIER on "Y" day to act as Liason Officers. One of these will be detailed by the Officer Commanding 20th. Northd. Fusiliers (1st. Tyneside Scottish) and one by the Officer Commanding 22nd. Northd. Fuslrs. (3rd. Tyneside Scottish).

The following Officers will be detailed as Liason Officers from this Brigade and will report on "Y" day to the Brigades concerned.

To 101st. Inf. Bde.   Officer to be detailed by
                             O.C. 1st. Bn. Tyneside
                             Scottish.

To. 23rd. Inf. Bde.   Officer to be detailed by
                             O.C. 4th. Tyneside Scottish.

<u>20 Officers per battalion only are to go into action on Z day. Officers in excess of this number are to report to the Transport lines of their units on "Y" day.</u>

These officers do not include those detailed as Liason or other duties of a similar nature.

Position of Advanced Report Centres.

47. Advanced Report Centres will be:-

Divisional Headquarters. MOULIN VIVIER.
with a Command Post in the line connecting
ALCOCK'S AVENUE to [illegible] AVENUE, about W.30.d.4.8

101st. Inf. Bde.   W.20.d.?.7?.
102nd. Inf. Bde.   W.24.b.5.1.
103rd. Inf. Bde.   W.24.d.?.?.
with a command post for the use of the G.O.C.
102nd. and 103rd. Inf. Bdes. in the vicinity of
KINZAUR STREET.

MISCELLANEOUS.

48. (i). No papers or orders are to be carried by officer or men taking part in the attack except the new 1/5000 German Trench map, and the 1/20,000 Map Sheet 57d. S.E. All messages and reports will refer to one or other of these maps. ~~Reference system must be used in conjunction with the numbers on the 1/5000 map in communicating to formations outside the III Corps.~~

(ii). ~~Hand~~ grenades are difficult to replenish; they must not be thrown indiscriminately.

(iii) Captured machine guns must be collected or damaged.

~~(iv). Men in the ranks are not to fall out to assist back wounded.~~

~~(v). Tools as well as ammunition must be recovered~~ during the advance from wounded men and carried forward.

(vi). Pipers will accompany their companies.

(vii). All maps &c. referred to in these orders are to be seen at Bde. Headquarters.

~~49. Acknowledge.~~

[signature]
Major.
BRIGADE-MAJOR.
102nd. (TYNESIDE SCOTTISH) BRIGADE.

18/6/16.

SECRET.
102nd (TYNESIDE SCOTTISH) BDE.
OPERATION ORDER NO. 32.
Dated 19/6/16.

The following additions and amendments are made to this Brigade Operation Order No. 32, of the 16th. inst.

COPIES NOS. 1 to 8.

1. Page 3, para. 3, line 3, add new para:-

   " from -65 to Zero on Z day there will be a
   " concentrated bombardment on enemy's trench
   " system, localities, strong points, billets and
   " gun positions, the subsequent bombardment will
   " be in accordance with the programme Appendices
   " A and A1.

2. Page 3 last para. delete as far as "infantry can advance" (on page 4) and substitute:-

   "The Heavy Artillery will lift straight back from
   "line to line as shown in Appendix A1. The Field
   "Artillery will rake back from line to line as shown
   "in Appendix A".

3. Page 4, para. 5. "SMOKE". Delete para 5 (a) and substitute

   "5 (a). If the wind is favourable. discharges of
   "smoke will take place duringk the last ten minutes
   " of all the concentrated bombardments which are to
   " be carried out on V.W.X. & Y days.
   " Instructions as regards these barrages are contained
   " in Appendix C".

   Para 5 (b) (i) line 2. for "60 bombs" substitute "120 bombs".

   Para 5. (b). (2) Delete the words:-

   "by two 4" Stokes Mortars - 40 bombs allowed"

   and substitute:-   "by P bombs"   500 allowed."

   At the end of para add:-

   "The O.C. G Company R... will arrange for the
   "discharge of P bombs and will report to the G.O.C.
   "102nd. Inf. Bde. For details see Appendix C1"

4. Page 7. Para 16, line 5. After the word "captured" add:-

   "The 207th. and 208th. Field Coy R.E. affiliated to
   "the 101st. and 102nd. Brigade will later be
   "withdrawn and come under the orders of the C.R.E."

5. Page 11 sub. para (d).   Delete.

6. Page 12. para 25, line 5. after the word 'objective' add:-

   "the enemy's intermediate line marked yellow on
   "map A."

AMENDMENT.
OPERATION ORDER NO. 32
of 19/6/16.

Add to Paragraph 2:

The assaulting columns will, prior to the assault, occupy a frontage as follows:-

RIGHT ASSAULTING BATTALION.

From junction X.20.d. & X.20.b. to INCH STREET (inclusive).

LEFT ASSAULTING COLUMN.

From a point 40 yards North of KIRKCALDY ST. to STANDISH ST. (exclusive).

To admit of the leading line of the left assaulting column being within 200 yards of the enemy's front trench at Zero hour, the column will start at 3 minutes before Zero, not 2 minutes as previously ordered.

Major.
BRIGADE-MAJOR.
19:6:16. 102nd. (TYNESIDE SCOTTISH) BRIGADE.

OPERATION ORDER 32.
dated 18/6/16.
Appendix B.

PROGRAMME FOR THE DISCHARGE OF GAS.

With reference to the above the O.C. units in the line and the Officer commanding the 102nd. Machine Gun Company will arrange to commence firing 5 minutes exactly prior to the time fixed for the discharge of gas, which time (and date) will be fixed later.

The Officer commanding the 22nd. Northumberland Fusiliers (3rd. Tyneside Scottish) Battalion will detail an Officer to fire the rockets from TARA REDOUBT; and the Officer Commanding 23rd. Northumberland Fusiliers (4th. Tyneside Scottish) the rockets from USNA REDOUBT.

These officers to report to BRIGADE HEADQUARTERS, at 9-30 am. on the 21st. inst.

The will have to get into touch with the Officer Commanding "G" company R.E. at 7 RUE DE VIVIER, ALBERT, and arrange with him as regards his informing them by wire from the front trenches of the termination of the discharge of gas, so that no time may be lost in sending up the rockets at +1.28 - the time ordered.

Major,
BRIGADE MAJOR.
102nd. (TYNESIDE SCOTTISH) BDE.

102nd. Bde. Hqrs.
20:6:16.

OPERATION ORDER 32.
Dated 18/8/15.

Appendix C.

1. With reference to the above, The Officer Commanding 21st. Northumberland Fusiliers (2nd. Tyneside Scottish), Coy. 18th. (Pioneer) Battn., 23rd. Northumberland Fusiliers, (4th. Tyneside Scottish), and 20th. Northumberland Fusiliers (1st. Tyneside Scottish), will each detail 1 Officer, 11 N.C.Os and 22 men to find the 11 parties required from each of the above units.

The N.C.Os will parade and be marched down to the Headquarters of the O.C. "G" Coy. R.E., 7 RUE DE.VIVIER, at 10 am tomorrow 21st. inst. and will receive instructions from that officer, they will subsequently be required to instruct the men who form their party in regard to the duties in connection with smoke.

[margin note: The Officer to be there at the same time]

These N.C.Os and men must be shown exactly the positions they will take up in the trenches when a discharge of smoke is ordered. Officers Commanding units will have to consult the O.C. G. Coy R.E. on this point.

2. The Candles and P.Bombs can be drawn from Brigade Headquarters by units concerned, shortly; they have not yet been received from the Division.

The candles are very susceptible to damp and must be wrapped up in waterproof sheets prior to being put into the dugout, and kept in the waterproof sheets until they are actually lighted. A shower of rain on them while they are being carried from the dugout to their place in the trench is liable to render them useless.

3. The Brigade Signalling Officer will make all arrangements for giving daily the correct time to the O.Cs units concerned. The loan of watches, under regimental arrangements, to the N.C.Os in charge of parties would greatly facilitate the correct timing.

4. Officers commanding units in the front line will consult together as regards the best joint method of using the dummies referred to and will inform the Brigade Commander as to the action they propose.

RE APPENDIX C1.

The attention of the Officer commanding the company 18th. N.F.(Pioneers), is called to Para. (b). 24 men will be required for this duty and should be detailed beforehand.

102nd.Bde.H.Q.
20:6:16.

Major
BRIGADE-MAJOR.
102nd.(Tyneside Scottish) BDE.

SECRET.

OPERATION ORDER NO. 32.   Dated 18/6/16.
APPENDIX C.

The following amendments are to be made in appendix C.

(i). The liberation of smoke during the preliminary bombardment will now be limited to:-

    on W day. from 10.10. am. to 10.20 am.
        X day.   "   5.40. am. to 5.50. am.
        Y day.   "   7.10. am. to 7.20. am.

Para. 1 of Appendix C to be amended accordingly.

(ii).   This will entail the following amendments in the body of the order.

Para. 6. (a). to be amended to read.

"If the wind is favourable, discharges of smoke will
"take place during the last 10 minutes of the
"concentrated bombardments on W.X. and Y days mentioned
in appendix C.

                                         Major,
                                    Brigade-Major,
23/6/16.   102nd. (Tyneside Scottish) Bde.

SECRET.
Ref. Sheet 57D N.E. 1/20,000.   T A B L E "J" (Contd:)   Issued with O.O. No. 35

DATE.	UNIT.	FROM	TO	REMARKS.
1916 JUNE 27/28th.	22nd N.F. (3rd TYNESIDE SCOTTISH) Bd.Qrs. & 4 Platoons 8 Platoons 2 Platoons	SUNKEN GARDEN BRESLE USNA/TARA Line.	FORWARD AREA. USNA/TARA Line. FORWARD AREA.	
"	23rd N.F. (4th TYNESIDE SCOTTISH) 4 Platoons 4 Platoons	FIR WOOD. Remain in USNA/TARA Line.	USNA/TARA Line.	
"	208th FIELD COY. R.E.	DERNANCOURT	USNA/TARA Line.	
28/29th.	22nd N.F. (3rd TYNESIDE SCOTTISH) 2 Coys	USNA/TARA Line	Position of Assembly.	Via PERTH AVENUE - To be clear of USNA/TARA Line by 10:30 p.m.
"	23rd N.F. (4th TYNESIDE SCOTTISH) 2 Coys	USNA/TARA Line.	Position of Assembly.	To be clear of USNA/TARA Line by 10:45 p.m. Via ST. ANDREWS AVENUE.
"	208th FIELD COY. R.E.	USNA/TARA Line.	ST. ANDREWS AVENUE. Position of Assembly.	To be clear of USNA/TARA Line by 11 p.m.

[signature]
BRIGADE MAJOR. Major.

102nd (TYNESIDE SCOTTISH) BRIGADE.

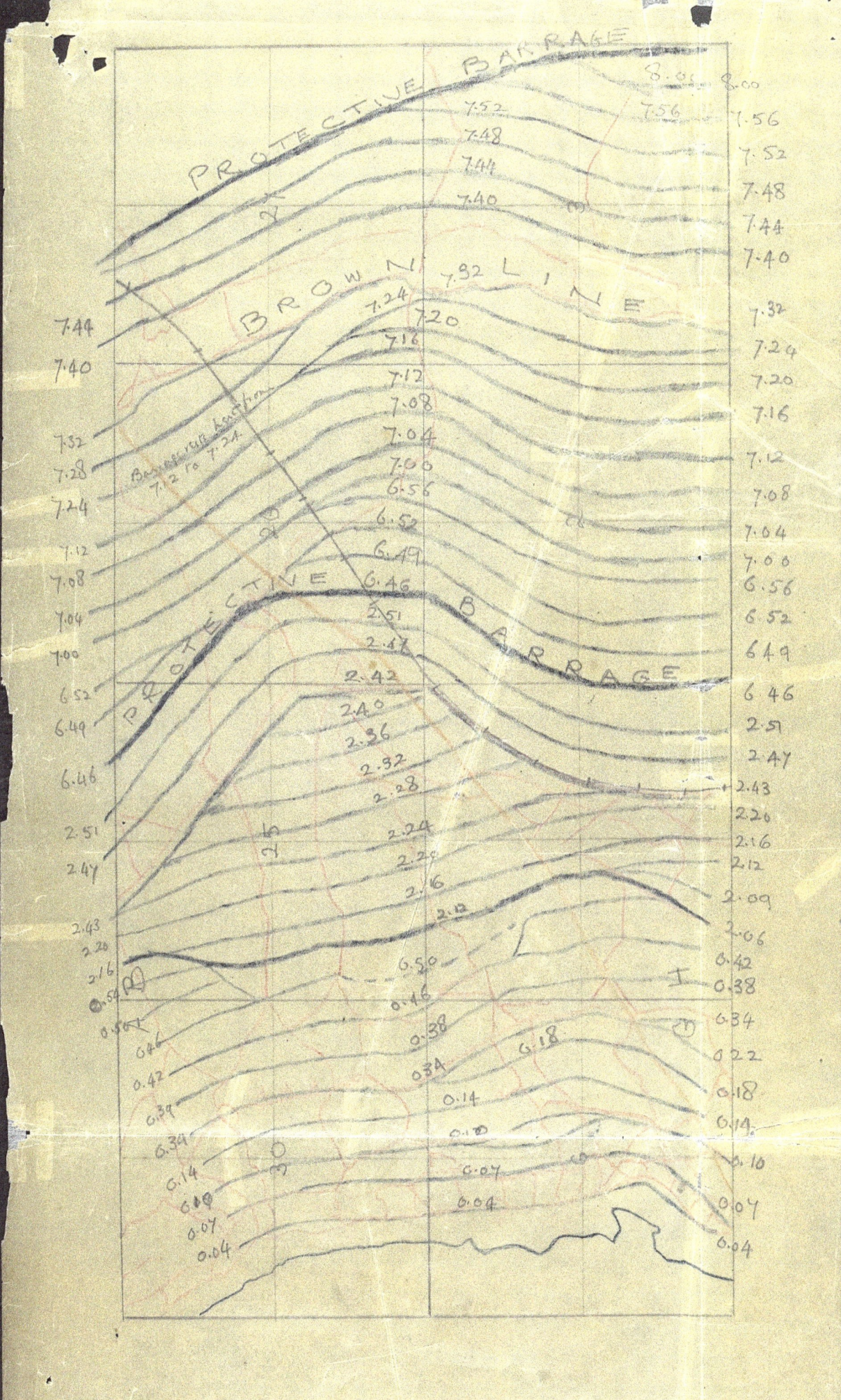

66TH DIVISION
TRAINING CADRES

34 DIV

23RD BN NORTHUM'D FUS

AUG - DEC 1918

July 1918 to 1919 MAR

~~From~~ 34 DIV

102 Bde

Served with 197 Bde

L of C from Sept 1918

Army Form C. 2118.

16/39

JULY 1918. WAR DIARY VOL VII

INTELLIGENCE SUMMARY.
(Erase heading not required.)

23rd North'n Regt.

Instructions regarding War Diaries and Intelligence
Summaries are contained in F. S. Regs., Part II.
and the Staff Manual respectively. Title pages
will be prepared in manuscript.

Place	Date	Hour	Summary of Events and Information	Remarks and references to Appendices
Mourmelon	1st		Training A.E.F still. Lost squadron class	
	2		Rumours of armode (nothing like a change)	
	3		H.Q. work. Americans start packing up.	
	4		Move to Bouvincourt – Billets quite good.	
	5		Sleep jolly as men	
	6		Commence work – squad school started again	
	7		Managed by some instructors & stores from Divison	
	8		Major Atkins Leavenots Ref. arrived to help in musketry	
	9		Continuance of training	
	10		do	
	11		do. Squad Ypres annexe to help with class	
	12		do	
	13		do	
	14		C.O. goes on leave. Ackman day in the papers	
	15		Training as usual	
	16		do	

WAR DIARY or INTELLIGENCE SUMMARY

Army Form C. 2118.

JULY 1918 VOL VII cont

23rd month 9 m.f.

Hour, Date, Place	Summary of Events and Information	Remarks and references to Appendices
LENS. II.		
Morning 17	Rumours of another move. A.E.F. is	
18	to work all preparation for move (some baggage)	
19	Transfer to Duars – fed up I note to want.	
	A good time held to see one	
Nautchequi 20	A.E.F. made break made up for which	
21		
22	Very little to do – are I working more than ever	
23	do	
24	do	
25	do	
26	do	
27	do	
28	do	
Maynicourt en Courte 29	And yet another move – Coron or baggage. C.O. from here	Major Jenkins Lt Col
30	Take over supervision 310 Regt A.E.F.	Comm'd 23rd month finish in
31	End I am miserable, monch – all want to be	
	made up – scrapping the town after here this.	

CONFIDENTIAL

WAR DIARY

OF

23rd Batt'n Northum'd Fus

From Aug 1st 1916
To 31st

Vol No 1

Army Form C. 2118.

WAR DIARY Vol. 8

August 1918

INTELLIGENCE SUMMARY.
(Erase heading not required.)

23rd (S) Bn. Northumberland Fusiliers

Instructions regarding War Diaries and Intelligence Summaries are contained in F. S. Regs., Part II. and the Staff Manual respectively. Title pages will be prepared in manuscript.

Date, Place	Summary of Events and Information	Remarks and references to Appendices
LENS II		
1st August Magnicourt-Cote	Continued preparations of 310th Regt A.E.F.	
2nd "	do	
3rd "	Entrained at Tinques for Audruicq	
4th " Licques	Arrived at Licques	
5th "	Awaiting orders	
6th "	do	
7th "	do	
8th "	do	
9th "	do	
10th "	do	
11th "	do	
12th "	116th Bde Rifle Meeting 1st Day	
13th "	do 2nd Day	
14th "	Move is probable	
15th "	Entrained at Northorque. Transferred to 66th Division, 198th Bde	

Army Form C. 2118.

August 1918 WAR DIARY
INTELLIGENCE SUMMARY.
(Erase heading not required.)

Vol. 9 (contd)
23rd (S) Bn. Northumberland Fusiliers

Date, Place	Summary of Events and Information	Remarks and references to Appendices
Ref Map: DIEPPE 16		
16th August. Abancourt	Arrived at Abancourt Camp	
17th "	Awaiting Orders	
18th "	do	
19th "	do	
20th "	do	
21st "	do	
22nd "	do	
23rd " Hendicourt	Moved to Hendicourt Camp	
24th "	Preparing camp to receive reinforcements	
25th "	do	
26th "	do	
27th "	do	
28th "	do	
29th "	do	
30th "	do	
31st "	do.	

CONFIDENTIAL

WAR DIARY

OF

23rd. NORTHUMBERLAND FUSILIERS.

From 1st. Septr. 1918 to 30th. September 1918.

(VOLUMNE 9)

..................Lt-Col.Comdng.,
23rd. Northumberland Fusiliers..

SEPT: 1918 WAR DIARY VOL. 9.

INTELLIGENCE SUMMARY.

(Erase heading not required.)

Army Form C. 2118.

23rd (s) Bn North'n

Instructions regarding War Diaries and Intelligence Summaries are contained in F. S. Regs., Part II. and the Staff Manual respectively. Title pages will be prepared in manuscript.

Hour, Date, Place	Summary of Events and Information	Remarks and references to Appendices
HAUDRICOURT		
1st to 18th	Aweekly Malarial Reinforcements Building Camp Medical Officer arrived	OR5
13th	"	
15th	departed to MARTIN EGLISE	
18th	8 O.Rs (malarial) arrived (Jame: Yorkshire)	
19th	61 " do	
20th	33 " (Manchester)	
21st + 22nd	Continuing work on new Camp - began clearing Rough Lack of material	
23rd + 24th	Lt Col hewis B.S.O. m.c. 610 to 21st Divison	
25th	Start working on Camps. 252 O.Rs in camp In inflict	
	Major Calthorpe Suffolk Regt takes over Command	
	Capt mcl. Murray Jnr to 15th Batt Yorks	
26th to 29th	Working on Camps left Brown comment	
30th	Lt Col P Q & Landon Gordon Highlanders to Command of the Battalion	
	Major Calthorpe goes back to unit	

J Dalrymple Lt Col
Comm'g 23rd North'n

Forms/C. 2118/11.

CONFIDENTIAL.

WAR DIARY.

of

23rd. BN. NORTHUMBERLAND FUSILIERS.

From 1ST OCTOBER, 1918.   To. 31ST OCTOBER, 1918.

(Volume 10).

Army Form C. 2118.

WAR DIARY
or
INTELLIGENCE SUMMARY.

(Erase heading not required.) 23rd (S) Bn. Northumberland Fus

October 1918   VOL. 10

Place	Date	Hour	Summary of Events and Information	Remarks and references to Appendices
No 1 I.B.D.E. 1st 23rd Reception Camp.	1 to 31		Section and Platoon Training (Programme) afternoons devoted to sports	
	15th		Capt. and adjt. A. Stanley proceeded to join 2nd Bn Lincolns	
	19th		452 O.R's stay in camp for night	
	20th		26 Reinforcements (Warrant) arrived	
	24th		Draft of 152 O.R. to 14th and 50th Divisions	
	28th		Some officers (Senior Subalterns) posted to other units	

Confidential

War Diary

of

23rd North'd Fusiliers

From 1st November, 1918.   To 30th November, 1918.

(Volume II)

for O.C. 23rd W Lenard 2/Lt. & a/Adjt.
Northumberland Fusiliers.

November 1918   Vol. II.

Army Form C. 2118.

WAR DIARY
or
INTELLIGENCE SUMMARY.
(Erase heading not required.)   23rd (S) Br Northumberland Fus.

Instructions regarding War Diaries and Intelligence Summaries are contained in F. S. Regs., Part II. and the Staff Manual respectively. Title pages will be prepared in manuscript.

Place	Date	Hour	Summary of Events and Information	Remarks and references to Appendices
No 1 I.G.B. and Reception Camp	1st to 31st		Progressive training carried out in section and platoon work, intensive digging &c.	W.G.
	1st		2/Lieut (a/cap) F.M. Wordsman and 2/Lt O.W. Howie proceeded to join 15th D.L.I.	
	2nd		41 O.R's reinforcements (Balance) arrive	
	5th		-do- -do-	
	8th		Draft of 59 O.R's to 50th and 66th Divisions.	
	11th		Major Smith (Worcestershire Reg) posted to this Regt.	
	12th		2/Lt (a/cap) R.M. Hunnicutt proceeded to join 15th D.L.I.	
	12th		All parades for the day cancelled by Brig. General I/c M.G. D.S.O. to celebrate armistice signed on the 11th Nov. 1918.	
	13th		2/and Lieut J.B. Taylor (A. and S. Highlanders) posted to this Batt.	
	15th		2/and Lieut J.G. Beck proceeded to join 15th D.L.I.	
	16th		2/and Lieut G.W. Wortland (Gordon Highlanders) posted to this Batt.	
	25th		Draft of 4 O.R's to 29th and 55th Divisions	
	26th		Draft of 17 O.R's to 2nd and 66th Divisions	
	30th		Draft of 2 O.R's to 66th Division	
	30th		Total strength of reinforcements of this date 150 O.R's	

27 Confidential

WAR DIARY of
23° Northumberland Fusiliers.

From 1st December 1918   20 - 31st December 1918.

(Volume 12)

Wenarth, 2/Lieut & Adjt
for O/C 23 Northumberland Fus.

December 1918   Vol 12

Army Form C. 2118.

WAR DIARY
or
INTELLIGENCE SUMMARY.
(Erase heading not required.) 23rd (S) Bn Northumberland Fusiliers

Instructions regarding War Diaries and Intelligence Summaries are contained in F. S. Regs. Part II. and the Staff Manual respectively. Title pages will be prepared in manuscript.

Place	Date	Hour	Summary of Events and Information	Remarks and references to Appendices
No 1 I.B.C. One Reception Camp	1st to 3rd		Progressive training carried out with Malaria Reinforcements	
	3rd		All Malaria reinforcements (163 O.R.s) transferred to 16th Sherwood Foresters. Mr Taylor & Westland also sent to 16th Sherwood Foresters. Major Hunt to 10th Lincolns	
	4th to 9th		Awaiting orders for move. Nothing to do.	
	10th		Left Hardecourt (advance it) with Cadre and transport for Havre, arriving in the evening, and accommodated at No 2 Rest Camp.	
	14th		Orders to proceed to No 1 Rest Camp, Section B to assist in demobilisation of mining Personnel men. Lt Col. D.R.F. Swordes (C.O. of this batt.) appointed Camp Commandant.	
	15		Commenced functioning, and during the night and the following day, the 16th, 22 Officers and 1202 O.R. arrived. All ranks arriving in this Camp for demobilisation are sent to three disposal areas in U.K. (formerly divisions and subdivisions). We function every third day	

WAR DIARY
or
INTELLIGENCE SUMMARY.
(Erase heading not required.) 23rd (S) Br Northumberland Fusiliers

December 1918 Vol. 12

Army Form C. 2118.

Instructions regarding War Diaries and Intelligence Summaries are contained in F.S. Regs., Part II. and the Staff Manual respectively. Title pages will be prepared in manuscript.

Place	Date	Hour	Summary of Events and Information	Remarks and references to Appendices
No 1 Rest Camp Sec B Havre.	1918 Dec 20th		28 Officers and 1725 O.R's sent from this camp for demobilization.	
	22		Major Hunt transferred from 10th Lincolns to this Batn.	
	24		22 Officers and 806 O.R's entrained from this camp for demobilization.	
	25		Christmas Day was observed as a holiday. Dinners provided by B.E.F. and was very satisfactory. Each man was presented with pipe, pouch and tobacco.	
	29		32 Officers and 1440 O.R's sent away to UK for demobilization from now onwards we only take in men for demobilization as no dispersal area.	
	30		10 Officers and 360 O.R's embarked from this Camp.	
	31		7 - 344 -	
	31		To date we have sent 16 drafts from our Cadre establishment and our strength is 10 Officers and 37 O.R's	

4 Confidential

WAR DIARY
23rd Northumberland Fusiliers

From 1st January 1919 to 31st January 1919
(Volume 13)

[signature]
for O.C. 23rd Northumberland Fusiliers

Army Form C. 2118.

WAR DIARY
or
INTELLIGENCE SUMMARY.

(Erase heading not required.) 23rd (A) 8th Northumberland

Vol 13

Instructions regarding War Diaries and Intelligence Summaries are contained in F. S. Regs., Part II. and the Staff Manual respectively. Title pages will be prepared in manuscript.

Place	Date	Hour	Summary of Events and Information	Remarks and references to Appendices
Hoars	1919 Jan 1st-31		During the whole of the month we have been engaged on demobilization at no 1 Despatching Camp. Men despersed stations in the U.K. as fireworks by no 23rd Northumberland Georgetown Kinross Hopetoun Broxburn & Upon the numbers despatched every each day, but the average is 800.	
	2nd		Lt Col Innes A. DSO 5th Bn Northumberland Fusilier joined this battalion to take over command vice Lt Col 2A? Dooley posted to 9th Bn Borders 4th. The command to take effect from the 1st Feb.	

C O N F I D E N T I A L

W A R   D I A R Y
23rd. NORTHUMBERLAND FUSILIERS

From 1st. February 1919   To: 28th. February 1919
            (Volumne 14)

.... Major
for O.C. 23rd. Northd. Fusiliers.

WAR DIARY or INTELLIGENCE SUMMARY

Army Form C. 2118.

23rd (S) Bn. Royal Fusiliers VOL 14

Place	Date	Hour	Summary of Events and Information	Remarks and references to Appendices
HAVRE.	Feby 1 to 28.		During the whole of the month, the Battn. was engaged on demobilisation at NO 1 Despatching Camp, HAVRE. The appointment of Lieut Col A. Irwin D.S.O. to command the Battn. was cancelled, Lieut Col J.R.E Swarbs, Gordon Highlanders retaining the command. Lieut Col Irwin left on the 17th to assume command of the 18th Bn Lancashire Fusiliers. A Battn. dinner was held at the Grand Hotel on the 1st, present 5 Officers & 16 other Ranks. Capt R.M Hunteroto & Lieut J.E. Beck rejoined the Battn. from 15th Bn Durham Light Infantry. Capt J.A Bailey & 2/Lt H Clarke proceeded to U.K. for demobilisation.	

Army Form C. 2118.

WAR DIARY
or
INTELLIGENCE SUMMARY.

(Erase heading not required.) 23rd (S) B⁻ Northumberland Fus⁻

Vol 39

Instructions regarding War Diaries and Intelligence Summaries are contained in F. S. Regs., Part II. and the Staff Manual respectively. Title pages will be prepared in manuscript.

Place	Date	Hour	Summary of Events and Information	Remarks and references to Appendices
Havre	March 1st to 31st		During the whole of the month the battalion has continued to work at No 1 Despatching Camp Havre.	
	13		7 O.R's arrived for this Bat⁻ and were taken on the strength.	
	20		12 O.R's reinforcements arrived for this Bat⁻ but authority for posting has not yet been received	

T2134. Wt. W708—776. 500000. 4/15. Sir J. C. & S.

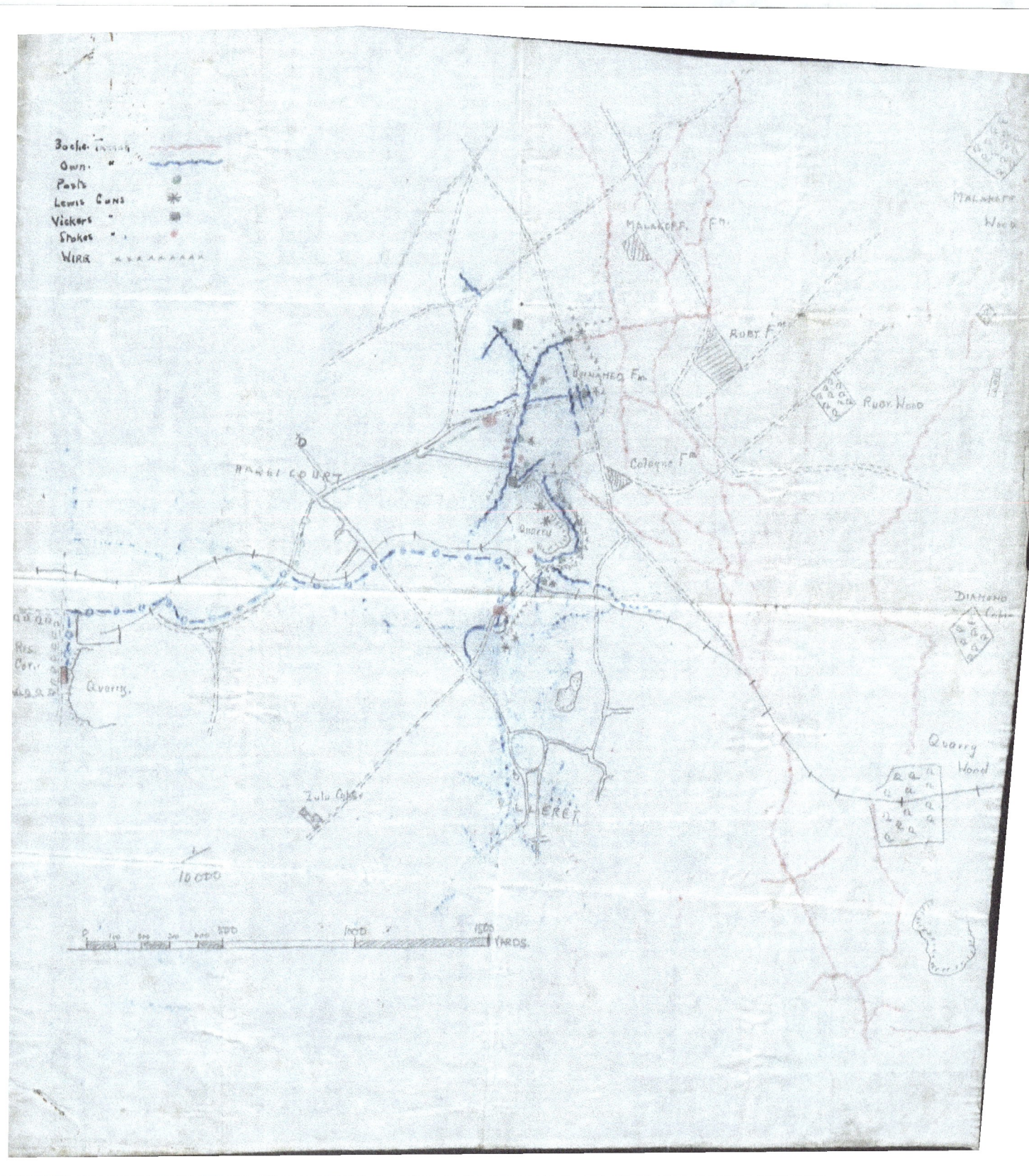

www.ingramcontent.com/pod-product-compliance
Lightning Source LLC
Chambersburg PA
CBHW080813010526
44111CB00015B/2549